THE
BIRTH OF
FRANCE

THE BIRTH OF FRANCE

Warriors, Bishops and Long-Haired Kings

KATHARINE SCHERMAN

PARAGON HOUSE
New York

First paperback edition, 1989

Published in the United States by

Paragon House
90 Fifth Avenue
New York, NY 10011

Grateful acknowledgment is made to the following for permission to reprint previously published material:

Cherry Valley Editions: Poems from *A Basket of Chestnuts: From the Miscelianea of Venantius Fortunatus*, translated by Geoffrey Cook. Copyright © 1981. Published by Cherry Valley Editions.
Coronado Press: Excerpts from *Liber Historiae Francorum*, ed. and trans. by Bernard S. Bachrach. Reprinted by permission.
Penguin Books Ltd.: Excerpts from *The History of the Franks* by Gregory of Tours, translated with an introduction by Lewis Thorpe (Penguin Classics, 1974.) Copyright © 1974 by Lewis Thorpe.

Library of Congress Cataloging-in-Publication Data

Scherman, Katharine.
    The birth of France : warriors, bishops, and long-haired kings /
Katharine Scherman. — 1st pbk. ed.
        p.   cm.
    Bibliography: p.
    Includes index.
    ISBN 1-55778-174-5 (pbk.)
    1. Franks—France—History. 2. France—Kings and rulers.
3. France—History—To 987. I. Title.
[DC64.S34 1989]
944—dc19

88-14697
CIP

Manufactured in the United States of America

FOR AXEL

CONTENTS

THE MEROVINGIAN KINGS*

Clovis I
481–511

Theodoric I
King of Metz
511–534

Theudebert I
King of Metz
534–548

Theudebald
King of Metz
548–555

Chlodomer
King of Orléans
511–524

Childebert
King of Paris
511–558

Lothair I
King of Soissons
511–558
King of all Franks
558–561

Sigibert I
King of Austrasia
561–575

Charibert I
King of Paris
561–567

Guntram
King of Burgundy
561–592

Chilperic I
King of Soissons
561–584

Childebert II
King of Austrasia
575–595
King of Burgundy
593–595

Lothair II
King of Neustria
584–613
King of all Franks
613–629

Theudebert II
King of Austrasia
595–612

Theodoric II
King of Burgundy
595–613
King of Austrasia
612–613

Dagobert I
King of Austrasia
623–628
King of all Franks
629–639

Charibert II
King of Aquitaine
629–632

Sigibert II
King of Austrasia
King of Burgundy
613

Sigibert III
King of Austrasia
632–656

Clovis II
King of Neustria
and Burgundy
639–657

Dagobert II
King of Austrasia
674–678

Lothair IV
King of Austrasia
717–719

Lothair III
King of Neustria
657–661
King of all Franks
656–661

Childeric I
King of Austrasia
661–675
King of all Franks
673–675

Theodoric III
King of Neustria
673–698
King of all Franks
675–691

Chilperic II
King of Neustria
715–720
King of all Franks
719–720

Clovis III
King of all Franks
691–695

Childebert III
King of all Franks
695–711

Childeric II
King of all Franks
743–751
(deposed by Pepin the Short)

Dagobert III
King of all Franks
711–716

Theodoric IV
King of all Franks
720–737

*Dates given are those of their reigns.

THE
BIRTH OF
FRANCE

THE
FORGOTTEN
KINGS

A plain square-columned Romanesque gateway gives on the tree-shaded cloister of the old monastery of Saint Médard at the edge of Soissons in France. Within all is still; not even a cat disturbs the grass. On one side are the featureless buildings of the school that occupies the site of the medieval abbey. On the other is a low roofless structure, all that remains of the sixth- to ninth-century church. A short flight of crooked stone steps, weeds growing in their cracks, leads down to the crypt. It is dark and cold; sunlight creeping through narrow round-arched window openings cannot penetrate far into the underground gloom. The crypt, intact though neglected, consists of seven small chapels opening off a central gallery. Each holds a sarcophagus, empty, open and unmarked. The cells are bare of decoration; only one of them has, on each side of its entrance, the now empty arched and pillared niche that once held the figure of a saint.

The crypt is too quiet. The city seems far away and the place breathes of death in a distant age. More poignant, not only death is here but Lethe. The living world has forgotten this place.

But it was one of France's shrines. "At this time [about 560], while Lothair was still reigning as King, Saint Médard the Bishop ended a lifetime of good works and died full of days and famed for his holiness. King Lothair had him buried with great pomp in the city of Soissons, and began to build over his remains the church which his son Sigibert later completed and embellished. At Médard's holy tomb I myself have seen the chains and shackles of prisoners burst asunder and lie broken on the ground."[1] One of the bare sarcophagi once held these miraculous bones.

A year after Saint Médard's death, it was the turn of King Lothair himself. The Merovingian king of all the Franks died on the first anniversary of the burning to death, on his order, of his rebellious son. Lothair's own imminent death outraged him: "What manner of King can be in charge of Heaven, if He is prepared to finish off great monarchs like me in this fashion?" Another of the blank coffins is Lothair's only memorial.

In 575 Sigibert, another of Lothair's sons, was stabbed with poisoned knives by two servants in the pay of his brother's wife. Her husband, relieved of a young and active enemy and free of direct responsibility for his removal, had Sigibert's body ceremoniously interred at the church of Saint Médard beside his father.

These few sentences, written in the sixth century by Saint Gregory of Tours, bishop, historian, friend and often critic of some of the kings of Frankish Gaul, are a sudden sharp lightning flash revealing a glimpse of that long-ago alien world. The unquestioning faith that saw miracles performed by the bones of saints, the flickering Christianity of a Teutonic chief closer in spirit to the forests of Germany than to the fading calmness of Roman-ordered Gaul, the slaying of a young hero by the treachery of a barbaric queen—these highlight an era much farther removed from today's world than that of the complex, decaying Roman structure it replaced.

However dissociated from us they appear, these credulous saints and savage kings and queens stand at the edge of our history. Their period, which we call the Dark Ages, was in truth the beginning of Europe as we now know it. The universal Roman Empire was dissolving; into the gap stepped the floating barbarian populations that had been alternately harassing and buttressing the failing giant. Gradually they settled, if uneasily and changeably, within definable boundaries that would later be called national. To the Latin-speaking citizenry of Gaul and Spain and Italy the new masters were alarmingly virile and ignorant. But they offered a robust contrast to the corrupt officials who had been slackly managing the affairs of the empire at its edges, out of touch with the central government at Constantinople. The German tribal chiefs and their rustic warriors, on the other hand, found much to admire and imitate in the civilized subject peoples whom they ruled with a forceful but not always insensitive hand. The blending was for the most part neither bloody nor abrupt.

In fact the Franks, by the time they had become the acknowledged masters of most of Roman Gaul, had little resemblance to their tribal forebears for whom battle was the chief purpose of a man's life, and who chose their leaders solely for their skill and courage in combat. By the sixth century, the onetime tribal chieftains had to deal with matters of peace instead of contention. Their problems were those of a settled agricultural population. Their mentors were the lords of a church whose ideological keystone—in contrast to that of the old German wielder of thunderbolts—was love for one's brother. The Frankish leaders, originally elected by their peers only for the duration of a specific fight or raid, had become hereditary monarchs with absolute personal power. These long-haired kings of the Merovingian dynasty governed an area considerably larger than present-day France. If they had not ironed out all traces of their warrior heritage, they had acquired essential new skills in statesmanship and diplomacy. Saint Médard, who lay beside them at Soissons, was a bishop of high education and noble stock, with a Gallo-Roman mother. He was also their adviser and their ally. For a few generations the Merovingian royal line was the most important political fact of Western Europe.

The Dark Ages are dark indeed if one looks for traces of classical learning, poetry and dialectic, refined sculpture or noble architecture. It was a disordered time, as any period of extreme change must be, and there was little tranquillity for the cultivation of the gentle arts. But out of it arose a new world. The Frankish tribes and their kings were both at the forefront and the center of this world: they were the successful barbarians, the organic link between the classical universal world of Rome and the discrete kingdoms of medieval Europe. However turbulent their history, from the regnancy of these sanguinary warriors and their unsoftened women grew the nation of France.

In the process of developing the future, the Franks were being transmuted by the past. Behind their success in Gaul were the prior accomplishments of the Romans and their Celtic subjects: out of this synthesis Gaul had developed into the most cultivated and flourishing province of the Western Empire. The Franks, inheriting this happy land, acquired much of the organization and a little of the polish of their predecessors.

On the other side, from the regions north and east of Gaul, the

German peoples brought the democratic spirit of a tribal society, a fearless and independent temper and genuine esteem for the honor of women. These qualities were, in those days, quite un-Latin, and they were a gust of fresh air in a demoralized world.

The catalyst was Christianity. The Roman political organization was deteriorating and the still-barbarian conquerors were ignorant of the techniques of handling their diverse new lands. The Church structure had survived the wreck of the Western Empire. In Frankish Gaul, after the conversion of Clovis, the fifth-century Merovingian conqueror, the Catholic order not only endured, it grew in vigor and effectiveness. The bishops, conservators of classical learning and inheritors of the best Roman tradition of public service, were counsellors and educators to the rough-textured new masters. The Catholic Church became the ally and the main prop of the Merovingian and later of the Carolingian dynasties; it provided the bridge from the Greco-Roman era to that of medieval Europe. In the Middle Ages its structure would become rigid and its power monstrous. But in the troublous centuries after the fall of the Western Empire it was the essential web of civilization over a chaotic and amorphous new world.

PART I

WARRIORS AND BISHOPS

CHAPTER ONE

ROMAN GAUL

During the four centuries before Caesar added Gaul to the Roman Empire it was the heart of the Celtic domains in Europe. As the strongest power north of the Mediterranean the Celts were a persistent menace to Greece and Rome. In the fifth century B.C. Rome made an alliance with the Greek colony of Massilia (Marseilles) for mutual defense. It was Rome's first toehold in Gaul, and the beginning of the contest between Romans and Celts for the dominion of northern Europe.

At about the same time the Romans began to eye the pleasing land to the north, the Celts were looking southward. They had become so successful in Gaul that their population had grown unmanageably large.[1] Their ruler appointed two enterprising young men as leaders of migrations to seek a home elsewhere. Among the migrating tribes were members of the Arverni (who gave their name to Auvergne), people of southern Gaul who would later face Caesar in nearly successful defiance.

In 390 B.C. a division of the wanderers crossed the Alps, and for the first time Celt met Roman in open conflict. Under the leadership of a warrior named Brennus the Celts defeated a Roman army at Allia, about twelve miles from Rome. Brennus then went on to attack Rome, an event surrounded by engaging legend. The Citadel, walled except for a precipice on one side, seemed impregnable until the besiegers caught sight of the footprints of a Roman messenger who had scaled the cliff face. The Celts, following his track, crept up the natural wall at night so quietly that even the sentries' dogs did not hear them. But a flock of geese was more alert. Sacred to Juno, the birds had been permitted to remain alive, despite the near-starvation of the Romans. The geese honked and flapped their wings, waking one soldier. He ran to the edge and surprised the first of the attackers at the crest. The Roman pushed the Celt off, and he crashed into those below him, sending them off the hillside like a stack of cards. The vigilance of the geese did not relieve the siege, and the impasse was resolved by a ransom of a thousand pounds of gold. The bribe, disgraceful to the Romans, was made more bitter by the insolence of Brennus, who, when the Romans claimed the Celtic weights were dishonest, threw his sword atop the pile of gold, saying "Woe to the conquered!"

Eventually the Romans defeated the Celtic invaders and drove them to the territory between the Alps and the Po River, an area that became known as Cisalpine Gaul. For about forty years they were fractious neighbors. In the Celtic manner, some of their disputes with the Romans were decided by single combat between champions. The Celts finally opted for peace, and in a pattern that was repeated throughout the history of the Roman conquests, the erstwhile enemy living on Roman soil was fully accepted by his tolerant master. The Celtic settlers, quick-witted and adaptable, with an Indo-European language similar to Latin, gradually became respectable Roman subjects well on the way to full citizenship.

The unassimilated Celts of Gaul were a different matter. To understand what the Romans faced at the time of Caesar's conquest of Gaul—and to appreciate the character of Roman Gaul at the time of its fusion with the Teutonic kingdoms of the Merovingians—we need to look at the Celts themselves, those extraordinary people who had most of Europe under their loose hegemony, yet never successfully challenged the Roman Empire.

The Celts are a branch of the Indo-European family from which most of the present-day European, Middle Eastern and Indian races are descended. Probably originating in the plains of western Russia, the ancestors of the Celts settled in the Alpine region of Austria and Switzerland. There, between 1300 and 600 B.C., they built a coherent society. But at no point in their history were the Celts a separate, blood-pure race. They were a blend of many peoples—an amalgam of adventurers, traders, farmers and fighters bonded by intermarriage, similarity of religion, custom and language—who developed a valid sense of identity. In short, they were a nationality.

Their development was given a strong impetus by the onset of the Iron Age, which reached the Celtic cradle around 900 B.C. The new technology in the hands of a driving and talented people, as well as their growing sense of nationality, gave the Celts an urge for expansion beyond their borders. Beginning about 500 B.C. the rest of Europe became increasingly familiar with roving bands of shaggy-haired, mustachioed, half-naked warriors irresistibly armed and mounted, who unleashed a wild, unnerving fury in battle. The fragmentary raiding resolved into a wholesale drive to conquer, and by the beginning of the third century B.C. the Celts were Europe's dominant power, their sway extending south to Italy, east to Rumania, Yugoslavia, Bulgaria, Thrace and Macedonia, and north through France and southern and central Germany, into the British Isles. This period of the Celts' ascendancy is known as the La Tène era, from the site in western Switzerland where the first artifacts were identified.

The Romans considered the Celts oafish and unkempt barbarians unable or unwilling to speak a civilized language or to write any language at all.* But the Celtic society that developed in the five centuries before Christ had a degree of accomplishment far beyond anything yet seen in that part of the world. Its strength of national feeling, despite the wide territory, was probably due to the ecclesiastical nature of the state. In their hierarchical society, aristocratic warriors shared the highest place with druids, who were priests, philosophers, teachers, judges and poets. The druids were the only educated class, and it was inevitable that they would influence, and sometimes usurp, the authority of the secular governments. The druids guarded their privileged position closely. Though they could write, they preferred to transmit their lore orally to chosen disciples; to record it would have lessened its magic. They did not want an educated congregation: the less available the mysteries, the more potent their effect. The result was a deeply religious populace, unified by its faith as were none of the other, more primitive barbarian peoples of Europe.

Since nothing was written down, not much is known of Celtic

---

*The Greeks originally coined the word "barbarian" from the "ba-ba-ba" sounds uttered by those they considered too uncouth to be able to learn Greek—including the Romans.

beliefs. The little we have comes from cloistered Irish scribes who started as early as the sixth century A.D. to record the oral lore of their countrymen—reproducing it in a surprisingly earthy and un-Christianized manner. The functions of their complex hierarchy of deities corresponds noticeably with those of the Greek, Roman and Teutonic pantheons, all of them derived from common Indo-European ancestors.

Music and poetry, in the regard of these warlike pagans, reached a level almost divine. Eloquence was valued as highly as bravery in battle, and could stay the arm of the most furious fighter. The god of literature was Ogmios, described as an old man who drew after him a crowd of people held by little chains of gold and amber, attached from his tongue to their ears.[2] The Celts were less proficient in the graphic arts, with the exception of fine metalwork. Artists covered the smallest surfaces of pots, weapons and personal ornaments with mazes of arabesques, arches and curving tendrils entwining stylized plants, animal figures and faces, a multiplication of detail so precise that it seemed the artists must have worked with magnifiers.

The people were endlessly inventive in the conveniences of daily life. Their smiths, who learned to cast soft iron and developed a new kind of brass, made a variety of excellent utensils and tools. Their carpenters and wheelwrights, as well as fashioning the swiftest and most elegant chariots, originated barrels and buckets that replaced pottery jugs over most of northern Europe. They introduced into the West trousers for men: since they operated chiefly on horseback, these were a Celtic necessity. They lightened the labor of the farmer and his wife with the invention of the scythe and the rotary hand mill for grinding grain—but their interest in agriculture hardly went beyond the preparation of grain for beer. The labor of the settled farmer seemed intolerably tedious to this race of dashing fighters.

The Celts were skillful sailors and innovative shipbuilders. They developed a sailing ship, unusual in that time of oared vessels, which they used both for trade and war; and they were the first regularly to ply the Atlantic Ocean.*

Though their level of education was high, their sense of justice strong and lively and their devotion to poetry fervent, the Celts were

---

*In Christian times the Celts of Ireland sailed to Iceland in their leather curraghs, establishing monastic communities there; and according to Norse saga-history they even reached the shores of North America.

mainly notorious for their fearsome aptitude as fighters, and their startling appearance. Their long red hair, white skin and great height were alarming to the small dark southern people into whose world they intruded. Even more dismaying were their manners in battle: the furious rush of horsemen and horse-drawn chariots, the shouted chanting of harsh voices, the discordant music of horns, the rhythmic beating of swords against shields. Before going into combat they whipped up a war spirit with ritualistic imitations of battle, and by the time they were ready to go they were so overheated with frenzy that many threw off their chain mail and launched into the fray naked. They had no fear of death: it was but "the midpoint of a long life"[3] and their spirits would survive in another body, or perhaps in a re-creation of the present one.

Fighting was the heart's blood of the Celts. Yet with all their audacity as warriors their mental outlook was imbued with grace and honesty. They honored their women and were generous and hospitable to strangers. They were an outdoor people, loving and understanding the ways of nature. Having few towns they had not learned the decadent luxuries nor the accompanying miseries entailed in urban living. Their moral code was uncluttered by sophistry and their lifestyle was spontaneous.

Their virtues bred flaws, and deep in the Celtic character lay the seeds of their downfall. Free, individualistic and proud, they could not envision the concept of cooperation that is essential to a strongly organized central government. They never managed—in fact they never even tried—to make a working empire out of the vast territories they dominated. Though they were tenuously united by the druidical hierarchy, their political structure was weak, ordered around the family and rarely going beyond the clan. In character they were too sure of themselves. Their natural superiority was great, and they appear to have had a distaste for the hard work of expanding it in the direction of self-government.

In the second century B.C. Rome's interest in Gaul accelerated. The extensive Roman domains were beginning to fray at the edges. Barbarian tribes, pushed out of their homelands by climactic conditions or by the pressure of other groups, were spilling over the ill-kept boundaries. Rome needed to round out her empire and secure her borders. Gaul was one of the uneasy sectors; besides, it was an alluring land of rich pastures, deep forests and great navigable rivers.

On their side the Celts saw imperial Rome as a threat to their supremacy in northern Europe. The two powers clashed several times on their common border before the uncohesive Celtic structure finally shattered under the impact of the Roman military and administrative machines. In 150 B.C. the Arverni gathered other Celtic tribes into a temporary union and challenged the Romans settled in Mediterranean Gaul.

The Auvergne is a country of contrasts: young volcanic mountains strewn with nearly impassable lava fields, hot springs from the magma not far below the earth's surface, protected, fertile river valleys and broad pasture lands. It is easily defensible: its narrow, hidden mountain defiles are classic territory for guerilla warfare. On this occasion, however, the Celts were defeated by the Romans, and in 123 B.C. Rome established a military post, Aquae Sextiae (Aix-en-Provence), at the southern edge of Arvernian territory.

In 121 B.C. the Celts made another essay at united opposition, again led by the Arverni. This time they were vanquished by Emperor Domitius, with the assistance of African elephants. The emperor then annexed a slice of southern Gaul from the Rhône Valley to Geneva, as well as the arc of the Mediterranean coastline between Rhône and the Pyrenees. After parading around his conquered territories on an elephant, Domitius brought his spoils to Rome. In the victory parade marched the captured Arvernian chief, in full Celtic war dress of animal skins, bronze breastplate and woolen cloak fastened with an elaborate bronze fibula, his long hair flowing free in back under the high bronze helmet and plaited in two braids beside his mustachioed face.

Domitius's victory over the Arverni marked the beginning of the Roman province of Gaul. In 118 B.C. this conquest was consolidated by the foundation of Narbo Martius (Narbonne), Rome's first citizen colony in Celtic Gaul. At the same time the Romans built their first road in Gaul, with the primary object of establishing land communication between Italy and their Spanish colonies. Sixty years later Gaius Julius Caesar continued where Domitius left off until Celtic Gaul was completely absorbed into the Roman Empire.[4]

In 58 B.C. Caesar was made proconsul of both the Roman Gallic provinces, Cisalpine and Transalpine Gaul. His command extended north to the Cebenna Mountains (the Cévennes in Languedoc) and Lake Lemanus (Lake Léman), and he had to deal not only with the hostile Celts* north of his border but with the newer and more dangerous waves of Germans under the able leadership of the Suevian Ariovistus. Ariovistus used the perennial quarrels among the Celtic tribes as an opportunity to annex part of Alsace; he then got himself confirmed in Rome as king of this region and Friend and Ally of the Roman People. His actions discomposed the Aedui, a Celtic tribe of the Alsace, who were also allies of Rome, and they sent a call for help to the new proconsul. Caesar welcomed the opportunity to make Rome's presence felt in northern Gaul. Disregarding the questionable ethics of balking one alley, he raced to Alsace with his legions and secured the boundaries of the other, the weaker Aeduis.

With his troops legitimately in Outer Gaul, Caesar decided to extend his activities. His motives for invasion were a combination of personal ambition and political foresight. He perceived that Gaul's future belonged not to the Celts but either to the Germans or the Romans; and he intended its destiny to be Roman. Celtic Gaul at this time included most of present-day France, Belgium, the Rhineland and much of the Netherlands and Switzerland. To the Romans, confined in Europe to the already overpopulated regions of narrow Italy and part of Spain, the rich, varied land of the Celts seemed boundless—a new world wherein the decaying Roman economy could regenerate itself and flourish indefinitely.

The native Celtic inhabitants did not worry Caesar. Though they had a complex society and a large population, their political and social organization had no basic unity. Because their technical development was far behind that of the Romans, they would be easily defeatable in battle in spite of their ferocity. Beyond these weaknesses lay the ultimate failure of a civilization. The Celtic nation had come to the end of its extraordinary rise. It had lost its original primitive virtues and had not succeeded in attaining the discernment and sophisticated judgment of an advancing culture. The Celts, who had dominated most of Europe for so long, were falling apart, destroyed by internal dissension and lack of motivation. Though Caesar observed the fatal weakness of a civilization in decline, he knew the

---

*The names "Celt" and "Gaul" were used interchangeably by contemporary Romans. Caesar differentiates, writing that only part of Gaul was definitely "Celtic," but it is not clear what he meant by this designation. There was so much confusion at the time, along with so little knowledge, that in the interests of clarity we will refer to all the tribes of Caesar's Gaul as Celts.

Celts to be an alert, inventive, responsive people ready for progress under experienced direction.

In his campaigns, which lasted seven years, from 58 to 51 B.C., Caesar confounded the enemy with swift marches and sudden strikes made possible by prodigious feats of engineering as the advancing troops built roads and bridges to facilitate their progress. Though the Celtic tribes outnumbered the invader, they had not learned the value of cohesion even in a desperate situation. The Celtic method of warfare depended upon individual duels between soldiers. Against the measured advance of the legions this was no more than a brave way of dying.

Near the end, in 52 B.C. under the leadership of the Arvernian chief, Vercingetorix, they rallied in a concerted attempt to repel the Romans. Vercingetorix used ruthless tactics to discipline his rowdy conscripts and to train them to act as a unit, in the Roman style. He rewarded and entreated those ready to learn, executed cowards or burned them at the stake, and as an example to waverers, punished minor faults by cutting off an ear or gouging out an eye. With his armies charmed or terrorized into order, the tough young leader was ready to engage the Romans.

After some minor skirmishes Vercingetorix, avoiding a pitched battle, retreated into the wild and rough country south of today's Clermont-Ferrand. He made camp in the fortified Arvernian town of Gergovia, located on a steep hilltop plateau twenty-four hundred feet above the plain where the Roman legions had halted. The Celtic settlement is long gone, destroyed by the Romans after the conquest of Gaul. But the plain of Gergovia remains untouched, except for a tall stone monument, and the structure of the battle is clear. The hilltop field is well defensible, its only access up steep basalt outcroppings. One can still see the grass-grown humps that were the Arvernian earthworks, and the gorse-filled ruts of the ancient tracks. The Romans scrambled up the rocks surprising the Celts in the encampment they had considered impregnable. The Celts fled in disarray, but Caesar at once recalled his troops. He preferred a judicious retreat to a possible victory accompanied by the certain loss of many men. Some of his soldiers heeded the trumpets, others chose not to. Sure that they could dispose of the disordered Celtic soldiery, the disobedient troops advanced to attack the town. Hand-to-hand fighting ensued; but the exhausted Romans could not cope with the fresh Celtic troops and finally, after the loss of seven hundred men, had to withdraw to their camp below. Caesar praised their heroism but condemned their poor discipline: "I want obedience and self-restraint from my soldiers, just as much as courage in the face of danger."

Vercingetorix himself chose the final battleground, the Field of Alesia, near the present-day town of Alyse-Sainte-Reine in Burgundy. The defeat of the Romans at Gergovia had strengthened Celtic unity: the Celts felt that another decisive rout would push Caesar and his legions forever out of Gaul. There was unusual agreement among the tribes. Vercingetorix had forces from most of the central clans under his banner, and his army (according to Caesar) far outnumbered that of the Romans.

Like Gergovia, the hilltop field of Alesia seemed easily defensible to Vercingetorix, and its fortress was well supplied. But this time the Celtic leader miscalculated. He was prepared for fighting below the walls of the fortress; instead he found himself locked in. Caesar built siege works all around the base of the hill, and in a short time Vercingetorix's big army had exhausted the garrison supplies. The soldiers became so demoralized that one of their leaders advocated cannibalism as an alternative to surrender. In the fierce battle that finally ensued—in which Caesar himself took part, conspicuous to his own men and the enemy alike in the scarlet cloak he always wore in action—the Celtic troops were thoroughly routed and many of them simply ran away and went home.

Their leader chose to sacrifice himself for the ultimate honor of his nation. Rather than flee, Vercingetorix put himself into the hands of his remaining soldiers, saying, "I did not undertake the war for private ends, but in the cause of national liberty. And since I must now accept my fate, I place myself at your disposal. Make amends to the Romans by killing me or surrender me alive as you think best." They delivered him to Caesar. Vercingetorix saluted the conqueror and surrendered his arms and his horse. The Roman general paid tribute to his enemy's qualities of leadership and courage, but did not spare him the customary Roman humiliation. Caesar allowed him to languish in prison for six years, then exhibited him in a victory parade through the streets of Rome. He was publicly executed at the foot of the Capitol for high treason against the Roman nation.

Vercingetorix represented the Celtic nation's final and best attempt at unified resistance. He had been the rallying point, the last hope, for a civilization which was already doomed. He is a figure of tragedy—too late and, in a way, too gallant. If he had saved himself after Alesia he might have been able to preserve the Celts' fragile unity for a few more years. But at the end he sacrificed that unity for the sake of a heroic gesture. "It is characteristic of the Celtic nation," wrote the historian Theodor Mommsen, "that its greatest man was after all merely a knight."[5]

The compatriots of Vercingetorix did not lose their country. They lost the war and their ascendancy in continental Europe. But in the tradition of Roman conquerors, Caesar was a considerate victor. Out of concern for his own exhausted troops he brought the war to a speedy close. His main goal, in the three years that remained of his ten-year governorship, was to leave a tranquil province as his legacy, peaceful within and secure on its borders. In only one direction was he ruthless: he brutally chastised the remaining insurgents, ordering that one whole rebellious Celtic garrison have the right hands cut off as a deterrent to further revolts. "His clemency was so well known," Caesar wrote of himself, "that no one would think him a cruel man if for once he took severe measures."

In general Caesar treated the conquered people with indulgence, respecting their political and religious institutions while he saw to their gradual Romanization. He put into office men favorable to Rome, admitted Celts of high rank into Roman citizenship and established the Roman monetary system. Above all he introduced the Latin language, with its consequent boon of writing. Along the far edges of Gaul he made allies of the people whom he could not subjugate. These included the Celtic territory of Armorica (Brittany)—which would survive both the Merovingian conquests and Charlemagne's consolidation—and the still nomadic Teutons to the north and east. The latter were the most potent threat to Rome's hegemony; Caesar minimized their dangerous antagonism by colonizing the tribes along the frontier and enrolling them as friends of Rome, to act as buffers to the encroachments of those beyond.

Although these measures were only beginnings, Caesar was wise beyond his century. He laid the groundwork for a Roman Europe that would fuse the continuing classical Greco-Roman tradition with the fresh Celtic-Teutonic ethos. The conquered Celts approached him halfway. Though Caesar had given the deathblow to their society, they were a far from decadent people. Resilient by nature and apparently undismayed by their military defeat, they collaborated readily with the conquerors. As an example, the tribal deity of the Arvernians, the god of the mountain Puy-de-Dôme, a solitary volcanic cone towering over Clermont-Ferrand, turned Roman. He became Mercury, the Roman patron of astronomy and the god of merchants, two aspects of an advanced civilization.

Within a hundred years the new province was the shining light of the Roman Empire, and for four centuries, until the Western Empire fell, Gaul was the main preserver of the classical world against the barbarian onslaughts. So strong was the vitality of the young province that even after the fall of the empire it retained its Roman outlines.

Much of Gaul's vigor derived from its rich and varied countryside. Despite its size, communication was made easy by the great river systems, the Rhône, the Loire, the Seine and the Rhine. Even the mountain ranges of the east and central south were not impassable. The extensive forests were a source of timber as well as of food and shelter for hogs; the plains were planted to grain, the valleys to orchards and vegetables; the uplands provided pastures for horses, sheep and cattle—a large source of wealth for Celtic Gaul. The southern regions rivaled Italy in wine and olive production—to the extent that when Rome had established her first foothold north of the Alps in the second century B.C., the local inhabitants were forbidden this lucrative husbandry. A little later Italian wine traders established a brisk exchange with the intemperate northern Celts, trading one jar of wine for a slave.

Trade and agriculture provided the new Roman province with material prosperity. Towns gradually developed; but in the beginning the Romans found the country too big and the people too rustic to be organized into a web of cities, as in Italy. Administration was ordered around the tribe and its territory. The pre-Roman Celts, country-dwellers, had few towns and these were no more than expanded marketplaces. Many of them were known by the name of the local tribe: Verdun from the Verodunenses, Amiens from the Ambiani, Poitiers from the Pictones, Reims from the Remi. Others had original Celtic names, as Burdigala (Bordeaux) and Lugdunum (Lyons), named for Lug, the chief Celtic god. It was Roman policy to de-emphasize local mores and implant the concept of empire; with this aim they often tacked an emperor's name to the old Celtic gathering-places, as Augustodunum (Hill of Augustus), which became Autun, and Colonia Agrippinensis, shortened to Cologne. But the Celts (or Gallo-Romans as they came to be called), cooperative as they generally were, clung to their sense of historical identity. They tended to slough off the characterless Roman names and return to the older appellations: the Roman Caesarodunum, for instance, slipped back to its original nomenclature of Tours, the capital of the Turones, and Roman Limonum revived its Celtic name of Poitiers.

Material wealth, Roman organization and above all peace stimulated the growth of the Celtic marketplaces into towns. With the evolution of urban life came an intellectual flowering, and some of the towns became university cities sheltering the best of Roman culture. The Romans had to draw on the Celtic aristocracy for the government of Gaul, and for this they needed an educated citizenry. They established schools in many of the towns and the Celts, anxious to direct their own land, responded with enthusiasm. They had always had a profound respect for education, and with a supple new language and a splendid new way of using it—writing—their schools developed into the finest in the empire. By the time of the fall of the Western Empire in the fifth century, Gaul had become its intellectual heart.

The Romans, utilizing the best of native tradition, established their schools over the druidical seats of learning. Autun, one of the earliest of the Gallo-Roman schools, had been a druidical seminary where the young nobility was trained in the study of the traditional oral lore. Besides Autun there were schools in many of the main cities— Toulouse, Vienne, Lyons, Reims, Bordeaux, Arles, Trier, Marseilles— where students took rhetorical training, the equivalent of today's university course. The studies included the classics; and while Roman Gaul produced only a few noteworthy poets, its scholars were largely responsible for the preservation of ancient literature through the centuries of ignorance that followed Rome's demise in the West.

One of Rome's lasting gifts to her conquered land was the Latin language. The new citizens learned Latin in the Gallo-Roman schools, and with the ingrained Celtic fondness for poetry and rhetoric, became known all over the empire for their eloquence. Public speaking was far more important then than it is today: it took the place of newspapers and magazines. The gift of extemporaneous oratory was a valuable asset, and Gallo-Romans became the most brilliant rhetoricians and the most sought-after teachers. Skill in oratory was vital for advancement in the Roman civil service; many

Gallo-Romans became leading statesmen. Among these was Gnaeus Julius Agricola, a Narbonnese who studied at Marseilles, rose to become governor of Aquitania and in A.D. 77 was elected consul and sent to Britain as governor. There he first subdued, then effectively civilized the newly conquered island.

In the field of literature the Gallo-Roman output, though large, was not memorable. The troubled decades of Rome's final decline in the West were not conducive to creative freshness, and its literary excellence lay more in style than in content. Several poets stand out—while not for their creative genius—for the deft charm of their writing, and for their relevance to their age.

Among these is Decius Magnus Ausonius, a poet and teacher of the fourth century: a Gallo-Roman aristocrat who, though true to the Roman tradition of public service, remained intellectually aloof from the violence of the break-up of his world. He was born about 309 in Saintes, educated in nearby Bordeaux, and in his early twenties set up a school of rhetoric there, that he ran for thirty years. His prestige grew to the extent that he was summoned by Emperor Valentinian I to tutor his son Gratian at the imperial court at Trier. When Gratian became emperor in 375 he rewarded his teacher with the prefecture of Gaul, and a year later with the consulship. Gratian was murdered in 383, and Ausonius, now in his seventies, retired to his family demesne at Saintes.

During these years usurping emperors were set up and defeated; legitimate emperors were murdered; Frankish tribes overflowed violently across the border of northern Gaul; whole terrified populations fled west out of the regions of the Danube from the rampaging Huns, displacing the Gallo-Roman inhabitants of the province as well as the German *foederati**** newly rooted in the land. Yet no echo of this activity rings in either Ausonius's quaintly detailed catalog poems of nature and geography, nor in his charming, provincial letters. His is always the voice of a happy rural gentlemen serenely at ease with his world.

His writing is the expression of a man who has been a teacher all his life. It is in the old Celtic and Teutonic tradition of teaching by mnemosis, a throwback to the time when the outstanding attribute of

Foederati were barbarian settlers on Roman territory who had been awarded, usually *ipso facto*, the status of allies of the empire.

a scholar was his well-muscled brain, developed by the exercise of memorizing. In that time, before writing simplified learning, poetry was the rule, even for documents of state, because rhythm and alliteration were aids to memory. Even in the fourth century A.D. memorization was a prevalent teaching device: books were few and precious before the time of the monasteries and their busy scriptoria.

But the objective of teaching does not make for sensitive poetry, and Ausonius does not shine in the area of emotional subtlety. The aim of his poetry was to teach, as in "Mosella," an idyll of the river, classifying its watery inhabitants and the dwellers along its banks. His orderly poems are hardly more than verse, but as methods of instruction they have an appealing charm—the poet had to make education pleasurable to the son of an emperor. Ausonius's letters also reflect the mind of the teacher and classifier, as a spirited disquisition on the subject of oysters.

This lyrical frivolity seems out of place in the context of the empire's impending doom, particularly from a highly placed politician who should have been aware of the fragility of his world. But awareness of that very instability may have decided Ausonius to retreat into an idyll of natural trivialities, to stem the tide for a while among his own friends, and to direct their view toward the unchanging beauty of small things.

Despite the scholarly retirement of his aging years, Ausonius was a true child of his time. He lived on the edge of two eras but did not suffer from the dichotomy between them. His leisurely, expansive style has a classic Latin graciousness, and his concerns, those of the well-to-do Gallo-Roman country gentleman, were not yet out of place in fourth-century Gaul. He was also a Christian, and this was relatively unusual among his class in Gaul, where paganism kept its hold, especially in rural areas like Saintes. Ausonius was a Christian of the early Gallo-Roman type: a cultivated, reasoned gentleman who believed mildly in Christ but knew nothing about the ascetic movement just entering Gaul, nor of the inflamed conflict over the nature of the deity that was tearing the East apart. His faith was not that of the enthusiastic convert but that of the intellectual who practices a balanced moderation in all areas of life. After the morning prayer, he wrote in *Ephemeris*, "Now God has been prayed to enough."[6] His kind of Christianity would not outlive the fire of asceticism and monasticism that would engulf Europe when the barbarians decisively replaced the Romans as masters of the West.

In the following century Roman authority crumbled all over Europe, and no power strong enough to take its place had yet arisen. Gaul suffered from the piecemeal erosion: bands of insurgent peasants plagued the Loire Valley; Franks infiltrated the northern regions from their Flemish settlements; Burgundians invaded the Savoie and Alemanni entered the Alsace; Visigoths came up from Spain to harry and finally to conquer Aquitaine; Britons inundated Armorica, in flight from Angles, Saxons and Jutes; Saxon and Frisian pirates made hit-and-run raids up Gaul's northern rivers.

In the middle of the fifth century a worse disaster than all these hit the Western Empire: the invasion of the Huns. Panic-stricken citizens as well as barbarians stampeded out of the eastern regions before Attila's advance, to compound the disorder in Gaul. Less than ten years later, Rome had hardly a foothold left in her best province. In 476 the puppet emperor, Romulus Augustulus, was deposed by Odoacer, a Teutonic warrior from Denmark who had been a general in the Roman army. There was no longer a Roman Empire in the West.

Into this shattered world came the last of the Gallo-Roman intellectuals, Gaius Apollinaris Sidonius, bishop of Clermont-Ferrand, poet and litterateur, and courageous defender of his beloved Auvergne. He was born about 430 in Lyon, into a family that was among the highest aristocracy. His father and his grandfather had held the office of praetorian prefect in Gaul, and both his mother and his wife were related to the family of Avitus, prefect of Gaul, later to be elected emperor in the West. These two strong women successively dominated the family, after the fashion of most aristocratic Gallic households. When Avitus was called to Rome as emperor in 455, Sidonius went with him. Avitus was the recipient of Sidonius's first panegyric, a popular type of pragmatic composition. Throughout his life Sidonius would produce panegyrics, even dedicating them to politics diametrically opposed to his own. His fluent encomiums, more journalism than literature, are graphic documents of fifth-century Gallic leaders and mores.

Avitus was deposed and assassinated a year after his election, and Sidonius, returning to Lyon, participated in a Gallic revolt against Majorian, a former soldier, who became emperor in 457. Sidonius successfully produced a panegyric intended to secure the new emperor's pardon for the insurrectionary Lyonnais.

In 469 Sidonius was made bishop of Clermont-Ferrand, the main city of Auvergne. It was a bad time for the Gallo-Romans. Roman emperors had been succeeding one another almost yearly, by deposition or murder, and the barbarians were taking advantage of Roman weakness. Majorian, who was murdered in 461, was the last Roman emperor to concern himself with Gaul. His deputy, General Aegidius, ruled over a small realm, Soissons, in the valley of the Seine. By the time Sidonius became bishop, Soissons was the sole remnant of the great northern dominion Caesar had bequeathed to Rome nearly five hundred years before.

Among the chieftains parceling out Gaul was the Visigothic king of Spain, Euric. Although a converted Christian of the Arian persuasion, Euric was a particularly barbarous conqueror. When he took Arles and Marseilles, "without more ado he cut off the heads of all who would not subscribe to his heretical opinions, he imprisoned the priests, and the bishops he either drove into exile or had executed. He ordered the doorways of the churches to be blocked with briars so that the very difficulty of finding one's way in might encourage men to forget their Christian faith."[7] Euric then proceeded to Auvergne, where he besieged Clermont-Ferrand unsuccessfully for three years. The city's defense was organized and led by its intrepid bishop, Sidonius, who penned a passionate plea for aid to his nephew Ecdicius, son of Emperor Avitus: "It is for you that the last breath of freedom is waiting, drawn by the citizens in their dying agonies. Whatever we have to look to—whether hope or despair—still our resolve is to have you among us to be our leader."[8] Ecdicius responded gallantly, bringing his little troop of commandos through the line of siege and entering the city amid the fervent acclaim of its citizens.

The heroic defense of Clermont-Ferrand was a lost effort. In 475 a minor and cowardly emperor, Julius Nepos (next to last Roman emperor in the West), agreed to cede Clermont-Ferrand to King Euric in return for Arles and Marseilles, cities more important to Rome. The bargain was wasted: Euric soon returned to Provence and the cities were lost for good. The shabby surrender of his town inspired Sidonius to a bitter lament: "Was it, in expectation of this glorious peace, that we tore out the plants growing in the crannies of the walls for food, often through our ignorance infected by poisonous weeds? O, break off by some means these shameful peace negotiations. If need be we would gladly prolong the siege and go on fighting and starving."

After the surrender Sidonius was imprisoned for two years. On his release, through the offices of a highly placed friend, he was surprisingly allowed by King Euric to return to his bishopric at Clermont-Ferrand. This inspired a graceful panegyric to the late enemy, though he had been an enemy not only in the political sphere but in the spiritual as well. Before his Gallic conquests Euric had been a fanatical persecutor of Catholics. Possibly he now saw the need, like other barbarian leaders, for the continuity of religion in the territories he had so peremptorily wrested from their historic affiliation. With the break-up of the Roman bureaucracy the structure of daily life was threatened with disintegration. The only trace left of the Roman organism was the Catholic Church, and the only men with administrative experience were the bishops. Sidonius, a Roman official turned bishop, would be of crucial importance to the new rulers of Gaul. Euric, faced with the administration of a large and hostile territory, saw the value of having this responsible and popular bishop on his side.

Sidonius made it easy for Euric. From his writings it may be deduced that he did not believe that spiritual preoccupations were a proper subject for the pen, nor even quite seemly in a working bishop. The austere discipline of the monastic orders and the exaltation of self-immolation were concepts alien to Sidonius's learned and worldly background. He was a conscientious bishop but a practical one, whose main concern was to administer his see.

Sidonius was an active bishop until his death in 488. Four years before, Euric had died, leaving his kingdom to his weak young son, Alaric II. The Visigothic dominion in Gaul at this time reached from the Pyrenees to the Loire, and east to the Rhône. Euric, after his initial brutality, had given it a measure of stability. He was the first to codify Visigothic law, he governed in the Roman manner, and his language of state was the Latin vernacular. But he clung to his Arian heresy, and despite his able rule he could not win the hearts of his Catholic Gallo-Roman subjects. Alaric II could not sustain the balance Euric had achieved, and before long the Visigothic conquests in Gaul would revert to the new masters of that land, the Catholic Franks.

Life in Sidonius's time, according to his letters, was pleasant and polite. One can see, in his description of a country Sunday after church, the breadth of leisure that Gallo-Roman life in the south still afforded. "Here some of us sat down under the shadow of a vine whose hanging foliage made a shady canopy. Others sat on the green turf, which was fragrant with flowers. Conversation ensued, pleasant, jesting, bantering, and a specially happy feature of it was that there was no mention of officials or of taxes. [Then] we raised a two-fold clamor, demanding according to our ages either ball or a gaming-board. Our most charming and delightful brother, Dominicius, had seized the dice and was busy shaking them, as a sort of trumpet-call summoning the players to the battle of the box."

This kind of indulgence in innocent frivolity would not outlast the century. It was long finished in the parts of Gaul where the Roman influence was not so strong. North of Provence and Auvergne the religious contour of Gaul was already showing signs of the unqualified piety of the Middle Ages, foreshadowed by the ascetic Martin of Tours nearly a century before Sidonius. Who is to say now which attitude was the more meritorious, the happy moderation of Sidonius or the unassuming spirituality of Martin? If the calm Gallo-Roman attitude had prevailed, European Christianity might have bypassed the bigoted, deliberate ignorance of the early Middle Ages and the appalling excesses of the Crusades and the Inquisition. But much would have been lost to us. We would not have had the art: the innocently devout stone carvings and hieratic painted wood Virgins of the Romanesque, the slender spires and arches of the Gothic era that embody the spirit of prayer. Gallo-Roman pragmatists could not comprehend these transcendent symbols of faith. The art of the Middle Ages grew out of an undoubting, naive devoutness antithetic to the reasoned cultivation of people like the bishop of Clermont-Ferrand.

Sidonius was almost an anachronism even in his day, yet his love of learning and literature, and of the already archaic Roman culture endears him to us. His personality comes through his articulate and often tart sentences. As an entrenched Gallo-Roman landowner with a distinguished lineage he was scornful of barbarians, especially Germans: "Why do you bid me compose a song dedicated to Venus, placed as I am among long-haired hordes, having to endure German speech, praising oft with wry face the song of the gluttonous Burgundian who spreads rancid butter on his hair. You don't have a reek of garlic and foul onions discharged upon you at early morn."

He is critical of doctors: "With their attendance and disagreements, their ignorance, and constant attentions, they over-anxiously kill off many patients," and gently witty at the expense of a fellow poet-orator, to whom "no one was sufficiently distasteful to call forth his curses, yet no one congenial enough to escape his abuse." Above all he loved his home, though he could rarely take his peace there. In the midst of stress and vicissitude the family estate was the place his heart was drawn to.

Sidonius's writing is a bright tapestry of Gallo-Roman life. The sharply drawn characters are not only landowners of his own class but merchants, Jews (for whom he had an enlightened regard remarkable in his time), fugitives and priests, along with bishops and emperors and barbarian chieftains. He is fluently urbane, and yet he exhibits throughout an honest integrity. One can see him, smiling and civil, standing at the far side looking at us understandingly across the Middle Ages. The valley in between is much more shadowy to us than his flowered Auvergne countryside.

Long before the time of Sidonius the polite world he celebrated had begun to rot. In the late third and fourth centuries the empire was entering into the financial and moral decline that would end with its abdication in the West. And although it remained a center of Roman culture and learning, Gaul was not spared the spreading corrosion of the Roman Empire. It was a period of currency inflation, increasingly uncontrollable crime, corruption in high places and inertia in the face of the growing barbarian menace. The cumulative effect was a pervasive demoralization of Roman society.

Much of the empire's distress came from the intolerable conditions of its tax structure. The *curials* (landowners liable for civil service) was responsible for the collection of taxes. It had been a matter of pride for a Roman citizen to be in this class: he took his duties seriously and discharged them with honor. But his responsibility had become insupportable as the empire reached unwieldy dimensions and needed ever more money to finance its enormous bureaucracy and the armies that protected its frontiers. At the same time there was widespread rural depopulation due to recurrent plague, military conscription and the crushing taxes themselves. Agriculture was declining: arable land was abandoned in many areas and the soil exhausted in others. As agriculture faltered, industry and commerce suffered, and there were not enough resources to supply the administration's bottomless needs.

The tax collectors were caught in the middle. Every year a required amount of money had to be paid into the treasury regardless of how it was raised, and whatever the curials could not collect had to come out of their own pockets. In desperation they became oppressors. With no recourse against the tax evasions of the rich, they hounded the ever poorer subsistence farmers. The law required the curials to fulfill their civil service; and at the same time forbade them to change either their position or their domicile. They were not allowed to enlist in the army or to enter the Church or the law. A few could escape the intolerable situation by getting themselves elected to the Senate, where they were not liable for civil service. The majority of curials went under, forsook their property or were dispossessed and had to enter the protection of a rich landowner in return for work. There they had a measure of security, at the cost of personal liberty. The middle class of the empire was being destroyed as the free provincial landed gentry was reduced to the status of serfs. In its place were an ever smaller and richer upper class and a vast lower population of dependent tenants and workers with wretched prospects and no incentive. The working classes, like the middle class, were chained by a rigid caste system, the most baneful aspect of the later Roman Empire. The poll tax law barred even those in trades and professions from changing their positions, and locked every worker irrevocably into his station. The result was a bleak apathy to the present and to the future.

The western part of the empire suffered more than the eastern because of the barbarian pressure on all its fronts. In 330, Constantine chose Byzantium as the site of New Rome, or Constantinople. He was forced to divide the empire because of its unmanageable size and because old Rome was too far west and too close to the encroaching barbarians to be a secure location for the center of government. But the transfer of the imperial capital increased the strength of the eastern part of the empire at the expense of the exposed western section.

The morbid condition of the armies exacerbated this condition. The Roman troops were no longer the loyal, disciplined legions of Caesar's time. The soft Roman youths of the fourth and fifth centuries had a horror of soldiering and sometimes cut off the fingers of their right hands or otherwise mutilated themselves to avoid military service. There was a preponderance of German *foederati*, callous and unreliable mercenaries, in the imperial armies. They gave their shallow allegiance only to their mostly German leaders, who also had no particular loyalty to the distant, abstract empire they served.

One of the first and most alarming symptoms of Rome's moral failure had been the rise in third-century Gaul of the Bagaudae, a peasant army made up of members of the rural lower class and the dispossessed middle class. They were goaded by famine, pestilence, excessive taxes and judicial oppression to rebel against Roman rule. Though its beginnings were spontaneous the movement attracted malcontents of all kinds and it soon took a criminal turn. Fugitive slaves and malefactors whose only desire was escape were gathered by army deserters into bands with a semblance of military organization, but whose object became straight banditry. The bands trained as fighting units under self-styled "emperors," some of whom were products of several generations of brigandage, their families rich in cattle and slaves taken in raids. Among the more egregious outrages, an army of marauders entered and sacked the city of Autun after a long siege. In 287 Maximian, a general later chosen as emperor of the West, succeeded in quelling the revolts and breaking up the rebel armies. The disbanded outlaws slipped away into the mountains and forests and continued their raiding well into the fifth century.

The Bagaudae were a flagrant sign of a fundamental revolution in Western Europe, attenuated over several centuries, as the classical order of the Greco-Roman world decomposed and in its place the barbarian kingdoms and the Christian Church, the twin structures of the Dark Ages, emerged. In 410 Alaric and his Visigoths sacked Rome, sending a cataclysmic shock through the western world, "when the bright light of all the world was put out, when the Roman Empire was decapitated, and the whole world perished in one city."[9] In 476 the German *foederati* general, Odoacer, destroyed the last vestige of imperial authority in Rome, and Italy became but another barbarian kingdom.

Between the sack of Rome and the deposition of the last Western emperor, there came a tempest out of the East: the Huns, under Attila, crossed the Rhine and invaded Gaul.

The origin of this Asian people is not positively known. Probably they were the Hiong-nu, a race dominant in Mongolia in the third century B.C. For several centuries they harried the Chinese empire under the Han dynasty, where they enjoyed a reputation as formidable raiders expert on horseback, bestial to women and children, wantonly destructive of the lands they crossed, terrible in war and slothful in peace—and grotesquely ugly. In the first century A.D. they were defeated by the Han dynasty and ceased molesting China. Over the next three centuries the strongest and most pugnacious of the Huns began moving westward across Russia. In the middle of the fourth century A.D. they appeared on the European horizon. In 372 they invaded Scythia (today's Rumania), and spread rapidly from there across the plains of Hungary.

With their invasion of the Roman Empire the legends began.[10] The Huns had arisen, wrote Jordanes, sixth-century historian of the Gothic nations, when Filimer, king of the Goths, discovered witches among his people and banished them to the swampy hinterlands. "There the unclean spirits, who beheld them as they wandered through the wilderness, bestowed their embraces upon them and begat this savage race, which dwelt at first in the swamps, a stunted and puny tribe, scarcely human and having no language save one which bore but slight resemblance to human speech." The historian conceded that the Huns had a subsequent partial development, were skilled horsemen, and experts with the bow and arrow.

But the trifling advance in the culture pattern of the Huns did not improve their appearance, which unstrung all whose paths they crossed. For most Europeans this was the first encounter with Orientals. They were appalled by the Huns' slitted eyes, flat noses and broad hairless cheeks, which appeared to them as deliberate deformities. "They had a sort of shapeless lump, not a head, with pin-holes rather than eyes. They are cruel to their children on the very day they are born. For they cut the cheeks of the males with a sword, so that before they receive the nourishment of milk they must learn to endure wounds. Hence they grow old beardless, and their young men are without comeliness."

In 434 Attila became the king of the Huns. Even in his time Attila was a near-legendary figure.* "He was a man born into the world to shake the nations, the scourge of all lands." But those who visited this dreaded leader in his tent village in Pannonia (probably near today's Tokaj in northern Hungary) found that his manner of life was both simple and dignified. In the wooden house that was his "palace" Attila received ambassadors while seated on a wooden chair; at banquets he ate plain meat from a wooden platter—although his guests were served luxurious food on silver dishes and drank from

---

*Attila appears in the *Nibelungenlied* and other medieval sagas, his name slightly changed and his disposition benevolent.

golden goblets.[11] He dressed simply—his only concession to physical vanity was to be clean—and his sword and his horse's bridle were unadorned.

In his early years as king of the Huns he had hired himself out as a mercenary in the pay of the emperor at Constantinople, helping Roman generals fight other barbarians. In this capacity he became a close associate of the Roman general Aetius, a Scythian who had risen in the service of the empire to become virtual ruler of the Western Empire. Aetius had spent some youthful years as a hostage at the Hunnic court, so the Mongolians were not so outlandish to him as to most of his countrymen. He and Attila, both successful generals, were respectful of one another's military expertise. Both were also of barbarian birth, and became personal friends in their joint defense of the empire.

The friendship lasted only as long as Attila remained in the East. He had demanded an exorbitant tribute for leaving Constantinople alone. In 450 the emperor in the East refused to pay it any more, and Attila, casting about for ways to retaliate, found two good pretexts for invading the West.

Valentinian III, emperor in the West, had a half sister, Honoria, who was enduring a carefully monitored girlhood at the court of Ravenna. Bored with her circumscribed life, she became pregnant by her chamberlain. She was sent in disgrace to Constantinople, where she came under the restrictive vigilance of her ever-praying step-cousins, and was betrothed to a dull and respectable consul. Regarding her prospects as intolerable, the princess offered herself to Attila, her antithesis in every aspect—a man who worshipped the god of war symbolized by an iron scimitar, whose appearance was repulsive to western eyes, whose language was unintelligible and who, besides, already had a number of living wives. The Hunnic leader accepted the offer with alacrity and sent a ring of betrothal to Honoria's brother, the Western emperor. The token was accompanied by the demand that his bride's half share of the Western Empire, which she had forfeited on her adventure with the chamberlain, should be restored to him as her lawful husband. Valentinian turned him down on all counts, and instantly married his sister to her dusty fiancé.

This was Attila's first excuse for invading the West. His intention was reinforced by a feud between two German leaders, one of whom, an ally of Attila, enlisted the Hun's aid. Attila, therefore, in the double guise of champion of a wronged princess and defender of a threatened ally, used these claims to see what he could realize in western Europe. He led his massive army across the plains of Hungary and the forests of eastern Germany from Tokaj to Mannheim, a distance of six or seven hundred miles. Disaffected *foederati* and unassimilated barbarians swelled his forces as they passed, and by the time they reached the Rhine in 451, Attila's forces numbered about five hundred thousand.

Attila's march across Europe, a wantonly destructive progress, marked the end of his accord with Aetius. Aetius was an ambitious barbarian who yet believed in the maintenance of the Roman Empire as the only viable government of Europe. Attila, equally ambitious, believed in nothing but himself. The lands devastated and the people despoiled in the wake of his conquests demonstrated that the Hunnic leader had no interest in any order at all. Aetius knew that the inundation of Europe by the Hunnic hordes would bring paralyzing chaos. The German conquerors—Ostrogoths, Visigoths, Burgundians and Franks—who were beginning to reshape Europe into new kingdoms on the groundwork of the Roman structure, would be annihilated.

The Huns' entry into Gaul started with the destruction of Trier and the burning of Metz. The army swept westward, sacking towns, laying waste farmlands, murdering and raping. There is some semilegendary evidence, despite the wholesale panic recorded by contemporaries, that Attila's advance was not absolutely ungovernable: he was turned aside from Paris by Saint Geneviève, who led the people of the city in a crusade of prayer and fasting (and consequently became the patron saint of Paris); and he was persuaded to spare Troyes by Saint Lupus, who, taken hostage, succeeded in converting his brutish captor to Christianity. But in general the Hun's progress was irresistible until he reached the fortified town of Orléans.

He was shaking the walls with his battering rams, and the people within were prostrated in prayer, when he learned of the approach of Aetius and his allies from the south. Attila's main strength was in his horsemen, and he knew that he needed open country in order to be effective. He withdrew his armies northeast, to the Catalaunian Plains, the flat farming country east of Paris. (In a historical echo this region, the main battleground of World War I, would be the farthest area of German penetration.) There, in 451, took place the battle which decided the course of European history.

The battle lasted one day. The details are obscure, and legend has taken the place of lost fact—as that the spirits of the slain warriors fought on in the air above the field. Jordanes states that one hundred sixty five thousand men were killed on both sides, and gives a lurid picture: "That portion of the earth became the threshing-floor of countless races. Hand to hand they clashed in battle, and the fight grew fierce, confused, monstrous, unrelenting—a fight whose like no ancient time has ever recorded. A brook flowing between low banks through the plain was not flooded by showers, as brooks usually rise, but was swollen by a strange stream and turned into a torrent by the increase of blood. Those whose wounds drove them to slake their parching thirst drank water mingled with gore."

Among the allies of Rome was a small band of Franks, making on this day their first recorded appearance as *foederati*. Their leader was Merovech, the eponym of the Merovingian dynasty. Merovech's brother fought on the side of Attila; for in this battle German fought German. Some of those under the banner of Attila were Roman allies discontented with the corrupt rule of the empire; many were impressed subjects from the Hunnic leader's lands. Attila's empire at the time he invaded Gaul included most of central Europe, where the population was mainly Teutonic.

The outcome of the battle was a draw; even Jordanes was unable to claim victory for the side of virtue. But it resulted in Attila's losing his zest for the further demolition of Gaul. He retreated in good order with the remains of his army, and went back to Pannonia. The following year he invaded Italy, where he leveled the city of Aquileia at the head of the Adriatic, and reduced Padua and other northern cities to heaps of stones and ashes. (One fortuitous result of Attila's annihilative progress through Italy was that the few fleeing inhabitants of Aquileia, joined by survivors of other razed cities, took refuge on the waterlogged islands in the Adriatic, where later would rise the Republic of Venice.) Attila was stopped finally, say the pious chroniclers, by the intercession of Pope Leo the Great, his pleas aided by the materialization of Saints Peter and Paul, who threatened instant death if the Hun did not desist from his ruinous course. The more likely eventuality was that Attila's men were decimated by famine and disease in the country they themselves had scourged, and the remnants were unmercifully harried by Aetius's auxiliaries. Exhausted, they went back home. In 453 Attila took a new young bride, and he died on their wedding night, of a stroke brought on by too much revelry.

For seventy-nine years, from 372 to 453, the Huns had held Europe in fear. When Attila died the menace evaporated. He was the unifying force of the immense Hunnic realm, which extended from the Caucasus to the Rhine and from Thrace to the Danube. After his death the kingdom, held together by his efficient brute power, disintegrated as his many sons quarreled among themselves. The uncohesive nation broke up into small bands and disappeared as a force in history. Some of the Huns stayed in eastern Europe; most, it is thought, went back to Russia and settled north of the Caspian Sea.

Aetius died a year after Attila. The Roman general was slain, with no reason but jealousy, by the hand of Emperor Valentinian III— whose beset realm Aetius had spent his strength buttressing and at the end had saved from disaster. As Aetius presented the emperor with a bill for his services Valentinian jumped from his throne, shouted treason and ran him through with his sword—the first time he had ever drawn it. Valentinian himself was assassinated in the following year by a senator whose wife he had violated.

The chief fighters in the conflict that decided Europe's future were dead within two years of its resolution. One relatively minor figure remained: Merovech still lived, with the remnants of his brave band of Franks, the inheritors of ravaged Gaul. Within two generations his descendants would transform the waning star of the Roman Empire into the dominant kingdom of the early Middle Ages.

CHAPTER TWO

THE
GERMANS

"The Germans I regard as aboriginal, and not mixed at all with other races. [For] who would leave Asia, or Africa, or Italy for Germany, with its wild country, its inclement skies, its sullen manners and aspect, unless indeed it were his home?"[1] So wrote Gaius Cornelius Tacitus at the end of the first century A.D. from his own home under the soft Roman sky.

The Germans were not a new phenomenon in Tacitus's lifetime: they had been a familiar menace around the Empire's northern borders for at least two centuries. But they still struck the Roman mind with a mixture of fear and contempt, along with a half-acknowledged yearning for the elemental purity and the heedless valor that made their lives enviably simple. To the literati, the rough German warrior and his chaste partner-wife were the "noble savages" of their time, an attractive alternate to the effete youth of Rome and her decadent, amoral women. Tacitus's account of the German mores was the fruit of four years' sojourn among them, and it is as accurate as was possible to a contemporary historian with little to go on but personal observation. Still, while not a conscious idealization, it presented a heroic image of the man of the wild woods, with the clear intention of pointing a sermonizing finger at his antithesis in Rome.

From a realistic viewpoint, a very large storm was gathering in the north. Caesar and others before him recognized this, but in their day it seemed fully possible for Rome to weather it. Unfortunately, the expedients with which they protected themselves were temporary. There were too many Germans, and they kept on coming. From time to time the encroaching tribes were soothed with treaties and gifts of land; and already groups of partly tamed *foederati*, presumably loyal to the empire, were filling empty spaces in the Roman armies.

The creeping flood of Germans was the latest manifestation of mass migrations going back into prehistory. Even though the "wild country" was their home, the Germans from time to time had found its climate intolerably disagreeable. About 500 B.C. the climate of northern Europe began to chill, and long winters and short wet summers made life in those regions insupportable. People began moving southward and the first Germans appeared at the limits of civilized Europe. These movements were not the aggressive forays that would harass the empire in later centuries, but long trains of oxcarts carrying the goods and families of trekkers escaping a homeland no longer endurable.

Around the second century B.C. the cosmic pulse of weather caused new shifts. A warm cycle resulted in the melting of glaciers in the north, with consequent widespread flooding and subsidence of land along the Baltic Sea. Solid land became island, arable field and pasture turned to salt marsh. Again there were forced migrations. The restless tribes moved south and west along the edges of the Roman Empire. They displaced already established German settlements, whose members, forced out, created a continual roiling of populations and an irresistible undertow to the south.

Celtic Gaul, as the most northerly of the cultivated domains bordering on the German lands, received the brunt of the impact. German tribes were settled, uneasily and inconstantly, along the whole Gallic border. To discourage attacks by their wandering brother Germans they made a practice of laying waste all the land for miles around their rude settlements. In any case they were less interested in agriculture than in raid and battle, and the rich land across the river was alluring. They began inching over, to the dismay of their long-established and softened cousins, the Celts, and to the alarmed attention of the Romans entrenched in Transalpine Gaul to the south.

But the Germans of the second and first centuries B.C. were not yet a serious menace to the empire. The northern barbarians, even those who had settled along the Rhine and come under the influence of

Celtic and Roman traders, were still living by standards set in the time of their free-roving fathers. They were shaped by their environment—the sea and the forest—and the elemental facts of their existence developed in them self-reliance, a sense of isolation and a mystical oneness with nature. These in turn led to their insouciant acceptance of danger, their defiance of fate and their independence of spirit. Alongside this semireligious idealism were traits consequent on the unceasing struggle simply to stay alive: hard realism and facile recourse to cruelty and violence.

The basis of their society was the family. As they gradually ceased wandering and began to settle in the more benign sections of their generally harsh country, the nuclear family grew into an extended sibling group, or tribe, which included non-blood relatives and adopted outsiders.

Some tribes had a chief known as a *kuning* (king), a Teutonic word meaning man of the kin. While the Germans were still nomadic and ordered to the enlarged family group the king's position was largely honorary, and it was not hereditary: he was elected from one of the noble families of the tribe. He was mainly a peacetime leader with judicial and sacral functions; in some cases he was also a war chieftain. But his position was dependent on the will of the entire male body of the clan, in whose hands were all the main decisions as well as the overall welfare of the community. The warriors assembled in a field either at the full or the new moon, coming uncoerced and fully armed, at their own tempo. At the meetings they resolved on war, dispensed justice and, if necessary, elected a new king. They ritualized their choice by raising him on a shield and carrying him around the field. This democratic congress became known as the *campus martius*, and it survived, with some long intermissions, until the time of Charlemagne.

The German sense of justice was strong and its dispensing rough and immediate. The crime was usually punished according to its kind. Traitors and deserters, whose iniquity should be exposed, were hanged from trees. Other offenses must be hidden: cowards and those "stained with abominable vices" were bound in a cage of woven twigs and thrown into the bog. Lesser offenders were usually chastised by fines of horses or cattle. Half the fine was paid to the community, the other half to the victim or his relatives.

Of more immediate consequence than the king was the military leader, elected by the clan for a specific raid or battle, during which he would have the power of life and death over his followers. The chosen leader called on the assembled warriors for volunteers, and the young men who ventured with him, forming an association known as the *comitatus* (a Latin word meaning a body of companions), were ready to defend and protect him to the death. Everlasting disgrace, wrote Tacitus, faced one who left the field alive, on which the master had been slain. Though the chief fought for victory, his vassals fought for him. These dedicated fighters were not necessarily of the clan. If a tribe was too long at peace its restive youths, seeking a more interestingly perilous life, would leave the community for one where combat was still everyday fare. "The sloth of prolonged peace is odious to their race," wrote Tacitus. The fraternity of the comitatus gave them, besides an escape from boredom, a quick return in spoils far preferable to the tame round of toil at home. Though they might pay for it in blood, the adventurers thought less of that than of the ensuing glory.

The comitatus was the only institution for which freemen crossed the tribal line: not only did the volunteer leave the encompassing shelter of the family but he might find himself fighting his own kin. With his oath of fidelity he had forsworn all the old tribal values; his single-minded allegiance to one man was a substitute for what he had relinquished. This obsessive fealty was a spur to the enterprising leader who, with his rootless young fanatics, could extend his field of operations well beyond the single undertaking for which his clan had chosen him. The hero-leader and his band of loyal companions were the vanguard of the eventual barbarian penetration of the empire: they were alternatively the raiding, looting scourges of the border; the advance seekers of fresh pastures for their compatriots back in the woods; or the hired mercenaries, of great skill and dubious reliability, of the Roman armies. They also became the nucleus of confederacies which would challenge Roman supremacy in the western provinces. The comitatus, vital in the years when the Germans were establishing footholds in Roman Europe, endured into the era of German supremacy: the *comites* became the antrustions—voluntary followers—the chosen companions and defenders of the Merovingian kings.

While many of the young men were out winning their places in the sagas their countrymen in the hinterland pursued lives of unsparing simplicity. In common with other seminomadic barbarians the Germans had a manly distaste for tilling the soil, and their domestic pursuits were mainly pastoral. Herds of undersized cattle constituted their chief wealth, and milk, cheese and meat their main diet. They tended to stay in one place only until the pasture gave out; and necessity was reinforced by their traditional attitude to the land. No one owned land; temporary holdings were assigned to each family at the discretion of the chief, to be withdrawn the following year. The result (and also the purpose, according to Caesar) was to prevent people from settling into the placidity of soil cultivation and losing their fine enthusiasm for war. They would begin building comfortable houses, and then they would no longer be hardened by exposure to the climate as they were in their mud-and-wattle huts. Even more insidious, they would begin to make an adequate living: this would soften their moral fiber. A further deterrent was the tribal practice of decimating the countryside around the settlement: besides foiling invasions by the neighbors this effectively frustrated potential home-makers.

The same approach was manifested also in their regard for chastity. Continence was expected: it was not only disgraceful, it was un-healthy for a young man to have intercourse with a woman before the age of twenty. Abstinence, they believed, made the youth grow taller, stronger and more muscular.

The German attitude toward women echoed this belief. Though women had no political or property rights they were surrounded by an atmosphere of reverence almost religious—a view probably deriv-ing from an earlier, more peaceable society when the fertility cult was paramount. Priestesses and female seers were venerated and consulted by the most temeritous leaders. Though the German wife could not go to the assemblies where her armed relatives arranged the fates of her husband and her sons, she was with them when they went to battle. She brought food and encouragement to the field; she tended the wounded and comforted the dying; she rallied the failing courage of her men by representing with tears and bared bosom the horrors of captivity.

The marriage state was held in deep respect. When a woman married—well past adolescence, like her bridegroom—she became the property of her husband. She could be sure, however, that she would share him with no one else, either within or outside the law. Monogamy was obligatory. Though theoretically her husband owned her and could do as he liked with his possession, in practice her relatives would see to it that he did not abuse his right. She herself—

his untimid partner who did not shrink from the smell of blood and the sound of battle and who ran the household in peacetime, doing most of the heavy work—was not a chattel to be unwisely handled.

Before the wedding the couple exchanged gifts. The future bride received from her betrothed no feminine trinkets, no gowns or household linens, but a horse, a shield, a lance and a sword. As her contribution to the future of their household she presented him with more weapons. The relatives gathered round to view the exchange, and if they judged the prospective family adequately prepared for a lifetime dedicated to armed conflict, the wedding took place.

It was likely to be a happily noisy affair, taking place out of doors, with dancing, singing and immoderate eating and drinking. If it was an aristocratic marriage the guests were gorgeously dressed. The men wore short, many-colored tunics, leaving their legs bare above the heavy laced boots. Around the waist was a broad deerskin belt studded with bronze bosses, and over the shoulders a cloak of bright-colored wool or matched animal skins. On their bare arms they might wear a massive gold arm band, and around their necks a twisted gold torque; fastening the cloak at the shoulder was a gold fibula adorned with precious stones. Their jewelry was crudely fashioned, in contrast to the intricate Byzantine adornment of the same period, but it had a simple grace, the expression of a people natively artistic. The men's hair, unbound, flowed over their shoulders, and their faces were shaven but for long mustaches. The woman's basic garment was a long straight underdress of fine skins or wool; over it she wore an embroidered linen tunic attached at the shoulders with brooches and circled with an embossed leather belt. Her hair fell loose, and was bound across the forehead with a fillet of twisted gold wire. For all the splendor of their dress the wedding party guests were not overnice; and added to their normal rankness was the effluvium of the food they ate—wild onions and ripe venison—and the rancid butter with which they oiled their hair.

Once married, the woman's body and soul were forever dedicated: her husband and her household were her total life. In contrast to her Roman counterpart she was "uncorrupted by the allurements of public shows or the stimulant of feastings." In fact she had little leisure to be seduced by anything that we would call pleasure. She was a drudge. While her husband's only domestic concern was the protection and defense of his property, she worked in the field, tended the herds, managed the household, suckled her yearly babies and reared them after a fashion. Though her husband idealized her as a demigoddess and valued her, in practical terms, as his indispensable helpmeet, their partnership was not that of equals. When he was not off fighting or depredating along the border he was hunting. When he came home from the forest or the battleground he spent the idle hours feasting, drinking, quarreling with his intemperate companions and listening to bards extemporize on his exploits.

The honor of the German tribesman's wife was paramount to his self-respect. If he dared not mistreat her he was also extremely sensitive of her chastity. Though adultery was rare (it is probable, as Gibbon remarks, that the physical allurements of these doughty women were not such that temptation readily came their way[2]), it was harshly punished when it occurred. The husband, in the presence of her relatives, cut off the sinner's hair, stripped her naked and flung her out of the house; then he flogged her publicly through the village. After this she was blindfolded and thrown into the bog with a hide collar around her neck, an end similar to that of the most contemptible male miscreants.

The women bore as many children as possible. Though there was no law against limiting the number of offspring or destroying unwanted babies, these practices were severely discountenanced. From birth the children were familiar with the milieu that would dominate their lives. When the women accompanied their men to war the entourage included all the children down to the suckling babies. Back at home no nursemaid came between mother and child. She nursed him herself and when he left her arms she saw to his daily care, such as it was. Sketchily clothed and unsoftened by warm baths, the children played and slept on the dirt floor of the hut. In summers they could bathe in the river; all through their youth the sexes bathed together, so that the facts of sex, though not the experience, were familiar to them. They grew up sturdy, unfastidious and totally democratic, the master's children undifferentiated from those of the slave until age and calling separated them.

Starting at birth the Germans were free in a way no Roman could ever know again. It was small wonder that those who had no direct experience of the underside—the dirty, dismal huts, the uncouth children, the violent and slothful young men, the ever-drudging young women, the general squalor of a life devoid of all the little luxuries lightly taken for granted in Rome—should see in these tall, arrogant, healthy outlanders a lost ideal of proud and confident freedom.

The Germans' religion was the reflection of their temporal lives. Combining pragmatism with poetic idealism, they invested with divinity only the things they could see. Those that influenced them most—the sun, the moon, fire, the earth—were personified by their higher gods. Lesser divinities inhabited trees, fountains and rivers; unfriendly dwarfs lived in caves and river beds; the most dreaded enemy, the frost giants, threatened them always from beyond the boundary of their present world—from the inclement north whence their forefathers had fled. The exodus was unrecorded except in race memory, but the fear which had driven them south was perpetuated as a war in which the gods were fated to defeat.

All their deities, amiable and disagreeable alike, were as fallible as their human counterparts, and the careers of gods and earthlings were inextricably mixed. The skalds—the oral historians—tended to exaggerate, in deference to their paying customers. In their tales the fates of the mortal heroes became so entangled with celestial affairs that in the end they were all part of the same great epic. A primary key to the Teutonic character was the pervasive gloominess of the religious outlook—the blood feuds of the gods, the deceit and treachery through which they compassed the destruction of the mortals involved with them, the hard hand of fate, against which they fought in vain, knowing always that Ragnarok, the doom of the world, lay at the end.

Their long, involved drama, romantic and earthy at the same time, has come down to us chiefly through the agency of Christian writers of the medieval period. Though these priest-scholars had not the intention, as had their singing predecessors, to entertain a battle-weary, mead-sodden clientele, they had another bias: the shadow of Christianity lies over the pagan drama. The cruel motives of the gods are qualified by awakening conscience, and the despair of the final holocaust is mitigated by the promise of redemption. These attributes were no part of the pre-Christian German mentality. A tender conscience and the expectation of elevated bliss hereafter were alien to the mind of the tribal German. He regarded aggression as the whole spectrum of terrestrial life; and his projection of an afterlife took him no further than the feasting-table at Valhalla, identical to that below though better spread, and a continuation of the habitual hostilities, with nobody dying. In spite of the Christian drift, however, the medieval sagas give us a picture of a people's mentality as seen through their religion, a clear-etched portrait that would otherwise have been erased by time.

At the time this religion was at the height of its practice it was known only piecemeal to such Roman writers as Tacitus and Caesar. They gave the German deities Latin names and classical attributes. This was understandable, for there is a cousinship among all the Indo-European male gods—the war gods and the sky gods—and their careers have striking similarities. Like the Christians later, the Roman observers did not recognize that gods change with their environment; that they are, after all, but alter egos of their worshippers. Though the Roman observers could not have a panoramic perspective of the Germans' religious beliefs, they noted the visible practices. The Germans had no religious organization as advanced as the oligarchy of the Celtic priesthood. But there were authoritative individuals who performed the liaison offices between Midgard and Asgard (earth and heaven), who consecrated, sacrificed and foretold. They also judged in cases of sins against the community, which were regarded as offenses to the gods. These men and women depended especially on augury because the results were visible: the Germans had a practical attitude toward their gods. Superstition was pandemic, and it would persist, ineradicably pagan, for centuries after the conversion to Christianity.

Methods of divination included human sacrifice: in a ritual of the Cimbri and Teutones, for example, the victim, usually a prisoner of war, had his throat cut over a large caldron of water, and the priestess made the prophesy from the eddying patterns of blood.

As they had no priest caste, neither had they temples. The closest they came to a consecrated place of worship was a grove of trees imbued with dread sanctity by generations of human sacrifice. Before they came in contact with the Romans they set little store by pictorial art, and few of their deities were represented in human form. An exception was the goddess of the earth, Erda, a survival of a submerged religion. Erda was common to most of the tribes; she had probably been a fertility goddess worshipped by the megalithic peoples of Europe before the Indo-Europeans brought in their sanguinary male deities. The goddess lived on a holy island in the North Sea, where a sacred grove sheltered the covered chariot in which she sat. Once a year her special priest—the only one permitted to touch her—walked by her side as her chariot was drawn around the countryside by heifers (the practice was later appropriated by Christians on feast days connected with female saints). That was a season of peace: there was no battle and no one went armed. Wherever she went there was festival, until at length the goddess, "weary of human intercourse," was returned to her island. There a ceremony of purification took place in a holy lake. The slaves who administered the bath were immediately drowned. No one remained who could tell of the rite except the goddess's priest, who was silent.

With mystery wrapping them in a penumbra of terror, the potency of the ancient female deities was preserved. The more recent male gods had a more open existence, their worship being represented by symbols rather than by secret ritual. Some of the symbols are common to other religions, such as the tree of life, or tree of knowledge. In Teutonic mythology Wotan, god of war and of poetry (an expression of the duality of the Teutonic character), immolated himself head down on the great ash tree, Yggdrasil, for the sake of bringing runes (i.e., learning) to mankind.[3] The deeper purpose of his self-sacrifice is lost in the darkness of time. Even if the Christian scribe could guess it he was not going to attribute to a pagan god a motive with direct similarity to the Crucifixion. However, the nearly universal tree was transposed to the cross as the Christians took over a symbol that was meaningful to their predecessors.

As Wotan was the expression of the highest Teutonic idealism, Loki, the god of fire, was the evil genius of the pantheon, the personification of the dark side of the German nature. He is a liar and a breaker of faith; but he is nevertheless one of the gods, foster brother and companion to Wotan, and he is essential to them. Being the son of a giant he could deal with the forces of evil—the dwarfs and the frost giants—whose aim encompassed the destruction of the gods. Loki knew how to trick them, buy them off, gain favors from them. The purer gods decried the chicanery—and accepted it. For a long time Loki's badness was condoned on account of his usefulness. But in the end he directed his wiles against the gods themselves, accomplishing the slaying of Wotan's son, Baldur, god of love and peace—Loki's diametric opposite. For this act the fire god was caught by Thor and imprisoned for eternity in a cave, where he was bound with iron chains to three pointed rocks. Above his head a suspended serpent forever drips venom onto his face. His wife catches it in a cup, but some reaches him, and then his agonized writhing produces earthquakes.

But the gods had not destroyed their enemies. Loki's children by his giantess wife were leading participants in the final battle, Ragnarok, when the gods were destroyed along with the worlds they had created. Then, "heaven was cleft in twain, the stars were hurled from the heavens, the sea rushed over the earth and the tottering mountains tumbled headlong from their foundations."

Loki's qualities suggest that he was a member of an older pantheon, as were his relatives, the giants, displaced by the younger gods and transmuted by their worshippers into evil spirits. The Christians would similarly demote the pagan gods to the rank of devils. It is a curious fact, however, that the Teutons allowed this one fallen angel, the cleverest and the most baneful of them all, to remain a god. Whatever his origin, Loki represents a strand of viciousness in the Teutonic soul, a cunning cruelty which seems at odds with the heroic image observed by the Romans. This inherent taint goes together with the grim Teutonic pessimism underlying the entire saga of the gods: the certainty that the forces of evil would in the end overcome and destroy the bright spirit of mankind.

This was the character of the people who would challenge Rome for the domination of Europe: a race with a strong spirit of individual freedom allied to romantic idealism and reckless defiance of fate; on the reverse side, deep-rooted gloom, and callousness extending to cruelty. These extremes were alien to the trim Roman mind typified by the systematic universality of the empire. But the Germans were becoming the second power in Europe, and the antipathy of the two cultures were bound to result in a decisive contest.

The conflict began nearly a century before Caesar's conquest of Gaul. The Celtic star was still high in the second century B.C., and the older inhabitants of Gaul had progressed far beyond the tribal pattern of the German invaders. The Celts had a strong if disjointed sense of nationality, where the newcomers were still operating from a seminomadic, family-based set of mores; and Celtic inventiveness had lifted their culture to a plane of convenience unknown to the hunter race. But these settled veterans of early migratory waves had lost the vigor that had given them dominion over most of Europe—a toughness still held in full measure by the fresher Teutons. The Celts were hard put to repel the raiding warriors and their combative families, who found the temperate Gallic countryside preferable to the dank woods and marshes of home.

The Celts needed help, and Rome, already anchored in southern Gaul, became a willing ally in the effort to secure the Rhine border. But the Rhine was a feeble barrier to the continuing stream of barbarian tribes, who combined a natural disposition to belligerence with a real and pressing need for a new home. About 120 B.C. the Cimbri, a Germanic people driven by storms and floods from their homeland in Jutland, moved into the Alpine regions, and in 109 B.C. they crossed the Rhine. Together with some other German tribes they overran all of Celtic Gaul and moved against the new Roman province of Transalpine Gaul, founded a decade before. Between 109 and 105 they defeated five Roman armies, but in 102 they were finally routed. Many were killed; the survivors who did not escape were taken to Italy as slaves, an insufferable fate for a free German warrior.

Aggressively as the Germans had battled, they were not yet ready to outfight the efficient Roman military machine, nor to defy the might and prestige of the Roman Empire. But they were progressing: by the first century B.C. they had begun to learn the advantages of confederation. Between 70 and 65 B.C. a united threat came from across the Rhine that had a far-reaching effect on the future of Gaul. Several Celtic tribes in the region of Alsace were engaged in an endless quarrel. Resorting to the dangerous expedient of hiring foreigners to fight their battles, one of the tribes invited an army of fifteen-thousand mercenaries from a confederacy of German tribes known to them as the Suevi (wandering people). Under the leadership of Ariovistus this band was hovering, ready, on the border of West Germany. After an easy victory in 61 B.C., Ariovistus took over part of Alsace and opened the border to waves of German settlers, amounting to about one hundred twenty thousand. For the first time the Germans had a solid base in Gaul, and they had achieved it by a German rarity, a working confederacy. The German tribes had resisted united action even more obstinately than their Celtic cousins. But this time they had one to organize and inspire them—an audacious leader whose aim was to establish a German kingdom on the soil of Gaul, and who thus anticipated the fact. By now the Romans had a parallel design, though they chose to regard the German tribes as interlopers, coveting what never could be theirs by right.

France would have had a different history if the brash genius Ariovistus had not come up against the wiser genius Caesar. Ariovistus, like his comtemporary Vercingetorix, was one of the great failed hero-leaders of history. But where the Celt tried futilely to pull together the threads of a fraying civilization, the German led a people in the ascendant—a pugnacious race following a magnetic dream of the future.

Ariovistus's nearly successful defiance of Caesar was a preview of the long struggle of the Germans against the decaying might of the Western Empire. But by the time of the final dissolution Rome would have had nearly five centuries in which to put her indelible imprint on the country that would become France. The Germans would inherit, along with the failing political structure, an enduring culture.

Now, in 58 B.C., it was Caesar's task to make a beginning.[4] In 59, Caesar, as consul in Rome, had recommended to the Senate that Ariovistus be named king and "Friend" of the empire in *de facto* recognition of his occupation of Alsace. Caesar recognized the dangerous strength of the new German confederacy, and the growing menace of the barbarian tribes, now in continuous motion along the entire Rhine border. He aimed at the temporary appeasement of Ariovistus, the most immediate threat, in order to keep Roman hands free for fighting in other areas. When Caesar became proconsul of Gaul the following year he was at once involved with the problems in the Alsace region. He decided to use his interference there as an excuse to confront Ariovistus.

Caesar came up against an impudent defiance unfamiliar to any Roman of his century. His ostensible reason for facing the German leader was the appeal of the local Celts against what they claimed was intolerable oppression. Not only had they to pay tribute to the new ruler, wrote Caesar, but "Ariovistus had shown himself an arrogant and cruel tyrant. The man was an ill-tempered, headstrong savage and it was impossible to endure his tyranny any longer."

The headstrong savage, when ordered imperiously to meet with Caesar, replied: "'If I wanted anything from Caesar, I should go to him; so if he wants anything of me, he must come to me.' He could not imagine," continues Caesar, "what business Caesar, or the Romans at all for that matter, had in the part of Gaul which was his by right of conquest. Since he did not dictate to them how they were to exercise their rights, he ought not to be interfered with in the exercise of his. Let him attack whenever he pleases. He will discover what German valor is capable of. We have never known defeat, we have superb training in arms, and for fourteen years have never sheltered beneath a roof."

Caesar laid preparations to meet this abrupt challenge, occupying and preparing to defend Vesontio (Besançon), a well-fortified military and trading center which was threatened by the German troops. Here he encountered another difficulty to this date almost unknown to Roman generals: panic among his own soldiers. They too had heard Ariovistus's boasts; further, in conversation with the merchants of Vesontio, they had word of the prowess of the barbarian fighters and the terror inspired by their very visages. Some of Caesar's soldiers "alleged some urgent reason for leaving camp." Others stayed, but "at times they could not help shedding tears, skulking in their tents."

Caesar rallied his troops, recalling the many other times the Romans had met the Germans with success and adding that he would move against the enemy that very night, with no one to follow him, if need be, but his loyal tenth legion. The appeal to their honor heartened his soldiers and they prepared to take the field.

Battle was joined near the present town of Mulhouse about fifteen miles west of the Rhine. Close behind the German troops were their baggage trains along with their women and children, including the wife and daughters of the German leader. The armies approached one another so swiftly that they clashed at once in hand-to-hand fighting, the Roman soldiers actually throwing themselves on the wall of shields put up by the German phalanxes, wrenching the shields out of the enemy's hands and stabbing them from above. The Romans in the end prevailed, and the German army broke and fled back to the Rhine. Many drowned trying to swim the river; many more were hunted down and killed. Among the few who reached safety was Ariovistus, who found a little boat moored at the river's edge, and escaped to the other side, deserting his women, three of whom were killed and the fourth captured by Roman cavalry. This defeated hero lacked the proud and pointless heroism of Vercingetorix. But saving his own skin did not further Ariovistus's ambitions, for the Romans heard nothing further from him. The tribal Germans attached themselves to a leader only as long as he was successful and admirable. Ariovistus was no longer either.

With this one short engagement the lines of western Europe were drawn for the next five centuries. The natural boundary of the Rhine became the political boundary of the Western Empire. The Suevi retreated to the interior of Germany. The German tribes already settled on the west bank of the Rhine were enlisted by Caesar as the defenders of the frontier: their self-interest in protecting their homes would make them good guardians against encroaching fellow-Germans. With his boundaries now secured on the east Caesar could turn his attention to the subjugation of the tottering structure of Celtic Gaul, the final step in the rounding off of Rome's Western Empire.

At the time Caesar defeated Ariovistus the Germans still had no organization capable of a decisive challenge to the Roman Empire. The Suevian confederacy was nothing more than a wartime expedient. But the Germans were learning. From their earliest contacts they had developed a sound respect for their southern neighbors. In dealing with the Romans they retained their pride but forewent their rashness; admired the best yet refrained from servile imitation. They learned what they needed to know. They recognized the practiced agility of the legions; they observed also the devious mentality of the Roman leaders: one day they would slay their prisoners or sell them into slavery, the next day bribe and flatter them into joining the imperial army to fight their compatriots.

It had been a Roman policy since the time of the Republic to invite the border tribes to become *foederati* in the Roman territory they had already appropriated. In part this was insurance against their less tamed countrymen; but also there was no choice. By the first century A.D. the population of parts of the western provinces, particularly that of northeastern Gaul, was predominantly German. As it was obvious to any Roman in the field that the Germans made superlative soldiers, these partly Romanized settlers soon became the mainstay of Rome's armies in the West. They were her best soldiers—brave, skillful and ambitious—but they were not necessarily loyal to the empire. Though some of their leaders, like Stilicho, rose to positions of power, for the most part the Germans did not absorb the Roman outlook along with their adopted polity. Their Romanization inevitably became dangerous to their hosts, for these alien citizens came to rival and excel Rome in the fields which were her forte. They learned military tactics and strategy, and above all they learned the value of united action. When Roman treachery disappointed or offended a Rome-educated chieftain he took his acquired knowledge to the tribal meeting and advised his compatriots. Out of these gatherings of newly educated warriors arose the confederacies that evidenced the first stirrings of national solidarity. In the beginning the objectives were only immediate: to throw off the Roman yoke and at the same time harvest booty from the rich towns across the Rhine. Among other signs of encroaching civilization, the Germans were acquiring a taste for Gallo-Roman luxuries.

In A.D. 9 a confederacy was formed with this simple and immediate intent. The ensuing clash was not an important battle in itself, and it could easily have been won by the Romans under other circumstances. But its resolution was out of proportion to the slightness of the motives: the consequence was a turning point in the course of European history.

Emperor Augustus, like Caesar before him, understood the increasing threat of the German tribes on Gaul's eastern border. Caesar had been too wise to try to conquer beyond the Rhine, knowing that to pursue the fluid German tribes into their own territory would be sending his legions into a quagmire. His policy had been to make a neutral buffer of the border tribes, an admittedly temporary expedient. Unlike his predecessor, Augustus sought to Romanize the interior, hoping thus to free his western European provinces forever from the barbarian menace. He had the dream of establishing a new province of Roman Germany. In 16 B.C., as a first step, he sent two of his ablest generals, his stepsons Drusus and Tiberius, to subdue the fractious tribes along the northern Rhine border. They succeeded brilliantly, and by 9 B.C. Drusus had reached the Elbe, where trophies were set up to mark the farthest point yet reached by a Roman army in German territory. Fortresses were raised along the Elbe and Weser rivers, and Augustus's hope of a Roman Germany began to materialize.

That same year, at thirty, Drusus died of a fall from his horse. The task of consolidating his conquests and keeping the newly subjugated tribes under control fell to Tiberius. He also was elected to further the ultimate Roman aim of connecting the new frontier with the Danube, to integrate the line of empire all along the eastern European frontier. Tiberius was now the first soldier of the empire, and it seemed that his future, as well as that of Roman Germany, was assured. Then in A.D. 6, without adequate explanation, he announced his decision to retire to Rhodes and study. Quintilius Varus succeeded him as military governor of the new province. Varus was a vain man of luxurious habits and low sensibilities, and he at once began to uproot the old German customs. His acts alienated Germans who had been friendly to Rome, and before the end of his first year their hostility had begun to breed a dangerous unity.

One of the German tribes brought into Rome's orbit was the Cherusci. Its chief, Hermann, had been educated in Rome, had served in the Roman army and had been knighted. His tribe, inhabiting the basin of the Weser, was one of those considered to be successfully integrated into the new province. Hermann, about twenty-five at the time of Varus's appointment, was initially friendly to the new governor, simply because he was Roman. But in A.D. 9, after a few years of Varus's high-handed measures, the young chief roused his people to revolt. Other tribes joined in a league to eject the Romans and restore the old liberties.

In the service of Rome Hermann had learned that it was hopeless for untrained native warriors to assault the entrenched Romans. Insinuating himself into the governor's confidence, he persuaded Varus to move his headquarters east to the Weser basin, where he would be more vulnerable. Then Hermann arranged a local uprising. Varus set out to subdue it with three legions amounting to twenty-seven thousand men. The Cherusci, led by Hermann, formed his rearguard; though Varus's advisers had warned him of treachery, Hermann had cajoled the Roman governor into trust. Between Varus and his objective lay the Teutoburger Wald hills. The troops, unfamiliar with the terrain, became entangled in the dense underbrush of the hill of Teut (now Grotenburg). Their German allies melted into the forest and roused the nearby tribes with horn and fire signals. The hordes fell on the Romans and Varus, still under the spell of Hermann's flattery, persisted in regarding the attack as a rude brand of German horseplay. With his soldiers dropping all around him he at last realized what was happening, and withdrew his troops, with great difficulty, to an open plateau. Though personally brave he was incapable of giving orders. In the ensuing battle his confused and disheartened soldiers were overwhelmed by the natives and slaughtered almost to a man. Varus took probably the only sensible course of his life: he died a soldier's death, falling on his sword.

With the destruction of the legions Hermann had thrown the Romans out of Germany—forever, as it transpired. Emperor Augustus was getting old—he was seventy-two at the time of the Battle of the Teutoburger Wald—and the year before he had been distressed by a much more serious blaze of revolt all over Pannonia and Dalmatia. With the loss of his legions in Germany and the death of Varus, following the disaster on his Danube boundary, the emperor, profoundly discouraged, gave up his dream of Roman Germany. He decided to abandon Drusus's Elbe frontier and Tiberius's work of consolidation among the tribes, to withdraw the frontier back to the Rhine and to follow henceforth a strictly defensive policy. He strengthened the Rhine and Danube frontiers with fortified walls, an act which secured relative peace to the empire until about A.D. 200. He contented himself with a single act of vengeance for the lost legions: he sent Germanicus Caesar, Drusus's son, to subdue Hermann, which the young soldier did in two vigorous battles.

Hermann's subsequent history was sad, but inevitable, because his people still had not learned the true lessons of confederation. They refused to accept military defeat as the forerunner of cooperation with the victor, and they continued to fight for their ancient freedoms. But when they won a battle they did not know what to do with the peace they had earned, and they could not yet tolerate the anomaly of a peacetime leader. Hermann, demeaned by his defeat by Germanicus, could not keep his hold over his people. Unable to cope with a situation which did not require warfare, he became involved in squabbles among the tribes. He incurred jealousies within his own tribe, and in A.D. 19, aged thirty-six, he was murdered by his kinsmen.

The Battle of the Teutoburger Wald was a small conflict in terms of the history of warfare, and it could easily have been averted, or later repaired, by the skill and good sense of Tiberius or Germanicus. Lost through the incapacity of one man, it marked the end of the idea of Roman Germany. To later Germans it commemorated their rejection of the ideal of universal empire. Hermann, a half-Romanized chieftain who wasn't big enough for his role, was romanticized into a symbol of Germany's refusal to accept imperial domination—and along with it the cultivation of the ages.

At the site of his battle stands Hermann's fifty-two-foot effigy, sculpted in beaten copper, brandishing a twenty-three-foot sword in eternally proud defiance. To modern eyes he is a symbol, not of heroism, but of retrogression. As a result of the Battle of the Teutoburger Wald civilization in Europe took a long step backward, and the repercussions have been echoing ever since. Among the most baneful is the unending animosity between France and Germany—Latin and Teuton—which has disrupted Europe with recurrent violence over the centuries.

But the Romans could not have stemmed the tide of the Germans. There would be other Hermanns in the irresistible advance: the barbarians had a fresh, ambitious energy that would inevitably prevail. Imperial Rome had no defense against their youth.

A more formidable revolt broke out sixty years later under Civilis, chief of the Batavi, a tribe living in today's Netherlands. Gathering Germans and Celts into a temporary confederacy, Civilis and his allies nearly succeeded in detaching Gaul from the empire. Although he failed, he was an augur of the future: under his leadership the notion of a separate empire of Gaul was first advanced.

Claudius Civilis (known only by his Roman name) was a prince of his nation who, like Hermann, had been educated in Rome and trained in the Roman army.[5] He turned against his mentors when his brother was executed on a false charge and he himself was put in chains and sent to Emperor Nero. He was acquitted but remained under suspicion. When Nero died, in A.D. 68, the empire was disputed between Vitellius and Vespasian. In A.D. 69, under cover of recruiting allies for Vitellius, Civilis roused his people to rebellion. He used as a goad the corrupt usages of recruiting officials: some of these made a practice of conscripting the old and ill in order to exact bribes to excuse them; others pressed into service very young boys whom they then used for debauchery. Working on the local resentment, Civilis called the chiefs and boldest warriors to a banquet in a sacred grove, where he exhorted them to throw off the bonds of Roman slavery. Warmed by the food and drink that accompanied the leader's eloquence, the assembly took ritual vows of alliance. Civilis's cause was further strengthened by the cooperation of a young seeress, Veleda, to whom the German tribes accorded a near-divine status. Veleda lived in a high tower, and she safeguarded her sanctity by refusing to see anyone but a near relative who acted as intermediary priest, conveying questions and answers up and down the tower.

Most of Civilis's troops were Roman-trained. His own Batavians had for many years been supplying men and arms to the empire. They had fought ably in Britain, and at home they possessed a select body of cavalry trained to swim the rivers with their arms and horses. Civilis's insurrection lasted over a year, and at first the Germans were spectacularly successful. The skill of their seasoned troops, and their intimacy with the watery terrain of their homeland, foiled the Roman soldiers. The Batavians provoked battle in a marsh which they had created by throwing an oblique dam over the Rhine. The lightly armed natives, used to bogs, found no obstacle, where the Romans, heavily accoutered, were rendered helpless. The Batavians captured twenty-four Roman boats with the aid of defectors at the oars. They starved out and then leveled an important Roman garrison near the Rhine, massacring the survivors. They forced the capitulation of Cologne, one of Rome's oldest colonies in northeastern Gaul. Their successes brought them allies, both in Germany and in Gaul. Finally, two of the commanders of the Gallic legions were persuaded to defect and join Civilis. Gaul, effectively severed from the empire, was ready to declare itself independent.

At this point Civilis, wise beyond his time, declined to set himself and his Batavians over Gaul as conquerors: "We have not taken up arms in order that the Batavi may rule over the nations," he told the Gallic troops still under Roman command. "Far from us be such arrogance! Accept our alliance. I am ready to join your ranks, whether you would prefer me to be your general or your comrade." (Though he had sound political instincts, the German leader was not beyond allowing himself the occasional barbarian relapse: he set up Roman prisoners as targets for the arrows and javelins of his little son.)

But despite their temporary success the Germans were contesting an empire still mighty. While Civilis was scoring his victories, Vitellius, emperor less than a year, unambitious and too good-natured to be an effective leader, tried to resign his title and was killed by disaffected Roman soldiers. The new emperor, Vespasian, sent his best general, Petilius Cerialis, to deal with the Gallo-German insurgency. Cerialis began with tact. He did not punish the legions that had defected, but lectured them: "Do you fancy yourselves dearer in the eyes of Civilis and the Batavi than your fathers and grandfathers were to their ancestors? Liberty, indeed, and the like specious names are their pretexts; but never did any man seek to enslave his fellow and secure dominion for himself without using the very same words. Should the Romans be driven out, what can result but war? By the prosperity and order of eight hundred years has this fabric of empire been consolidated, nor can it be overthrown without destroying those who overthrow it." The very spirit of Rome spoke out of his words, and the Celts, more attuned to submission than to revolution, abandoned their less susceptible allies.

After winning back the Celtic legions, Cerialis attacked the Germans. He freed Cologne and defeated Civilis in a decisive battle at Trier. But the Roman general knew that military victory gave him only a temporary advantage. He began to woo the Batavi away from their leader, pointing out that their allies had submitted, that the leadership of Civilis had brought them nothing but defeat, and that if they did not accept Roman rule "the vengeance of heaven" would be upon them. The last threat he reinforced with firm advice to the seeress Veleda that she would be better off if her prophesies from now on favored Rome over the Germans. He promised, meanwhile, to pardon Civilis, knowing that a defeated German leader had no stature among his people. The Batavi hardly wavered. They debated briefly among themselves, lamenting the loss of freedom but blaming their leader for their reverses. Civilis had no choice but to give up.

Here the story of Civilis ends abruptly and the rebel leader drops out of history. But more than his predecessors Civilis had a focal place in the organic development of Europe. Ariovistus and Hermann, skillful warriors with no talent for peace, have been immortalized as symbols of haughty German obstinacy. Their direction was regressive. Civilis made a bold step into the future, anticipating a Gaul—still four hundred years away—that would be a union of Germans and Gallo-Romans. But in Civilis's time German unity melted away under adversity, and the farseeing leader was impotent in the face of defeat. Neither martyr nor victor, his shade has succumbed to the oblivion of unconcern.

For more than a hundred years after Civilis's abortive revolution there was relative peace in the western part of the empire. Rome wisely stayed away from the treacherous ground of northeastern Europe, respecting her self-imposed limits, the fortified west banks of the Rhine and the Danube. But peace gave the barbarians as well as the empire breathing space. While the Romans left them alone the German tribes had leisure to progress in the direction envisioned by Civilis and, in a more primitive way, by Ariovistus and Hermann. Their social structure, based on the extended family, began to develop into the more advanced form of tribal confederacies loosely organized under a leader who was operative in peace as well as in war.

One of these groups was composed of several tribes living on the right bank of the Rhine in today's Belgium, Holland and West Germany. Civilis's tribe, the Batavi, was among them, as were the tribes of Hermann's Cheruscan league. The pith of the group was, it is believed, the Sicambrians, or Salians (so called for their home on the Sala River, the old name for the Yssel in the central Netherlands).

The composition of the confederacy fluctuated with the still-nomadic tendencies of the tribes, as did the definition of their territory, but by the third century A.D. they had become a recognizable union. The Romans gave the name "Francia" to the lands they inhabited: not France as we know it, but the right bank of the Rhine from the area of Njimegen in the Netherlands to that of Coblenz in West Germany. In 241 they were first called "Franks" by the historian Flavius Vopiscus.[6] The name may have derived from the Celtic word *franc* (generally, "free"), or from the Teutonic word *franci* (formidable), an adjective applied by the Romans to the Sicambrians whether foe or ally.

Throughout the third and fourth centuries the Sicambrian league or, as we shall now call them, the Frankish confederacy, engaged itself in a continuing series of attacks on northeastern Gaul—the Roman provinces of Gallia Belgica and Germania Inferior. They were among the less advanced of the Teutons: they used neither horses nor armor, and went into battle half-naked in the old barbarian style, carrying only a primitive casting hatchet. But they had a stubborn belligerence and an unquenchable desire to live in Gaul. Seasoned Roman generals kept defeating them in set battle, pushing them back over the border, killing them, according to Roman reports, by the hundreds of thousands—and still they kept reappearing in as great strength as ever. In 276 they swept all the way down to the Pyrenees, capturing sixty Gallic cities. Probus, soldier-emperor, freed the cities, drove the invaders back into their northern marshes and annihilated, it is said, four hundred thousand of them. For nearly a generation after this the Frankish confederacy appeared to be prostrate, and Franks, despite their familiar reputation for perfidy, were recruited to guard the Romans' Rhine border.

In the early part of the fourth century Constantine the Great inflicted a conclusive defeat on the Franks on their own home ground. He transported a multitude of prisoners—those, it was claimed, too faithless for military service and too stubborn for slavery—to Trier, where they were thrown to the lions in the circus to the delighted applause of the citizenry (which was Christian). This occurrence brought more Franks up in arms, and hostile encounters became routine. Constantine's son, Constantius, continued his father's military policy and duplicated his successes, with a similar lack of result. In these years, however, various pretenders to the imperial throne saw fit to enlist the aid of northern barbarians by rewarding them with Gallic lands. So the Franks began to achieve their heart's desire without the aid of their casting axes.

But they wanted much more than the scraps handed out by impermanent usurpers. Though not yet an agricultural people the Franks, eyeing the comfortable living of their southern neighbors, were by degrees relaxing their scorn for the drudgery of the plowman. In 355, while Constantius was still emperor, a tremendous invasion of land-hungry barbarians started all along Rome's northern frontier from Strasbourg to the North Sea. At this critical juncture Constantius drafted his young cousin, Flavius Claudius Julianus, to take command of the armies of the West as Caesar. When he was called to his duties Julian, then twenty-four years old, had had no experience in war or politics. He was still at school in Athens, where he was studying philosophy and absorbing the art, literature and mythology of ancient Greece. Julian was the son of a half brother of Constantine the Great. Most of his male relatives had been murdered by order of Constantine's sons when they came into power, to prevent possible rivalry for the imperial throne. Anguished by the coldblooded atrocity—perpetrated by Christian emperors—Julian abjured the Christian religion and embraced a pagan neoplatonism popular among Greek philosophers.

In Gaul he kept his apostasy hidden in deference to the influential bishops, and devoted newly discovered talents to the task of clearing the province of barbarians. He endeared himself to his troops from the beginning by his courage in battle, his friendly manner and the austerity of his life-style, which was in sharp contrast to the profligacy of the sons of Constantine.

Along with his personal charm the young philosophy student proved himself a military genius. With a comparatively small force he threw the invading Franks back over their border, freed the Gallo-Roman cities they had occupied and recovered the left bank of the Rhine from Strasbourg to Cologne. Then he rebuilt the fortifications, which the Franks, hating walled towns, had leveled and burned.

In the third of his four years in Gaul Julian went on to pacify Toxandria, in northern Gaul. Here he had a different situation to deal with. In the earlier Frankish invasion halted by Probus a hundred years before, one group of the Salian (Sicambrian) tribe had stayed in Roman Gaul and managed to retain a foothold in this section of Germania Inferior (today's provinces of Limberg and

Brabant in Belgium). By the time Julian reoccupied Toxandria their descendants, inheriting the fields and pastures, had given up the character of roving warriors and turned into farmers. Julian observed that these determined squatters would make better allies than enemies. In 358 he confirmed them in their occupation and made them *foederati:* they were to enjoy limited Roman citizenship, and were liable to pay an annual tribute of cattle and to be conscripted into the army. This was the first recognized permanent settlement of Franks in Roman Gaul.

Julian withdrew his troops from active campaign in the winter months and spent the intervals overhauling the Roman administration of Gaul and reforming its financial structure. Taxes, he maintained, if honestly collected and efficiently applied, would yield sufficient to keep both the military and the civil machinery running smoothly. He administered the province from his Gallic capital of Lutetia,* a Celtic-Roman town on an island in the Seine (now the Île de la Cité in Paris), of which he wrote with affection: "I happened to be at winter quarters at my beloved Lutetia—for that is how the Celts call the capital of the Parisii (a Celtic tribe). It is a small island lying in the river; a wall entirely surrounds it, and wooden bridges lead to it on both sides. The river seldom rises and falls, and it provides water which is very clear to the eye and very pleasant for one who wishes to drink. The winter, too, is rather mild there, perhaps from the warmth of the ocean, which is not more than ninety miles distant. A good kind of vine grows thereabouts, and some people have even managed to make fig trees grow by covering them in winter."[7]

The Parisii had lived on the island in the Seine since the third century B.C., and their descendants, the Gallo-Romans, built the walled town in the first century A.D. Some structures from Roman times still stand: the baths in the Musée Cluny and the amphitheater nearby. Nothing remains above ground on Julian's island, either of the city or of the palace from which he administered the province. Most of the palace area is covered today by the awesomely authoritative Palais de Justice; the oldest building on the site is Saint Louis's ethereal thirteenth-century Sainte Chapelle. But a few steps away part of Julian's Lutetia still exists under the court of the Cathedral of Notre Dame. In the enormous, dim, excavated area are some of the

---

*The first mention of the name Lutetia is by Julius Caesar in 53 B.C. In Julian's time it first assumed the name Paris, although Julian continued to call it Lutetia.

massive stones that were part of the Gallo-Roman wall, fragments of streets and houses of the time, and the portal of the Roman temple which in the sixth century became the porch of the Merovingian Cathedral of Saint Stephen, predecessor of Notre Dame.

In this town that he loved Julian, busy as he was with governmental detail, found time to study and write, crystallizing the ideas on philosophy and morals that he would later attempt to impose on the empire as a substitute for Christian theology. He also began to assemble the library that would later, in Constantinople, accumulate to one hundred twenty thousand books (all destroyed in an accidental fire in the fifth century).

Constantius had installed Julian as Caesar in Gaul partly to counteract the presence of possibly disloyal Frankish *foederati* generals. He began to see that he had created for himself a far more dangerous menace. Julian was the idol of the soldiers—and in the fourth century the army was the king-maker. In 359, therefore, the emperor essayed to geld this threat by ordering Julian's finest troops to remove at once to the eastern front, where war with Persia was a chronic condition. Julian was prepared to accept the order from his superior, but his troops mutinied and declared him Augustus. He made perfunctory objections before yielding, and in 361 he marched east at the head of his devoted army. Before Julian could challenge the incumbent emperor, Constantius died, and Julian succeeded pacfically to the throne his soldiers had been prepared to confer on him with arms.

When Julian became emperor, the last of the line of Constantine, he moved permanently to Constantinople, and the remaining two years of his life had little relevance in the West. Starting at his death Christian historians alternately damned and ridiculed this earnest, attractive and enlightened young emperor. Julian's fatal fault was his apostasy at a time of selfconscious Christian escalation.

Julian's sanction of the occupation of Toxandria by the Salian Franks was official recognition of a historic inevitability. The encroachments of the Franks on Roman Gaul had started in the form of raids. By the fourth century they had acquired the character of a population drift. In forays out of their marshy or forested hinterlands they disturbed a people who were contentedly harvesting the wealth of the soil. The serenity of this civilized land, so vulnerable and so rich, was a compelling attraction to the adventurers.

Further, the Franks were being pushed from behind. The Saxons, who lived to their east, had formed a rival league and fostered a contentious hatred of their neighbors. Because they were in the way of Saxon penetration of the felicitous land to the south, the tentative Frankish settlements were ceaselessly harassed. The eastern barbarians were easily as courageous as the Franks and even less tame. With the Saxons importuning them on one side and the Gallic farmlands luring them on the other, the Franks naturally gravitated southward, to the pleasant land that was so easy to appropriate.

They became ever bolder as the Roman defenses weakened. More and more Roman legions were withdrawn, and those that remained were infiltrated with Frankish soldiers. More fatal than Rome's military weakness was the demoralization of the empire, particularly at its perimeter. The corruption of the provincial administration had depressed in the colonials any respect for or identification with the empire. Compounded with this was the loss of Gallic identity: Rome had for so long quelled the leanings of the natives toward their own cultural background that the Gallic citizenry had become apathetic. The Gallic landowners no longer had any national feeling, not caring under whose dominion they existed. Often, in fact, they welcomed the rough grip of the barbarian as an alleviation from the grasping hand of the Roman tax collector.

The land that Julian had conceded to the Frankish tribes who already lived there was poor, boggy country compared with that immediately to the south. The river valleys of the Scheldt and the Lys were open avenues to the fertile fields and pastures of Gallia Belgica. But the Gallo-Roman farmers were rich only in land. The invaders found nothing to take: the only potential wealth was in the soil. Eventually, perforce, the Franks had to take up the despised toil of peasants.

By the middle of the fifth century, Frankish settlers had occupied the areas of Thérouanne, Arras, Cambrai and Tournai, in today's northwestern France and Belgium. The immigrants probably met little opposition. In fact one sector of the population probably welcomed them: the rural lower class. The Roman caste system had locked the poorer farmers into the position of serfs; they had no incentive, no hope and no future. The new landowners, in contrast to their forerunners, were honorable and straightforward. The land was being worked again and the peasants had a new dignity. The people of the occupied towns may have been worried, but here, too, the

Franks, no longer adventurers, caused little disruption. The Teutons traditionally disliked town life, and stayed away.

All in all, the barbarians brought health into a country that was suffering more than most from the moral decay of the Western Empire. The gradual occupation of Gaul by the Franks had the character of replacing rather than destroying the old order.

As the marauders metamorphosed into farmers their political focus began to change. In place of the war leaders, who had been elected for temporary purposes, the *kuning*, or king, head of the clan and a peacetime leader, began to emerge as the political principal. Though still dependent on the will of the *Campus Martius* he tended with the years of peace to arrange it so that the high station stayed in his family.

Along with the king's honorary duties went his responsibility to deal with the Romans: to arrange payment of tribute, negotiate peace terms after battles and otherwise act in a diplomatic role. It was preferable, therefore, that the chieftain display other qualities besides battle courage and a strong throwing arm. As the position of king became hereditary the family tended to grow in aristocratic stature; the sons received an education of sorts and learned to speak some Latin, so that when they succeeded to the family position they could deal on nearly equal terms with Roman officialdom. The *kuning* dynasties grew haphazardly into traditional kingships. Most of these dynasties were ephemeral, flourishing and fading with the destinies of their people. The Salian Franks held on to their leading family and in the sixth century began to call its scions Merovingians and to represent them as the first and only kings of the Franks.

It is impossible to pinpoint pre-fifth-century individuals of this family that was to become supreme. The Frankish settlements were still transitory and their political arrangements changeable. But it is surmised that the chieftains ruling in various parts of Gaul taken over by the Franks were members of one family, represented in half-legendary oral history by "King Faramund,"[8] founder of the Merovingian dynasty.

The first member of this ruling clan to be historically identified was Clodion, in the pages of the sixth-century *History of the Franks*, by Gregory of Tours: "Clodion was a man of high birth and marked ability among his people, who was King of the Franks."[9] This efficient wartime *kuning* lived in Dispargum (probably today's Lens in Belgium, about thirty miles southwest of Brussels), in the territory of Germania

Inferior ceded to the Franks by Julian in 358. About 431 Clodion crossed the great Roman road that ran from Bavay in northwestern France to Cologne in West Germany and marked the northwestern boundary of the empire (it is today the linguistic frontier between France and Belgium). This strongly fortified line had for years resisted the intrusions of the barbarians, but Clodion breached it and invaded the territory of Arras in Belgica Secunda. He was routed by Aetius and retreated. In 445 he crossed the border again, defeated the Romans at Camaracum (Cambrai) and took possession of all the country around, down to the Somme. Though two years later he was bested once more by Aetius and passed out of history, Clodion's impact was indelible. By the beginning of the sixth century, despite the desperate heroism of the Gallo-Roman defenders, the Franks would be in possession of most of Rome's northern Gallic provinces and a good part of her southern with Clodion's descendants as their chosen kings.

One hundred and fifty years passed between Julian's cession to the Franks of a piece of Roman Gaul and the last major campaign of the Merovingian conqueror Clovis. Much besides warfare lay behind the extraordinary success story of this relatively minor barbarian confederacy. There was the conversion of the warring invaders to landowners and farmers. There was the settlers' gradual acceptance of coexistence with the Gallo-Romans. Above all, there was Clovis's espousal of the Roman Catholic faith.

CHAPTER THREE
CHRISTIANITY

In the autumn of A.D. 312 Constantine, not yet emperor, led his army rapidly over the seven-thousand-foot pass of Mont Cenis from Gaul into Italy, to confront Maxentius, oppressive ruler of the western part of the empire. The armies faced each other near Saxa Rubra in the plain of the Tiber, just north of Rome. Maxentius's force (it is written by Constantine's biographer) was much larger, but its men were softened by their term of easy license in the capital. Constantine's tough, elite little army was veteran of six years of warfare, under his skilled leadership, against the Picts and the Scots in Britain and the Franks in Gaul. The challenger's immediate objective was the passage across the Tiber by way of the Milvian Bridge, and his ultimate goal was Rome, nine miles south. On the eve of the battle Constantine saw in the sky a cross of light over the sun. Written in stars around it were the words (in Greek): "By this sign shalt thou conquer."

Like generals before and after him faced with entrenched and superior forces—a situation where audacity must be seconded by luck—Constantine was calling for heavenly assistance. A few years before he would have called on one of the pantheon whose members were specifically concerned with the quarrels of mortals. At this moment it probably made little difference to Constantine that he was invoking the help of a God whose worship was based on brotherly love, meekness and the abandonment of temporal ambition. In three centuries the compelling appeal of Jesus' words had spread through the foundations of the Roman Empire, and the Christian ethos had become a stronger force in Constantine's world than that of the old sky gods.

Constantine's appeal worked. With an army inspirited as much by their general's daring skill as by the *chi rho*, the monogram of Christ, he had ordered them to paint on their shields, they attacked the enemy from four sides, crumpling Maxentius's right wing and sweeping his left wing into the Tiber. Maxentius was killed along with a large part of his army.

Constantine's heavenly vision, followed by victory, convinced him that he was a favorite of the God of the Christians. A few months later, at Milan, he proclaimed equal rights for all religions and restored the Christian property which had been confiscated by his predecessors. In the following years he went much further than mere toleration. He became an activist in the new religion, personally arbitrating Church disputes; and he was abundantly generous in his gifts. Though the emperor probably superimposed the Christian creed over the pagan sun-worship fashionable in his day, he was nevertheless a conscientious and energetic Christian.

It is not our place here to view the momentous effects on the Church, both good and bad, of the Edict of Milan. We are concerned rather with the origins of the hegemonic Catholic Church in Europe. When the Roman Empire fell apart in the West nothing was left but the outlines; the only viable survivor of the old universal order was the Church. The Church was not only still alive; it throve with the new order. The barbarian chieftains, metamorphosed to established monarchs of large, static populations, soon discovered the extreme usefulness of the bishops. These men, as eager to help as to proselytize, knew how to run things in the efficient Roman manner. The Church filled the empty spaces in the web of empire. Its priests advised, scolded and bolstered the new rulers who thought as they did, and effectively undermined those who embraced heresy. They educated the children, assumed the remains of the imperial bureaucratic structure in the towns and the countryside, organized the defenses of the cities against attackers and even fought alongside the civilians. While doing all this they passed on to us, through the Dark Ages, a fragment of classical civilization.

This was the Church that arose from the Edict of Milan. The pre-Constantine Church had been a harbor for the poor and wretched, a retreat for the wealthy surfeited by a materialistic society, and an underground enemy of the Roman polity, denouncing the emperor as Antichrist. With Constantine's conversion it became the religion of the empire. The inescapable consequences were power, wealth and worldliness: the Church came somewhat to resemble the empire that had adopted it. The Church of the fourth and fifth centuries was not nearly so closely related to the peaceable teachings of its founder as to the enterprise of the leader who fought with the conviction that God fought beside him.

One hundred and eighty-four years after the Battle of the Milvian Bridge, Clovis, king of some of the Franks but not yet of all of them, entreated the support of Constantine's God during a battle on the outcome of which his future career depended. Again it worked— history does not record the unsuccessful bargains with God. The resultant partnership between the Franks and the Catholic Church was the decisive factor in the ascendancy of the Frankish kingdoms under the Merovingians and later under Charlemagne.

Christianity appealed to the meek and miserable in all lands. Acknowledging no authority but that of an indefinable, omnipotent God, the new religion was an invisible threat to the tidily interlaced bureaucracy of Rome. But the early efforts to stamp it out only made it stronger. The glories of martyrdom added to the young faith the dimension of passion, and laid the basis for a new mythology, the hierarchy of saints. The appealing and ardent faith spread rapidly, an unquenchable underground force. In A.D. 50 Saint Paul preached the gospel in Europe for the first time. When he came to Rome in 62 he found Christians already there. By 250, long before Constantine's Edict of Milan, there were about a hundred clandestine bishoprics in Italy.

Gaul was still out of the mainstream, and its exposure to the new thought was slower. But the province was good ground for a healthy religious culture. There poetic, inventive Celt had combined with pragmatic Roman to produce an eminently civilized breed, the Gallo-Romans. To these people excess was disagreeable, yet they had the sensitivity for inspired religious devotion.

In the middle of the second century Gaul's first bishopric was established in the thriving trade center of Lyons, to minister to its community of Greek-speaking Christians and the scattering of others in the surrounding countryside. In 177 Emperor Marcus Aurelius instigated an intense persecution of Christians. The Greek community at Lyons suffered: in the anti-Christian riots, its first bishop,

Pothinus, then aged ninety, was publicly humiliated, stoned, imprisoned, tortured repeatedly and finally executed. His place was taken by his presbyter, Irenaeus (which means "peacemaker"), a Greek from Smyrna, born about 130, who had probably been sent to Gaul as a missionary. His episcopate included the sees of Lyons, Vienne and others in southern Gaul, and he administered his large diocese with practical kindliness, extending it considerably: according to Gregory of Tours, "he converted the whole city [of Lyons] to Christianity."[1]

As a concerned pastor Irenaeus was preoccupied with the teaching of the unfading truths of the gospels, and he communicated his message with a warmhearted earnestness that endeared him to his flock. He justified his name by being a tireless peacemaker: possessed of tolerance rare in a second-century Greek Christian, he understood that minor differences in creed could only strengthen the faith that formed the Church's underlying unity. In a time of shifting danger, when the lives and welfare of Christians were at the mercy of a hostile authority, his upright honesty, his kindness and his instinct to compromise made him a spiritual citadel.

No prejudice attached to Irenaeus because of his eastern origin— even in the West, Greek was still the official ecclesiastical language. But Irenaeus believed that the words of Jesus should not be tied to one language or culture. At a time when the usual Greco-Roman attitude toward barbarians was a combination of scorn and ostracism, the considerate bishop chose to ignore fashion and preach to his rural constituents in Celtic.

Though he was effective in the spread of Christianity in Gaul, Irenaeus is not so much remembered for his fatherly ministry as for his defense of the Apostolic tradition and the genuineness of the gospels, against the widespread heresy known as Gnosticism. This movement was a complex of Oriental mystery cults that relied on revelation and superstitious rites, and denied both the humanity of Christ and the authority of the gospels. The success of the heresy forced the Church Fathers to gather their thoughts together to define the foundations of their religion; in so doing they solidified its structure. They began to build an organized hierarchy tracing its descent directly from the apostles; they delineated the exact extent of the Scriptures; and they started to enforce strict doctrinal discipline. Their systematization would result in the rigidly homogeneous Catholic Church of the Middle Ages, but in the second century it was an imperative defensive action.

Bishop Irenaeus, as one of the defenders, was an early architect of the Church. With unequivocal reasoning he asserted the humanity of Christ and the reality of the apostolic succession. Gnosticism was at its height during Irenaeus's lifetime. By the time of his death its vogue had waned, due partly to his resolute exposition of the historical roots of the Faith, and partly to the growing strength of the Christian hierarchy and the simple appeal of the gospels.

Irenaeus was not a Christian philosopher, though he is listed among the Fathers of the Church. His contributions were practical: with his old-fashioned morality he was strong as a marble column, and his logical defense of the Faith was an important step in the evolution of Western Christianity.

Alongside the definition of Church doctrine was the growth of a Christian intelligentsia. Constantine's edict of toleration brought the religion out of hiding. The recognition of Christianity as the state religion meant wealth and standing to its ministers, and this attracted the elite. Men with a classical education came to predominate in ecclesiastical inner circles. The primitive Church, appealing to the illiterate poor, necessarily used a homely language. Now that it had become socially acceptable, not only the expression but the whole outlook changed. The original humble purity was lost but in its stead was a gain: the melding of classical tradition with the austere lessons of the early Christians. In the East there were Basil of Cappadocia and Gregory of Nyssa; in Africa Clement of Alexandria, Origen and Athanasius; in Europe Hilary of Poitiers, Ambrose and Jerome, and their heir, Augustine, whose ideas dominated Christian thought in the West for a thousand years. These were educated men of the Greco-Roman aristocracy, some of them predating the Edict of Milan. For even before Constantine officially approved it, Christianity had crept into the upper echelons of Roman society, many of whose members found the compulsory pagan worship sterile and perfunctory. Constantine was not ahead of his time; a wise statesman, he went along with it, legalizing what was already there.

Christianity in Gaul, at the time of Constantine's conversion, was still provincial. The best education was classical pagan, but even here Gaul lagged behind the highly cultivated East. Gallic scholars who converted discarded their rhetorical training along with the old gods; they restricted themselves to instructing Christian neophytes in basic Gospel truths unadorned by philosophic connotation. The character of Western Christianity, formed by the limited perspective of these early teachers, would retain an inflexible simplicity: this was one of the differences that widened the gulf between West and East.

An exception to the naïve directness of Gallic teachers was provided by Lactantius, a Gallo-Roman by adoption and one of the earliest Christian authors: an educated aesthete, teacher and writer in the classical Latin style. Born about 240 near Carthage, he received there an education based on Neoplatonism, a late form of paganism akin to Christian thought. Lactantius did not cross the line to Christianity until he was about sixty. A few years before that he had been called by Emperor Diocletian to teach Latin rhetoric at the Greek imperial court at Nicomedia. When Diocletian issued his first edict against Christians in 303, Lactantius, now a converted Christian, resigned his post. He did not flaunt his voluntary abdication nor did he seek the ostentation of martyrdom; he withdrew from public life and lived in quiet penury, remaining steadfast in his faith and helping others in worse straits. At this time he began his Christian literary work.

Constantine had been at Diocletian's palace in Nicomedia at the same time Lactantius was teaching there, and they became friends. In 313, after his conversion, the emperor appointed the Christian savant tutor to his eldest son at Trier, the Roman capital of Gaul. Lactantius's last years were happy: he was back in the West, speaking Latin again after the lonely Greek years, in an honored position, instructing a ready young pupil in a villa in the serene Moselle Valley.

When Constantine moved the capital of the empire to Byzantium Lactantius did not accompany the court. He died about 320, somewhat out of the stream, and his writings were largely ignored in the centuries following, overshadowed by the achievements of the intellectual giants of the later fourth century. Lactantius had been new in a field where everyone else was new. His intent was to blend classical thought with Christian theology. He failed because he had neither the philosophic insight nor the knowledge to rationalize the subtleties of Christianity.

In the fifteenth century his work was revived by Erasmus. In a time of mental inelasticity in the Catholic Church the Dutch humanist found Lactantius's emphasis on the classical humanities refreshing and his felicitous third-century Latin pleasing.

Lactantius had demonstrated that a classical education could be made to work in a Christian context. Through his influence a Gallic school of Christian writers began to flourish in the fourth century. Among these the leading intellect was Hilary of Poitiers, the first Latin theologian before the age of Augustine. Hilary had the further distinction of being the first Gallic Christian thinker born and educated in Gaul. In his writings he is reticent about his antecedents, but it is evident that he had a fine education, and that his parents were high-ranking pagans. His education included the Greek philosophers as well as the Latin classics. The educated classes in the Western Empire were by this time nearly bilingual; since the removal of the capital to Constantinople Greek was becoming equal to Latin as the official language of the empire.

Hilary's knowledge was wide, including, besides the required grammar, rhetoric and logic, a grounding in natural history. Scattered through his writings are allusions to scientific subjects such as troglodytes, topazes, fig trees, worms ("born without the ordinary process of conception"), and surgical anesthesia ("the soul can be lulled to sleep by drugs, thus the flesh does not heed the deep thrust of the knife").[2]

Hilary was born in or near Poitiers, about 315. Nothing is known of the years before he became a Christian, not even by what road he approached the faith, but he was converted about 350, after his first youth was past. His grounding in Greek philosophy influenced his Christian thinking, as is evident in his strong attraction to the Greek fathers of the Alexandrian school, particularly Origen, whom Hilary regarded as his master. The philosophic logic of the great Christian platonist, as well as his emphasis on man's essential dignity and freedom of will, were probably the most decisive influences on Hilary's reasoning.

The earliest positively known fact of Hilary's career is his unanimous election as the first bishop of Poitiers, about 353, but it is not known whether or not he was chosen directly from lay life. He probably was; in fourth-century Gaul the responsibilities of a vast, newly created diocese like Poitiers required the superior education and experience found only among the elite laity.

Christianity had come early to Poitiers. By the third century a Christian community was established there, and its first church, the oldest Christian building in France, still stands—the Baptistery of Saint John, a sturdy brick Roman structure we will view in detail in a later chapter. Like others in the West, the see of which Poitiers was the center was geographically enormous. In the heavily Christianized, densely populous East every town had its bishop; in contrast Hilary was almost alone in southern Gaul, his nearest peer being Saturninus, the bishop of Arles. His position was strong, but remote: it was impossible for anyone, even a bishop with Hilary's enthusiastic zeal and attractive personality, to excite personal devotion among such a widely scattered flock. He did his best: he was amiable and gracious, and he was an indefatigable worker.

He was also outspoken, ready to jump into controversy when confronted with what he saw as fatal Christian error. His years of study and ratiocination had convinced him of his moral and theological correctness, and he was a tenacious fighter, disregarding the possible inconveniences to himself of challenging entrenched bishops, and even emperors. Almost immediately after his election to the see of Poitiers he involved himself in a righteous but solo battle with Bishop Saturninus. Saturninus was of the Arian persuasion, as was his patron, Emperor Constantius, third son of Constantine the Great.

The Arian heresy was to be of crucial importance in the history of post-imperial Europe. In order to understand this, as well as the context of Hilary's imprudent crusade, we will go back briefly to its originator, Arius, a priest of Alexandria in the time of Constantine the Great. He was an honest, pious scholar with no vestige of heretical avant-garde in his perspective. Shortly before 320 this well-meaning priest had developed a theory of the origin of Christ: God was eternal, unknowable and indivisible, so Christ, born mortal, could not be God in the same sense. Before He created the rest of the world God had created His Son from nothing, endowing him with divinity. Arius saw himself as a devout monotheist. It did not occur to him that his logic led him to a pagan conclusion: since his Christ could not be the equal of God the Father, and yet was divine, he was no more than a lesser god. The rationale was immediately attractive, especially to pagans, who saw no difficulty in worshipping a demigod. Within a short time Arius's conception caused such a furor in Alexandria, a city noted for its outsized furors, that Arius was excommunicated. But he was popular (among other talents he was a composer of hymns, and edified the lower classes with his theological propaganda songs), and he found powerful supporters within and outside Alexandria. Tempers ran so high that Emperor Constantine finally felt he had to take a hand.

In the beginning the emperor had viewed the controversy with negative tolerance: he could not understand why the warring priests would not argue out the finer points of the nature of Christ in logical discourse, like civilized Greek philosophers, instead of making a public commotion over a battle of semantics. But his attempt to make the two sides engage in sane dialectic had no effect, and in 325 he called a council of bishops from West and East at Nicaea, a lake town in today's northern Turkey. Though it was the first ecumenical council in history, only six bishops were attracted from the distant West, while the eastern bishops, always disputatious and politically minded, turned out in force, some 250 to 300 attending. The emperor himself guided the discussions. The main business of the council was to define the nature of Christ in a creed that could be accepted unanimously. The result was a compromise that satisfied no one. The main burden of the final resolution was the affirmation that God the Father and God the Son were of the same essence. The concept was designed to confute Arius's definition of Father and Son as of two separate identities.

Eventually this theory of the codivinity of Father and Son would become the central tenet of the Nicene Creed, the basis of Christian orthodoxy—but not in the fourth century, when hair-splitting over the meanings of words was a noisy, corrosive and unending battle. Arianism was by no means dead as a result of the Council of Nicaea. Constantine's sons and the succeeding emperors varied, some being of the Arian persuasion, some following the dictates of Nicaea. Whichever group of bishops went along with the notions of the current emperor threw out all the dissenting bishops to the accompaniment of unedifying abuse, causing extreme confusion among their flocks. The un-Christian, cantankerous atmosphere persisted for more than half a century. Finally, in 381, the Orthodox emperor Theodosius the Great resolved to end it. He called a council at Constantinople, during which the Orthodox faith, based on the Nicene Creed, was declared the state religion of the empire. In the East, Arianism officially existed no longer.

The end of Arius himself was pathetic. While his theory and the debates it excited were still very much alive, he himself was considered negligible by both sides. About 336, sick and defeated, the old priest begged Constantine to allow him to return to his home city to receive the sacraments there before he died. His wish was granted, but while walking in the street a few days before the ceremony Arius suddenly fell dead. As he was over seventy-five the occurrence was not unexpected, but a legend arose some twenty years later, circulated by his enemies, giving a less prosaic explanation. By the judgment of God the heretic had been struck down on the eve of absolution in the following manner: He "emptied out his entrails through his back passage in the lavatory, and while he was occupied in emptying his bowels he lost his soul instead."[3]

In the fourth century the conflict over the nature of Christ was nearly non-existent in the Western Empire, and the Nicene Creed was barely heard of, let alone understood in its theological implications. But at about the same time that Arianism was effectively suppressed in the East a variant of it was gaining a strong foothold in the West.

In the early part of that century a young Goth from Dacia (today's Rumania), named Ulfilas, went to live in Constantinople, where he received a Christian education. At this time the Christian schools of the East were teaching the Arian heresy: there was an Arian emperor on the throne and it was politic to believe as he did. Subsequently Ulfilas was consecrated missionary bishop to his people. A naïve and ardent Christian innocent of politics, Ulfilas went back to proselytize his pagan compatriots, taking his heresy with him—unaware that with the next emperor his beliefs would be declared unacceptable. In Dacia, Ulfilas's Christian converts incurred the antagonism of the pagan Visigothic leader, and the missionary was forced to migrate with his people to lower Moesia, south of the Danube (today's Bulgaria). There Ulfilas labored for thirty years, during the course of which he translated the Bible into the Gothic language. There was no written form of Gothic except in runes, so Ulfilas invented a new alphabet of twenty-four letters, based on the Greek, with some Runic characters to express sounds which did not exist in Greek and Latin pronunciation. Ulfilas's Gothic Bible gave his people in written form what they had heretofore had only orally, and Christian conversion among the barbarians made a great leap forward. By the end of the fourth century not only the Goths but all the barbarians who now dominated the kingdoms of Europe and North Africa had become Christians—of the Arian heresy. Only the Franks, still an obscure rural confederacy confined to northern Gaul, remained pagan. The rulers of the Vandals, Visigoths, Ostrogoths, Burgundians, Suevians and Herulians tried to impress their religious deviation on their

Roman subjects, sometimes intemperately, sometimes with moderation, but never with success. The orthodox Christian convictions of
the subject peoples—the majority of the population—were only
hardened by opposition, and the rulers had to contend with the
obstacle of an ever discontented populace.

In 496, a century later than the other conquering barbarians,
Christianity reached the Franks through the conversion of their
leader, Clovis. Clovis's religion, under the influence of his Catholic
queen and the instruction of his forceful bishops, was the orthodox
version. Overnight the Frankish chief became the champion of all the
beset Catholics of Europe, and the Frankish kingdom, at ease with its
Gallo-Roman subjects, began its ascent to the position of the
dominant power west of Constantinople.

We return to the fourth century and to Bishop Hilary's incautious
effort to bring into the West the controversy that was splintering the
East. Though the Nicene Creed was by this time (the 350's) nearly
thirty years old, the doctrinal issues it purported to settle had little
relevance in the West. The ordinary priest, uneducated and conservative, accepted the simple Christian truths without analysis, and even
the more worldly bishops perceived no essential difference between
Catholic and Arian. Hilary himself had not yet heard of the creed.
But Arianism was widespread in Gaul, and he saw its danger: that it
was an insidious heresy which attacked the very heart of Christianity.
As we have seen Hilary began his campaign with an attack on one of
the emperor's favorites, Bishop Saturninus of Arles. At the same time
the Poitiers zealot wrote a letter to the emperor openly protesting the
interference of the state in religious affairs. Constantius did not
receive Hilary's partisan presumption kindly. The emperor's position
in Gaul was precarious: his cousin Julian was the popular hero, and
he still played the part of an orthodox Catholic. Hilary's letter
appeared to the emperor an invitation to the Catholics of the West to
support a pretender who thought as they did. Further, Constantius
had acquired from his father, Constantine the Great, the notion that
the Roman emperor was the deputy of God on earth. It was for him
to tell Gallic bishops what to do, not the other way around.

In 356 Hilary was summoned to appear before a synod of bishops
called by Saturninus. There he was tried, not on his faith but on his
political contumacy. His attempt to bring into the trial the perils of

the Arian heresy was ignored, and he was exiled to the East for civil interference.

The sentence was for Hilary an invitation to spend a holiday in the promised land. Phrygia, the province of his exile, was adjacent to Cappadocia, the intellectual center of Christian thinking. The Gallic exile, ever predisposed to Greek modes of thought, had a firsthand opportunity to indulge his inclination. In the congenial and enlightened air of the Greek East, Hilary studied the complexities of the Arian controversy; and he explained these for the benefit of the unaware West in his most important work, the treatise *On the Trinity*.

Along with study, discourse and writing, Hilary continued to administer his diocese by correspondence. His people, regarding him as a martyr suffering for his faith, raised money to support him and sent delegations to assure him of their unfailing loyalty. With material comfort, intellectual stimulation and leisure to think and to write, Hilary enjoyed an idyllic exile. But his sojourn in the most civilized region of the Empire could not indefinitely satisfy the active bishop. He wrote another letter to Emperor Constantius containing, among other tactless declarations, the opinion that the West was the home of the true creed. The emperor reacted, not with indignation, but with prudence: he restored Hilary to his diocese. His reasoning was that the bishop would find himself so busy with the affairs of his see that he would have no extra energy to be vexatious.

The emperor's tact was wasted: on his way home, a triumphal progress through an admiring Italy, the unregenerate bishop composed an *Invective against Constantius*. The emperor had no time to react; he died in 361, right after its publication. Julian, who had been acclaimed emperor by his armies just before his cousin's death, had no longer a remote interest in the refinements of Christian doctrine. But in deference to his powerful Gallic Catholic supporters he listened to Hilary and saw to the deposition of Bishop Saturninus of Arles; and that "very bad man, of an evil and corrupt character, was convicted of many unspeakable crimes, and cast out of the Church."[4]

Hilary's solo battle to free his province of heresy gave the subsequent Merovingian dynasty an edge over the Arian regimes of Spain and Italy. His effect on political history as a fighter was more lasting than his effort on ecclesiastical history as a philosopher. Hilary was a sagacious theologian, but his innovative thought was overshadowed by the later work of Ambrose of Milan and Augustine of Hippo. Following Hilary's lead, these masters of religious logic expressed themselves with more flowing ease, to a more receptive audience. Even in his own time Hilary was not widely read. His ideas, profoundly logical as they are, make turgid reading. The rhetorical schools of the later empire had become degenerately refined, and Hilary never got away from his education. His overweight prose defeated even scholarly Jerome: "Adorned as he is with the flowers of Greek rhetoric, he sometimes entangles himself in long periods and offers by no means easy reading."[5]

Hilary's one excursion into popular literature was the writing of hymns. He loved music in church; it was a fine way to fight the devil. "Every adversary must needs be affrighted, the devil routed, death conquered in the faith of the Resurrection, by such jubilant utterance of our exultant voice."[6] Besides foiling Satan, the old fighter's hymns made warfare against heresy: he aimed to combat the musical popularity of Arius with equally singable propaganda for the orthodox faithful. Unfortunately none of Hilary's hymns is reliably extant; soon after his death they were superseded by those of Ambrose.

Even the death of the bishop of Poitiers, in about 367, failed to attract the chroniclers. It is not known exactly when or how he died: no attendant priest wrote down his last words, no miracle accompanied the winging of his soul to heaven, no votaries fought for shreds of his garment. These were such everyday occurrences on the occasions of fourth-century holy deaths that it is evident that the fiery bishop was forgotten even while he was still alive.

But Hilary's influence on western Christianity was more effective than the people of his time realized. Religion in the West was still a matter of uninformed and unthinking traditional faith. With his sound Greek training and his agile mind Hilary brought to it the beginnings of intellectual awareness. And the ardent, angry faith he brought to the battle against heresy was a prime component of the later ascendancy of Catholic Frankish Gaul.

Hilary was the forerunner in the contest against ignorance and heresy in the West. In the decades after his death three great writers and thinkers, Jerome, Ambrose and Augustine, following the lead of the Gallic fighter-theologian, set the Roman Catholic Church in the pattern it was to hold through the Middle Ages.

Though Hilary's death passed unnoticed his memory is enshrined in his own town, in the noble church of Saint-Hilaire-le-Grand. This church, erected in the eleventh century over the chapel he had built to house his tomb, combines delicate ornamental detail with massive proportions in a manner typically Romanesque. Soaring rows of columns lead the eye to the decorated arch of the crypt wherein lies the modern reliquary. High above, on a column capital, the saint lies on his little bedstead, eyes closed and mouth downturned. Four worshipful figures surround him, three of them reading books—presumably Hilary's. Above them hovers the naked soul, its head and feet held by two smiling angels. The scene has an archaic sweetness.

Alongside the intellectual growth of Christianity in Gaul ran the parallel stream of monasticism, a withdrawal from the world of warring kings and argumentative clerics. While the bishops, activists in the contemporary scene, ran their sprawling dioceses, engaged in controversy, preached, comforted and admonished, another kind of evolution, equally consequential, was occurring within the silent precincts of cloister walls.

Gallic monasticism had its antecedents in the East, where retreat to the desert for a deeper contact with the world of the spirit was far older than Christianity. The primitive Church, isolated and persecuted, had no need for an escape in order to find God—it was austere from necessity. Mortification of the flesh was a fact of daily life and martyrdom was not sought but imposed. With Constantine's edict of tolerance, Christianity could come out in the open and clothe itself in respectability. Enriched by imperial gifts and acceptable to the middle and upper classes, the Church soon grew into a worldliness out of contact with its roots. A few purer souls, looking for a return from materialism to the stern virtues of the primitive Church, followed the example of pre-Christian anchorites and withdrew to the deserts of Africa and the Middle East. There they sought, in solitary contemplation, the ethereal joy of surrender to God. Since martyrdom was a condition of the past, they aspired to reach this blessed state by mortifying their flesh: "I kill [my body] lest it should kill me."[7]

It was an escape, and as with other kinds of escape, the motives were not always good nor the practices wholesome. Many aimed only to flee the clutches of taxes and military conscription. Others sought a notoriety they could not attain at home, indulging in freakish acts of self-mortification to draw attention to their superior sanctity: they led the life of animals, feeding on grass and eschewing clothing; they wore iron belts; they subjected their bodies to poisonous insects. Among the more notorious was Simon Stylites, who, expelled from a monastery for overdoing his penances, lived for some years chained to a stone inside a cistern infested with worms. Then he built himself a pillar in the Syrian desert and sat on it, surrounded by devotees, until he died thirty years later. Still another motivation was political: the scum of the cities, congregating in the desert as "monks," were gathered by demagogues into bands, to act as armies when Church conflicts degenerated into brawls, a frequent occurrence in the volatile African cities.

But the core was sound, and the lives of the best of the holy hermits are records of an extraordinary goodness. If they contributed nothing to the Church in the way of doctrine or philosophy, they gave back the primal simplicity of faith that had been failing. Few of them were intellectual, in fact most were illiterate. But they were humane and gentle, they spoke with the wisdom of the heart tempered with humor, and when they prayed all knew that God listened, for their faith was absolute.

The beauties and rewards of the solitary life were introduced to the lay public in the mid-fourth century by Athanasius, contemporary and friend of Saint Anthony. His appealing *Life of Saint Anthony* represents the Egyptian saint, the first authentic Christian hermit, as a healthy solitary who deplored both self-maceration and idleness, and succeeded in living, according to his biographer, from 251 until 356. But Anthony devised for his soul a lonely, arduous discipline, and very few had the strength to live as he did, alone in the Egyptian desert. The yellow hills, rolling in empty monotony to a dusty horizon, the inescapable sun, the frigid starlight—the appearance of eternity was too literal even for the very pious.

A contemporary of Anthony, Pachomius (292–346), recognized that if men were occasionally together they could more easily tolerate being mostly alone. He organized would-be anchorites into a community at Tabennesis, in the area of Thebes, where they were subject to rules, liable to obedience to a superior and dependent upon one another. The movement acquired a new perspective when Basil of Cappadocia (330–379), regarding the hermit life as self-defeating, taught that the highest aim of the religious was the exercise of brotherly love. His monks were not to immure themselves in the scenery but to labor, like Jesus, among the wretched. His monastery, in the teeming city of Caesarea (in today's central Turkey), included a hospital, a school and an almshouse. Basil tempered the military severity of Pachomius's discipline with humanity; his is still the basic rule of eastern monasticism.

Basil's moderated monastic rule did not reach Gaul until early in the fifth century, but a rudimentary monastic movement had arisen there earlier, inspired by travelers' exaggerated accounts of the glowing sanctity of the desert hermits. Athanasius's *Life of Saint Anthony* gave the movement a positive impetus. But the strenuous asceticism of the East was unsuitable for Gallo-Romans both temperamentally and physically. Athanasius had written that "fasting is the food of angels."[8] "It is unkind," complained one of his readers, "to try to force us Gauls to live after the fashion of angels; and yet, through my own liking for eating, I could believe that even the angels are in the habit of eating, and we are, in one word, Gauls."[9]

However some attempted to reproduce in the chilly forests of Gaul the frugal rapture of the desert fathers, sleeping in tree trunks or caves, wearing skin tunics and sabots and living on barley meal and wild herbs. Around a holy hermit would gather hopeful disciples, and the saint, untaught and inexperienced, was constrained to make his retreat the center of an institution. There was no written rule nor monastic tradition. Discipline was impossible: impatient young men embraced the difficult austerity of cenobitic life expecting to develop halos overnight, grew bored or distressed and drifted back to society. Monks kept their personal belongings; if chastised for this, or for any other infringement of communal life, they simply departed.

There was one great figure in early Gallic monasticism: Saint Martin, who founded his first institution at Ligugé, near Poitiers, in 360. Martin left no written rule, and it is not known how his monastery functioned. Aside from Ligugé, the monastic movement was still in a primitive and incoherent state in the early part of the fifth century when John Cassian, the towering genius of early Gallic monasticism, put order into it.

Cassian came of a cultivated Christian Provençal family, and he spent the years of his young manhood in the East, where he had journeyed to learn from the anchorites themselves the ways of desert monasticism. Realizing that in its pristine state the desert cult would not suit either the Gallic climate or the Gallic character, Cassian devised a gentler rule. He wrote two books, *Institutes of the Coenobia* and *Conferences*, with the aim of acquainting the West with the usages of eastern monasticism and of modulating its practices for western aspirants. His concept of monastic life became

the model for Benedict of Nursia in the sixth century; and Benedict's rule in turn became the accepted monastic practice all over
medieval Europe.*

Among the philosophies Cassian studied in the East the most far-
reaching influence on his thinking was that of Evagrius, a religious
writer known as the father of spirituality. From Evagrius came the
concept of the seven deadly sins, which would be one of the main
tenets of the moral theology of the Middle Ages. In Latin usage they
were: pride, covetousness, lust, envy, gluttony, anger and sloth.
Cassian's battle against the last would be the spring of the great
medieval flowering of monasticism.

Sloth, known to Cassian as *accidie* (acedia), is defined as spiritual
torpor and apathy, and it was an occupational disease of contempla-
tives. Through the ages it would be an insistent concern of abbots: it
was insidious, feeding on itself, and it led, above all the other faults,
to breaches of discipline and finally to abandonment of the monastic
life. When the disease "has taken possession of some unhappy soul,"
wrote Cassian, "it produces disgust with the cell, and disdain and
contempt of the brethren who dwell with him. He cries up distant
monasteries and describes such places as better suited for salvation,
and he paints the intercourse with the brethren there as sweet and
full of spiritual life. On the other hand, everything about him is
rough, and there is nothing edifying among the brethren. Then
besides this he looks about anxiously this way and that, and sighs
that none of the brethren come to see him, and often goes in and out
of his cell, and frequently gazes up at the sun, as if it was too slow in
setting."[10]

The cure for acedia is work, and from this premise arose the
momentous impact of medieval European monasticism on its world.
Cassian enjoins his monks to labor with their hands until they are
weary, for "a monk who works is attacked by but one devil; but an
idler is tormented by countless spirits."

From the simple charge to work grew the toil that transformed
western monasticism. Desert monasticism had had the quality of
ingrown contemplation in which the main concern was the selfish
care of the single soul. With Cassian and his successors began the
development toward the highly specialized industry of the medieval

*An admirer of Cassian, Benedict required his *Collationes* (*Conferences*) to be read
aloud at lunch; hence *colazione*, the Italian word for "lunch."

monk, part of an industrial and intellectual complex the equivalent
of a corporation or a university today. Cassian's monks were sent into
the fields to cure their idleness: out of their mandatory toil grew the
agricultural revolution of the Middle Ages. That they should not sulk
in their cells they were required to spend several hours each day in the
scriptorium painstakingly copying manuscripts of whose meaning
most of them probably had little comprehension: from this grew the
great monastic libraries, and the illuminated manuscripts whose
intricate beauty is an artistic marvel.

The original monastic ideal brought by Cassian from the desert
cells of Egypt and Palestine did not envision any sort of learning and
culture; in fact it was unambiguously anti-intellectual. The intentions
of Cassian and his successors never encompassed scholarly pursuits.
It was not in the monkish ideation that their retreats should become
the repositories of classical culture and they themselves the only
transmitters of the learning of the ancients. But through the chaos of
the barbarian invasions, the break-up of the Western Empire and the
following difficult years of Europe's rebirth, the monks undesignedly
became the heirs of Greece and Rome.

Following Cassian's dictum that a monk must work in order to eat,
there were few parasitic monks in the West. Also there were few
disconsolate countenances in monasteries. The prevailing atmosphere
was one of cheerfulness, the product of an orderly and useful life. This
too was the gift of Cassian: the abstruse mysticism and harsh self-
denial of the East was filtered through his common sense, to give the
contemplative life a homely western naturalness. It has been argued
that the overwhelming popularity of monastic retreat was a bad thing
for the West: a large part of the lay masculine population was diverted
from the service of Rome to the service of Christ at the time the
failing empire needed the active devotion of its able-bodied citizenry.
The barbarians were taking over, infiltrating the army and the civil
service, spilling across the borders with importunity, seeking, no
longer loot but arable land. And Rome's *jeunesse dorée* was hiding in
monasteries. This is a hindsight view: to modern thought the
profound search for God that occupied philosophical minds in the
fourth and fifth centuries has no sensible relevance compared with
the hard facts of Alaric, Ataulf, Gaiseric and Odoacer, the barbarian
leaders who were rudely deciding Europe's future. In their own lights,
however, the theologians were not negative, advocating escape from a

terrible world, but positive, trying to build a fuller and richer one. They were rewarded, and in the end the barbarians did not defeat them but were transmuted by them.

There was another side to the recoil from secular life. When the Franks sacked Trier early in the fifth century the horrors of the raid were described by one of the survivors: "I have seen corpses lying about everywhere, naked, torn. The deadly stench of the bodies wrought a plague among the living. Death breathed out from death. What happened after? The handful of the nobility who had escaped death demanded circuses of the emperor as a supreme remedy for the destruction of the city. Where, I ask, will they be held? On the mounds and the ashes, on the bones and blood of your dead? If my human frailty would suffer me, I wish I could shout out even beyond the limits of my strength and make my voice echo throughout the world: shame on you, ye Roman people everywhere, shame on the lives you lead. It is our vicious lives alone that have conquered us."[11]

It is understandable that so many young men were turning away from the service of the empire to immure themselves in monasteries or to take priestly vows. They were not fleeing the barbarians but escaping from their own kind. Disgusted with the frivolous indifference of the elite to the suffering of those not so wealthy or lucky, these young men found honesty and humanity only within the walls of cloisters. In many ways the Western Empire brought about its own downfall. But the Roman citizens who survived to take over the reins in the barbarian kingdoms were those whose forerunners had elected to abjure secular service at a time when the empire seemed to need them most: the priests, monks and bishops.

Toward the end of the fourth century, when Cassian was interviewing the anchorites and cenobites of Egypt, Honoratus, cosseted scion of an aristocratic Gallo-Roman family of Gallia Belgica, gave away his hunting horses, discarded his silken garments, cut his long hair and set sail for Greece to learn at first hand how to be a monk.

A youth of outgoing sweetness and good humor, Honoratus had been the light of his parents' life. They had dreamed of seeing him married and following in his father's footsteps as consul in northern Gaul. But Honoratus, dedicated to God from early boyhood, had pursued a Christian course in the face of all opposition, giving away his pocket money and his jewelry, and honoring his clerical teachers as his true fathers. He resisted the temptations of a gay aristocratic life that were deliberately put in his way by his relatives, who "feared to have snatched from them a kind of ornament owned by the whole family."[12] Knowing that he must be stern with himself while still young, Honoratus remarked later: "It is easier to uproot a sapling than to cut down a sturdy tree."

When he came of age Honoratus renounced his birthright and committed himself unequivocally to a religious life. In Greece he absorbed the teachings of the clear-witted father of Greek monasticism, Basil of Cappadocia. Basil's rule would form the basis for the illustrious and happy institution Honoratus later founded in southern Gaul.

On his return to Gaul Honoratus chose for his retreat the small island of Lérins (now Saint Honorat, near Cannes), because he was sure no one would disturb him on this waterless waste, inhabited only by venomous snakes. The army of serpents, it is said, fell back at the approach of the hermit—who soon found that he could be a hermit no longer. So many flocked to the once-shunned island to speak with the holy man and experience the healing power of his compassion that he was constrained to establish "a kind of camp of God." In about 410, Lérins became a monastery; and even during Honoratus's lifetime it gained a reputation for sanctity and learning unequaled in Gaul.

Honoratus's unsparing self-discipline did not change his sunny nature. He remained blessed with a kindliness that made him loved alike by the simplest and the most erudite of his disciples. Among the adages in which he liked to indulge was a paraphrase of Psalm 105: "Let the hearts of those who seek the Lord be gay." He took much trouble to ensure that none of his monks became depressed, treating each with separate concern, arranging tactfully that the overactive would not be burdened with too much labor nor the slower become slothful with inaction. Though always ailing himself he was tireless in his solicitude, visiting the sick when he was sicker, observing fasts and night watches with the strongest. His mind was ever on his charges: "This one," he would say, "is feeling the cold; that one broods; *he* finds the work heavy; that food doesn't suit *him*." Guests at the monastery were many, and warmly welcomed; the richer ones brought money and gifts, immediately disposed of among the needier. On one occasion there was only one gold piece left; Honoratus gave it to a passing beggar, saying, "If our treasury has nothing left to bring out, you may be sure there is someone not far off with something he is bringing in."

In 426 he was elected bishop of Arles, southern Gaul's chief religious center, as successor to one Patroclus who had been accused of simony, then murdered. In an atmosphere of tempestuous disharmony Honoratus, who had left Lérins reluctantly, reasoned with the feuders and knit them together in mutual forgiveness. But the strain was too much for his frail health, and three years later he succumbed. His cousin Hilary (his biographer, who would succeed him as bishop of Arles) sat by his bedside weeping, to be tenderly chided by the dying man: "Why are you weeping over the inevitable lot of men? My departure ought not to find you so unready for it, when it has not found *me* unready." At the end those who surrounded him tried to keep him awake, that he might not sink into a death-sleep. "I am surprised," he said, "that, when I am so weary after so many sleepless hours, you should take such a serious view of my sleepiness!" He added "that he would allow us to be a nuisance, since we were looking after him. He had almost used up his life before his sweetness."

His body was stripped nearly naked on its way to the grave, the mourners scrambling for threads of the holy garments. The custom of vandalizing the dead for relics was still new, and the indecent ardor with which it was indulged attests to the survival of heathen usage even in the sophisticated Greco-Roman surroundings of southern Gaul. It is indicative of the age that so civilized an observer as Hilary sees in the uncouth despoliation only an added tribute to the saint.

Honoratus left no written rule, no treatises or sermons, and his spoken words exist only in the adulatory pages of his successor. His sole legacy was the enduring luster of his foundation. While he was still its abbot, Lérins had become a haven for scholarly exiles. In the early years of the fifth century, Frankish invaders devastated the northern cities of Trier, Mainz, Cologne and Rheims, and much of Aquitaine. Educated laymen as well as priests, fleeing the barbarians, found at Lérins a congenial atmosphere that derived in part from the cheerful benevolence that was the legacy of its first abbot, and in part from its Greek antecedents. Southern Provence was blessed with the melding of three cultures: Celtic, Roman and Greek. Long before the Romans had impressed their mores on the imaginative Celts, Gaul's Mediterranean area had been a Greek colony. Intellectual life had a historic continuity there, reaching back to classical Greece and enduring after Greece's decline, through intercourse with the enlightened communities of North Africa. Continuing the tradition, Lérins

produced some of the finest thinkers and writers of the time, and it
was renowned as a literary center well into the sixth century, when
the educational standards of Frankish Gaul were otherwise at a low
ebb. Not only writers and philosophers found the atmosphere of
Lérins stimulating, the spiritual education it afforded produced a host
of excellent churchmen, giving it the reputation of a "nursery of
bishops."[13]

France's patron saint, Martin, predated Cassian and Honoratus as
a monastic founder. His monastery, Ligugé, was the first in Gaul to be
organized under a rule. Existing at the same time as the haphazard
groups of hermit cells loosely based on hearsay from the East, Ligugé
was known as a model of disciplined virtue.

But in aura if not in time, Saint Martin belongs to a later period
than the intellectual ecclesiastics of Provence. Though he was probably better educated than his biographer gives him credit for, little of
the fourth-century scholarly classicism clings to his history, and he
left no writings by which he can authentically be characterized. To
posterity he is a creature of the early Middle Ages, enveloped in the
cloud of magical holiness that began to form around him soon after
his death. In 397, the year Martin died, his disciple, Sulpicius
Severus, wrote an affectionate, miracle-filled biography.[14] The legend
of Martin's sanctity was inflated through succeeding centuries, until
its subject was magnified into a larger-than-life immortal not unlike
Ireland's Saint Patrick.* The unquestioning reverence with which
Martin was regarded obscured his true position as a pillar of the
Gallic Church: a preacher and converter of pagans, a considerate
abbot and an active bishop.

In another parallel with English-born Saint Patrick, Martin was not
a native of the country that adopted him as its particular saint. He
was born in about 316 in Pannonia, to solidly middle-class heathen
parents. His father was a military tribune who, aiming to quench his
son's aberrant longing for the holy life, designed the boy to follow a
military career. But Martin would not be deflected. When only ten he
begged the local priest to give him religious instruction. At twelve he
tried to enter one of the unregulated eremitical orders that were

---

*Not all the readers of Sulpicius's biography were credulous; twenty years later
Cassian, pointedly disapproving, stated in the preface to his Institutes that he would
not "weave a tale of God's miracles and signs, which minister to the reader nothing
but astonishment and no instruction."[15]

proliferating in Europe in imitation of those in the Sahara; to their credit they turned him down as being too young. Martin's predilection for holiness annoyed his father so positively that when the boy turned fifteen and became eligible for military service, he reported his son to the authorities. Martin was seized, put in chains and forced to take the military oath. Though never cowardly he was an atypical soldier, forgoing the customary army vices and kind and humble with his companions. He even treated his servant as master, cleaning his boots and waiting on him at meals.

Military duty took him to northern Gaul under the command of Julian, who was fighting the Franks in the area of Amiens. There it was that Martin got his heavenly call. It was an inclement midwinter day when the young soldier, now twenty years old, met a poor man with little clothing who was begging the passersby at the town gates to have pity on him. Martin had no warm clothing left but his cloak, having already given away everything else. This he rent in two parts with his sword, and gave half to the beggar. "Some of the bystanders laughed, because he was now an unsightly object." (A careless appearance was to bring scorn on Martin throughout his life, to his unconcern.) That night a vision came to him in his sleep, of Christ with the visage of the beggar, clad in the half cloak. Martin—with complete absence of vanity—saw the divine apparition as a manifest signal of his true calling, and went at once to be baptized.

When Julian called his army together to brief them for a battle with the barbarians Martin boldly announced that he would no longer serve: he had become a soldier of Christ, he said, and it was no longer lawful for him to fight. The general accused him of cowardice, and Martin answered by volunteering to stand unarmed between the battle lines; then, protected only by the sign of the Cross, he would walk untouched through the enemy ranks. Julian prepared to accommodate him by throwing him in prison until the battle should commence, when he would be taken at his word. But the young hero did not have to redeem his pledge because the enemy unexpectedly sued for peace—an eventuality attributed by Martin's biographer to the intervention of Christ. His career as a secular soldier decisively ended, Martin went to Poitiers to enroll himself as a disciple of Bishop Hilary. The bishop recognized the potential of the unassuming but determined spiritual fighter and brought him into the office of the diaconate. He wished Martin to conduct divine service but the neophyte refused, saying that he was unworthy. Hilary, a discerning man, perceived that he could only advance his protégé by giving him an office that would appear demeaning. He made Martin an exorcist, the second lowest office in the clerical hierarchy (the first being that of lector, or reader of lessons in the church service). Martin, ever modest, did not refuse in case it should be thought he disdained the office. He became attached to Hilary, however, as a kind of alter ego. In their complementary roles Hilary, an intellectual aristocrat, worked among the educated elite whom he essayed to convert away from Arianism by reason. Martin's orbit was missionary work among the simpleminded pagan peasantry.

During the vicissitudes of Hilary's anti-Arian campaign Martin was his master's active assistant, and he was just as valiantly tactless. Finally, near the end of Hilary's life, the two were allowed to settle peaceably in Poitiers. Hilary gave Martin some land at Ligugé, near the city, and in 360 Martin founded his monastery there. Martin's rule is no longer extant—if he ever wrote it down—and probably this early foundation was rudimentary in comparison with Cassian's highly organized houses. But presumably Martin ran a trim and respected establishment, for after twelve years as abbot he was called, in 372, to be bishop of Tours.

Already in Martin's time the city on the Loire was the political and economic center of western Gaul. It had been the chief settlement of a Celtic tribe, the Turones, and the Romans recognized its potential value to their Gallic dominions. The Touraine countryside is flat and fertile, the climate pleasant, and the broad, quietly flowing Loire ideal for river traffic. The settlement was a stop on the main thoroughfare between Spain and Aquitaine and the empire's northern Gallic provinces, and the Romans built five roads centering in the town. About 375, Emperor Gratian made it the capital of the central province of Lugdunensis Tertia (Touraine, Le Maine, Anjou and Armorica).

There had been Christians in Touraine while Christianity was still a clandestine religion. In about 240, more than half a century before the Edict of Milan, Saint Gatian, a companion of Saint Denis and an early apostle to the Gauls, came to the area. He preached there for fifty years, and is known as the first bishop of Tours.

Tours today is a big bustling city of industry, agriculture and tourism. The old city, between the Loire and the Cher, is overlaid by the new, and the remnants of earlier centuries are hard to see. Martin's Tours has vanished beneath sixteen centuries of building.

Two beautiful eleventh- to thirteenth-century towers, the Tour Charlemagne and the Tour de l'Horloge, are the only remnants of the great Romanesque Basilica of Saint Martin which replaced the fifth-century sanctuary leveled by the Normans.

The election of Martin to this already important episcopate was accomplished by nearly unanimous vote of the citizenry. He had been unwilling to leave his monastery, until a dissembling *tourangeau* begged him on his knees to visit his ailing wife. Unable to refuse an appeal to his mercy, Martin went forth to find himself the captive of an eager crowd, a kind of guard to escort him, whether he would or no, to the city. There multitudes, not only from the town but from the surrounding countryside, lined the streets to give him their votes. Whatever his private wishes, Martin was the people's choice.

Martin was not the only one who was reluctant: from the start of his career the Gallic bishops had both scorned and feared him and all he stood for. The entrenched bishops objected to monasticism in general—they felt that it was anticlerical, and that it set a dangerous example of austerity. In particular they disapproved of this resolutely informal, undauntable monk. Overtly they frowned, not on Martin's ideology but on his appearance, holding "that Martin's person was contemptible, that he was a man despicable in countenance, that his clothing was mean, and his hair disgusting." The aspersions brought only ridicule upon the critics, for Martin was beloved.

And however unkempt his facade he made a good bishop. Unassuming and homely, he was devoted to the least of his flock, yet he met the formal demands of his office with dignified courtesy. He had innate nobility, even though he preferred rather to sit on a three-legged stool than on the bishop's throne.

But sometimes Martin needed repose. In his heart still a monk, he founded a small monastery about two miles outside Tours, at Marmoutier. There the Loire flows close to a steep hillside, and Martin's secret place could be approached only by a single-file passage up the rock scarp. He constructed his cell of branches, and his monks lived in similar huts or in caves they hollowed out of the overhanging cliff. The life was austere: they lived alone and in silence except for the times of prayer and the one simple daily meal, and they were clad in garments of camel's hair in imitation of John the Baptist. Yet among the eighty monks many were gently bred and used to luxury. One of their number was Martin's subsequent biographer, Sulpicius Severus, a rich Aquitanian nobleman.

Marmoutier Abbey is still there, and the Loire still flows past it, nearly touching its gates in flood. It is closed to the public; behind the severely graceful thirteenth-century gatehouse are Martin's narrow path up the rock face and the caves of his aristocratic monks, hidden, as in his lifetime, from the intruder.

Martin could not spend much time in his riverside retreat. He involved himself in the public affairs of his time and place, interceding on behalf of political prisoners and treating successfully with emperors in ecclesiastical matters. Though never aggressive he was spiritedly determined, as in his interview with Emperor Valentinian I. When the emperor, taking his cue from the haughty bishops, refused to see him, Martin had recourse to the familiar weapons of the holy man: sackcloth and ashes, fasting and nightly prayer vigils. An angel appeared to inform him that the royal gates would open to him of themselves, and so they did. Martin came into the presence of the emperor, who did not condescend to rise "until fire covered the royal seat, and flames seized on the part of the body that sat on it." Then the emperor jumped from his throne, and granted all of Martin's requests without asking what they were.

Though effectively bold in high places, Bishop Martin's first concern was with the poor farmers of the countryside. Most of these were pagan, all were illiterate, and Martin's appeal to them was a combination of sympathy and dispatch. His rough-and-ready miracles appealed to a credulous rural people. Some of his prodigies were healing; others entailed the destruction of heathen temples. Once he set about personally chopping down a sacred pine tree. Assuring the protesting worshippers that the spirit of the tree was a devil, not a god, he volunteered to stand in the way of the tree if they themselves would cut it down. They bound the saint in the path of the tree and began, with glee, to proceed to the Christian's annihilation. When the tree tottered toward him the saint held up his hand in the sign of the Cross. The tree spun around and fell to the opposite side, almost crushing the rustics. They all decided to be saved at once, and Martin built a church over the roots of the heathen tree. As a rule he was not a temple smasher: sensible and eloquent, he usually prevailed on the farmers to do the job themselves.

He performed wonders which had already, in his biographer's time, come to be routine: many of the miracles turn up regularly in the lives of the saints, others have natural explanations. Sulpicius records them with an appealing narrative skill, often stressing the bizarre and macabre, always infusing his tales with the compassionate sweetness of his hero's nature.

Martin raised the dead to life, as in the case of a slave who hanged himself: the saint stretched himself upon the lifeless body, praying, and, "Ere long, the deceased, with life beaming in his countenance, and with his heavy eyes fixed on Martin's face, is aroused." He exorcised devils, including one which "gnashed with his teeth and, with gaping mouth, was threatening to bite, [when] Martin inserted his fingers into his mouth, and said, 'If you possess any power, devour these.' While he had no power of escaping by the mouth, he was cast out by means of a defluxion of the belly, leaving disgusting traces behind him."

Martin endeared himself to the country people with pastoral specialties: he banished hail from a district that had suffered from it for twenty years. After the saint's death the hail, bewailing his loss, returned with extra violence. He exorcised a demon from a cow; enjoined a dog to stop barking and disturbing the neighbors; directed a serpent swimming toward the bank on which he stood to turn around and swim to the opposite shore.

Besides the fantasy-magic of his subject's actions, Martin's biographer deliberately stresses the saint's humble nature. Sulpicius, though genuinely convinced of his master's supernatural excellence, was also a pamphleteer. He expressed the growing dissatisfaction of the populace with the wealthy, influential aristocracy of the higher clergy, depicting Martin as a man of the common people, a symbol of the protest against the elite Gallo-Roman upper class. The democratic figure of Saint Martin appealed to a people largely not Roman, with little background of the classical tradition. Another objective was to break the ties with the antique Mediterranean world by establishing the existence of an authentic Gallic saint whose effective piety surpassed even that of the eastern ascetics. In a mild way Sulpicius was a revolutionary.

But Martin was not. Sulpicius's engaging tales of saintly marvels, for all their ulterior purpose, cannot entirely obscure the true lineaments of their star. Sulpicius was, for his time, an honest biographer, and a real Martin sometimes shines through the fog of saintly romance. Martin was well educated: "How prompt and ready [he was] in solving questions connected with Scripture! I never heard from any other lips such exhibition of knowledge and genius, or such specimens of good and pure speech." This passage, amidst the miracles, is not extraordinary: after all, Martin was an aide to that quintessential scholar and aristocrat, Hilary of Poitiers. He had enough scholarship to understand the religious disputes of his day: he successfully intervened with the emperor on behalf of some Spanish clerics persecuted for an arcane heresy far from Tours. He supported Hilary in the Arian controversy, and for this he must have had more than a superficial comprehension of the philosophical fallacy of the heresy.

The biographer throws another surprising light on his hero when he reveals Martin's distrust of the relic cult. In the fourth century, dead saints had become the foci of popular religion: the most egregious wonders occurred at their graves, and their detritus was an object of greed. Martin's exposure of fakery in this area is unexpected. The saint went to an altar over the sepulcher of a supposed martyr whose ghostly emanations were exciting the reverences of the local farmers. There he prayed energetically until the shade of a man appeared and admitted in a clear voice that he had been a robber beheaded for his crimes, and that he had nothing in common with the martyrs. Martin ordered the altar to be removed, "and thus he delivered the people from the error of this superstition."

Martin died in about 397 at Candes, thirty-three miles west of Tours at the confluence of the Loire and the Vienne—now, as it probably was then, a small quiet village. Its church, replacing the one where Martin spent his last hours, rises from the wide bend of the riverbank in an odd, attractive combination of extravagant Romanesque carving and grim Gothic fortification. The bishop had journeyed there, though ill of a fever, to calm a clerical dispute, and his death, like his life, was unassumingly fearless: "Thou didst neither fear to die nor refuse to live." He had hardly breathed his last when the people of Poitiers and Tours entered on a competition over which city should get the body, not yet cold. Like quarreling children they each claimed ownership. "As a monk he is ours," said the *poitevins.* "We entrusted him to you, but we demand him back." The *tourangeaux* countered that "God took him away from you, but only so that He might give him to us. If you claim him because you have his monastery, then you must know this, that his first monastery was in Milan."* "They argued until night came, when the body was locked

*Before he went to Gaul to become Hilary's disciple Martin had lived briefly in Milan, whence he was driven by its Arian bishop.

into a room and the door guarded by representatives of the dispu-
tants. "The men of Poitiers," continues the narrator, "planned to
carry off the body as soon as morning came, but [they] all fell asleep
in the middle of the night, and when the men of Tours saw that, they
took the mortal clay and passed it out through the window."[16]

This story is told straight-faced by the historian Gregory of Tours,
who not only sees nothing unseemly in the deathbed contention but
views it as God's doing that all the guardian poitevins fell asleep at
once. Saint Martin unquestionably belonged to Tours, thought the
loyal *tourangeau*. By the sixth century, when Gregory lived and wrote,
the presence of a dead saint was infinitely more valuable than the
milieu of his lifetime.

Martin's cult began at his death, and by the time of King Clovis's
baptism a century later he had become the consummate Gallic Saint.
Clovis endowed the church at Tours with a great treasure and
appropriated Martin as his personal patron. This act, uniting the
barbarian conqueror with Gaul's most beloved representative of
Christianity, would enhance the prestige of Clovis's new kingdom.

Martin was one among several nationally revered saints who, as
they became part of the mythology of Frankish Gaul, lost their
humanness in a nimbus of legend. The real Martin is occasionally
visible because his biographer had known him. The cult of the third-
century martyr, Saint Denis, called by the Parisians "Monsieur Saint
Denis," arose much later than his mortal existence. His history was
transmitted orally by the monks of the Abbey of Saint Denis, the
institution founded over his shrine, and was not recorded on
parchment until six centuries after his death. The accounts were then
collected and indited by Hilduin, abbot of Saint Denis, and his pupil,
Hincmar, both of whom had a political motivation in advancing the
renown of their founding saint. The resultant medley is a fascinating
study in pious confusion. It typifies the development in Frankish
Gaul, as in the rest of Europe, of the simplistic faith of the early
Middle Ages. Long gone was the clear-eyed rationality of John
Cassian and Hilary of Poitiers, scholars still in contact with Greco-
Roman culture. It must be added in defense of Hilduin and Hincmar,
otherwise reputable men of letters, that they acted on order of the
Carolingian king, Louis the Pious, and that they intended honestly
to do no more than collect the oral residue of several centuries.

In the first place the ninth-century chroniclers perpetuated and solidified a change in the dates of the actual Denis (the French spelling of the Latin Dionysius), confusing him with the first-century Dionysius the Areopagite, who is said to have been Paul's first convert. The Greek Dionysius, himself partly legendary, became further confused with an anonymous scholar who was later known as the pseudo-Dionysius the Areopagite, a fifth-century monk and Neoplatonic theologian.

From this scrambled identity emerged the outsized figure of France's most influential and most nebulous saint. The little we know of the real Saint Denis is recorded by Gregory of Tours, who described him as one of seven apostles sent by the pope in the middle of the third century to seven cities of Gaul. This was in the time of Emperor Decius, persecutor of Christians. Denis, whose assignment was Paris, "suffered repeated torture in Christ's name and then ended his earthly existence by the sword."[17] Of ascertainable fact there is no more.

Gregory adds to his one-sentence account a number of miracles attributed to the saint, evidence that even as early as the sixth century, Denis had become renowned as a wonder-worker who helped those in trouble and energetically guarded the precincts of his own tomb. In one case soldiers of King Sigibert (a grandson of Clovis) pillaged Saint Denis's church. One soldier climbed on the saint's tomb to seize a gold dove that hung above it. Losing his balance he fell with his feet on either side of the tomb and died of compression of the testicles, with his sword in his side.[18] Though this hardly constitutes a miracle it was regarded as proof that the spirit of the saint was veritably there, and vigilant.

By the ninth century, Saint Denis had been dematerialized to a figure with the hieratic aspect of a medieval fresco. While he was still in Greece as Saint Paul's disciple, runs the story, the apostle related to him an ecstatic vision he had experienced, which Denis recorded in a series of treatises on the celestial and ecclesiastical hierarchy. (These were actually composed by the fifth-century pseudo-Dionysius, and they would become the charter of medieval mysticism.) On the death of Saint Paul, Saint Denis, by now bishop of Athens, gave his position to a friend and went to Rome, where he was appointed missionary to the pagans in Gaul. His mission was successful: after proselytizing effectively in Arles he went to Paris, where he established a Christian community and became the first bishop of the city.

When Denis was an old man he fell victim to the Roman persecutions. The missionary, by now over one hundred and quite feeble, was subjected to a course of appalling tortures: he was beaten, placed on a grill in a furnace, given to a hungry lion, hung from a cross. He survived these ordeals, to be sentenced to death by beheading on the hill then known as Mons Martis and changed in the ninth century to Mons Martyrum (Montmartre) in honor of its holy sufferer. On the night before Saint Denis's death, angels administered the last sacrament through his cell window.

The next morning the executioner failed to succeed on the first try, slicing off only the top of the skull. The second blow succeeded. When his head touched the ground the martyr picked it up and walked away, and the head chanted psalms as he went, accompanied by a choir of angels. At the bottom of the hill he paused to wash his gory head in a spring. There, in the little grassy Square Suzanne-Buisson, pleasantly planted with flowers, a modern statue stands. The severe, classically-robed figure holds its mitered head neatly with both hands before its breast. The severed head is dignified—after all, it was chanting psalms. Below, a meager fountain sprinkles itself into a small pool. It is a scene for children and retired people, very genteel. The saint continued on his journey until he reached Catolacus (today's Saint Denis), five miles away, where he was interred.

By the late fifth century, long before the Saint Denis apocrypha developed, his cult was well under way. With a minimum of facts to support his legend, Denis became the patron saint, along with Martin, of the Merovingian and Carolingian dynasties. Later medieval kings, starting with Louis VI, le Gros, in 1124, marched to war under the monastery flag, the scarlet Oriflamme, with the battle cry, "Montjoye Saint Denis!"

Saint Denis and Saint Martin are classic examples of the metamorphosis of the holy man from reasoned theologian to romantic protagonist enveloped in an aureole of miracles. Two later saints may be added, who touch the outer edges of our history. Even through the hyperbole of their biographers these two have a discernible aura of fifth-century authenticity: the chief events of their lives are there, though sparse and viewed through the hedge of legend. The saints are Germain of Auxerre and Geneviève of Paris.

Germain was born about 378 at Auxerre, in western Burgundy. The Roman town, on a steep rise above the Yonne, was an important center on the Lyon-Boulogne route. Germain, of a noble family, had the benefit of the best Gallic education.[19] He went to Rome to study law and returned to Gaul to practice as a barrister. In recognition of his legal prowess, he was made governor of Armorica before he was thirty. At the end of his term he returned home to take part in the secular affairs of his town.

Though brought up a Christian, Germain was more interested in hunting than in church. He liked to hang the heads of the animals he had killed from the branches of a pear tree in the center of the city (a throwback to the Celtic custom of impaling the heads of slain enemies on the doorpost). His preceptor, Bishop Avator of Auxerre, after remonstrating vainly with his heathenish pupil, had the pear tree cut down. In a rage Germain resolved to kill the bishop, but was prevented by Avator's timely summons to Autun. There the bishop fell mortally ill, and in his fever he dreamed that Germain was to be his successor—a message he believed was from God. He had himself carried back to Auxerre, called his people to him, told them death was upon him and persuaded them to elect Germain. The young man was straightway seized, tonsured, clothed in religious habit and brought to the bishop, whose last act was to induct the captive into holy orders.

Though consecrated by force, Germain changed his way of life forthwith. "His wife was turned into his sister"; he eschewed wheat bread, wine, vinegar, oil and even salt, elected to spend his leisure hours in a cell dug in the ground and in other ways humiliated his body. With all his personal austerity Germain was a kindly and accessible bishop, lavish in hospitality and forthcoming with helpful miracles. In one case a tax collector was robbed and, liable to produce the tax money from his own pocket, appealed to the bishop for help. Germain suspected the thief and attempted to exorcise the devil which had prompted the robbery. When the victim resisted, the bishop took him to church and prayed for him before the congregation. At this the thief was levitated high into the air and, "yelling out the Bishop's name, confessed his crime."

Germain, trained in secular politics, was also an effective bishop, active in the affairs of his day and persuasive with secular leaders. So successful was he in his diocese that in 429 the pope sent him to Britain to combat heresy there and to give heart to the few and beleaguered orthodox Christians. Crossing the Channel, his ship came near to capsizing in a gale and Germain, seeing devils at work behind the winds, chided the ocean; the devils were routed and the waves subsided. In Britain his warmhearted preaching, combined with some simple miracles, rooted out the heresy and multiplied the faithful. The bishop's second visit to the island was marked by a spectacular military coup. The withdrawal of the Roman legions had left the native Britons prey to marauders. In one raid a combined force of Picts and Saxons marched against a much smaller defending army of Britons. Germain led the Britons to a ravine between two high hills and told them to shout "Alleluia!" three times in unison. The shouts echoed back and forth in the narrow valley and the enemy, thinking the very sky was falling on them, fled in panic.

The pope was impressed not so much by the martial adventure as by the successes of the Gallic bishop against the heretics. At Germain's urging, he sent Palladius to Ireland to convert the heathens. Palladius failed in his mission, being out of sympathy with the "wild and rough" Irish.[20] His place was taken, again on Germain's advice, by Patrick, who had been, it is written, his pupil in Auxerre.[21]

On his return to Auxerre, Germain, though near seventy and frail, took up the cause of his pre-ecclesiastical charges, the Armoricans. They had risen in revolt, and General Aetius had sent against them Roman-trained barbarian troops whose aim was plunder rather than chastisement. The Armoricans appealed to their erstwhile governor, and the ailing old man, still an adroit advocate, persuaded the barbarian leader to withhold his forces.

In 448 Germain followed his diplomatic success with a journey to Ravenna to plead with Galla Placidia, the dowager empress, to recall Aetius's troops permanently. His efforts were nullified by the Armoricans themselves, who rebelled again. Shortly thereafter Germain succumbed to age and illness. On his deathbed he asked the dowager empress to send his remains back to Auxerre. She duly had his body embalmed in spices and clothed in elegant vestments the saint would have disdained to wear in life. He was placed in a coffin of cypress wood and shipped home, where a magnificent funeral was held. The coffin is still there, under the Gothic church of Saint Germain, in the hole that Germain had had dug for his times of meditation.

Among Germain's Gallic protégées was a young woman, Geneviève, born about 422 in Nanterre (today a suburb of Paris). Geneviève had aspired to the religious life from the age of seven, and when she was fifteen she took the veil. Germain had known her since her early childhood, and when her parents died he supported Geneviève not only with his blessing but with material assistance, helping her to settle in Paris. Geneviève had visions, and she made unpalatable predictions, which the Parisians disliked to the point of making an attempt on her life. But the fulfillment of one of her forewarnings changed their attitude. A vision showed her the approach of Attila with his destructive army, and in 451 the prophesy came true. The terrified townspeople turned to the young nun, who exhorted them to beg God, in a course of fasting and prayer, to deter the Hun. In the event Attila changed his line of march, ultimately reaching the Catalaunian Plains northeast of Paris, where the decisive contest took place. The denouement established Geneviève as the savior of Paris. Henceforth her visions were unassailable and her help was always sought in crises.

In 464, the Frankish chieftain Childeric returned from exile to claim his kingdom. In his career of conquest he besieged Paris, and Geneviève went by boat up the Seine to Troyes to collect food for the beleaguered citizens. Her journey was accompanied by small rural miracles, and she returned home a heroine, bearing corn for her starved fellow townsmen. She even won the respect of Childeric, who, in 475, gave her permission to build a chapel at the burial place of Saint Denis outside Paris at Catolacus. This church was near the site of today's Cathedral of Saint Denis; it was also on or near a place sacred to pagans—excavations have disclosed that some of the stones of Geneviève's church had originally been part of a Gallo-Roman temple.

Geneviève lived more than eighty years, and toward the end of her life another Frankish king entered her orbit: Childeric's son Clovis, the first Merovingian to be converted to Christianity. In 496 she joined Bishop Rémy of Rheims in persuading the arrogant conqueror to bow his head to the priority of Christ. A few years later she prevailed on Clovis to build a church near Paris (the city was at that time still confined to the Île de la Cité), the Church of Saint Peter and Saint Paul. When she died, about 509, she was interred there, and the church was renamed Sainte Geneviève du Mont. In 1744 the building was replaced by the Panthéon, and during the Revolution Geneviève's remains were taken out and publicly burned. The relics that were saved were enshrined in the Gothic Church of Saint Étienne du Mont; and there they are today, within a stone sarcophagus which is in turn encased in a gaudy cage of burnished copper.

Germain and Geneviève bridge the period between imperial and barbarian Europe. Germain, Roman-trained and Roman-souled, reached out to the primitive Christians of Armorica and the British Isles, to touch them with the civilization of Roman Gaul. In the next generation Geneviève, child of a distraught period, laid her firm and gentle hand on the wolfish rulers of the new Frankish Gaul. Exemplified by these two, the cultivation of the Gallo-Roman Christian merged with the tough vitality of the pagan Frank.

PART II

THE LONG-HAIRED KINGS

CHAPTER FOUR

CLOVIS

"Let us set out the beginnings of the kings of the Franks and their origin and also the origins of the people and its deeds. [After the fall of Troy] Priam and Antenor, two Trojan princes, embarked on ships with twelve thousand of the men remaining from the Trojan army. They came to the banks of the Tanis [Don] River. They sailed into the Maeotian swamps, penetrated the frontiers of the Pannonias and began to build a city as their memorial. They called it Sicambria and lived there many years, growing into a great people."[1]

So wrote the unknown seventh-century authors of *Liber Historiae Francorum*, following the accepted early medieval practice of "synchronized history," in which the few known facts of a people's past are meshed into classical or Biblical epic. The method was to uplift the antecedents of a race whose actual past was lost in oral myth, but whose present-day accomplishments warranted them a respectable slot in the mainstream of history. The Franks' Trojan origin connected them by blood to the Romans, who claimed descent from Aeneas.

In fact, the chroniclers' flights of imagination do exist within a framework of history once they have the Franks settled in Pannonia. There the Romans employed them to drive the "perverse and rotten" Alans out of Pannonia, and "because of the hardness and daring of their hearts the Emperor Valentinian called the Trojans Franks. In the Attic tongue Frank means fierce." The "Franks" now rose against their allies and killed the Roman tax collectors, arousing the anger of the emperor, who sent a large force against them. The battle was a draw, but the Franks left the insecurity of Pannonia and traveled northwest "to the farthest reaches of the Rhine River where the Germans' strongholds are located. [After many years] they chose Faramund, and raised him up* as the long-haired king above them." This was the first time the Franks had had a single king, and the unauthenticated Faramund (whose name does not appear in written histories before the seventh century) was the direct ancestor of the dynasty of the Merovingians. The tentative date of his election was A.D. 418. "After King Faramund died they raised up into his father's kingdom Clodion, his long-haired son. At this time they began to have long-haired kings." The date was about 428.

The significance of the long hair was ritually connected to the tradition of the dynasty and, like the dynasty itself, had no remarkable attribute that assured royalty. All the patriarchal families of the Franks wore their hair long: it was the style of the pre-Roman aristocratic German. When the barbarians came in contact with the short-clipped Romans, the style fell out of use. But a few leaders flaunted their preference for the uneffete hairdress of their forefathers—now modified so the royal tresses hung in long braids on either side of the face. The traditional coiffure, adopted by the Merovingians as exclusively their own, was first noted in the sixth century by Gregory of Tours. He wrote that when the Franks left Pannonia and colonized the banks of the Rhine they "set up in each country district long-haired kings chosen from the foremost and most noble family of their race."[2] By Gregory's time it had become a symbolic act of Merovingian supremacy to forbid anyone but members of this family to have long hair. A scion of the house shorn of his locks was barred from the succession (although on occasion he presumptuously let his hair grow long again). So inextricably had their long hair become identified with this ruling family that the Merovingians have come down in history as the "Long-Haired Kings."

As well as remarking on their hairstyle Gregory was the first to refer to the Merovingian dynasty as if it had come full-fledged into the world as the single ruling family of the Franks. By the sixth century the dynasty was so successful that it was unthinkable that it had

---

*A reference to the raising on a shield of an elected chieftain by his warriors.

originally been but one among many families of rank from which the war leaders and kunings were chosen.

We have already met the long-haired hero Clodion, the first Frankish leader to occupy territory in Roman Gaul, taking Cambrai and pushing down to the Somme. The next recorded king after Clodion was Merovech, who may or may not have been his son. In a seventh-century history Merovech was awarded a legendary birth: "Clodion was sitting on the seashore together with his wife during the summertime when his spouse, while going into the sea to bathe, was attacked by a sea monster which was like a centaur. Having become pregnant at once, she gave birth to a son named Merovech."[3]

Merovech does have historical reality, appearing in person in contemporary Roman history: on the death of his father he went to Rome to gain support for succession to the kingship against his elder brother, who sought aid from Attila the Hun with the same design. "I have seen him," wrote the historian. "He was still very young, and we all remarked the fair hair which fell upon his shoulders."[4] In Rome he was honored with the friendship of Aetius, and subsequently we have seen him engaged with his band of Franks as allies of Rome in the battle of the Catalaunian Plains. His brother, on the losing side, is at the same time lost to history. Merovech still lives through his name, which later historians assigned to the family tree of his descendants — probably in deference to his Roman affiliation. By the sixth and seventh centuries this connection had become important for historical prestige.

After the death of Aetius in 454 Merovech broke the alliance with Rome, but he died in 456 or 457, too soon to pursue his father's policy of expansion. He was succeeded by his son, Childeric I. This prince was a doughty warrior, but at an early age he displayed the uninhibited sensuality that would be an unwholesome characteristic of most of his descendants, and would finally snuff out the line through debilitation. "His private life," wrote Gregory of Tours, "was one long debauch."[5]

So assiduously did Childeric pursue the daughters of his more influential subjects that they demanded his abdication. This would have meant little to the self-willed chieftain, but the added threat of assassination made him opt for prudence. He fled to Thuringia, across the Rhine, where another branch of Frankish tribes gave him sanctuary. A loyal friend stayed behind in Tournai, Childeric's capital, and each retained one half of a gold coin. The friend was to plead Childeric's cause with his ruffled subjects; when this had been successful he would send the exile his half of the coin as the signal to come home.

Meanwhile the Franks of northern Gaul, disgusted with their unruly leader, unanimously chose as their king the Roman patrician, Aegidius, ruler of the Roman enclave of Soissons, and the sole and lonely representative of imperial authority in Gaul. This interesting choice illustrates the drawing together of Romans and barbarians in western Europe under the menace of Attila. The barbarians who were *foederati* already identified themselves to a great extent with the empire. Those still outside the Roman pale recognized for the first time the horrible alternative: their safety, indeed their continued existence, lay in amity with the only central authority that remained, however rotten it had become. Amity did not mean subjugation, however: the union was an off-again on-again affair. What it did mean was that the brash warriors who were becoming the masters of Europe began to understand and to value the centripetal force of the old order, as well as to absorb a smattering of classical learning and a modicum of classical manners.

Aegidius was a Roman aristocrat of an old Gallo-Roman family, the Syagrii, who had great estates in the valley of the Seine and in Burgundy. Even after the fall of the Western Empire the Syagrii would manage to preserve most of their ancestral holdings. Loyal, brave, wise and wealthy, Aegidius had been the natural choice as Master of the Soldiery, in practice governor, of Rome's central Gallic dominion. By this time, the middle of the fifth century, Rome was losing her control of her southern Gallic lands to the enterprise of the Visigothic King Euric. Her only certain holding in Gaul was the realm of Soissons, an area bounded on the south by the Loire and on the north by the Somme, and including the cities of Rheims, Soissons and Paris. It was surrounded by raptorial barbarian kingdoms: the Visigoths held southern Gaul, the Burgundians and the Franks of West Germany abutted on the east and the Salian Franks of Belgium under Childeric had penetrated south to the Somme. Aegidius, cut off from contact with the empire, had behind him no authority but the ghost of imperial prestige and the long shadow of a great civilization to help him maintain the independence of his Roman island. That he managed to do so for seven years, and at the same time to be elected king of the Franks, is a tribute to his sagacity, courage and diplomatic skill.

He did not remain long king of the Franks. The reasons behind the restoration of Childeric in 464 are uncertain. A likely contributing cause is that the exiled chief had managed to gain the support of the court of Byzantium to reassert his claim to the rule of his people. Ignorant of the predatory guile of the Frankish exile, faraway Byzantium probably saw no danger in a barbarian king who was leader of a federate people and an ally of Rome. On the other hand, the eastern court might have been wary of Aegidius, a Roman soldier of patrician background, popular with the army, who could exploit his local strength to look toward the imperial throne. Aegidius was a potential insurrectionist; Childeric, at the moment, a trusted friend.

Even before Childeric came home Aegidius was in trouble. In an uphill fight he had been trying to defend southern Gaul against the incursions of the Visigoths of Spain. The Gallo-Roman inhabitants there tended to help the barbarians, whom they foresaw as their eventual masters, against the increasingly feeble imperial administration. With his army engaged in the south, Aegidius had to leave the northern sections undefended, and Germans from across the Rhine, including non-Romanized Franks, erupted into the Rhineland, sacking and burning Cologne, Trier and other Roman strongholds. Aegidius did his best, with an inadequate force, to repel the invasion, but there were too many Germans and he was forced back behind his own boundaries. Childeric, meanwhile, was on his way home: it is likely that the German attacks were planned, or at least actively abetted by him in a bid to regain his kingdom. Aegidius died soon afterward, in 464. He left his realm to his son, Syagrius, who, as Rex Romanorum,* would, incredibly, maintain the fragile imperial foothold for twenty-two years, until the inevitable inundation.

In the year of Aegidius's death Childeric returned to his kingdom. He did not return alone. The king of Thuringia, at whose court he had taken refuge, had a wife, Basina. The unregenerate Frank had seduced her and in the process captivated her. She followed him back to Tournai and announced that she was henceforth his. "I know you are a strong man" she said when he asked for an explanation. "I have therefore come to live with you. You can be sure that if I knew anyone else, even far across the sea, who was more capable than you, I should have sought him out and gone to live with him instead."[6] Basina was

---

*The title was conferred on him in the sixth century by Gregory of Tours. Syagrius was probably titled, like his father, Master of the Soldiery.

the first of a series of redoubtable Merovingian queens. Her enterprise evidently pleased the king, and he married her. These bold parents had an even bolder son, Clovis. A popular legend, recounted in the early seventh century, relates that the new queen roused her husband three times during their wedding night, telling him to go outside the palace and tell her what he saw. The first time he saw lions and leopards, the second time bears and wolves, the third time "lesser beasts." "Even so shall be thy descendants," said Basina.[7] The historian who recorded (and perhaps invented) this folk tale prediction wrote in the seventh century, when the Merovingian dynasty was in its downward slide.

Childeric was a forceful leader with an aptitude for diplomacy. Though Aegidius had been his rival for the leadership of the Franks, Childeric, once he got his throne back, cultivated an alliance with the Roman. When Syagrius inherited Soissons Childeric fought beside him against the intrusions of the Visigoths from the south, a continuing menace to both kingdoms. Syagrius's borders were further embarrassed on the north by the depredations of the Saxons, who were not after conquest so much as plunder. Their leader was Odoacer, who would become a force in imperial affairs and ten years later would deal the death blow to the Western Empire. At the time Childeric and Syagrius were allied against him, he was hardly more than a free-lance soldier and brigand, more nuisance than danger.

Childeric's respect for the boundaries of the little Roman kingdom of Soissons did not exclude his disposition for expansion in other directions. He had no scruples about his southern borders, and he extended his realm to the Loire, capturing Angers. In the course of his southern sweep he besieged Paris, where he had his aforementioned contact with the coercion of heaven in the person of Saint Geneviève.

By 481, when Childeric died, the Salian Franks were securely established in northern Gaul, no longer as conquerors but as settlers. The hunter-warriors of the forests had become landowners and farmers, soldiers in the imperial service, accepted allies of Rome. Their territory was not yet called a kingdom, and there is no evidence that either Rome or Childeric's own people called him king. It was only a century later that he was awarded the title in the pages of Gregory of Tours, with the object of elevating the Frankish past.

But the treasure found in Childeric's tomb at Tournai, recovered intact in 1653, is evidence of his consequence. This first unmistakably authentic Merovingian ruler was a respectable chief of state who had outgrown the status of mercenary soldier-cum-barbarian chieftain. His magnificent and beautifully crafted hoard points to a potent personage with contacts in the East and wealth and stature in the West.

Childeric left a stable foundation for his son Clovis to build on: a tradition of loyalty to the empire and a consequential position among the new powers of Europe. The only important advantage lacked by Childeric was Christianity. Clovis, the first Frankish king, became also the first Catholic Christian monarch in post-imperial Europe.

Clovis carried his inherited power to an extreme unpalatable today. Daring, ambitious and unscrupulous, he cared not by what perfidious tactics he accomplished his entirely credible aim: to unify the autonomous and discordant Frankish tribes into one nation under one leader. As a Catholic convert he carried out his most amoral actions with the approval and, on occasion, the active collaboration of the Gallic upper clergy.

Clovis's career of conquest started shortly after he succeeded, at age sixteen, to his father's position as leader of the Salian Franks. At his accession in 481 the land under the unquestioned control of his branch of the Franks consisted only of northwestern Gaul, south to Tournai (today's Belgium). It was hemmed in by powerful neighbors: the Burgundians under Gundobad, an ally of Rome with the title of Patrician; the Visigoths under the predatory Euric; the autonomous Roman enclave of Soissons, ruled by Syagrius; the determinedly independent Armoricans under a succession of more or less brigandish chieftains; and a floating population of pugnacious German tribes on the right bank of the Rhine, some of them Frankish, tough and unfriendly relatives of the Salian Franks of Gaul. Although Childeric had pushed his conquests to the Loire, the Franks were secure masters only of the area of their original settlements in Gallia Belgica. The army inherited by Clovis numbered no more than about six thousand men, but his father had shaped it into a disciplined band, courted by allies and feared by opponents. Childeric had known that a coordinated and agile striking force creates a reputation for invincibility.

In his teens Clovis had already understood that to survive in the barbarian world he had to conquer. Syagrius's Roman outpost was his first objective. That his father and the Roman ruler had been collaborators did not matter to Clovis—the alliance did not suit his convenience. It was logical for him to take this precarious realm first. In order to confirm his father's conquests to the south he needed to control the key cities of Soissons and Rheims, just over his southern border. Further, there were countrymen of Clovis living in the Roman belt who were no longer wholeheartedly Frankish. Syagrius had been rewarding those faithful to him with gifts of imperial land, regardless that they were not his to give. His beneficiaries were understandably more loyal to their landlord, the image of venerable Roman authority than to an unpredictable pagan youth somewhere to the north. A further consideration, if more be needed, was that Clovis's right to the land had just as firm a basis—or lack of it—as that of Syagrius. Since Odoacer had overthrown the Roman Empire in the West in 476 Syagrius had no emperor to whom he was responsible, and no true title to the land he had so valiantly held for twenty-two years.

Clovis was twenty-one when, in 486, he took Soissons. He raced through the forest of Ardennes and fell on the city, surprising Syagrius, whose forces were larger and just as well trained. The Roman soldiers fought bravely, but their army was cut to pieces and Syagrius fled for his life. He took refuge in Toulouse with Alaric II, the young Visigothic king who had succeeded to the throne of his father, Euric, in 484. Clovis demanded the surrender of the fugitive, with the alternative threat of war, and Alaric meekly gave him over, "for the Goths," wrote loyal Gregory of Tours, "are a timorous race."[8] (Alaric was barely ten years old.) Clovis imprisoned Syagrius and, as soon as he had consolidated his conquest of Soissons, ordered him executed in secret, probably to avoid an uprising of partisan anger in the new territory.

The defeat of Syagrius is a historical divide. Soissons, though independent and isolated, had been the last Gallic possession of the Roman Empire. When Clovis added it to the Frankish kingdom the final vestige of imperial authority in Gaul evaporated, and the history of France began.

Surprisingly, considering the ruthless temper of the conqueror, it began auspiciously. In Soissons Clovis demonstrated that he was more than an aggressive warrior. He set out to win over his new subjects, both Frankish and Gallo-Roman, so that he could count on their allegiance. From the beginning of his career of conquest he forbade his soldiers to loot and, as far as possible, he left Gallo-Romans in their administrative posts. Some landowners were displaced so he could reward his most trusted companions, and some treasure was taken to help finance the cost of the next advance. Since Clovis had had no possessions on his accession to the kingship, the judicious acquisition of spoils was mandatory, as was also the levying of tribute on vanquished neighbor kings. But there was no degradation of the conquered by an oppressive new aristocracy.

For one thing, there was no aristocracy. The only power in Clovis's century was the power of the king. This king, already wise at twenty-one, saw a contented people as a crucial attribute of a successful kingdom. The old Gallo-Roman families managed, with the approval of Clovis, to preserve much of their estates, and under the law they were in most respects equal to their conquerors. Their sons, if they did not serve in the government, went into the Church, where they exerted an increasing moral and secular influence on the new barbaric sovereignty. The empire was finished in Gaul, but thanks to the sagacity of her replacement, the Frankish chief, her heirs were still there, reembodying the outlines.

Clovis's realm now included the cities of Soissons, Paris, Rouen and Rheims. He went on to consolidate his father's advances south to the Loire and west to the borders of Armorica, whose population, stubbornly free even when it had been part of the Roman Empire, defied him. The influx of Christian Britons fleeing the incursions of the Angles and Saxons in Britain had converted Armorica;* the stubbornly Christian immigrants, under the leadership of a series of independent-minded chieftains, managed to hold back the offensive of the latest Thor worshipper. The rest of the northwestern territory, which Clovis succeeded in unifying under his single rule, came in later generations to be known as Neustria (New Land).

After Soissons Clovis proceeded to annex some of the petty principalities around his northern and eastern edges, and to exterminate their rulers. These were Frankish chieftains like himself, some of them related to him but lacking his brisk initiative. They included the kings of Thérouanne, Tongres and Thuringia, the land that had given his father sanctuary. By 491 he had most of Gallia Belgica and some of Germania Inferior under his control, and he had disposed of some potentially troublesome cousins.

Clovis was not so obsessed with conquest as to neglect his domestic

---

*In this century Armorica, its original Celtic name, began to be known as Brittany, for its latest Celtic immigrants.

future. He had mistresses, one of whom was the mother of his first son, Theodoric. But he was more foresighted than his father, and he did not allow himself to yield to the sensualism that had nearly arrested Childeric's career at its outset. He realized that an advantageous match would be expedient; and so did his Gallo-Roman advisers, particularly those in the Church.

In 493, when he was about twenty-eight, he made his choice. His courtship of Clotild, the niece of Gundobad, king of Burgundy, as narrated in the seventh century, has the flavor of a medieval romance.[9] In reality it was the outcome of a prearranged scheme stage-managed by some farsighted churchmen. Gundobad was a Christian king, but he was of the Arian persuasion. He was an easygoing heretic. Unlike Euric, the brutal king of Visigothic Spain and Aquitaine, Gundobad did not persecute his Catholic subjects. He even allowed two Catholic bishops a high place in his court, listened politely to their arguments on the Trinity and allowed them to educate the young ladies of his household. These ecclesiastics were in contact with their counterparts in Frankish Gaul, among whom the most influential with the Frankish king was Rémy, the popular bishop of Rheims. Rémy saw that it would be to the Church's advantage that Clovis should wed a princess who had been schooled in the Catholic faith and who was, besides, both strong-minded and pretty.

There was another party in the court of Burgundy which feared the effects of the alliance. Gundobad had expediently killed his brother, a rival to his throne, along with most of his family. A very young daughter, Clotild, was spared. She was brought up in Gundobad's court and educated under the direction of Bishop Avitus, one of the Catholic prelates tolerated by the Burgundian king. Clotild was still innocent, but Gundobad's counselors warned that Christian charity would mean nothing to the child if she married a bellicose leader. Clovis, they foresaw, would make her vengeance an excuse for attacking Burgundy.

Before King Gundobad could make up his mind, events were out of his hands: the Frankish and Burgundian churchmen had arranged the romance. Clovis had been told of the beautiful princess, runs the tale, and he resolved to make her his own without consulting her uncle. He sent an envoy who, in the ragged dress of a pilgrim, begged alms of the princess. Clotild received him in the manner of a Christian: in deference to his holy guise she washed his feet. As she knelt before him he whispered his secret message and gave her

Clovis's ring. The offer pleased the princess. She gave him her ring in return and warned him to hurry back to his master before Gundobad's wary advisers prevailed. Clovis at once sent a formal legation to Gundobad, offering his friendship in return for the bride, and the Burgundian king was afraid to refuse. Clotild left the palace in style, carried on a litter and accompanied by a rich dowry. No sooner was she on the road than her uncle, heeding his counselors at last, changed his mind and sent troops after her. Clotild ordered her Frankish escorts to dispense with the litter and put her on a horse. The advance pursuers caught up with her anyway and made off with her treasure. They were repulsed by her escorts, and the princess then directed that the land be devastated for twelve miles behind her to discourage further pursuit. Clotild might go to church on Sundays but the rest of the week she was as hardheaded as her Teutonic forebears. Clovis had chosen well.

Once married and pregnant, Clotild became forwardly Christian. Wanting their first child to be baptized, she delivered a sermon on the impotence of Clovis's gods.[10] "They haven't even been able to help themselves," she said, "let alone others. They are carved out of stone or wood or some old piece of metal. Saturn ran away from his own son to avoid being exiled from his own kingdom, and Jupiter had his fun with all his female relatives and couldn't even refrain from intercourse with his own sister.* You ought instead to worship Him who created at a word and out of nothing heaven and earth, the sea and all that therein is."

Clovis allowed his new wife to have her way, but when the baby boy died in the middle of the rite of baptism he reproached her: "If he had been dedicated in the name of my gods he would have lived; but now that he has been baptized in the name of your God he has not been able to live a single day." Clotild, unrepentant, boldly asserted that her God "has not found me completely unworthy, for He has deigned to welcome to His kingdom a child conceived in my womb, [and] in his white baptismal robes [he] will be nurtured in the sight of God."

When her second child was born Clotild again held out for baptism, and Clovis—merciless with his cousin kings—could not

*Either the historian, of solid Gallo-Roman background, supposes that the pre-Christian Franks worshipped the Roman gods or that, like the Celts, they had become sufficiently Romanized to adopt the names of the classical hierarchy.

oppose his queen. The barbaric Frank loved his wife deeply and undividedly; in addition, he respected, her education. Clotild was luckier this time: the baby ailed but, following energetic prayer, recovered. However, the queen still could not persuade her husband away from the worship of idols. To him they were perceptible, therefore efficacious. They had upheld him during his disposal of his relatives, and he could not believe that an unseeable, unknowable Spirit would be similarly accommodating.

In 496, the fifteenth year of his reign, Clovis was faced with a genuine danger. On his eastern border, inhabiting today's central Switzerland, was a warlike and unusually well-integrated tribe, the Allemans. As their name indicates they had originally been, like the Franks, a confederation of several German tribes. The Allemans had been battling Roman legions and harrying Roman borders with varying success for about two hundred years. In the fifth century, having destructively occupied Burgundian territory, they moved into Alsace and Lorraine and threatened the kingdom of Cologne, still unassimilated by Clovis. To protect his eastern border, Clovis went to the aid of Cologne's king, Sigibert, and they met the Allemans at Tolbiac (Zülpich), twenty-four miles southwest of Cologne.

The armies and their leaders were resourceful, but the Allemans had the best of it, forcing the Franks back and following up their anticipated victory with an impetuous rush at the retreating enemy. With his army in disarray and rapidly being annihilated, Clovis raised his eyes to heaven and invoked the aid of Clotild's God, offering reciprocity: "Jesus Christ, you who deign to give help to those in travail and victory to those who trust in you, I beg your help. I want to believe in you, but I must first be saved from my enemies. If you will give me victory I will be baptized in your name." The prayer discernibly worked. Even as he finished bespeaking Christ, the Allemans began to turn and run away. At that pivotal moment their king had fallen, and with the loss of the leader their aggression melted. They begged for the fighting to cease, and Clovis withheld his soldiers and granted truce. The Allemans never recovered their strength. After acknowledging Clovis as their overlord, they drifted or were driven south out of the Main Valley, and their threat to western Europe was dissipated.

Grateful that his appeal to heaven had succeeded, Clovis was true to his side of the bargain. He told Clotild that Christ had won him the victory over the Allemans, and announced that he was ready to accept Christianity—along with three thousand of his soldiers.

Though Clovis's conversion seems on the surface to have been activated more by ambition than by conviction, it required courage to take the step. Northern Gaul, Clovis's native land, was still almost entirely pagan, and the adjoining kingdom of Cologne had a firmly pagan chieftain. Only half of Clovis's army followed his lead; many of the remainder went over to his rivals. His kingdom was not yet stable, and he was surrounded by grasping adversaries. Conversion was a daring move. But it was a sagacious one: Clovis had a comprehension of the direction of history far transcending his tribal antecedents.

For one thing, the entire Gallic clergy now favored him. Among his advocates was Geneviève, already honored by the Parisians as their patron saint. The aging saint, who had prayed for the delivery of Paris from the siege of Clovis's father, now advised her fellow citizens to open the gates to the Catholic conqueror. Clovis's chief instructor in religion was Rémy, bishop of Rheims, friend of Queen Clotild. This strong-minded and gentle-mannered priest was a superb example of the survival of the Gallo-Roman ethos in barbarian Gaul, and of its increasing influence. He was born about 434 in Laon, northeast of Paris, of a wealthy, cultivated and intensely religious family (his mother, Celina, was later sainted). In 456, when he was only twenty-two, he was unanimously elected to the bishopric of Rheims. During his seventy-four years as bishop he witnessed the extinction of the Western Empire and the rise of the Frankish monarchy from its beginnings under the barbarian Childeric to its consolidation under the Christian sons of Clovis—a metamorphosis spanning three generations. Life in Rémy's near-century (he lived to be ninety-six) was like dwelling on the side of a live volcano; but tranquil of heart and firm of mind, he performed his episcopal duties with steadfast ardor. He was backed for many years by Queen Clotild, who knew him through her mentor, Bishop Avitus of Vienne. Rémy's miracles were many, though some were of a worldly nature. To cite one instance, Clovis had granted the bishop all the land he could go around during the king's midday sleep. One of his tenants, an incautious miller, refused to accept the new landlord, whereupon the mill wheel began to turn backward. No one evermore could make a mill wheel work in that place.

Rémy had come to the Church with great wealth and estates (all of which went to enrich his see), a superior education and a commanding presence even at a very young age. At the time of Clovis's conversion Rémy was about sixty-two: it was small wonder that his noble mien gave him an advantage over the impulsive young fighter. Awed beyond his wont, Clovis was a cooperative pupil, and he brought to the lessons his own primitive generosity: "If I had been there with my Franks," he said of the Crucifixion, "I would have avenged His injuries."[11]

The baptism took place in Bishop Rémy's church at Rheims, on Christmas Day, 503.* For the ceremony the main squares of the town were decorated with colored hangings and the church itself was decked with white linen, illumined with hundreds of candles and fragrant with incense. The sacrament was a ritual to delight the faithful and dazzle the pagan. Baptism was by immersion in a deep square pool in the middle of the church. When Clovis advanced to wash away his sins Rémy blessed him and pronounced: "Bow your head in meekness, Sicamber.† Worship what you have burned, burn what you have been wont to worship."

Clovis had been king and conqueror for fifteen years; during that time it is safe to say that no one had presumed to order him to do anything, let alone meekly. But thenceforth he would willingly and enthusiastically subject himself to the Church, the first exponent of the alliance between the kings of France and the Catholic Church—a union that would be so momentous an advantage to them both in the medieval power balance of Europe. Clovis was the forerunner of *le roi très chrétien*. His contemporaries regarded him as the spiritual child of Constantine.

The basilica of Saint Rémy now stands at the site of Clovis's baptism. It is an eleventh-century Romanesque church overlaid with twelfth-century primitive Gothic. In the soaring interior, arches rise upon arches, the lower ones rounded in the Roman style, the higher ones pointed; the effect is of a prayer to infinity. Over the center of the nave hangs a gigantic chandelier bearing ninety-six candles, which are lighted on the feast day of the saint in honor of the ninety-six years of his life. Saint Rémy himself is here, behind the altar, his

---

*Gregory of Tours put the date at 496. Writing at the end of the sixth century, when Merovingian strength was at its apex, Gregory makes this "constructive" change in order to confirm the connection between the Merovingian success in conquest and its Christianization, and to establish the role of its kings as the Christian saviors of Europe and the successors to the empire.
†A deprecating reference to Clovis's tribal ancestry.

simple stone sarcophagus encased in an ornate nineteenth-century gold casket. Behind it is a seventeenth-century stone carving of the baptism of Clovis. The bishop, an imposing figure elaborately garbed and stern of visage, holds his hand over the kneeling king, who is simply dressed and bareheaded. Clovis's head is not bent; aside from this, the conqueror looks young and meek.

The immediate result of his conversion was that Clovis became very popular with Catholics in his own land and all over Europe. Soon after his conversion the chiefs of Christian Brittany voluntarily ceded to the Catholic king what they had stubbornly withheld when he was still a heathen—their free fealty. Though Clovis did not subjugate his western neighbor (Brittany, unconquered by Caesar, would remain free of Merovingian domination, survive Charlemagne's consolidation, and keep its independence, with temporary lapses, for another thousand years, until 1491), the Breton towns, led by their bishops, offered a reciprocal alliance. For the duration of Clovis's reign the two nations coexisted in harmony, respecting one another's free-spirited bravery and, alone in continental Europe, sharing the Catholic faith.

The rest of the continent saw an insignificant barbarian chieftain, one among many, suddenly alight with the radiance of a consecrated hero. Most of the rulers in post-imperial Europe were of the Arian heresy, and the Catholic bishops, whether or not their church was under persecution, looked to the Frankish king as their deliverer. The king of Burgundy was notably easygoing with his dissenters, but Bishop Avitus, Queen Clotild's childhood teacher, looked for more than mere tolerance. His letter of congratulation to Clovis was a clear invitation: "Your faith is our triumph: every battle you fight is a victory for us."[12] It does not sound very Christian. But Avitus's blessing was in line with the prevailing attitude of his day—you won battles with the help of Jesus—nor did it vary from the reasoning of the Old Testament Israelites.

In any case Clovis did not need the hint. The Burgundian lands had been part of Gaul for centuries under imperial rule, and it was logical to Rome's presumptive successor that the province should again be united under one ruler. There is no contemporary indication that Clovis's Burgundian wife encouraged him. Given the Christian bias of the chroniclers the motive of revenge would have been immoral. But is likely that lively spirited Clotild, Christian or no, was content to see the murderer of her parents and her brothers brought low.

Since his marriage Clovis had been importuning King Gundobad for the treasure captured from Clotild's bridal party by the Burgundian pursuers. Gundobad had given way to pressure with bad grace, remarking to Clovis's envoy as he handed over gold, silver and jewels: "Is there anything else that remains, except perhaps that I divide my entire kingdom with Clovis?"[13] In 499 his ill-tempered prediction began to come true.

At this time Burgundy was jointly ruled by two brothers, Gundobad and Gotegisel. The extent and boundaries of Burgundian territory had been fluid since the Burgundian tribes first came down from Scandinavia (probably from Bornholm Island) in the second century B.C., to invade and settle parts of northeast Germany. By the fifth century A.D. Burgundian sovereignty encompassed all the land that is now Burgundy, and extended west to the Rhône and south into Provence; to the east it comprehended Savoie and the western part of Switzerland almost to Lake Constance. But the shape and size of the huge realm continued variable into Clovis's time.

Kings Gundobad and Gotegisel disliked and distrusted one another, in the fifth-century fashion of royal brothers. Clovis, with his usual vulpine diplomacy, set about to widen the rift. He was seconded in his design by the Catholic clergy in Burgundy, always ready to assist in the dislodging of an Arian ruler. Clovis made a secret pact with Gotegisel, promising to help him against his brother; in return the Burgundian would pay an annual tribute to the Franks. Clovis then marched his army against Gundobad, who unsuspectingly called his brother to his assistance. "Let us make a common front against this people which hates us," he appealed reasonably, "for if we are not united we shall suffer the fate which others have met before us."[14]

Battle was joined near Dijon on the banks of the Ouche—a slow-flowing tree-shaded river—and it was only then that Gundobad perceived his brother's treachery. His army was destroyed by the armies of the two other kings, and he fled, taking refuge in Avignon. Clovis followed him there but was deflected from violence by a clever envoy from Gundobad, who persuaded Clovis that it would be more constructive to treat with the fugitive than ruinously to attempt to pry him from his stronghold. "You are destroying the fields, spoiling the meadows, cutting up the vineyards, ruining the olive groves and ravaging the whole countryside, which is a very fruitful one. In doing

this you are causing no harm whatsoever to Gundobad. Why don't
you send an ultimatum to him to say that he must pay whatever
annual tribute you care to exact? In that way the region will be saved."

Clovis accepted the advice, and Gundobad was spared. He paid the
first year's tribute and thereafter, though he never bothered to pay
again, continued peaceably as king of Burgundy. The career of the
falsehearted brother had ended soon after the conclusion of the peace
treaty. Following the battle on the Ouche Gotegisel had retired,
satisfied with his role, to his capital at Vienne. There Gundobad later
pursued him, besieged the town, gained entry by a ruse and killed the
traitor in an Arian church (where the violation of sanctuary was
disregarded).

Burgundy remained free of Frankish control for the next thirty-
three years, partly because of the good sense of the Burgundian king.
Gundobad, though an Arian, knew that to retain the loyalty of his
people he had to please his Gallo-Roman subjects, who far outnumbered the Burgundians. He had always been deferential to the
Catholic hierarchy, but his subject population needed more than
token courtesy. The Gallo-Romans were the cultured intellectuals of
the realm, respected and imitated by their barbarian masters; they
also retained much of their ancient landed wealth. This vanquished
but still puissant majority required legal standing. Gundobad had
advanced far from his war-chieftain antecedents. He had been exiled
to Rome in his youth, and had learned there some of the niceties of
civilian administration. On his reprieve from the Frankish threat he
set about to codify Burgundian law, and he created a broad-minded
body of law, the Burgundian Code. This was not only highly civilized
in fifth-century terms, but it gave the Gallo-Romans virtual equality
with their rulers. His liberality did not go against the grain of his
native Burgundians: as a race they were good-natured and tolerant, in
contrast to most of the other Germanic tribes—including the Franks,
who were notorious for their truculent impatience. For the time being
the Gallo-Roman population of Burgundy was reconciled to being
ruled by a heretic barbarian.

Gundobad's good will could not by itself have kept his kingdom
inviolate. He had on his side Theodoric the Ostrogoth, king of Italy,
surnamed the Great, to whose compelling diplomacy even Clovis
yielded. Theodoric, a hero of medieval legend, was a paragon in real
life. He was the illegitimate yet acknowledged heir to the kingdom of
the Ostrogoths, then inhabiting Pannonia. At the age of eight he was

sent as hostage to the court at Constantinople, where he was exposed to a comprehensive education. True to his barbaric heritage he learned best the arts of war and least well the philosophic sciences. So effectively did he ignore the Greek part of his education that he remained illiterate all his life (though he loved music and good conversation at the dinner table).

Though the Ostrogoths in Pannonia were *foederati* they were not safe allies. Living in want at the edge of the voluptuous prosperity of Byzantium, they were a perpetual irritant. When Theodoric, already an adventurous conqueror, succeeded to their kingship in 475 he convinced Emperor Zeno of the potential danger of Ostrogothic ill will. Zeno, an indolent and cowardly ruler, found it more convenient to appease his mettlesome ally than to oppose him. He granted the Ostrogoths money and lands, and appointed them defenders of the lower Danube under Theodoric's command. He then blandished the young king with extravagant favors and, in the hope of entailing his permanent loyalty, adopted Theodoric as his son.

But the enterprising Goth had no taste for the hedonistic eastern capital. He requested his foster father to assign him sterner duties: specifically, to retake Italy from Odoacer, who in 476 had ejected the last western emperor and named himself king of Italy. "For it is better," said Theodoric, "that I, your servant and your son, should rule that kingdom, receiving it as a gift from you if I conquer, than that one whom you do not recognize should oppress your Senate with his tyrannical yoke and a part of the republic with slavery."[15]

Zeno had no choice but to accede to the reasonably phrased demand. In 489 Theodoric invaded Italy and easily defeated Odoacer, whose mercenaries were unequal to the sanguinary dedication of the Ostrogothic forces. While Odoacer barricaded himself in Ravenna, Theodoric liberated the country from the Alps to Sicily, reigning as king by right of conquest, unsanctioned by the eastern throne. This was not what Zeno had had in mind when he granted his foster son's request, and he postponed official recognition of Theodoric's usurpation of power. In 493 Ravenna surrendered to the Ostrogoth, and Odoacer was killed by the order (and possibly by the hand) of the latest barbarian ruler of Italy. In the same year Zeno died; and the new Roman emperor, faced with the fact of a popular and forceful savior in the remains of the Western Empire, unenthusiastically recognized Theodoric as king in the territory whose affairs he already commanded.

Once he had achieved his desire Theodoric abjured aggression and studied the arts of peace. He was a constructive king, reviving Italy's agriculture and mining industry, rebuilding her cities and repairing her roads. In religious matters he was tolerant, doing his utmost to conciliate his Italian subjects. Brought up in the Arian heresy, like most Goths, Theodoric was not a passionate believer, and allowed freedom to all creeds, even that of the Jews.* He was respectful to the pope, though not obsequious, appreciating the Italians' devotion to him as well as his increasing importance in the affairs of western Europe. As for the emperor at Byzantium, Theodoric tendered him a careful and ambiguous deference. Reared in Greco-Roman ways, he honored the personification of the empire and imitated Roman rule in his country. But he never presumed to covet the title of emperor. Under the name of hereditary king, however, he assumed all the prerogatives of an emperor in the West.

He ruled from Sicily to the Danube, from Sirmium to the Atlantic Ocean, and his sphere of influence stretched from Africa to the North Sea. With judicious marriages of himself and his children he enlisted the friendship of the rulers of the Franks (his wife was Clovis's sister), the Burgundians, the Visigoths, the Vandals and the Thuringians, all of them Arian monarchs except Clovis. Through these friendly alliances he maintained the balance of power in the West and took it on himself to arbitrate the quarrels of the touchy barbarian kings, who nearly always deferred to his realistic wisdom. Theodoric was the earliest proponent of an amicable coalition of independent European states. In nearly every case he mediated for peace, regarding battle as an undesirable last resort. "My own opinion," wrote Sidonius perceptively, "is that he dreads being feared."[16]

This was the prodigy among monarchs with whom Clovis was faced when he eyed Burgundy possessively. Clovis was younger than Theodoric by about ten years, but he had succeeded to his throne twelve years before Theodoric had assumed the rule of Italy, and his power was in crescendo, particularly since he now wore a savior's halo and the Catholic clergy in all the Arian-ruled kingdoms looked to

*When the Catholics of Ravenna, unable to find anything to hate in their lenient ruler, directed their frustrated hostility toward the Jews of the city, burning their synagogues, Theodoric directed the whole community to rebuild the temples; those who balked were whipped through the streets by the executioners.

him to lead them out of captivity. Clovis did not disdain diplomacy; but to him it was only a gateway to further aggression. Still, he was astute enough to be wary of offending Theodoric with his steel mesh of alliances and his wide popularity. There would come a time when Clovis's lesser descendants would gnaw at the domains of Theodoric's even feebler heirs. But before Theodoric died and the strength that held Italy together dissolved, the Franks, in common with the other European chiefs, restrained their intrusive ambitions. It may not have been fear but it was certainly respectful caution that kept Italy's borders secure during Theodoric's thirty-three-year reign.

It was to the Ostrogoth's interest and to the interest of the peace of Europe to retain an intact Burgundy between Italy and Frankish Gaul. So Gundobad was safe as long as Theodoric lived. Clovis had to turn in a direction which would not immediately disarrange the careful balance that the king of Italy had achieved.

In line with this aim Clovis entered on his last campaign in 507, against the Visigoths. The Franks and the Visigoths had been fighting over the dominion of southern Gaul since long before Clovis's conquering career. To one who wanted to master control of Gaul the provinces of Aquitaine and Provence were essential, particularly Aquitaine with its vital Loire Valley. The Visigothic king Euric had expanded the Spanish kingdom to include these territories. Their populations, firmly Catholic, were deeply committed to Roman thought and Roman ways. They had a history of resisting conquerors: their Celtic forebears had defied Caesar under Vercingetorix, and they themselves had held out with stubborn desperation against Euric. When Euric died in 484 he was succeeded by his son Alaric II—ninth in descent from Alaric I, who had shaken the Western Empire with the sack of Rome in 410. Alaric had been only a little boy when Clovis, slightly older, had demanded that he surrender Syagrius. He had grown into a weak king, fearful of his aggressive neighbor yet unwilling to placate his Gallic subjects. Though not as determined an oppressor as his father he made himself unpopular with his support of the Arian clergy against the Gallo-Roman Catholic bishops of his main cities.

This made it easier for Clovis, who now considered that he had a moral as well as a practical duty to eradicate the power of the heretic Visigoths in Gaul. His aims were abetted by his higher clergy, who wanted the Arian king confounded for the sake of their uncomfortable brethren in Gaul's southern provinces.

At first this was a war of words and intrigue. The Catholic clergy of Aquitaine actively campaigned in favor of the Frankish savior north of their border, while Alaric himself, apprehensive of his energetic neighbor, sought to keep peace by negotiation. He was aided by Theodoric of Italy, who is said to have arranged a meeting between the two kings. The meeting, chronicled by Gregory of Tours,[17] may have been a later invention. In any case it would have accomplished nothing, since Theodoric failed to back it up with military assistance and Clovis, who had already made up his mind, was always dedicated rather to action than to parley.

A more likely report is that Clovis conferred with his counsellors, when he is reported as saying: "I find it hard to go on seeing these Arians occupy a part of Gaul. With God's help let us invade them." Backed by his Catholic virtue and the blessing of his bishops he set out for the south, invoking the aid of the saints all the way to Poitiers, where his opponent nervously awaited him. In return he received miraculous signs of God's help. When the Frankish army entered Saint Martin's territory around Tours, Clovis forbade his soldiers to requisition anything from the local populace. One soldier disobeyed, stealing hay from a poor man. When the king heard of this he drew his sword and killed the soldier on the spot, saying, "It is no good expecting to win this fight if we offend Saint Martin." (Placating of saints aside, Clovis always maintained strict discipline in his army.) He sent messengers ahead of his march into Tours, to shower the saint's church with gifts. One of these was his favorite and fastest horse. After the battle he tried to get the horse back, offering one hundred gold pieces, but the animal refused to move. Clovis increased the premium to two hundred, and at once the horse trotted to him. "Indeed the blessed Martin is good in his help," said Clovis, "and careful in business."

As Clovis's messengers entered the church after the gift-giving, the precentor happened to be chanting Psalm 18: "For thou didst gird me with strength for the battle; tjou didst make my assailants sink under me." Acknowledging this open sign of the saint's favor Clovis thereupon adopted as his battle standard the "Chape de Saint-Martin," a flag bearing the saint's blue cloak. This would be the battle flag of the Merovingian dynasty until its demise, and Charlemagne would later fight under it.

Clovis was temporarily halted at the river Vienne, in flood from heavy rains, until in answer to his prayer a great doe forded the river "as if to lead them at God's command." When they approached Poitiers they saw a pillar of fire arise from Saint Hilary's church, a sign that that saint too had entered the lists against the heretic as he had so vigorously done in life.

Alaric was encamped at Vouillé, near Poitiers, and there the kings met in battle. It was a fierce, hand-to-hand engagement, but its end was foreordained. "The Goths fled," wrote Gregory, "as they were prone to do, and Clovis was the victor, for God was on his side." For all the historian's scorn, the Visigothic king showed himself no coward. He fought Clovis single-handed and was brought down by him. As he fell two of his henchmen rushed up and struck at Clovis with their spears. Clovis's leather corselet saved him, and his horse carried him out of danger.

Though Clovis had won the fight he did not utilize his victory to conquer all of southern Gaul. He sent his eldest son, Theodoric, south to subjugate Auvergne. Theodoric was a rougher conqueror than his father: in his advance he massacred, plundered, destroyed vineyards and took so many captives that the slave market would be glutted for three years thereafter.

While his son was raging through Auvergne Clovis rested his troops in Bordeaux. In the spring of 508 he went south again and took Toulouse, where he appropriated most of the treasure which Alaric I had looted when he sacked Rome a hundred years before. Clovis went on to besiege Carcassonne, at the same time his son was hammering at the gates of Arles. Father and son were stopped at last by the belated activity of the other Theodoric, the king of Italy. The Ostrogoth was alarmed by the easy victories of the Franks, which brought them close to northern Italy. He marched his troops over the Maritime Alps and drove the Frankish Theodoric out of Provence— which he then took the opportunity to annex for himself. Clovis realized that his projected occupation of southern Gaul was not propitious. He raised the siege of Carcassonne and prudently retreated north.

He then headed back to Tours, where he intended to give thanks and gifts to Saint Martin's sanctuary. Along the way he mopped up isolated areas where the Goths still held out. Among these was Angoulême, where "the Lord showed him such favor that the city walls collapsed of their own weight as he looked at them."

When Clovis got to Tours he found letters awaiting him from Anastasius I, the emperor in Constantinople, conferring on him the ranks of patrician and consul, honorary titles coveted by the ambitious arrivistes of barbarian Europe. These honors worked both ways: they were a symbol to the empire of continued sovereignty, and they imparted august overtones to newcomers with no backgrounds to their thrones but force. The recognition from Byzantium did not in any sense make Clovis a vassal of the emperor; his absolute rule of his people was inviolate. But the favor of imperial Rome, its center of government conveniently far away, was important to a king the majority of whose subjects still regarded themselves as Roman citizens. Proudly Clovis stood in Saint Martin's great new basilica (erected in 473), clad in a purple tunic and his military mantle, and let himself be crowned with a diadem. After the ceremony he rode through the streets of the city scattering gold and silver coins among the people.

The Roman investiture was consequential to Clovis not only because of the barbarian chieftain's awe of the ancient imperial prestige and his pleasure in its glamorous trappings. From a practical viewpoint he was now ruler of a large part of the original Western Empire. As the self-imposed heir he had to make a show of legitimate succession and to reinstate as far as possible the orderly conditions of his predecessors. In this area he needed the guidance of the educated Gallo-Romans. On another level he wanted to please his people so there would be serenity in his young kingdom. With all his native brutality Clovis was a practical ruler.

Although he naïvely relished his Roman honors Clovis never lost sight of his German antecedents. Even had Theodoric of Italy not been in his way he had no interest in becoming a Mediterranean power. His concerns lay with the northern lands he had conquered early in his career, whose borders were still uneasy. He needed an accessible base from which to operate. Tours was too far south and Tournai, the old capital of the Salian Franks, too distant from the rest of his now large kingdom. He chose Paris: the little walled city, still confined to the island in the Seine, was in the heart of Clovis's northwestern kingdom. It also gave him access to the Loire Valley to the south, to the original Frankish lands of Belgium and to those he had liberated from Frankish chieftains to the north and east. Further, Clovis liked the Roman associations of the city: two emperors, Julian the Apostate, in 359, and Valentinian I, in 365, had elected Paris as their winter headquarters.

In 508, not long after receiving his Roman accolades, Clovis moved his capital to Paris. He did not, like the Romans before him, hold court within the walls. The surrounding countryside encompassed game-filled forests broken by the occasional vineyards and grain fields of the Gallo-Romans. Clovis probably quartered a guard in the town and moved from one hunting lodge to another in the congenial woodlands.

In his personal life, too, Clovis was true to his barbarian background. He was a Christian because the Christian deity had proven more helpful in battle than the heathen; but his conformity to Christianity did not touch the core of his heathen soul. He remained an obstinate Frank in domestic affairs: he married a Germanic chieftain's daughter and not, as he could have done, a Roman aristocrat's, and all his children's names came out of the pre-Roman Teutonic past.

Clovis returned to Paris a much more consequential monarch than when he had gone south three years before. Though his territorial gains from this campaign were not extensive, he had got what he wanted: the important cities of the Loire Valley, security on his southern boundaries, the downing of an Arian rival to Gallic soil, and sizable spoils for his empty treasury.

Part of the Visigothic treasure Clovis had preempted in Toulouse he gave to Saint Martin's church at Tours in gratitude for the saint's help. Henceforth Martin was the Merovingians' guardian saint, and the remnant of his soldier's cloak their holiest relic. Clovis's homage to the saint—or more properly, to the living heirs of the saint's heavenly authority—was as vital as any of the monetary, territorial or honorary benefits. It signified the obeisance of the king to his bishops, and it marked the cementing of the focal alliance of church and state which had been initiated at Rheims when Bishop Rémy laid his hand on the young conqueror's head.

Clovis made another material contribution to Frankish stability. During the years after Vouillé, the last three years of his life, he issued the first written version of the *lex Salica,* the old German law by which the primitive tribes and, later, those affiliated with the empire as *foederati,* had ordered their lives.

In 358 Julian, formally ceding to the Salian Franks the Toxandrian land they had occupied for a hundred years, had made official settlers out of squatters. As the Franks became increasingly responsible citizens, settled landowning farmers influenced by the Gallo-Romans among whom they lived, they recognized the need for bringing legal order into their lives. In the early fifth century, writes the seventh-century annalist,[18] during the reign of the first long-haired king, Faramund, the ancient word-of-mouth law of the Frankish tribes was brought into line with the new respectable status of their descendants. Four sages of the Salians, Wisowast, Wisogast, Arogast and Salegast, were appointed, or appointed themselves (the mechanics of Frankish government in those years are obscure, along with the facts), to systematize the law.

Now Clovis, in the fifth generation after his semilegendary ancestor, expanded and codified the antique system to suit the magnitude and diversity of the united Frankish kingdom, and his own position as its central head. The work was executed by a team of Gallo-Roman lawyers and clerics, who clarified, rationalized and rendered into Latin (with some necessary Frankish words) the old Salic law. The code contains no pagan elements, but neither is it imbued with the precepts of Christianity. While Clovis ruled over a majority of Catholic Gallo-Romans, much of his Frankish minority, their titular masters, was not yet converted.

The code opens with a lofty prologue: "The illustrious Frankish people, founded by God, brave in war, firm in covenants of peace, high in purpose, superior in body, sound in integrity, distinguished in stature, bold, swift and fierce, converted to the Catholic faith and immune from heresy . . . This is the powerful people who, by fighting, shook from its neck the hard yoke of the Romans."[19] The code moves from grandiloquence straight into practical matters. It is mainly a penal code: as such it expresses the problems and iniquities of a rather small rural population, the conquerors, settled among a larger class of subject people.

The Teutonic concept of the law differed from the Roman, which was community-oriented. In Germanic law the criminal's first liability was to the victim, and only secondarily, through him, to the public weal. This dual vision of crime entailed the primary compensation of the injured, along with secondary indemnity to the constituted authority. In tribal times punishment had been effected by violence: the blood feud was the only method the free Teutons had of correcting crime and suppressing disorder. The new code instituted, in place of personal vengeance, a graded series of punishments for which the payment of wergild could be substituted. Wergild, literally man-payment, was a levy of money or goods on the criminal or his family, half to be paid to the victim or his family, the other half to the state. The amount was proportionate to the grossness of the offense, and to the sex, age, position and general usefulness of the damaged citizen.

The highest wergild was commanded by the antrustions, successors of the Teutonic *comites*, the king's personal followers. This was not because they were of a higher class but because they were in the direct service of the king, having sworn a voluntary oath of perpetual fealty. Frankish Gaul had no hereditary aristocracy: after the king came the entire body of freemen, differentiated by their occupation, not by their birth. The antrustions were chosen by the king from all classes, and their position was not hereditary. They lived at court, superintended palace affairs and held themselves ready for any task their master might assign them, including war. The amount due for the murder of an antrustion was six hundred solidi (one solidus, a Roman gold coin whose descendant was the sou, was equal to one cow, and often the fine was paid in livestock). If he was killed while fighting the king's battle his body was valued at twenty-four hundred solidi. An ordinary Frankish freeman was worth two hundred solidi, but if he was under twelve—a potential warrior—this was tripled. Similarly escalated was the fine for killing a girl over twelve—that is, capable of bearing children. If she was pregnant her price was seven hundred. This was more than that of a priest, whose heirs could collect only six hundred, but not as much as a bishop, assessed at nine hundred.

The life of a Roman landowner, at one hundred solidi, was worth no more than that of a German serf (a cultivator of the soil who paid rent in kind to his landlord and, though not a slave, could be sold). This was not an indication that the Roman, like the serf, was a non-free sub-citizen. The wergild of the serf was paid to his master, not to his family, while the Roman had a right equal to the German, both of redress and of personal liability. The lower wergild was the Frank's expression of his superior value as conqueror; but he guaranteed the equal freedom of his lesser subject. The Gallo-Romans retained their own laws, but they had to live also by the law of their technically superior neighbors. The lowest class in Gaul was the slave, whose master received only thirty solidi for his murder, somewhat more if he were skilled in an art or craft.

Below murder was a host of maledictions of greater or lesser atrocity, from rape and deliberate mutilation to thievery and insult. The minuteness of the inventory gives rise to the observation that this was indeed a barbarous age. But of course a penal code dealt exclusively with social violence. Its object, not its subject, was the majority of unventuresome citizenry existing guilelessly on farms and in peaceful middlesized towns. The Salic Law protected these honest citizens in their coming and going; it left no conceivable area of transgression unredressed.

Criminal mutilations included the cutting off of an ear or an unimportant finger: these were worth only one third of the value of the nose, thumb or second finger (the one which drew the bow), and one quarter that of an eye, which cost one hundred solidi. Castration and cutting out the tongue cost as much as the life of a Roman landowner.

The enumeration of thievery went from the flagrant to the picayune: in its lower categories were the stealing of a horse, a boat, a swineherd's bell, grapes or apples from a garden, an eel net, a hunting dog. It covered all kinds of poaching—misdeeds specially iniquitous to a people addicted to the hunt.

Among the punishable insults, to call a freeman a hare or a fox was only one-third as bad (three solidi) as to name a woman a harlot— unless she was one. Uninvited caresses were disfavored: to stroke a woman's hand or finger cost fifteen, to touch her bosom, thirty-five. Rape entailed a comparatively small wergild of sixty-two and a half. But adultery was severely penalized, bringing two hundred (from the man), and abortion was even more heavily indemnified. The discrepancy in the fines for these crimes is indicative of the Teutonic bias: though a woman's virtue was still honored as in tribal times, her chief value lay not in her person but in her potential as a mother.

If you could not pay, or refused to, a variety of punishments was prescribed, depending on the enormity of your crime and your position in society. If death were indicated this was performed by cleaving the skull with an axe, for the gentry; stoning, for the plebeian; hanging or drowning, for the coward, deserter or effeminate; for the slave, the slower, more degrading sentence of crucifying or breaking on the wheel. Punishments for lesser crimes included torture and mutilation: among the most heinous wrongdoing was property theft, for which the prepetrator could lose an eye for the first theft, a nose for the second, his life for the third. Flogging was a frequent chastisement. Worse than this were imprisonment and enslavement, dreaded above all by the free Franks. These measures were not quite so gruesome then as they seem today: to a people taught to despise death and toughened from babyhood to the endurance of pain and privation, payment was likely to be a more oppressive levy than most of its alternatives. The Franks were neither as rich as most of their Gallo-Roman subjects nor as used to wealth when they acquired it, nor, even in the upper classes, as softly civilized.

The accused was brought before the local court, which, if it decided on his guilt, decreed the amount of the wergild or the nature of its alternative. In the absence of witnesses no special effort was made to look for evidence. But the accused had two recourses to clear his name: oath and ordeal.

Oath was sacrosanct to a grotesque degree. It took place in a church over the tomb of a saint. If a man swore by the holy ashes and was lying, the saint's spirit, living and present, might call him to immediate and appropriate account. One man, relates Gregory of Tours, who had clearly burned down his neighbor's house and swore on Saint Martin's shrine that he had not, was at once incinerated by a flame which was seen to descend from heaven.[20] Another liar found his tongue paralyzed. In addition to the saint's immediate retribution the perjuror could be sure that worse awaited him after he had been literally snatched by the jaws of hell. Only the most egregiously greedy, ambitious or hard-boiled would take the chance of lifting his hands over the holy ashes in a lie.

Ordeal was another kind of appeal to the deity: this was not only sanctioned by the Church, it generally took place in church. Sometimes it was undergone by the accused alone. There was the hot water ordeal: after attending Mass and taking Communion he must insert his hand and arm into boiling water (blessed by the priest) and retrieve a ring therefrom. The scalded limb was bandaged for three days, and if the flesh had not by then recovered its normal aspect he was proven guilty. In the cold water ordeal he was thrown into a pond with his arm bound to his leg; if he floated he was guilty. In other devices for uncovering guilt the subject had to hold a hot iron bar, walk barefoot over heated plates or walk between two fires and emerge unblemished.

Other kinds of ordeals were contests between the defendant and the plaintiff, or between two possible culprits. The duel was one method: the defeated combatant was not only judged guilty, he lost his hand as well, and on occasion he was buried alive. In the ordeal by cross the contestants had to stand with their arms extended for the duration of the service, and whoever dropped his arms first was the culprit. (This practice, to our eyes the most harmless of all the Frankish legal expedients, was later forbidden as being sacrilegious.)

There was little in the code concerning civil law, most of that being administered under Roman law. The small section devoted to it dealt mainly with the inheritance of property. There were no wills: a man's personal property went equally to his children, male and female, while his real property descended only in the male line, each son receiving an equivalent portion. "Of Salic land no portion shall come to a woman; but the whole of the inheritance of the land shall come to the male sex."[21] In the fourteenth century the *lex Salica* was erroneously invoked to justify the barring of women and any descendants through the female line from succession to the throne of France, and later, to that of some German kingdoms and duchies. But the actual Salic law and its successive emendations from the time of Clovis to that of Charlemagne had no political provisions. There is nothing in reference to the rights of succession, and almost no word of the powers and prerogatives of the king—except the crucial proviso that he is the final legal resource.

Clovis's *lex Salica* is an expressive picture of the society it protected: wealthy farmers living more or less pacifically side by side with legally inferior but more civilized conquered neighbors. Their farms were diversified, with cultivated fields, livestock, orchards, gardens and vineyards. Hawks, hounds, beehives and fishing boats added a spice of variation to placid rusticity. There is little reference to town life: the urban *modus vivendi* was not attractive to these country-oriented families whose fairly recent forebears still hunted and roved for their livelihood. Most of the malfeasance took the form of straightforward physical violence: assault, theft, and outrage to women. The simple Frankish felon was not yet educated in the subtleties of urban crime and the degeneracy which ulcerates the edges of more complex societies. Though it covers exhaustively nearly every aspect of unsophisticated wrongdoing, the Salic law is fundamentally no more than a codification of a chaotic body of tribal common law. There is nothing in the code concerning general legal principles, little on the procedures of evidence and detection, almost nothing on the public institutions of law and administration, a minimum of attention to civil jurisdiction.

But simplistic as it is legally, its codification by Clovis is a landmark in the history of Frankish Gaul. He changed little in the unwritten customary law; the importance of his action is that for the first time in Frankish history kingly authority is exercised in backing up and implementing the ancient heritage of common law. It is a concrete expression of the unqualified prerogative of kingship, a concept new to the Franks. Traditionally their kings had been local chieftains elected by their warriors for the specific purpose of military enterprise; and their law had been developed for freemen and their leaders as equals, by these same warriors. Now the king, as supreme judge, was in practice outside the law.

Clovis's last years were not devoted exclusively to the sedentary occupations of peace. Though Vouillé had been his last full-scale military campaign it was not the end of his irredentist activities. There were still uncompleted tasks along his Germanic borders, where local Frankish leaders had not yet acknowledged his sovereignty. Early in his career he had obliterated most of the boundaries between his Francia* and the territories of other Frankish chieftains. Clovis believed that the petty kings of those few that were left ought to acknowledge but one king of all the Franks. Chloderic, who had fought with him at Vouillé, was the son of Sigibert the Lame, who ruled the Frankish kingdom of Cologne.[22] Sigibert had been a friend and ally throughout Clovis's ascendant career (he had been lamed from a wound in his knee when they had fought the Allemans together at Tolbiac in 496). But by now Clovis considered another Frankish king redundant. Gregory of Tours tells the story. Secretly Clovis summoned Sigibert's son to him and said: "Your father is old and he is lame. If he were to die, his kingdom would come to you of right, and my alliance would come with it." Chloderic accommodatingly murdered his father. As the new king he offered his fealty and part of his treasure to his benefactor. Clovis thanked him for his goodwill and said that his messengers would look over the treasure but would not take any of it. The envoys came and inspected everything. "It was in this coffer," said Chloderic, "that my father used to keep all his gold coins." "Plunge your hand right to the bottom," they answered, "to see how much is there." As he leaned forward to do this, one of the Franks split Chloderic's skull with his

*Francia was the name given by the Romans, in the third century, to the small Frankish homeland north of Roman Gaul. By Clovis's time, Francia had been enlarged to comprise the heart of Frankish Gaul, and it retained its Teutonic connotation, its area and boundaries fluctuating, throughout the Merovingian era.

double-headed ax. "This unworthy son," concludes the historian complacently, "thus shared the fate of his father."

Clovis went to Cologne, spoke sadly to the people of the unfortunate accidental deaths of their latest two kings and suggested that they should put themselves under his fatherly protection. The assembled warriors clashed their shields, shouted their approval, then in the old tribal way raised Clovis on a shield to proclaim him their king. "Day in and day out," Gregory concludes, "God submitted the enemies of Clovis to his dominion and increased his power, for he walked before Him with an upright heart and did what was pleasing in His sight." Gregory's judgment illustrates the manifest advantage of walking arm in arm with the Church. Though the historian was coolly, sometimes imprudently, critical of the Merovingian kings of his own day, the great Clovis, who had died twenty-nine years before Gregory was born, was sacrosanct, his most disgraceful treacheries transformed to crusades by the halo of spiritual correctness.

The next to go was Chararic, king of a group of Salian Franks in Gallia Belgica, and a cousin of Clovis. Chararic had done nothing to arouse the ire of his relative except to stay cautiously neutral in the long-ago conflict with Syagrius, waiting to see who would win. Clovis now elected to hold this against him. By a ruse he captured Chararic and his son and had their long hair cut off, which was supposed to emasculate their royalty. He then pushed them both into the Church, Chararic to be ordained as a priest, his son to be made a deacon. Chararic wept at their humiliation and his son, to comfort him, unwisely said, "These leaves have been cut from wood which is still green and not lacking in sap. They will soon grow again and be larger than ever." This unwise remark, repeated to Clovis, caused both father and son to lose not only their hair but their heads. Their kingdom and their treasure passed to Clovis.

Then came the turn of Ragnachar, king of Cambrai. The disposal of this relative is justified by Gregory, for he "was so sunk in debauchery that he could not even keep his hands off the women of his own family." His exasperated nobles responded readily to Clovis's bribe of arm bands and sword belts seemingly of gold, actually of gilded bronze. Then the deliverer marched into Cambrai with his army, and Ragnachar's nobles arrested their lord and brought him before Clovis with his arms bound behind his back. "Why have you disgraced our Frankish people by allowing yourself to be bound?" asked Clovis. "It would have been better for you had you died in battle." He thereupon slew Ragnachar with his ax. When the nobles who had betrayed their king found that their gifts from Clovis were fakes, they complained to him. "This is the sort of gold," answered Clovis, "which a man can expect when he deliberately lures his lord to death." He added that they were lucky only to have been cheated instead of, properly, tortured and executed. They quickly begged forgiveness and joined the throngs acknowledging Clovis as their master.

Clovis dispatched another handful of superfluous chieftains, consolidating his kingdom. Then be bemoaned the dearth of relatives: "'How sad a thing it is that I live among strangers like some solitary pilgrim, and that I have none of my own relations left to help me when disaster threatens!' He said this not because he grieved for their deaths, but because in his cunning way he hoped to find some relative still in the land of the living whom he could kill." The sixth-century historian, condoning treachery in a good cause, did not countenance hypocrisy.

This was the same Clovis who was respectful and generous to the Church and who had given his Gallo-Roman subjects equality under the law. Tolerant where it was advisable for the welfare of his kingdom, he was ruthless with the Franks of his own class. He trusted no Frankish chieftain: they were all, he judged, as ambitious and as treacherous as himself, but less competent. He cut them down before they could gather strength to challenge him, and by the end of his reign there was hardly a noble-born Frank left in the kingdom. The destruction of the old Teutonic aristocracy meant that no longer was the king the elected choice of his assembled warriors, subject to their checks and control. Politically he was henceforth supreme. In matters of the spirit he gave precedence to his bishops, and he sought the wisdom of his Gallo-Roman elders in administrative affairs. But his authority was absolute. There was a privileged class in the realm, the king's antrustions. But, as noted, this was not a hereditary noble caste: it was originated by the king, its members were of no special birth or background and they were subject unconditionally to his will. It would not take long for a new aristocracy to grow, created by the king himself, but it would be a hundred years before it could successfully challenge an entrenched, capricious, by now almost legendary dynasty.

It took Clovis the last four years of his life to eliminate his peers. He died in Paris in 511, aged about forty-six, having reigned for thirty years. He was buried in the Church of Saint Peter and Saint Paul, which he and Clotild had built at the instigation of Saint Geneviève. His effigy, though not his body, lies in the Cathedral of Saint Denis among the host of his fellow kings: a calm stone figure, bearded and crowned and holding a scepter, clad in the garments of the thirteenth century, when the carving was executed.

Clovis died in peace and presumably content. By his own lights he had accomplished a great deal. He had unified the tribal Franks into a coherent kingdom. He had introduced the true faith to his heathen domain and gone a long way toward liberating his neighbors from the domination of their heretical leaders. He had overcome or checked the adjacent rulers who had appropriated or threatened Gallic lands. He had triumphed over armies larger and more experienced than his. He had ruled his own land and his acquired territories fairly, and in many areas of administration he had deferred to the judgment of his spiritual masters, the Gallo-Roman bishops.

By the light of posterity Clovis was a brutal and unscrupulous conqueror, paying lip service to a Christ who was to him but a more efficacious war god, cleaving the skulls of enemies with his own ax, employing perfidy to encompass the downfall of other foes. In other words he was a fifth-century Teutonic warrior, no more and no less virtuous than the gently bred Catholic churchmen who spurred him on and praised the iniquity that promoted the faith.

He was also a consummately successful king, the author of Frankish supremacy and a founder of modern France. The sense of unity he bequeathed to disparate Frankish tribes would outlast the factional squabbles of his descendants, and would become the basis for a conscious sense of nationality.

Whatever the philosophical arguments of ends versus means, we cannot pass a valid judgment on barbarian-Christian Clovis by any standards we have developed over fifteen hundred years.

CHAPTER FIVE

THE
SONS OF
CLOVIS

As Clovis's roots were those of a Teutonic war leader, his strong family feeling was also in the tribal tradition, and he fostered the growing mystique of the Merovingian clan. His inclination was seconded by the Church, which not only approved of solid family establishments but supported the unquestioned ascendancy of the royal line. His sons, of the downright Teutonic names Theodoric, Chlodomer, Childebert and Lothair, divided the kingdom among them, under the Frankish law of inheritance.

In the beginning no sense of disunity followed this dubious arrangement: the brothers were amicably sharing the spoils that came to them naturally from their father's conquests. If anything the strength of the Merovingian dynasty was enhanced by its spread among four, each of whom was equally a Merovingian king in his own eyes and in those of his subjects, and who shared Clovis's belief in the integrity of the family. The rapport would not last. All four inherited in full their father's imperious temper, but little of his canniness. The inevitable self-destructive quarrels would echo through the generations.

Theodoric was the eldest, the son of a mother whose name is not recorded, mistress of Clovis before his marriage to Clotild. His portion was the biggest, and the most decidedly Frankish: the section sometimes called Francia, later to be named Austrasia. This comprised all the northeastern provinces of Gaul, bordering on the

Rhine, where the main population and language were Germanic. In Theodoric's time it was called the kingdom of Metz, and its capitals were the cities of Metz and Rheims. Theodoric also received a part of southern Gaul including Auvergne, which he himself had captured, and where he was deservedly unpopular.

The second brother, Chlodomer, eldest son of Queen Clotild, got the kingdom of Orléans, which later became part of Neustria. (Chlodomer's portion was, however, much smaller than the later division: the boundaries of the Frankish kingdoms fluctuated through the generations.) Chlodomer's Orléans reached south to the Loire, north to the English Channel, east to the edge of Burgundy and west to the border of Brittany. His capital was the city of Orléans.

The third brother, Childebert, was king of Paris, or Sens, ruling over that central portion of Gaul now generally comprising the Île de France. Its capital was Sens, about seventy miles southeast of Paris. His sovereignty reached down to Bordeaux, and he also had nominal dominion over Brittany.

The youngest, Lothair, got Soissons, which included, besides that last foothold of the Roman Empire in Gaul, the old Frankish lands in Gallia Belgica, with the cities of Tournai, Cambrai and Thérouanne. Its capital was Soissons.

It was probably Clotild who, in an attempt to foster harmony, designated as capitals of the four kingdoms cities in a near arc around Paris—all were less than one hundred miles from that central town except for Metz, the alternative capital of Theodoric's Austrasia. Anticipating the predictable clashes of her hotheaded, only semicivilized sons, it is likely that she was also the one who persuaded them to respect Paris as neutral territory, where they should meet for amicable counsel, sans armed escort.

The opportune location of Paris, already appreciated by the Romans and by Clovis, was enhanced by the positioning of the Merovingian capitals around it. Since Clovis had chosen it as his central base the city had grown. Besides the island town in the Seine, there was another village on the hills of the river's left bank. On its highest point Clovis had built the Church of Saint Peter and Saint Paul at the request of Saint Geneviève, seconded by Queen Clotild. The king had marked the area designated for it by throwing his hatchet: his throwing arm was so strong that the edifice was longer than Saint Martin's sanctuary at Tours (which was one hundred and sixty feet long, according to Gregory of Tours).[1] This splendid church, decorated with marble and mosaics and royally endowed, became a center of pilgrimage. To the north was another village, the Roman settlement of Catolacus, where Saint Denis's psalm-singing head had finally come to rest. When Clovis became king, Geneviève was still building her church over the martyr's shrine, the project allowed her by Clovis's father, Childeric; and even to the pagan boy-king the growing cult must have conveyed a potent sense of the saint's awful presence. This village too had become enlarged by pilgrims and the merchants to serve them. By the time of Clovis's death Paris, expanded to include these thriving towns, had gained repute not only as a strategic military center but as a nucleus of ecclesiastical activity.

By the time Clovis's sons succeeded to their kingdoms, then, Paris was a good choice as a meeting ground where temperamental kings could settle their differences in unarmed congress. During their lifetime its inviolability was respected—with one appalling exception.

Outside the neutral ground of Paris, however, the kings were relentlessly belligerent. They continued their father's policy of conquest with battle, rampage, treachery and near-fratricidal quarrels. But for all their impatient temper, their reigns ended with a bigger and more strongly consolidated Merovingian Gaul than had been realized under Clovis's single rule.

Three main areas of expansion were recognized by the brothers as logically essential. Southern Gaul was divided between the Visigoths of Spain and the Ostrogoths of Italy. Burgundy was still ruled by unconquered King Gundobad. And Thuringia, domain of another branch of the Franks on the right bank of the Rhine, had regained its independence since Clovis had dispatched its king early in his reign. The addition of these three provinces would handsomely round out Merovingian Gaul, extending it to what the brothers saw as its natural boundaries.

Clovis's eldest son, Theodoric, had subjugated Auvergne and Provence without mercy. Though the campaign was on orders of his father, the methods were the preference of the son. His men would rather have assaulted Burgundy, a country easy to invade and rich with potential loot. To prevent mutiny Theodoric promised them equal prizes in Auvergne, whose Gallo-Roman wealth was of fabulous proportions to a fighting Frank. Even though he was professedly freeing the southern cities from the hard hand of the ruling Arian Visigoths, the Auvergnian Catholics liked Theodoric as little as did the heretics; his ruthless predacity recognized no religious bounds. To compound his general unpopularity, he was invading a country of centuries-old pride and independence: its cities, historically self-governing, resented any attempt at outside domination, and its vast estates, worked by multitudes of obedient serfs, were themselves practically autonomous little Gallo-Roman kingdoms. Theodoric rode roughshod over this autarchy. The inhabitants, in terror, fled to their high wild mountains, to fortresses such as Salers—now a medieval-Renaissance walled town—on a high plateau at the edge of the sharp, volcanic mountains of the Cantal. In these fastnesses they defended themselves successfully against the invader. But they could not save their towns and their farms from Frankish rapacity. Though Auvergne ostensibly became part of Frankish Gaul, it was not long before the terrorized inhabitants recovered their spirits and revolted against their harsh masters.

Theodoric had a legitimate strategic objective in overrunning Auvergne: to join forces, across it, with the Burgundian king, Gundobad, temporarily his ally. The aim of the two kings was to annex the cities of the Rhône Valley and restore Provence, the jewel of Roman Gaul, as an integral part of Frankish Gaul. The armies, Frankish and Burgundian, met at Arles, and there Theodoric's ferocious advance was finally checked. The other Theodoric, the Ostrogoth, king of Italy, belatedly alarmed by the Frank's rapid conquest of the Rhône Valley and the consequent threat to Italy's alpine border, sent his troops to the relief of the beleaguered city. The battle outside the walls of Arles resulted in an absolute rout of the Frankish invaders by the Ostrogoth's seasoned fighters. The Franks and the Burgundians lost, it is written, thirty thousand men on the field.[2]

The besieged town itself was not wholly without sympathy for its attackers, and during the siege tempers rose and accusations flew between Catholics sympathetic to their coreligionists outside the walls, and Arians fearful of their fate if Arles should fall. A side effect of the partisan intrigue was the attitude of the Jews, wealthy and respected citizens of Arles, who actively leagued themselves with the Arian party. In sixth-century Europe Jews were prone to support whatever faction was anti-Catholic. Arian rulers left them to work and worship in peace, while Catholics, ever activist, were energetically intolerant of their differentness.

For another twenty-eight years Arles remained under Visigothic rule, as did Septimania, the land along the Mediterranean coast from the Rhône to the eastern end of the Pyrenees. Theodoric of Italy propped up the feeble government of the latest Visigothic child-king, his grandson Amalaric, whose father, Alaric II, Clovis had slain at Vouillé. Through this influence the Ostrogoth controlled not only Italy and Pannonia but Spain and southern Gaul. Outside of northern Gaul Theodoric the Great now had the main part of the erstwhile Western Empire, and he had nearly attained his ambition: a return to the old "Roman peace." The Franks and the Burgundians, punished for their pushiness, were cut off from the Mediterranean seaports. During the remainder of the Ostrogothic Theodoric's years they were contained in the north.

Foiled in the Midi, and the Frankish Theodoric looked for a pretext to annex Thuringia, another of the three objectives of Merovingian expansion.[3] He reached back sixty years to find an excuse. At that time, 451, the Thuringians had fought on the side of Attila the Hun in the battle of the Catalaunian Plains, opposing the Merovingian ancestor, Merovech, and the victorious Aetius. After the battle Merovech had followed the Hunnish army back to the borders of Thuringia. The Franks and the Thuringians had exchanged hostages, and the latter were alleged then to have perpetrated on their hostages the atrocities which Theodoric now produced as reasons to extermi-nate the present rulers of that land. The story was that the Thuringians hung young men by the muscles of their thighs from the branches of trees, where they slowly died. They tied the arms of young women to the necks of horses, then stampeded the horses so the girls were torn apart. They fastened others with stakes over the ruts of roads and ran wagons over them. Whether and when these bad deeds were committed, they were a useful propaganda device with which Theodoric could whet the sanguinary appetite of his soldiers.

Three brothers named Hermanfrid, Berthar and Baderic jointly ruled Thuringia in disaccord. Hermanfrid eliminated Berthar by killing him in battle. Then he himself succumbed to a combination of the machinations of his vindictive wife and the treachery of his Frankish neighbor. His wife served his dinner one night with only half the table laid. "A king who is deprived of half his kingdom," she explained, "deserves to find half his table bare." This so aroused Hermanfrid that he sent a message to Theodoric in Metz, inviting him to come and make war on his brother Baderic, the fee for his aid to be half of Hermanfrid's kingdom. The Frank accepted with alacrity, and in the ensuing battle the second brother, Baderic, was beheaded. Hermanfrid did not keep his word about sharing the kingdom with his ally. In 531 Theodoric once more dredged up the historic crimes to reinforce his displeasure at present perfidy. He moved against Thuringia, this time with the aid of his youngest brother, Lothair. The Thuringians dug ditches to trip the Frankish horses. This had the effect of angering the Franks beyond control, so that the subsequent battle had a disproportionate violence. The Thuringians, roundly defeated, fled across the river Unstrut, where they were killed with such abandon that "the river was piled high with their corpses and the Franks crossed over them to the other side as if they were walking on a bridge." Hermanfrid, forgiven by Theodoric, visited the Frankish king at Tolbiac, reassured by promises of safe-conduct along with expensive gifts. While the two kings walked in friendly conversation along the wall of the town, "somebody accidentally gave Hermanfrid a push, and he fell to the ground and died. Certain people have ventured to suggest that Theodoric may have had something to do with it." Thuringia was now part of Francia.

Theodoric's next objective was Burgundy the area of one of his father's few failures. He entered on this venture at the request of his half brother, Chlodomer, king of Orléans, Clotild's eldest son. They were encouraged to their campaign by the dowager queen, who, despite her Christian piety, harbored an undying resentment toward the family of her uncle Gundobad, the killer of her relatives. Gundobad had died in 516, and the kingdom was ruled by his sons, Sigismund and Godomar. In 522 Sigismund, goaded by a spiteful second wife, had one of his young sons strangled while he napped in the afternoon. Sigismund threw himself on the boy's body and wept for his guilt, then retired to a monastery to pray for his wicked soul. He had no immediate intention of giving up his share of the kingdom, but Frankish Chlodomer took the opportunity to dispose of him. When Sigismund emerged from his retreat he was faced with Chlodomer's army, captured with his wife and children, and held prisoner near Orléans. Chlodomer decided it would be politic to kill this family before taking on the second Burgundian brother. He was eloquently advised against this course by an abbot whose words he generally respected: "Whatever you do to Sigismund and his wife and children, the same will be done to your children and your wife and you yourself." Chlodomer, no more nor less Christian than the rest of the Merovingians, went ahead anyway, and had the whole family murdered and thrown down a well.

Then he called on his brother Theodoric to help him in the main objective, the taking of Burgundy. Theodoric had no special interest at stake here—it was not his grandparents who had been killed long ago in Burgundy—but he was never averse to a fight, and he recognized the desirability of a Frankish Burgundy removed from the tenacious network of the other Theodoric, the puissant king of Italy. The Frankish brothers routed Godomar's troops with ease. But when Chlodomer followed up the victory by chasing after the retreating Burgundians, the fleeing soldiers, recognizing him by his long hair, imitated his own rallying cry and tricked him into believing that his Frankish troops were ahead of him. Chlodomer rushed into the midst of the enemy, who cut off his head and raised it triumphantly on a stake. The abbot's promise of retribution for the murder of innocents had begun to come true.

The immediate result of the battle was that the Franks engaged in an orgy of destructive revenge, killing Godomar and every other Burgundian they could catch, and devastating the countryside. The further result, which came about only after a third invasion, in 532, was the decisive incorporation of Burgundy into Frankish Gaul. Chlodomer's three young sons inherited his kingdom. As minors they were taken under the protection of their grandmother, Dowager Queen Clotild, who loved them.

The activities of Clovis's third son, Childebert, king of Sens, were determined by his shifting alliances with his brothers. He was a shade more moral and clement than the other three, but his humaneness was offset by capricious disloyalty. He took part in the fraternal military campaigns, but was likely to change sides, supporting first one brother then another, according to expediency. He was exceptionally acquisitive, even for a Frank. But according to the lights of his time he was a good Christian: much of the treasure he detached over the heads of his brothers, from defeated opponents, he donated to the Church. Being a Catholic he was concerned at the disagreeable fate of his sister, Clotild, who had been married to the Arian Visigoth, Amalaric, now king of Spain and Septimania. This young man was mistreating his Frankish bride because she refused to abjure her Catholicism. When she went to church on Sundays he had her pelted with dung, and on occasion he struck her. At last, in 531, the suffering princess sent her brother a plea for help, along with a towel soaked with her blood. Childebert, with Christian concern, immediately responded by mobilizing his army and setting out for Spain. Amalaric had been under the strong-arm protection of his grandfather, Theodoric of Italy, but the great king had died five years before, in 526. In the event it gave Childebert the opportunity to amortize his errand of mercy by wresting some of southern Gaul from the weak young king on his way south. He liberated Auvergne; and its capital, Clermont-Ferrand, the proud Gallo-Roman city which had so often defied barbarian intrusion, was now irreversibly a Frankish possession.

Then Childebert proceeded to Barcelona to rescue his sister. King Amalaric was by this time so frightened that he prepared to take ship and leave the country. At the last moment he realized that he had left behind a treasure of precious stones. Going back for it he found himself blocked by Childebert's soldiers. He tried to take refuge in a church (Catholic) but was caught on the threshold by a thrown javelin, and died at once. Childebert, along with releasing his sister from her distressful environment, also removed Amalaric's hoard of gems and a sizable treasure of church chalices, plates and book bindings of gold decorated with jewels—all this later to be virtuously bestowed on churches and monasteries back home in Sens. The whole train set off for Paris, but Clotild died on the journey. She was buried next to her father in the Church of Saint Peter and Saint Paul on the Montagne Sainte-Geneviève.

Now this quasi-Christian, having paid his sop to God, engaged in a gory act hard to match even in his own time. The orphans of his brother Chlodomer, the three little boys living in Paris with their grandmother, Dowager Queen Clotild, were heirs to their father's realm of Orléans, and their inheritance was an attraction to their rapacious uncle. Childebert suspected that Clotild intended soon to have them crowned, and he would lose his chance to inherit their kingdom. He called secretly on his brother Lothair, the youngest of the sons of Clovis and Clotild, to help him decide how to deal with the menace of these children. Lothair hesitated not an instant, even though he knew their action would violate the agreed neutrality of Paris. The brothers met in that city and, having put it about that they intended to crown the young princes, asked Clotild to send the boys to them. Pleased and innocent, she fed the children and sent them to their sharkish uncles, who immediately sequestered them and locked their attendants in another room. One of the boys, eight-year-old Clodoald, escaped with the aid of brave servants. He subsequently cut off his hair, voluntarily banning himself from the succession, and elected to live out his life as a servant of God. Clodoald, now known as Saint Cloud, became a hermit and later built the monastery west of Paris that bears his name; there he died in 560.

The other two boys, aged seven and ten, were subjects of a brief discussion between their uncles as to which was the wiser course, to cut off their hair or to kill them. A messenger was sent to the queen, carrying a pair of scissors in one hand and a sword in the other. "Your two sons," he said, "seek your decision, gracious Queen, as to what should be done with the princes. Do you wish them to live with their hair cut short? Or would you prefer to see them killed?" Clotild, out of her mind with shock and grief, hardly knew what she said as she answered, "If they are not to ascend the throne, I would rather see them dead than with their hair cut short." The messenger ran back to his masters before she could come to herself. Lothair, not wasting a minute, "seized the older boy by the wrist, threw him to the ground, jabbed his dagger into his armpit and so murdered him with the utmost savagery. The younger lad threw himself at Childebert's feet and gripped him round the knees. 'Help me! Help me! dearest uncle,' he cried, 'lest I perish as my brother has done!'" Childebert, tears of belated compunction in his eyes, begged his brother to desist, offering him anything he wanted if he would spare the child. But by this time Lothair was uncontrollable. "'Make him let go,' he bellowed, 'or I will kill you instead! It was you who thought of this business! Now you are trying to rat on me!'" Childebert gave way, tore the child's arms from his knees and threw him to Lothair, who stabbed him through the ribs. The priestly historian offers no comment on this deed, beyond noting that "Lothair climbed on his horse and rode away, showing no remorse," and "Childebert skulked off to the outskirts of Paris."

Sorrowing Clotild followed the little corpses in funeral procession to the Church of Saint Peter and Saint Paul, where they were buried side by side. Then, relinquishing her royal heritage, she donated all her wealth to churches and monasteries and withdrew from the world. She spent the rest of her life as a penitent, dressed in the coarsest robes, living on bread and herbs and devoting herself to the care of the poor and sick. Her selfless dedication is the obverse side of the Merovingian nature: the pure and literal application of the teaching of the primitive Church. People like Clotild—the sixth century fostered a number of them among its highborn—add a dimension of light, like the sun shining in back of a cloud, to the dismal and stormy climate of post-imperial Europe.

So the curse laid on Chlodomer was worked out. A thread of doom and evil runs through the history of this family: the story reads like an ancient saga of blood and vengeance and the terrible power of fate. But the instruments of this particular prophesy, the two brutal brothers, were impervious to the morals of folktales: they benefited greatly thereby, and lived to a healthy old age. They divided the kingdom of the dead children between them, cutting out their half brother, Theodoric. At the moment he dared not object because he needed Lothair's help in his campaign against the Thuringians. Later he would try to emend the arbitrary appropriation. Clovis's sons had outstanding enterprise in one direction: the acquisition of one another's property.

Childebert died in 558, in the forty-seventh year of his reign, and was buried with honor in the Church of Saint Vincent. He himself had built this church in 542, in the fields outside Paris on the left bank of the Seine, to house a relic of the true Cross which he had brought back from Spain on his lucrative expedition to rescue his sister. The church was renamed Saint Germain des Prés in 576, when the bishop of Paris was buried there, and it became the burial place of subsequent Merovingian kings until 639, when King Dagobert rebuilt the Church of Saint Denis. Pilgrims transformed the rural area of Saint Germain des Prés, like those of Saint Denis and Mont Sainte-Geneviève, into an extension of the city. The tombs disappeared when the abbey was suppressed during the Revolution, and effigies of the long-haired kings, sans bodies, lie now at Saint Denis.

Childebert was not all bad. Besides his generosity to the Church—probably as much a matter of expedience and superstition as of conviction—he was the author, with his brother, Lothair, of an important amendment to the Salic law. This was the *Pactus pro Tenore Pacis*, pact for the keeping of peace: it provided that armed soldiery pursuing robber bands could cross the king's boundaries with impunity. The act provided essential protection for the community against lawless violence, a prevalent symptom of the bewildering and chaotic changes in rule. These fierce kings, heirs to the barbarian premise of conquest and plunder, were making the first tentative move toward the creation of a civilized authority. Their peacekeeping police force was a recognition that the wellbeing of the commonweal was a king's primary responsibility. Their departure from tradition betokened a concept of monarchy new to the Franks. Conquest, self-aggrandizement, cruelty and treachery were still abundantly present, particularly in their relations to one another. But there was besides a nascent conscience that being a ruler entailed more than an intemperate exercise of power.

Lothair, the youngest of Clovis's sons, was the most truculent and the most successful of them. One attribute of his success was that he outlived the other three. More pertinent, he possessed an adroit perceptiveness wanting in his siblings.

Lothair had shared in the campaigns of his brothers, and initiated some of his own. He had aided his oldest brother, Theodoric, in the subduing of the Thuringians, had attacked Burgundy along with Chlodomer, who was killed there, and with his brother Childebert invaded Spain. This campaign, undertaken in 542, had no purpose beyond predation, but it included a curious incident. The Franks, besieging the wealthy cathedral city of Saragossa, saw a procession of inhabitants clad in hair shirts marching around the outer wall chanting psalms, behind one who carried a tunic. They were followed by wailing women clad in black, with ashes in their free-flowing hair. It is hard to discern from the historian's account who were the more nonplussed, the besieging Catholic Franks or the defending heretic Goths. The besiegers, drawing back alarmed, asked a farmer what was happening. They were told that the townspeople were invoking the aid of their saint, the fourth-century martyr, Vincent,* and that it was his tunic, a potent relic, which they were carrying. The Franks, recovering themselves, asked for the blessed tunic, but it was refused by the Saragossa bishop. By this time, however, the baffled Gothic soldiery had fled the city, and the Catholic protesters welcomed the Franks as deliverers. After the customary havoc, which included the taking of a large amount of loot, the two Frankish kings departed from Spain.

We have already recounted Lothair's part in the murder of his brother's children and his subsequent arrogation of half their king-

---

*Spain's proto-martyr, Vincent, was arrested during the persecutions of Emperor Maximian, refused to honor the pagan gods and, according to unreliable account, was racked and roasted on a gridiron, then thrown into prison, where he died of his tortures in 304.

dom, to the exclusion of his oldest brother, Theodoric. Now Theodoric, having successfully enlisted Lothair's cooperation in the devastation of Thuringia, and no longer in need of his help, devised a clumsy assassination plot in revenge. He invited Lothair to come to him to talk over some matters. In preparation he hung a canvas from one wall to another in his courtyard and instructed armed men to stand behind it, ready to leap on the visitor. The canvas was too short, and when Lothair entered the courtyard he saw a row of military feet below the hanging. He said nothing, but kept his bodyguard around him. Theodoric, to cover his bungle, quickly offered his brother a large silver salver. After Lothair had departed with the gift Theodoric instructed his son to run after his uncle and retrieve it. Unaccountably, Lothair gave it back; but Theodoric's maladroit exercise did not improve the brothers' already shaky relations.

Not long after this, in 534, Theodoric died, having reigned twenty-three years. His throne of Metz (Austrasia) devolved on his son, Theudebert. Though this youth had the congenital Merovingian avarice, he was slightly more humane, kinder in victory than his uncles, and generous to the Church. He was a strong king, and he might have materially changed the history of the dynasty had he lived longer than his uncle Lothair. (He was not murdered, but died in a hunting accident in 548.) His successor was his son, Theudebald, a spiritless child who reigned only seven years before dying of a chronic illness. The heirs of Clovis were now down to his two surviving sons, Childebert and Lothair. By this time the doughty Childebert was a weak old man, and he had no children. Lothair, himself already seventy, was still aggressively master of his destiny. Besides, as the father of several ambitiously voracious sons, he saw no reason why he should not possess himself of the whole kingdom of Metz instead of making the customary fraternal division.

When he appropriated Metz he inherited the perennially troublesome Saxons, who were in temporary tribute to that northeastern kingdom. The conflict between Saxon and Frank went back to the barbarian invasions of Roman Gaul. In the fourth century the Franks, expanding successfully into Gallia Belgica, cut their rivals off from access to the Roman provinces to the south. The Saxons, frustrated on land, could maraud only by sea. They evolved into Europe's most efficient pirate menace until the advent of the Vikings: they were the scourge of the northern coasts, not only of Gaul but of Roman Britain. By 531 they possessed most of Britain; they con-

trolled the entire North Sea area and they were the prime respresenta-
tives of traditional northern paganism against the champions of
Christianity, the newly Catholic Franks. Clovis had left them alone,
his hands full with the reducing of his relatives and the consolidation
of his kingdom. His sons treated them circumspectly, forming a
détente, in which the Saxons helped them in the destruction of the
Thuringian kingdom. As a result of this campaign the Saxons
enlarged their dominion; and in return for Frankish support in
retaining their precarious hold, they put themselves under the
suzerainty of their *pro tempore* allies, paying an annual tribute. But
they were unwilling lieges, and in 555 they challenged their nominal
masters, refusing to hand over the annual tribute.

That was the year Lothair made himself king of Metz, and at the
moment of the Saxon defiance he was engaged in the traditional
king's progress around his new kingdom—in this case a tactic to
strengthen his not quite legitimate position. He dropped his royal
passage, mobilized his army and hastened to the eastern border of
Metz. The Saxons, intimidated by Lothair's instant retaliation, sent
messengers to the Frankish king apologizing for their default and
asking with unaccustomed meekness for an end to the continuous
warfare between the two Teutonic nations. The aging Lothair, who
had never yet shrunk from an open battle, had learned enough to
recognize the more durable value of a lasting peace. He accepted their
overtures. But his splenetic henchmen saw it differently. "We know
what liars they are," they said, "for they never do what they have
promised. We must attack them." Lothair countered them, calling in
God as his ally. His men, outraged at what they deemed the
cowardice of old age, insisted on battle even after the Saxons offered
"all their clothes, their cattle and the whole of their property. 'Take all
this,' they said, 'with half of all the territory we hold, only leave our
wives and little children free and let there be no war between us.'"

Lothair tried once more to reason with his lieutenants, finally
saying that if they insisted on advancing they would advance without
him. They turned on him, tore his tent apart and dragged him out,
swearing they would kill him if he refused to lead them. Lothair had
no recourse but to accede. The result was a shambles, with uncount-
able slaughter on both sides, and neither one victorious. In suing for
peace Lothair apologized to the foe, claiming that he had marched
against his will. Truce was established, but not for long.

This episode indicates the nascent insubordination of the warrior

elite, the rising class made up of antrustions and Frankish landowners, which would become the aristocracy of a later generation.
This group, asserting itself in concert against the hereditary king—
even the convincingly bloodthirsty Lothair—was a new circumstance
in Merovingian history. The phenomenon, at first peculiar to Austrasia, would grow to unmanageable proportions, undermining and
finally destroying the Merovingian kingship.

With the stability of his northern frontier uneasily patched Lothair
turned to a problem more profoundly disturbing to him than the
insubordination of his followers. This was the insurrectionary activity
of his son Chramn, the youngest of seven, and his father's favorite.
Handsome, spoiled and licentious, Chramn had never learned to
accept the authority of a strong-willed father. During the Saxon
troubles he had found opportunity to assert his mutinous disposition.

While Lothair had been busy with the rebellious Saxons his
brother Childebert had occupied himself with encouraging the
northern pirates to further incursions over Lothair's borders. The
Merovingian brothers always enjoyed hurting one another, and
Childebert was specifically irritated because Lothair had high-
handedly cut him out of the inheritance of Metz. At this juncture the
Auvergnians took the opportunity to revolt against their hated
Frankish masters. Lothair, involved with the Saxon insurrection in
the north, sent his son Chramn to pacify the southern realm. Once
the prince had quelled the rebellion he carried the pacification to
extreme lengths, installing himself at Clermont-Ferrand as a capricious despot. He insulted and threatened the bishop, frightening him
into exile. He summarily dismissed the count of the city, who sought
safety in the cathedral. The young tyrant broke the sacred law of
sanctuary and had the fugitive dragged out; the count escaped, but all
his goods were confiscated. Then Chramn gathered around him a
group of disreputable youths, mostly from the lower classes, and
proceeded to issue arbitrary decrees, including the forcible requisition
of the daughters of senators for the entertainment of himself and his
coterie.

Lothair had to remove his corrupt surrogate if he wanted to keep
his southern kingdom intact, but he was unable to bring himself to
chastise his son. Chramn was permitted to move to Poitiers, where he
continued his career of debauchery, to which was now added a
vindictive hatred for his father. He made vows of loyal affection to his

uncle Childebert and together they plotted to invade and lay waste the district around Rheims, Lothair's second city. The effort was halted by Childebert's death in 558. Left without his ally, Chramn made false overtures of obedience to his father, but soon his intrigues began again, finally arousing Lothair's exasperated anger. Threatened with punishment Chramn fled to Brittany, where he sought refuge with the count of this province, traditionally independent of Merovingian authority. Lothair pursued him there, and the Breton count advised the young refugee against engaging his mighty father in battle, offering, himself, to attack at night, when Lothair would be unprepared. Chramn spurned the counsel, and at dawn the two armies met. King Lothair advanced on his favorite son with sorrow in his heart and the words of David on his lips: "Look down, O Lord, and judge my cause, for I suffer injury unjustly at the hands of my son. Look down, O Lord, and make a fair decision, and pass again that judgment which You passed between Absalom and his father." The army of Chramn and his Breton protector was defeated, the Breton count was killed and Chramn fled to the seacoast, where ships awaited him. He suffered a last-minute pang of decent remorse and tried to rescue his wife and daughters, but the hesitation cost him his life. He and his family were captured, bound and shut in a wooden hut. There Chramn was held down and strangled with a cloth; then Lothair ordered the hut to be fired and the others were burned alive.

In an agony of remorse Lothair went to Saint Martin's church at Tours carrying rich gifts. With many a groan at his own wickedness he confessed his evil deeds to the saint and prayed for Martin's personal intercession with God.

This grievous saga, among others in Lothair's career, portrays him as a primitive, two-dimensional warlord of the Dark Ages. In actuality his character had a versatile complexity. To understand one of its facets, we must go back long before the tragedy of Chramn.

From his early youth Lothair had been captivated by women and, for the most part, irresistible to them. Though careful in his choice of legal mates, he managed to amass a number of them—the recorded count is six—who evidently lived in some sort of arranged amity under his various roofs. Regarding the marital customs of Merovingian royalty the Church largely ignored its doctrine of monogamy. Alliance with influential families and the procreation of sons were the prevailing concerns of the ruling kings. Provided they did not openly mistreat their wives, and provided the wives themselves remained unstained, the Church prudently sanctioned whatever conjugal arrangements suited their temporal lords. The Church even respected, perforce, traditional Frankish usage in royal concubinage: illegitimacy reflected no taint on the children. Merovingian blood was above stigma. It mattered not whether a child was the offspring of a princess or a serving maid, nor whether his mother was or was not orthodoxly married to his father. If the Merovingian father acknowledged his son, the child was a Merovingian too.

Lothair's first official wife was Ingund, a beautiful and lively woman who pleased him greatly and who became the mother of six of his eight children (he had one daughter in addition to his seven sons). In the first flush of their married happiness Ingund asked him to find a good husband for her sister, Arnegund. Aroused by his wife's account of the beauty of this maiden, Lothair went to visit Arnegund at her villa, and there married her himself. He made a frank report of this to Ingund, saying, "I have done my best to reward you for the sweet request which you put to me. I have looked everywhere for a wealthy and wise husband whom I could marry to your sister, but I could find no one more eligible than myself." He must have had a potent allure, for Ingund accepted the new ménage, only pleading that she might retain some of her husband's favor. Arnegund bore Lothair one son, Chilperic, who was destined to carry on, alone, the Merovingian dynasty.

Like many susceptible men Lothair was attracted by widows. One of his later wives was Guntheuc, widow of his brother Chlodomer; she became the mother of the ill-starred Chramn. He tried unsuccessfully to marry Vultetrada, widow of his great-nephew, Theudebald (the sickly youth who died after only seven years as king). Along with the forcible inheritance of his great-nephew's kingdom Lothair took possession of this girl, who could have been his granddaughter. After the seduction he wished to marry her. His bishops, to whom he was usually wise enough to listen, forbade it—not because of the suitor's other wives, nor on account of the hint of incest, nor even in protest against the incompatibility of their ages, but because she was a heretic, daughter of the king of the Lombards, an Arian. Reluctantly Lothair donated her to a brother-in-arms, Garivald, duke of Bavaria.

One of his few marital failures occurred after he and Theodoric had routed the Thuringians in 531. The booty they had divided between them included an eight-year-old girl, Radegund, daughter of one of the extirpated Thuringian kings. Her capture by the Franks was in part an act of mercy—she was assured of a short future at the hands of her coldblooded Thuringian relatives. But it happened that she was also a beautiful child, and there was an argument as to who should have her. The brothers drew lots, and Lothair won. He installed Radegund in one of his villas at Athies, on the Somme. There she was gently sequestered, like Deirdre and Isolde, until she should be old enough to wed her lord, who was nearly fifty at the time of her capture.

But Radegund was of a cooler disposition than those susceptible princesses of legend. Her education was in the hands of churchmen, and it comprised the formal neo-Roman literature of the time, with emphasis on the lives of the martyrs and the works of the Fathers of the Church. This polite and godly teaching did not train Radegund to be a Merovingian queen, but rather confirmed her girlish reticence, turning her, as she approached womanhood, to asceticism. Seven years after her capture Lothair came to claim his bride; he found a chilly spinster piously aloof to his masculinity. The only bridegroom desired by his carefully nurtured betrothed was Christ. Lothair, bold in love as in war, was not prepared to give her up, and they were wed at Soissons in 538, against Radegund's will. She carried her vocation intact into married life, eating only bread and herbs, and tending the most repugnantly diseased of the poorer citizenry. An unrestrained sensualist, like most of his clan, Lothair was frustrated by his ethereal bride, whose obstinate austerity would have aggravated the mildest husband; he was heard to complain that he had married a nun.[4] Radegund was his—in the sixth century a wife was owned by her husband—and his was the choice of how to deal with his touch-me-not queen. Foiled by her flinty chastity, he could have forced her or punished her. To his credit he made a compassionate decision. In common with his tribal forebears Lothair had a reverence for the honor of women. He had, further, a courtly streak, part religious, part empathetic. His response to Radegund's vocation has a quality of medieval knightliness: he gave up his queen, at first unwillingly, later with magnanimity.

The occasion of the final breach was Lothair's order to have Radegund's younger brother assassinated, to keep the shattered Thuringians from coalescing around an heir. Outraged, Radegund went to her spiritual mentor, Médard, bishop of Soissons. Médard was one of those finely educated Gallic patricians, with a well-born Frankish father and a Gallo-Roman mother, whose administrative

and advisory services were invaluable to the ruling dynasty. Radegund pleaded with Médard to free her from her marriage and
consecrate her. The bishop hesitated: the request was counter to his
regard for the sanctity of the marriage bond. His doubts were
reinforced by the action of her armed escort. Their disapprobation of
the sundering of a Frankish king from his wedded wife was more
physically compelling than that of the Church: they dragged the
bishop from the altar before he could veil the queen. Radegund was
forced to retire. Unpersuaded, she donned the habit of a nun and
approached Médard again, saying, "If you refuse to consecrate me,
fearing more a man than God, you will be held responsible for the
soul of one of your sheep, O Pastor!" Médard, shaken, laid his hands
on her and consecrated her deaconess. Radegund thereupon placed
on the altar the splendid royal apparel she had discarded, together
with her jewels. Then she traveled around central Gaul seeking a
place where she might found a convent. This king, exasperated at his
queen's defection, started out after her, intending to reseat her
forcibly on her throne. She wrote for help to Germain, who would
later become bishop of Paris. This prelate was fearless in his open
disapproval of royal immorality and three generations of Merovingian
kings tended to obey his strictures. Lothair heeded him and halted
his journey at Tours. There he penitently knelt before Saint Martin's
shrine and surrendered his claim on the aloof girl he had rescued long
before, who had captured his heart. His enduring regard for Radegund did not cease with her desertion: he settled great wealth on her,
and in 557 gave her his royal authority to found at Poitiers a convent,
which remained under his protection until the end of his life.

Lothair also demonstrated his respect for Bishop Médard, who had
been the instrument of his renunciation: on the bishop's death he
raised a great church over the tomb, where, as we have seen, Lothair
himself was later interred. The Frankish king's motivation went
beyond the love he still bore for his reluctant wife. In common with
all the semibarbarian rulers of his century he was in awe of the power
of the Church. In part this was a superstitious fear of retaliation from
above if he displeased its representatives on earth. In part it was a
realization of the material advantages of the Church's blessings on his
extraterritorial ambitions. Further, the educated Gallo-Roman bishops were indispensably useful in the administration of his enormous
properties. Lothair freely sought advice from Bishop Médard, Bishop
Germain of Paris and others of the higher clergy. When he did not

request it, it was given unasked—for it was to the bishops' advantage to sustain and strengthen the power of their Catholic king.

Lothair's fear of the wrath of heaven was exemplified in a clash with his bishops over the imposition of taxes on the larger dioceses. This was a rational effort on the part of the king to divert some of the disproportionate wealth of the Church to the secular coffers. He succeeded in intimidating most of the bishops into paying a third of their revenues to the treasury, but the bishop of Tours, Saint Martin's city, refused: "If you have made up your mind to seize what belongs to God, then the Lord will soon take your kingdom away from you." After delivering this ultimatum the bishop stalked off without saying goodbye, leaving the king trembling. Lothair had seen what happened to those who defied ecclesiastic predictions and, in expectation of literal and immediate punishment, he sent messengers laden with gifts after the bishop. With deep apologies for his thoughtless importunity, Lothair absolved Tours forever (during his lifetime) of tax liability.

Both for magnanimous and practical reasons Radegund's immaculacy was assured. Though she had been an inflexibly chaste wife, she was not emotionally frigid. The place of a husband and family in her heart was taken by her nuns and her dependents, the wretched poor of the city. In her convent she followed a sensible and compassionate rule modeled on that of Saint Honoratus, the sweet-tempered founder of Lérins: it made allowance for personal weaknesses and specifically warned against excessive asceticism. Radegund was warm-hearted and indulgent to a fault. Her convent, Holy Cross (so named when in 569, twelve years after its founding, the Byzantine emperor Justin II, sent Radegund a piece of the true Cross), was large, comfortable, even elegant, with gardens, baths and other luxuries more suitable to a wealthy villa than a retreat for unworldly penitents. Two hundred young women took the veil on the same day as their queen, most of them from highborn Gallo-Roman families, with a few royal Frankish ladies. They occupied their lives of renunciation with sewing, spinning, embroidery, reading and copying of manuscripts: a quiet, pleasant and leisurely existence out of reach of importunate husbands and unruly sons.

Radegund herself took no advantage of the comforts with which she surrounded her wellborn followers. She even eschewed the position of abbess, conferring this on Agnes, a young protegée she had trained; and herself never rose higher than a plain sister. Her convent life was characterized by rigorous, often degrading austerities, a repellent catalog undoubtedly exaggerated by her contemporary biographer—the enumeration of morbid detail was held to enhance the holiness of the subject. Her life was one of sleeping in ashes, living on vegetables, bread and water, and of menial drudgery: she cleaned the nuns' shoes, lit the fires, washed the dishes, even scrubbed the church floor with the skirt of her white habit. In self-chastisement she wore a hair shirt, branded her skin with a heated metal cross, carried iron chains and burned herself with live coals. One day a week the diseased and derelict of Poitiers were allowed within the convent walls. Radegund bathed each one herself, from louse-infested head to horny feet, dressed their sores and ulcers, was even known to clasp a leprous woman in her arms. Then she gave them fresh clothing and fed them the epicurean convent food she refused for herself. The excessive ministrations over, the sufferers were left to themselves, when they were wont to indulge in the rowdy behavior endemic to all classes in the unrestrained society of that day.

An occasional sister followed the mistress's lead, sometimes to a hysterical extreme. One nun who had seen a vision asked permission of Abbess Agnes to become a permanent recluse. The request was granted, a cell was prepared and Radegund herself led the sister there by the hand, followed by all the nuns in procession, carrying lamps and singing psalms. The anchorite kissed each of them farewell, and entered her cell, which was then bricked up. "There she now passes her days," wrote Gregory of Tours, who approved, "in prayers and holy reading."

This extreme proceeding was an exception among the delicately nurtured lady nuns. Most of Radegund's associates were radically disinclined to aberrant self-renunciation. Even the mistress herself, stringently as she essayed to contradict it in her daily habits, could not shed all her cultivated background. She had been well educated in her girlhood at Athies, and in the convent she humored her studious turn of mind, studying and reading late into the nights. She specified that two hours in the morning be devoted to the humane letters, and often, when the sisters were gathered together at meals or sedentary tasks, one was chosen to read aloud—tales of the miracle-filled lives of saints, devotional texts and similar elevating if unsophisticated contemporary literature. Radegund was usually present at these sessions, and inaugurated discussions among the sisters; she questioned them gently as to the meaning of what they had heard, and explained passages which, even in this simpleminded fare, were beyond the limited erudition of her charges.

The easeful life of Holy Cross included masculine company. For all her unforgiving austerity with herself, Radegund's mind hungered for more provocative challenge than the artless literature and innocent, insipid conversation of the convent's leisure hours. Her foundation was about thirty years old when the poet-priest Venantius Fortunatus came into her life and practically moved into her convent. The warm and reciprocal friendship of these two, though it remained on an intellectual plane, went beyond the purely spiritual intercourse of a nun and a priest. Fortunatus was a cultured, witty and fairly learned cosmopolitan, and he had a manner of graceful ease with the great of his world, whom he pleased with skillful, vivacious and exaggerated panegyric verse in the late Imperial style. He must also have been authentically pious, otherwise Radegund could not have accepted him so unreservedly, nor would he have been respected by so estimable a churchman as Bishop Gregory of Tours. And a deeply religious fount within him is revealed in his hymns which, unlike his fulsome encomiums, are strong, simple expressions of spiritual fervor. Two of them, "Vexilla Regis" and "Pange Lingua" (both still sung in the Catholic service), were probably composed on the occasion of the translation of the relic of the Cross to Radegund's convent.

Venantius Fortunatus was born about 530 in Treviso, Italy, and he was educated at Ravenna, the last Roman capital in the West. Although the city had been taken over as the residence of the Ostrogothic kings of Italy, it retained its Byzantine connections and its reputation as one of the few remaining seats of higher Roman education in the West. When Fortunatus studied there, Ravenna was again, temporarily, part of the empire, having been retaken by Justinian in 539. But Italy was swampy territory for a rather timid scholar, and in 564 the imminent threat of invasion by the Lombards drove Fortunatus across the Alps into Gaul. Ostensibly he went to give thanks to Saint Martin for a miracle cure. The poet's vision had been failing, probably from the strain of over-study, and he had applied to his eyes oil taken from a lamp burning before the altar of the Gallic saint in a Ravenna church. The results were happy, and Fortunatus undertook to thank the saint in person at Tours.

Crossing the Alps from northeastern Italy in 566, he entered Gaul near Metz, in Austrasia, then under the rule of Lothair's son Sigibert.

The Italian refugee was just in time for the king's wedding to the
Spanish princess Brunhild, and Fortunatus celebrated the event with
a long nuptial poem in Latin, probably incomprehensible to all the
company but the bluestocking bride. This feat gained Fortunatus the
patronage of Sigibert and his queen, with consequent entry to many
of the royal and aristocratic houses of Gaul.

After paying his respects at Saint Martin's shrine at Tours, and
incidentally gaining the generous and enduring friendship of Bishop
Gregory, Fortunatus went in 567 to Poitiers at the invitation of
Radegund. There, though he traveled widely, he put down roots for
the rest of his life. He did not actually live at Holy Cross, but he spent
much time there and was the advisor to the founder and her abbess,
Agnes, for twenty years, until Radegund's death. Radegund was near
fifty when Fortunatus came, and he habitually addressed her with
respectful reverence as "Mother." The attractive abbess, however, was
nearer the age of the poet, then in his thirties and not yet in orders.
The poems he addressed to her come close to an emotion more earthy
than spiritual. He was a self-confessed *bon vivant*: he loved good food,
wine, flowers and fruits, and he responded with sensuous and agile
grace to the favors bestowed on him by his appreciative lady friends.

His poetry on the subject of their gifts to one another reveals a
frankly hedonistic nature:

> From one of you
>   I receive delicacies
> from the other
>   nourishing fruits
> One of you surprises me with eggs
> the other gives me plums.
> White gifts
>   then little black gifts
>   are together proffered.
> I wish my stomach would be peaceful!
>   the food churns so . . .
> You ordered me fed two eggs in the evening
> I tell you the truth!
> I, myself!, ate four.

He is equally candid about his enjoyment and consequent rue after
too much wine:

Between many-colored delights and blended tastes
while I drowsed
> I ate
> I opened my mouth
> I closed my eyes, again
> and chewed
>> —dreaming of all the dainty dishes.

I have a confused head . . .
Believe me!
> Dear Ones
I'm not up to speaking spontaneously
nor am I able to write
neither to scribble a verse with a pen
(An inebriated muse produces a wavering hand . . .
This very table seems to swim!)

Mother and Sister
as I am able
> I'll produce a few pleasant verses
Although sleep pulls with a thousand reins
> Love compels me to write this poem.

It is not clear to which of his two friends the following little love letter was penned:

> If the breezy rain
>> would not prevent me
> without your knowledge
> your lover would visit you.
> I do not wish an hour's absence
> When I see light
> there is my love!

But the next one is unmistakably addressed to Radegund, who had absented herself for the Lenten days in one of her spells of self-immolation:

> You, the life of your sisters
> your mind in God
> you ignite your body
>> to nourish your soul
>> tending your annual vows

today
     have incarcerated yourself . . .

You forget time
     as if you were not desired by a lover
(Momentarily
     as I behold you
          I fantasize
          myself
          in that role)

But
     Let us marry your vow
and here
     in the spirit
          I accompany you
               in your cell
               in which it is forbidden to go.[5]

This voluptuous soul evidently had an inverse appeal to the chaste queen who had abdicated the pleasures that were her birthright. She must have loved the sensuous little poems and the worldly admirer who dedicated them to her. There must have been many hours of sophisticated conversation to tinge her ethereal life with earthly reality. The love, of course, was idealized: Fortunatus had become a dedicated priest. But in sixth-century Europe the Church and the clergy were inescapably tainted with the self-serving materialism which permeated all spheres of life; and this confessed sybarite was probably not the right man to be chaplain and adviser to the convent. The institution, with its aristocratic constituency, had had a worldly cast from its founding, and the too-fleshly priest exerted a persuasive influence in the same direction. Fortunatus's was not basically a good character: he had come, a needy scholar steeped in the postimperial decadence of Ravenna, to live by his wits among wealthy arrivistes. His attractive personality and dexterous wit served him well: singing for his supper (including sycophantic songs in honor of some despicable rogues), he gained the flattered friendship of the highest of the land, from bishops and counts to kings and queens.

However supple his morals, Fortunatus was useful to Radegund for the very breadth of his acquaintance. After the death of Radegund's ex-husband, Lothair, the convent no longer enjoyed freehanded royal protection. Its stability was endangered by the convulsive bickering of Lothair's sons, jealously intriguing with and against one another. Poitiers came several times under different rule, and the atmosphere of the city was perennially nervous. Its bishop, a warm friend of Radegund, had died, and the new bishop was indifferent, on occasion openly inimical. Radegund appealed to Sigibert, Lothair's son, now king of Austrasia. With the active help of Fortunatus, a court favorite, Holy Cross was put under Sigibert's direct protection.

Radegund outlived her husband by twenty-six years. In 587 she died. Her embalmed body, displayed in an open coffin, was carried to its resting place past the walls of the convent lined with weeping nuns whose lamentations so affected the chanting clergy who carried the bier that they could hardly sing the words of the antiphons. She was sainted soon after her death.

Her body still lies in the beautiful part-Romanesque, part-Angevin Gothic church that was erected over the original sixth-century chapel of the nuns' burial ground. The graceful Romanesque choir has fat columns brightly decorated with foliage, Bible stories and secular imagery. Beneath it is a small, dark, round-arched crypt, from its style a vestige of Radegund's original chapel. In its entry stands a florid seventeenth-century stone statue of the saint (given by Anne of Austria in thanksgiving when her prayers for her sick son, the future Louis XIV, were answered). Almost filling the crypt is Radegund's bier, its stone slabs simply decorated with abstract sixth-century curlicues. Radegund's spirit holds court almost unattended in her great dark crumbling church. Most of the time the church is closed to the public (Poitiers had three other magnificent churches, and there is evidently not enough money to keep Saint Radegund's sanctuary in repair). The rare times it is opened for a service attendance is limited to a few elderly ladies of the parish. Holy Cross convent itself has disappeared. On its site now rises an airy modern museum housing, as well as several *beaux-arts* rooms, a small but fine collection of Celtic, Roman and Merovingian artifacts, including Radegund's oaken reading desk.

After Radegund's death it became apparent that there was much more amiss with the convent than was caused by political ferment outside it. Even during the saint's lifetime there were signs of erosion within the walls. Agnes seems to have been a weak abbess, powerless to handle her imperious charges; and the self-indulgent Fortunatus, as the convent's adviser, was not the man to care about the enforcement of even reasonable discipline among ladies equally accustomed to a soft life. After the death of the founder, convent morale began to disintegrate and rebellion sprouted. No one knows what became of Abbess Agnes, whose name disappears from the historians' records. Her place was taken by a lady named Leubovera who, according to the complainants, was no lady. Her chief flaw, apparently, was that she had low manners, not being of an aristocratic family. The dissidents were led by two Merovingian princesses: Clotild, daughter of Charibert, a son of Lothair, and her cousin, Basina, daughter of Chilperic, another of Lothair's sons. These royal women were female counterparts of their arbitrary brothers and fathers, and neither was a willing nun. (Basina had been forced into the convent by the machinations of her father's vindictive wife, Fredegund, a verifiable fairytale stepmother; this queen wanted no female competition around her.) The two wayward princesses walked out of the convent at the head of forty rebellious nuns, and their revolt, which included physical assaults on the convent's personnel, ran a disorderly course for an incredible two years. At the end the protesters finally succeeded in having Abbess Leubovera brought to trial. The charges were grotesque: the abbess had a man in the nunnery, whom she dressed in women's clothing and kept for her own pleasure. She had a number of other men castrated, to surround herself with eunuchs like a Byzantine queen. She played backgammon; held engagement parties in the nunnery; had a dress made for her niece out of an altar-cloth; had a necklace fashioned from the gold leaf of the same altar-cloth; provided wretched food and inadequate clothing for the sisters; and allowed other people (servants) to use their bathroom. All these allegations were satisfactorily refuted (the abbess's defense for playing backgammon was that the sainted Radegund, though she played no games, saw no canonical reason against the sisters so innocently entertaining themselves). Except for some minor indiscretions Leubovera was completely exonerated, and reinstated as abbess, with the tactful hint that she mend her plebeian manners so that her snobbish charges should find nothing to criticize. Clotild, the ringleader, was expelled, no doubt to her relief, and went back to secular life, her future secured with the gift of a large estate from one of her king-uncles. There was no place for Basina in her father's household, so she asked to be allowed to return to the convent, claiming that she was repentant. Her plea was granted, provided that she observe the Rule and refrain from sniping at her abbess.

Fortunatus does not appear at all in this disgraceful narrative; Radegund is in her tomb; and Agnes, as noted, has vanished. But there is no doubt that the personalities of these three were at the root of the disorder. At one pole was the old epicure with his late-empire horizon, who lived and practiced a humanism almost pagan; and good-natured, ineffective Abbess Agnes. At the opposite pole was Radegund, so otherworldly that she was beyond imitation even by the most pious of sisters. Against this combination even the very mild rule of Holy Cross was ineffectual.

The disorientation of this one convent, though an extreme case, is a microcosm of the state of the Gallic Church in the sixth century. Abbots and bishops, forced to deal with headstrong masters, were inevitably touched by their barbarism, and the Church existed in a state of uneasy compromise. The grossest materialism warred with withdrawn, often neurotic asceticism, and there seemed no room for the balanced monastic spirituality of an earlier age. The distortion was counteracted only once in our period, by the strong, pure genius of an Irish missionary-abbot, Columbanus (whom we shall meet in a later chapter), who refused to compromise.

The women in the Holy Cross case suffered: Agnes sank out of view, probably disgraced, and Leubovera's position, at the mercy of her capricious wards, remained precarious. But Fortunatus came out of it with a halo: five years before his death in 610 he was made bishop of Poitiers, and he is now a saint in the Catholic calendar.

In 558, after the death of the last of his brothers, Lothair became king of all the Franks, as well as overlord of several adjoining realms which acknowledged Frankish suzerainty. Greater Gaul was not only formidably big, its components were ruled by leaders whose ferocious liveliness required unceasing military attention. Lothair never shirked martial responsibility, and he held his bulky empire together by force until his death three years later. In the years of the first three generations of Merovingian kings, kingship had a different connotation than it would develop in the early Middle Ages. In feudal times the monarchy would be but the top of a pyramid of powerful local liege lords, who pledged allegiance and generally ran things their own way. In Lothair's day the elective kingship of the tribal era had hardened into a hereditary monarchy. But he still, as in tribal times, ruled over a population of freemen none of whom was technically superior to any other except at the king's direct pleasure. All were equally subject to his supreme power—which he could maintain only by virtue of his combat virtuosity and his masterful personality. This had been a workable concept when the Germans were a group of seminomadic autonomous tribes hunting and raiding for a living, tending sheep in slack times, and each acknowledging only its immediate war leader. It had begun to be unfeasible when Clovis, expanding the old tribal life-style, agglomerated his relatives' discrete chiefdoms into one great supertribe. Clovis's sovereignty was made even more unwieldy by the ramification of a subject population, much larger than that of the conquering Franks, of Gallo-Romans used to the skills and complexities of imperial bureaucracy.

But Clovis had found a way of handling his cumbrous domain. When he became a Catholic Christian he received the enthusiastic approval of those most influential Gallo-Romans, the higher clergy. Clovis, who had respect for the tradition of the empire, listened readily to the advice of its heirs. His heirs, in turn, found the bishops indispensable. With the expert and educated cooperation of their bishops the Merovingian kings learned how to administer their realms in the Roman style, through the law. This enhanced the power of the king by giving him a legal method of expressing his wishes. It also lifted him out of the reach of justice, for the Salic law provided no limits to royal prerogative. Both the heritage of imperial Rome and the hierarchy of the Church favored the absolute ruler. The early Merovingian kings, habituated by conquest to domineering, took easily to the counsel of their respected subjects, the higher clergy. Unchecked power in the hands of men who, to begin with, had a minimum of control over their passions could have been disastrous. The Frankish kings, as we have seen, gave way too easily to the misuse of their prerogative—but generally only in their dealings with each other. As leaders of men—and they were first of all warrior-kings—they knew the natural limits of authority. Clovis and his sons and his grandsons knew how vital it was to keep the loyalty of their subjects. They made the Merovingian kingship so successful that the dynasty would retain the unquestioning devotion of the mass of people long after it had lost all effectiveness.

For the last three years of his life Lothair was virtual emperor in Frankish Gaul, a territory by now much larger than old Roman Gaul.

But there still remained a Roman Empire in the East, and for thirty-four of Lothair's fifty-year reign its ruler was Justinian. The complex personality of this last Roman conqueror in western Europe, his dramatic accomplishments and the dubious means he employed to realize them, were the subjects of historians' arguments during his lifetime, and are still debated today. Justinian was the first truly Byzantine emperor: he transformed the classical Greek and Roman ideals into the Greco-Roman, or Byzantine spirit. We cannot here discuss his influence on culture, on the law and on the Church, but will confine our account to his impact on the Europe of the Merovingians.

In the sixth century Europe was divided between the Roman Empire and the Teutonic kingdoms, the Empire retaining most of the southeast and the Germans the northwest. Between these spheres was Italy, actually the kingdom of the Ostrogoths but still ostensibly under the aegis of the Roman emperor. Italy would be the last battleground between the old order and the new.

Among the convolutions of Justinian's labyrinthine character was his penchant, while destroying the old ways (for instance, he closed the philosophy schools of Athens, last sanctuaries of the Greek classical tradition), for reestablishing the past glory of the empire with its center at Rome. His general, Belisarius, was to be the hero of this enterprise. Belisarius had saved Justinian's throne for him by crushing a rebellion in Constantinople, and had gone on to retake Africa from the Vandals in 534. The following year he easily conquered Sicily in the first step toward the mastery of Italy.

For the next step, the penetration of the peninsula itself, Justinian needed the support, or at least the neutrality, of the Merovingian kings on Italy's northern edge. He spent a large sum of money for their promise of active help. But the Ostrogothic king of Italy, Witigis, in desperate self-defense, offered the Franks more. His predecessor, Theodoric the Great, it may be remembered, had taken over Provence in 507. Now, twenty-nine years later, in 536, the heir of Theodoric of Italy gave up this land, along with a sizable gift of cash, to the heirs of Clovis. The rich, traditionally Roman cities of Provence, including the vital Mediterranean ports of Nice and Marseilles, were at last irretrievably Frankish. The realm was divided between Clovis's surviving sons, Childebert and Lothair, and one grandson, Theudebert, son of Clovis's eldest.

Witigis thus bought neutrality from his dangerous neighbors.

Justinian, recognizing the strength of his enemy's bargain, accepted the facts: he acknowledged the supremacy of the Merovingian dynasty in all of Gaul, formally legalizing a situation which had existed empirically since long before he was born. Frankish Gaul was now officially an independent kingdom. Among other symbols of authority its king was allowed to mint his own gold coins. Instead of bearing the head of the emperor, like the coins of all Rome's satellites, Frankish coins now displayed that of Theudebert, Clovis's oldest grandson.

Though Witigis the Ostrogoth thought he had secured immunity, the Franks were treacherous as well as greedy. Theudebert easily ignored a promise which stood in the way of his ambition. Having fallen heir to a large part of Provence, he did not see why he should not append some of Italy as well. The same year, 536, that Witigis ceded his Gallic territories, the Frankish king led his army south over the Alps into the Italian plain. They came on the rear of Witigis's army, drawn up in battle array against the Byzantine forces. The Ostrogoths thought a friendly army was behind them, and they were cut to pieces by the axes of the falsehearted ally—who began by slaughtering all their women and children and throwing their bodies in the river. The Byzantine troops, cheered by the Franks' apparent shift of alignment, were dealt with in the same fashion, and Theudebert became master of most of northern Italy. But it turned out that he was master of nothing. In their march south his Franks had devastated the countryside. They bogged down in the marshes of Venetia, overcome by starvation and dysentery; there a third of them died. Painfully the remainder made its way north and straggled back through the Alps. Italy, for the moment, was safe from the Franks.

Justinian's ephemeral dream of a restored Rome brought financial and manpower woes which drastically weakened the empire. It cost Italy even dearer. For Justinian succeeded: his generals, first Belisarius and later Narses, overthrew the kingdom of the Ostrogoths. The kings who had succeeded the great Theodoric had been too weak to maintain their hold over a hostile population. But the Roman generals could not consolidate their military victories. They received no support from war-impoverished Constantinople, and their emperor, unaccountably fickle, lost his enthusiasm for the Italian project.

The campaigns had exhausted and demoralized the country. Italy was dangerously weakened by plague and the destruction of war:

agricultural lands, abandoned, were reverting to wilderness; landed proprietors, taxed beyond endurance, had sunk into the condition of serfs. The country people were starving: corpses were found with their emaciated fingers in the soil where they had died trying to dig up blades of grass; one woman, offering lodging to the homeless, had killed and eaten seventeen of her guests before the eighteenth caught her almost in the act.

The country was open to the invasion of the Lombards, a Teutonic people originally from the lower basin of the Elbe, who had moved into southern Austria and Pannonia, just over the Rhaetian Alps from Italy. Justinian had bribed the Lombards with land and money to help him against the Ostrogoths in his reconquest of Italy; thus encouraged, they came to stay. They were tough and impertinent allies: they would never, like the Ostrogoths whom they replaced, bow to the emperor far away over the sea, nor pay polite court to his exarch in Ravenna. Their leader, King Alboin, though slightly Christianized (his people had been converted to the Arian heresy late in the fifth century), was at heart an unregenerate barbarian—he was later murdered by his wife, whose father's skull he used as his drinking cup.

Taking advantage of the weakness of the country the Lombards proceeded from the status of allies to that of conquerors. In 568 they overran the peninsula. A few towns managed to buy exemption: Rome, Ravenna and other ports with access to help from across the Adriatic. But Rome, which Justinian had dreamed of revitalizing as the center of the Western Empire, was reduced to the rank of a provincial town, its buildings destroyed, its populace impoverished. The Church, with the shadow of the ancient authority behind it, was the only symbol left of imperial Rome; and its bishop, the Pope, was the city's only recourse for leadership and protection.

Some years after the Lombard invasion, in 590, Gregory I, the Great, became pope, and he set out to regenerate Rome by acting as her advocate with the Arian conqueror. The Catholic Church in Italy had great temporal wealth through estates inherited from its aristocratic episcopal families. Gregory drew freely on these riches to buy immunity for Rome from the depredations of Italy's new masters. Out of the ruin of old Rome he began to build the Eternal City. Starting with his work, the Roman Empire in Europe would be replaced by the spiritual empire—which came to be temporal as well— whose reigning seigneur was the bishop of Rome.

As for the Ostrogoths, with the defeat and dethronement of their leader and the destruction of their army, they passed out of Italian history, in fact out of history altogether. And Justinian's western conquests were revealed as the chimera they had been from their inception: Italy had suffered too much to be of any material value to his empire. Further, it was obvious that, for all the grandeur of Justinian's concept of the re-creation of the Western Empire, the phantom unity could never be maintained. The young, importunate kingdoms of Europe could no longer be relegated to the status of subservient allies, nor could their leaders be bought off or eliminated. Western Europe was irrevocably dissociated from the Roman Empire. For the remaining nine hundred years of its existence that empire was limited to the boundaries of Byzantium.

It had taken Belisarius and Narses nineteen years, from 535 to 554, to complete the reconquest of Italy. Less than fifteen years later Rome had once more, and finally, lost her western empire. By this time, 568, the main actors in the Italian wars were dead: Justinian had died that same year, Belisarius in 565, Witigis long before the war was over, in 542. The actors in the wings, the Merovingian brothers, the sons of Clovis, and their nephew, were dead, too. An entire new cast had come on the stage, to engage in the long, continuing exercise of battle, conquest, intrigue and murder that was the melodrama of the birth of Europe.

Lothair was the last of Clovis's sons to die. In 561, aged seventy-seven, he succumbed to a fever after an intemperate bout of hunting. Combative to the end, his last words were an enraged cry against the God who had dared to lay low the great king. His remaining four sons bore his body to the church of Saint Médard at Soissons. His sarcophagus is still there, its resting place a crypt open to the rain and wind and the coming and going of nesting birds.

Perhaps he deserves to be forgotten. The sons of Clovis were a rough lot, grossly self-indulgent, brutal with one another, deceitful, unendingly contentious. The spirit of their barbarian forefathers was still strong in them: the mentality of a race in whom cunning, courage and cruelty mingled, to whom military prowess and the unrestrained mastery of conquest were more compelling than the recognition of a higher moral power. Christianity had made small mark on them, and in their Gaul the enlightenment of classical Greece and Rome slid further into oblivion.

But they were there, and Rome was not; and in a roughhewn manner they began to organize their land into a new shape—the shape that would be France. For they were kings under the law, no longer under the rule of the battle axe. However they might strike at one another they were the ultimate and only guardians of the peace and welfare of their people. They were absolute rulers but they were also, in the mores of their era, legitimate rulers.

CHAPTER SIX

GREGORY'S KINGS

The tempers and motives of Clovis's sons can be inferred only from their deeds, as recorded by historians who wrote after they died. As a result they are monochromatic figures both greater and lesser than real life. For the sons of Lothair we no longer have to read between the lines. These are the kings who reigned in the lifetime of Gregory of Tours, and they are the chief subjects of his spirited, opinionated *History of the Franks*.[1] Gregory's people are earthborn: he knew them well and he saw them with a clear eye. We hear them speak and we see them act, meanly or honorably but always humanly. We know all about these passionate, imperfect kings and queens, backsliding bishops, scoundrelly counts, ambitious and hardhearted royal courtesans—everything except, unfortunately, what they looked like.

Lothair left his kingdom jointly to his four sons: Charibert, Sigibert, Guntram, and Chilperic. They started quarreling as soon as they had finished laying their father in his grave at Soissons.

At the time of their accession Frankish Gaul was divided into five territories ethnically and historically distinct; but the boundaries of these lands shifted constantly in tune with the victories and defeats of the squabbling brothers. The two kingdoms of Neustria in the northwest and Austrasia in the northeast were predominantly Frankish: they constituted Francia, the heart of the Merovingian empire. Aquitania and Provence, in the center and south, were the ancient domains of the empire, and the majority of their populations were

Gallo-Roman. Burgundy, on the east, was sui generis: mainly Germanic but not Frankish, it was a nearly autonomous kingdom.

The fighting started before there was time to divide the kingdoms reasonably. The provoker was Chilperic, the evil genius of Gregory's tale. Chilperic was the most grasping and ill-intentioned of the four, yet at the same time the most gifted and progressive. He was the half brother of the other three surviving sons of Lothair* and he disliked them all. Either he had a bad heredity or he was jealous, for he never ceased fighting them openly or undermining them secretly. Immediately following Lothair's death this presumptuous prince attached his father's treasury and marched into Paris, intending to seize its throne. He was checked at once by his irritated brothers; all four of them then sat down and fairly apportioned their inheritance. Charibert I became king of the Paris-Sens area, the central plain that had been the Roman realm of Syagrius. Sigibert I received the kingdom of Metz (Austrasia). Guntram became king of Burgundy and Chilperic I received Soissons (Neustria). The southern provinces were arbitrarily partitioned among the four kings, who bickered throughout their reigns over the sovereignty of these rich, hard-to-reach territories.

The chief protagonists of the family conflict were Sigibert of Austrasia and Chilperic of Neustria. Their feud was more than a personality clash: its fundamental cause was the tension between the two kingdoms of Francia. In general characteristics the regions were similar, both being primarily Teutonic. Yet they had disparities distinct enough to generate spontaneous and bitter rivalry. Austrasia was the least civilized part of Frankish Gaul, and at the same time the most robust and powerful. Its most conspicuous quality was its overriding Germanness: there dwelt most of the Frankish families that were beginning to rise to power in this century, and the Teutonic language and mores were paramount. In Neustria, the northwest sector, Latin language and culture had penetrated to a greater degree and there was some dichotomy of perspective. At the beginning of the reigns of Lothair's sons the differences between the two kingdoms were not as pronounced as they would become. The contention appeared to contemporaries to be no more than the cat-and-dog rivalry of the brothers, and the later unforgiving vendetta of their queens, Brunhild and Fredegund. No one foresaw that this early

---

*As the son of Arnegund, sister of Lothair's first wife, Ingund, who bore the other three, he was also their first cousin.

unpleasantness would develop into the focal struggle that would result in the emergence of the forefathers of Charlemagne and the pattern of France to come.

The rest of Frankish Gaul was peripherally involved in the interminable northern battle. The subject peoples of Aquitaine and Provence did not actively join the conflict, nor did they fight one another. But their fealties shifted from one suzerainty to another of their fractious Frankish masters, and their lands suffered exceedingly from royal rapacity. Burgundy remained outside much of the fraternal quarreling. Its king, Guntram, called by Gregory "good king Guntram," seemed to have caught some of the cheerful spirit of the Burgundian people. He was less feral than his brothers, even to the point of being cowardly, and he sometimes assumed the thankless role of peacemaker among them. Nevertheless he was recognizably a Merovingian: the latent barbarism surfaced in an occasional act of irrational cruelty.

The brothers assumed their proper reigns in 561, and by 562 they were fighting again. Sigibert had to defend his eastern border against the Avars,* who had spilled over the limits of their alarming empire in eastern Europe, to invade Thuringia and threaten Francia. While Sigibert's attention was focused eastward his brother Chilperic attacked Rheims, his second city, and captured some other Austrasian towns. Sigibert, momentarily successful against the Avars, turned on his brother and captured Chilperic's own capital of Soissons, taking his son, Theudebert, captive. He kept the young man prisoner for a year, then released him on the promise that he would never again fight against his uncle—a promise lightly forgotten.

After the initial spat between Chilperic and Sigibert the brothers were briefly unbelligerent with one another, being preoccupied with the affairs of their kingdoms. It was with their marriages that disturbances arose again. The history of the next thirty years is dominated by their women, Queen Brunhild and Queen Fredegund.

The marital affairs of the other brothers, Charibert and Guntram, although disorderly were not historically crucial. Charibert, king of

*The Avars were an Asiatic people, probably a race of Turks, called "Huns" by contemporary historians. Although they had no known relation to the fifth-century Huns of Attila, they caused a similar paralysis in their enemies: they were credited with winning battles by magic, making phantom figures dance before the eyes of the Frankish soldiers.

Paris and Sens, has but a short space in this narrative, because he died six years after he succeeded to his throne. His brief career was unrelievedly bad, according to the chronicler. Some of his badness had to do with his dislike of the clergy, which may explain Gregory's condemnation of him. In a dispute over the bishopric in the city of Saintes he went so far as to expel a priest who had come to him as an intermediary, sending him off in a car filled with thorns.

Charibert pursued a disreputable marital career. He had a legitimate and respectable wife named Ingoberg, but he was attracted to two of her servants, Marcovefa and Merofled, daughters of a laborer. Ingoberg tried to recover her husband's attentions by arousing his disdain for these lowborn girls: she put their father visibly to work preparing wool for the royal household. Charibert was so angry at her meddling that he dismissed her and married Merofled. He soon tired of his new wife and put her aside, taking as mistress, and later marrying, the daughter of one of his shepherds, a young woman named Theudechild. He then turned to the other servant girl, Marcovefa, who in the meantime had taken the veil. Charibert, flouting the Church, married her nevertheless, and they were both excommunicated. "She was struck by the judgment of God, and died," wrote Gregory. Shortly afterwards, in 567, King Charibert himself died. The remaining widow, Theudechild, the shepherd's daughter, whose upward mobility knew no bounds of modesty, offered her hand and most of her late husband's treasure to King Guntram of Burgundy. Her overture was agreeably received, but when she arrived at his court she found that it was her treasure and not her person that was in favor. Guntram sequestered the treasure "that it should not remain in the control of this woman who was unworthy of my brother's bed," and sent her to a nunnery at Arles. She revolted at the hard life of fasts and vigils, and planned to run away, hoping to ally herself with a Spanish Goth who was willing to accept her with what wealth remained to her. The abbess caught her at the gates with all her baggage, had her mercilessly beaten and locked her up in her cell. "There she remained until her dying day," wrote Gregory with relish, "suffering awful anguish."

King Guntram of Burgundy also had an undiscerning taste in women. He had a mistress who bore him a son. Later he married a woman named Marcatrude who killed this boy with a poisoned drink in order to ensure the birthright of her own son. Soon after this

Marcatrude's little boy died "by the judgment of God," and King Guntram thought it advisable to dismiss her. He then married a dreadful woman named Austrechild, daughter of a servant. Some years later, when she was dying of dysentery, she expressed the last wish that others might die with her so that the lamentation at her funeral would be magnified. Those she chose were her two doctors, whose skill had failed to cure her of that usually fatal illness. " 'I beg you,' " she said to her husband, " 'that you will cut their throats the moment that my eyes have closed in death. They must not be permitted to glory in my dying. When my friends grieve for me, let their friends grieve for them too.' " Cowardly Guntram did not dare contravene his wife's dying wish, and he ordered the execution of the innocent doctors. This was not a period favorable for doctors, who were usually regarded either as quacks or sorcerers. The bones of saints, threads from their garments, oil from their altar lamps, dust from their biers, were considered more trustworthy remedies for all types of suffering than the tainted hands of Satan-trained scientists. So far had the curiosity for knowledge diminished from the perspective of Hippocrates.

The third brother, Sigibert, appears to have had a more upright character than the others. He was an able warrior, an intelligent ruler and, an anomaly in those days, a faithful husband. Though he was overfond of battle, a Frankish king had little choice in those years if he wanted to keep his boundaries intact than to violate the boundaries of his equally rapacious brother kings.

Now Sigibert, observing the degrading untidiness of his brothers' marital affairs, decided to make a careful choice. The king of Spain had two beautiful and accomplished daughters, Brunhild and Galswinth. Visigothic Spain in this century was politically weak, ruled by a succession of impotent kings at the mercy of their nobles and hated by the Catholic majority because of their tyrannical Arianism. But this same majority, Roman by birth and tradition, made Spain the most civilized of the European kingdoms. Arian or not, its rulers were well educated as well as wealthy, and their daughters were popular choices among the surrounding royal houses. Sigibert sent messengers laden with gifts to the Spanish court to ask for the hand of Brunhild. The Frankish offer was accepted promptly: the king of Spain was glad to have the aid of this Merovingian brother in defense against the acquisitiveness of the other three. As king of Austrasia, Gaul's most German sector, Sigibert did not covet the southern provinces, and his active friendship would be useful to the Spanish ruler.

Sigibert chose well. "This young woman," wrote Gregory, "was elegant in all that she did, lovely to look at, chaste and decorous in her behavior, wise in her generation and of good address." Graced with a large dowry the princess traveled to Metz where, in 566, she was married with great ceremony. Present at the wedding celebration was Radegund's priest-poet, Venantius Fortunatus, a recent refugee from troubled Italy. He took the opportunity to cultivate new friends by producing an encomium to the king and his bride.

Fortunatus praised, among other qualities, the monogamous passion of the bridegroom, "burnt by the torch of Cupid's bow" but, "by matrimonial law happy with one embrace, and faithful to a chaste marriage bed." He went on to laud the receptiveness of the bride: "the virgin swelling into flower, ready to please with her first nuptial joys, and not restrained by shyness." He added a lengthy peroration on the mature judgment of the Frankish king, his moderation in peace and triumph in war; and followed this with a flowery apotheosis of the Spanish princess: "brighter than the lights of jewels, a second Venus born," in whose face "lilies mix with roses." He continues, "Sapphire, clear diamond, crystals, emerald, jasper—all yield to the new jewel Spain has begotten."[2]

Fortunatus's honey-tongued panegyric, composed in Latin, in the polished late-Empire style of rhetorical verse the poet had learned in Ravenna, was directed to the delectation of the educated bride. Brunhild was skilled enough in Latin so that in later years she could correspond with Pope Gregory the Great. The rest of the audience, from the king downward, was illiterate. Even the clergy present at the wedding, with the exception of one or two educated Gallo-Roman bishops, had not the classical background to cope with Fortunatus's high-wrought verbosity. The arcane verse, however, ingratiated the author, as it was intended to do, with the royal household. It was a useful introduction to his successful career as the poet laureate, so to speak, of Francia.

Brunhild had been brought up in the Arian heresy professed by her Visigothic family, but she listened willingly to the reasoning of the Frankish bishops and duly adopted the Catholic creed. In later years she would harden into an autocratic backer of the clerical status quo in her adopted country, but in the promising early days the gesture seemed no more than a gracious submission to her husband's way of life.

Even discounting the elevated flourish of the poet and the bias of the bishop-historian in favor of an activist Catholic queen, the young Brunhild shines through the murk of sixth-century Gaul with a quality of humanity notoriously absent in most of her royal contemporaries. She was probably mentally superior to her coarse-grained warrior husband; clearly, also, she possessed an appealing femininity. But she was unfailingly loyal, devoting herself to his interests until his tragic early death. She was a wise mother: she saw to it that her son, Childebert, received as good an education as was possible in Teutonic Austrasia; more important, she fostered in him a high moral standard unconventional among the self-indulgent Merovingian princes. As the vicissitudes of a difficult life toughened and embittered her, Brunhild's attitude toward the younger generation changed. She would exert a malign influence over her grandsons. But it was the cruelty of events that transformed her. Even in the last years, when her attractive youth was gone and we see her only through the eyes of inimical historians, there are visible traces of nobility, wisdom, generosity, even human tenderness.

None of these sympathetic qualities are discernible in Brunhild's lifetime rival, Queen Fredegund of Neustria. Chilperic, the king of Neustria, who had started his reign with a gratuitous act of hostility to Sigibert, now appreciatively eyed the felicity as well as the wealth of his brother's new Spanish connection. Chilperic asked for and was granted the hand of Brunhild's sister, Galswinth, an equally cultivated and desirable princess.

But Chilperic had not, like Sigibert, kept himself chaste in preparation for the ideal marriage. He already had at least one wife, Audovera, who had borne him three sons and a daughter. Audovera had a maidservant named Fredegund, who early in the marriage captured the heart, mind and will of the king. Unfortunately we have no physical description of Fredegund, but the young handmaid must have had a magnetic charm, for she made willing slaves of nearly every man who came in contact with her—with the notable exception of Bishop Gregory, who openly detested her. Alluring as she clearly was, she was a woman of no conscience: vindictive, mercilessly ambitious and, from the start, faithless to her husband. Fredegund was of a base mentality, although she possessed a sharp cunning that developed into political brilliance. Her experience in the background management of her infatuated husband's kingdom while he was alive, and her assumption of power after his death, gave her competence as a ruler, in the areas where her personal status was not threatened.

Fredegund was homicidally jealous of the women in her paramour's household, starting with Queen Audovera, whose legitimate position she coveted. Audovera gave birth to a daughter when Chilperic was away, and Fredegund tricked her into having the child baptized without a godmother. Church law forbade that a mother herself should receive the baby from the font, but Audovera, an innocent queen, was not aware of the rule. When Chilperic returned, and was informed by Fredegund of his queen's lapse, he said to his mistress, "If I cannot sleep with her, I will sleep with you."[3] He used the excuse of his wife's guileless negligence to exile her to a nunnery, and married Fredegund at once. The new queen made sure of her tenure by having her ex-rival murdered within the walls of her convent retreat. In time Audovera's daughter, Basina, grew old enough to appear a threat, and, as we have seen, her stepmother caused her to be banished to Radegund's Convent of the Holy Cross at Poitiers. Basina was not murdered, but she was never invited back home again.

Fredegund even resented her own daughter Rigunth. This young woman, however, invited trouble, being as ill-natured as her mother, and equally promiscuous. Rigunth indulged in the practice of insulting her mother, an exercise as rational as poking a viper with her finger. The girl claimed that, having royal blood, she, not her mother, should be the mistress of her father's household, and that Fredegund "ought to revert to her original rank of serving-woman." Fredegund reacted by inviting her daughter to look into her personal treasure-chest to pick out whatever jewelry she fancied. Then she slammed the lid on the girl's neck and pressed down until Rigunth's eyes stood out of her head. The lethal undertaking failed, owing to the presence of mind of a servant, who screamed for help. Fredegund was never brought to account, either for this or for other more successful felonious enterprises.

Fredegund was faced with an authentic threat when Chilperic resolved to marry the Spanish princess, Galswinth, with the promise to her father that he would put away his other wives. Galswinth, like her sister Brunhild, was well endowed in all ways, and Chilperic, wrote the historian cynically, "loved her very dearly, for she had brought a large dowry with her." Still enthralled by Fredegund,

Chilperic had not the will to expel her outright, and she remained in the household, insulting the new queen until Galswinth complained to her husband. Chilperic was not sympathetic, and the wretched queen begged to be allowed to go home to Spain, offering to leave all her treasure behind. Chilperic pretended to soothe her; and allowed himself to be prodded by Fredegund into ordering a servant to garrot the queen in her sleep. He wept at Galswinth's death, and a few days later took Fredegund back into his bed.

The coldblooded murder intensified the enmity that already existed between Sigibert and Chilperic, by bringing their queens into the conflict. With the entry of these tenacious women into the family discord a feud was initiated that lasted thirty years. The two women were implacable in their hatred of one another and ruthless in their continuing vengeance. Through their machinations three generations of Merovingian kings ruled in unending strife and intrigue, to the extreme detriment of themselves and Frankish Gaul. It is tempting to lay the downfall of the Merovingian dynasty at the door of the unforgiving hostility of Brunhild and Fredegund. But the currents of history that were forming during the latter part of the sixth century would accelerate into a flood that would finally engulf the kings of the Dark Ages regardless of their personal merits or inadequacies.

The conspiracies, treacheries, shifting alliances and mutual animosity arising out of the quarrel of the two queens made the history of this period a labyrinth. The boundaries of the kingdoms of Gaul changed continuously during the next thirty years, but no outside expansion of any consequence occurred. Gaul had reached its maximum size under the Merovingians during the reigns of the previous generation. Clovis's grandsons were too busy plotting and defending themselves against one another to add to the already unwieldy empire.

Even in their own time the pointless civil wars were noted and deplored: "What are you doing?" wrote Gregory of Tours. "You have everything you want! Your homes are full of luxuries, there are vast supplies of wine, grain and oil in your store-houses, and in your treasuries the gold and silver are piled high. Only one thing is lacking: you cannot keep peace. The Franks ought, indeed, to have been warned by the sad fate of their earlier kings who, through their inability ever to agree with each other, were killed by their enemies.

Beware, then, of discord, beware of civil wars, which are destroying you and your people."

The historian's prophetic words were ignored by the self-absorbed rulers, who went heedless into disaster. Gregory was wrong in the motivation: it was not that the kings were uncommonly covetous, ambitious or even innately quarrelsome. They were goaded by two relentless women who had a power one does not usually associate with a masculine-dominated society.

An even more potent determinant in the creeping dissipation of Merovingian authority was the emergence of a new aristocracy, some of it responsible and public-spirited, much of it factious and self-seeking. The power of this class grew unchecked, though contemporary historians did not recognize it. They are outspoken against the unruly disposition of individual counts, but they attribute this to the general ungodliness rather than to a national drift.

The origins of the new aristocracy lay back in the time of Clovis. The conqueror had uprooted the remnants of the old Teutonic nobility in Gaul. Vanquishing in battle, or murdering one by one the chieftains who might inhibit his single control, he had destroyed the entire upper sector of the Frankish population of Gaul. When he was through there was no hereditary class of nobles: under Salic law all freemen of Frankish descent were equal. But already in his lifetime a new aristocracy began to grow. The big diversified kingdom was cumbersome for a king—even for several kings—to handle alone; and the need for delegation of authority engendered a new upper class. It developed from various sources. One was the class of Gallo-Roman gentry, owners of great hereditary estates, whose members had a tradition of public service. The superior education and ingrained authority of these patricians made them natural choices as aides to inexperienced, semibarbarian princes. The bishops, the judges and many of the local governors were drawn from this group: in addition to their inherited family wealth they now acquired political power. Alongside this secure and ancient aristocracy was the privileged class of antrustions, the king's closest companions and men-at-arms. These men had no hereditary rank and were not above the law, but they tended to arrogate special license to themselves, and as their prestige grew so did their power.

The king was further the source of another nascent nobility: the new landowners. The various conquests of the early Merovingians left them in possession of huge public lands. They rewarded their generals and their favorites with land, or gave land to bribe those whose loyalty needed insuring. Land gifts were specified, in some cases, only for a term of years, in others for a lifetime grant. But no condition of military service was attached, as in later feudal tenure, and the grant could be revoked by the king. This class of new landowners was both Frankish and Gallo-Roman.

Within two generations, then, after Clovis's excision of the hereditary German aristocracy, there had arisen a new power class in Gaul, based variously on landed wealth, kings' favor and official position. This was the tide that was rising, unnoticed, while Brunhild and Fredegund pursued their vendetta and their husbands followed their lead with battle and plunder.

The first phase of the feud ended with the death of Brunhild's husband, King Sigibert of Austrasia. The events which led up to this theatrical finale display the appalling blend of perfidy and violence that distinguished most of the contests of these kings. One wonders, not for the first time, what qualities the Merovingians possessed that enabled them to retain for so many generations the unquestioning loyalty of the majority of the population.

In 573 Chilperic, spurred by Fredegund, went to war against Sigibert, aiming to bite off a piece of Austrasia. Sigibert, with the ready support of Brunhild, responded with spirit. In preparation for the contest Fredegund, who never scrupled to use her sex as a tool, did her part by ingratiating herself with the king of Burgundy. Guntram was enchanted by his sister-in-law (whom he would later denominate as "that enemy of God and man") and promised to help his brother Chilperic in the campaign against Sigibert. Fredegund could bewitch Guntram but she couldn't keep him loyal. He would change his allegiance as soon as it seemed expedient to do so.

With the Burgundians, he thought, behind him, Chilperic sent his son Theudebert to the western part of Sigibert's realm, to invest the cities of Tours and Poitiers. (Theudebert was the young man whom Sigibert had pardoned in an earlier rift, on the assurance that he would never again make war on his uncle.) Theudebert not only captured the two cities, but his soldiers, after desolating the surrounding countryside, burned churches, stole their holy vessels, killed clergymen, leveled the monasteries of men and "disported themselves at those of girls."[4]

His father, Chilperic, meanwhile, stormed through the country around Rheims, Sigibert's second capital city, burning and destroying. Enraged, Sigibert performed one of the few imprudent acts of his reign. He called in pagan Teuton mercenaries from beyond the Rhine border, men without conscience, mercy or loyalty to anyone, and marched them into Paris, from which neutral ground they were to bring to subjection his brother and his nephew. Sigibert soon found that he could not control these men at all, and he called them off before his ruinous plan could take effect. His change of heart was due partly to belated shame and partly to the pleas of Brunhild, backed by those of Germain, bishop of Paris, to spare the city. Enthusiastically as Brunhild supported her husband against her hated in-laws, she balked at ruffianism.

Even without his barbaric allies Sigibert confounded his enemies on all fronts. He defeated his nephew Theudebert, who was killed in battle, and induced his Burgundian brother Guntram to disregard his promise to Chilperic and sign a peace pact with himself. Though Chilperic escaped by fleeing to Tournai and locking the gates behind him, he nearly lost his kingdom. As a consummate indignity to the defeated king, the people of his realm, tired of murder, rape, looting and burning at the instigation of a king who never won any battles, offered their fealty to Sigibert.

Sigibert was irresistibly tempted and prepared to besiege his brother in Tournai, to make a final subjection. Bishop Germain of Paris tried to deflect him: "If you set out with the intention of sparing your brother's life, you will return alive and victorious. If you have any other plans in mind, you will die. That is what God announced through the mouth of Solomon: 'Whoso diggeth a pit [for his brother] shall fall therein.'" Sigibert had listened in the past to this wise voice, but now, anticipating victory, he was too elated to heed. Before setting out for Tournai he went to Vitry, east of Paris, where Chilperic's mutinous army awaited him: there the warriors raised him on a shield in their midst in the old tribal symbol of his election as their king.

At the pinnacle of Sigibert's triumph retribution struck. Fredegund was aghast at the complete rout of her husband, on which would inevitably follow the discomfiture of herself. She bought two ruffians with promises of money and honors if they succeeded, alms to the saints if they failed. She gave them drugged wine to drink, to sedate their fears, supplied them with poison for their knives and sent them off to Sigibert's victory celebration at Vitry. As the warriors carried the king through the assembly on the shield, the assassins approached him as if to make a request. He bent toward them to hear their words, and they drew their knives and stabbed him from both sides. "He cried out and fell, giving up his spirit, and died."[5] The murderers were killed at once.

The body of the slain king lay for a whole day untouched where it had fallen, while Chilperic cowered at Tournai in expectation of the final siege. There Queen Fredegund came to assure him that she had snatched victory out of catastrophe. Happily relieved, Chilperic left his hideout and went to Vitry to honor his dead brother. Sigibert's body, dressed in royal robes, was solemnly buried at the church of Saint Médard at Soissons. The year was 575. Sigibert was forty years old, and had reigned for fourteen years.

The mortal quarrel of the two queens and the downfall of Sigibert found their way, in much altered form, into the medieval German epic *Nibelungenlied*. The true story of the calamitous interaction of these kings and queens is no less tragic than its poetic reflection. They performed their harrowing roles in a climate of residual barbarism. We have to keep reminding ourselves that Sigibert and Chilperic and their terrifying queens can never be judged by the moral standards of a more fastidious age. They are the intermediates, pagan in nature though nominally Christian, between the cultivated decadence of dying Rome and the spirituality of the early Middle Ages.

After the death of her husband, Brunhild, regent for her five-year-old son, Childebert, began her twenty-eight-year career as deputy ruler of Austrasia and later Burgundy, a course that would toughen her into the virago of whom we read in the seventh-century annal, *Chronicle of Fredegar*. The authors of this work, resident in Burgundy, were partial to the newly powerful nobility, especially to the family that would produce Charlemagne. They had an understandable prejudice against the aging, imperious queen. Viewed with cooler perspective, Brunhild was trying to uphold the rights of her inadequate sons, grandsons and great-grandsons against the rising star of the Mayors of the Palace, representatives of the nobility. She persisted almost against reason, and the aristocracy could not forgive her. Despite the hostility of their spokesmen, Brunhild repeatedly, through the long hard years, demonstrated an instinct for ethical rightness and a sensitivity in personal relations. These qualities are not evident in the character of her rival, Queen Fredegund, who had from beginning to end the morals of a cat.

For the moment we will leave the two queens and look at Burgundy, which played so large a part in their history. As we have noted, Burgundy, though an integral component of the Merovingian empire, was neither Frankish nor Gallo-Roman. It had existed for about a century as an independent kingdom before being absorbed, in 532, into the Francia of Clovis's sons. It still retained its individual personality: that of a generally peaceful, fortunate land of rich cornfields and vineyards (the latter already famous in Roman times), and a people of equable temper. Much of the native content derived from the excellence of the Burgundian Code, composed and issued by the Burgundian king Gundobad early in the sixth century. Its present Merovingian king, Guntram, inheriting his throne in 561, reconstructed the kingdom along Frankish lines, but it retained its happy spirit under this singularly affable and peace-loving member of the Merovingian quartet.

Guntram was popular with the Church. It blinked at his duplicity and his occasional acts of brutality because he gave generously and was genially deferential to his bishops. At dinner with Gregory of Tours, for instance, Guntram "talked of God, of building new churches, of succoring the poor. From time to time he laughed out loud, as he coined some witty phrase, thereby ensuring that we shared his happiness." Even more evidential of his character, he was beloved by his people: he was accessible and clement, and went among them freely. The bubonic plague, rising on the Nile and spreading over the mideast, periodically swept over Gaul and Italy. In 588, late in Guntram's reign, it reached Marseilles, at that time under the suzerainty of Burgundy. The king went south and walked among his suffering people, ordering them to assemble in church for the special three-day supplication ceremony of Rogations. More practically, he commanded that they should eat and drink nothing but wheaten bread and pure water. In those days of blank ignorance of the concomitance of filth and disease, his advice was remarkable—and it worked. People followed him in the streets, begging for his help. One woman ripped a few threads from his cloak, infused them in water and fed them to her dying child, who then arose, cured. The courageous compassion of King Guntram in this disaster was one of the factors contributing to his canonization. The sixth century was conspicuously low on genuine candidates for the calendar of saints.

Although Guntram's faults, in the eyes of his clerical friends, did not outweigh his virtues, he could act in ways notably unsaintly. He was known to yield to momentary fits of senseless fury as on the day he was hunting in the forests of the Vosges and came across a recently killed aurochs, a European bison. Guntram was outraged: poaching was more than an indiscretion when committed in the preserves of royalty. He questioned the forester, who told him that the miscreant had been Chundo, Guntram's own chamberlain. Chundo was arrested, loaded with chains and accused. He denied his guilt and was granted trial by combat—under Salic law a method of discovering the truth in the absence of evidence. The chamberlain appointed his nephew as his surrogate; the other duelist was his accuser, the forester. The combatants succeeded in killing each other messily, and poor Chundo, unexonerated, made a dash for the sanctuary of a nearby church. The king shouted for his capture, and the unfortunate man was caught before he crossed the holy threshold, tied to a stake and stoned to death. "Afterward," wrote Gregory mildly, "the king was sorry that he had lost his temper and that for such a trifling offense he had recklessly killed a faithful servant."

In another direction Guntram exhibited a less than exemplary quality: his surrender to martial timidity. He was afraid of war—a curious attribute in a Merovingian king—and he did not lead his own armies. As a result his generals had no respect for their commander-in-chief, and they allowed their men to run wild. This was not an anomaly in the sixth century. Clovis had controlled his men with a strong hand, commanding their respect. His sons, also participant warriors, usually managed to lead their men to victory. But in their time the soldiers' continued loyalty required promises of booty and a free hand in the cities. By the third generation military discipline had deteriorated to the point that Clovis's grandsons lost nearly every battle they engaged in; and their fraternal contests usually ended in a mishmash. But the unbridled brigandage of Guntram's armies shocked even his contemporaries. The king of Burgundy made a pretense of audacity against the Visigoths, who still held Septimania: "It is a shameful thing," said Guntram in a weak echo of his grandfather's words before Vouillé, "that the territory of these horrible Goths should extend into Gaul." The king thereupon sent his army, without him, to rectify the situation. The soldiers marauded even through their own Gallic territory, destroying crops and herds, burning farms, plundering churches, slaughtering the clergy along with the civil population. When they reached the south they found the Provençal towns well fortified against them. Preferring the easy plunder of helpless farmlands to the long boredom of siege, they rampaged all over the soft countryside, cutting down the olive groves and destroying the vineyards. Having denuded the land to the point where they had nothing to eat, they turned around to march home by a different route, again despoiling their own country as they went.

King Guntram's army arrived back in Burgundy a thin shadow of the strong force that had set out. More than five thousand died, it is written, many of starvation, many by the hand of farmers aggravated to desperation. King Guntram, bold in anger within his safe palace, called his generals in, excoriated them (mostly for the plunder of churches) and demanded an explanation. The generals were frank: "No man fears the king," they said. "The entire population is steeped in vice and all delight in doing evil." Guntram had no answer to this but to announce that evildoers in general would be prosecuted. He was saved from further embarrassment by the arrival of a messenger who announced that Reccared, the son of the king of Spain, had invaded Toulouse. Guntram had no recourse but to send another army back down south. It was easily defeated by the rising young prince—who would soon become Spain's first competent monarch since Euric a hundred years before, and who would make the crucial decision to bring Spain's ruling house into the Catholic fold.

Occasionally Guntram's timidity was almost pathetic. Assassination was a familiar political weapon: Sigibert had been killed on order of Fredegund to prevent the imminent downfall of her husband; later Chilperic himself would fall by a murderer's hand for the convenience, it was said, of his own Fredegund. Even good king Guntram was not immune: an attempt was made in church by an assailant who clumsily allowed the knife to slip out of his hand before it touched the king. The man was caught (with another dagger in his other hand), bound and tortured, after which King Guntram let him go free, "for he held it to be impious to kill a man who had been taken prisoner in a church."

The king had felt it unnecessary to have protection within the sanctuary of church, but all his other comings and goings were shielded by an armed guard. Still he was frightened. One Sunday at Mass he rose and appealed to the congregation: " 'I ask you to remain loyal to me, instead of assassinating me. Give me three years at least in which to bring up these two nephews of mine, [the sons of his slain brothers, Sigibert and Chilperic] for otherwise it might well happen that I should be killed while they were still small children, and then there would be no full-grown man of my line to protect you.' The entire population prayed to God for his safety." Guntram was the longest-lived of the four brothers and he died in bed after a reign of thirty-one years.

Guntram's instincts of compassion and moderation in less disorderly times might have authentically earned him the title of the "Good King." Outside of a monastery these traits were unusual in chaotic postimperial Europe: in those years a king, if he had not the temperament of a warrior, had to resort to intrigue and treachery to hold his own. More than the others Guntram tried to do what was right, attempting to mediate between his warring brothers and, after their deaths, to calm his perpetually angry sisters-in-law. In 577 Guntram's only two sons (children of the atrocious Austrechild) died of that common killer, dysentery. Five years later Guntram proposed to adopt Childebert, son of the widowed Queen Brunhild, then about twelve years old. In gracious ceremony he said: " 'For my sins I have the misfortune to be left childless. This, then, is my request, that you, my nephew, should be considered as my son.' He placed Childebert on his throne and made over to him his entire realm. 'Let one single shield protect us both,' he said, 'and a single spear defend us. Even if I still have sons, I will look upon you as one of them, so that the same loving kindness which I promise you today, may remain between you and them.' " After the death of his brother Chilperic, Guntram similarly adopted one of his sons. The Burgundian king's motives were kindly: at no time did he try to annex either the territories or the treasures of these children.

Guntram had not been so heedful in protecting Childebert's mother, Brunhild, when, in 575, she was abruptly widowed. Temporarily entranced by Fredegund, he left his other sister-in-law to cope with her bereavement alone. Brunhild was living in Paris at the time of her husband's murder. Chilperic, defying the neutrality of that city, marched there at once. He banished Brunhild to a convent at Rouen, appropriated her treasure and tried to lay his hands on her son, Childebert, heir to the throne of Austrasia, with the intention of destroying him. The little boy was rescued by one of the dukes of the realm, who, according to the chronicler, caused him to be put in a game bag and passed out the window to a servant. The child was taken to Metz, the capital of his father's kingdom, and there he was acknowledged king of Austrasia by the assembled nobles.

Though this action seemed to be motivated by loyalty to the family of their deceased king, it had another side. Sigibert, a strong monarch, had had the intention of suppressing the rising ambitions of his nobility. He even had the insolent idea of subjecting them to taxation. With his little son in their care, under the regency of a Mayor of the Palace, they aimed to rule the kingdom and protect their immemorial Teutonic liberties. The office of Mayor of the Palace, filled by a member of the nobility, had been created to assist the king in his dealings with that class. In the last quarter of the sixth century this personage was reversing the intent and becoming the defender of the interests of his own class, which often ran counter to those of the monarchy. But the time of the nobles had not yet come: they reckoned without Childebert's mother.

At the moment, however, Brunhild was defenseless. She never was a helpless woman, but in Rouen, beside herself with grief and anxiety and temporarily friendless, she was driven to make one of her few mistakes. Chilperic had a son, Merovech, by his first wife, Audovera. At this time Audovera was still alive, living in Rouen at the same convent as Brunhild. Merovech went to Rouen, allegedly to visit his mother; in doing so he disobeyed his father, who had ordered him to mount an attack on Poitiers. Merovech's real reason for the visit was to console his aunt Brunhild, hardly older than he and attractive in her sorrow. The prince quite exceeded his mission of comforting her; he married her. The union was consecrated by the bishop of Rouen, Praetextatus—who subsequently paid with his life, by order of Queen Fredegund, for his rashness.

King Chilperic marched on Rouen at once, angry at his son's defiance of his order, and even more so at his impetuous marriage to the enemy woman. He used the excuse that it was against canonical law to marry one's aunt—a brazen pretext in a man with Chilperic's cavalier attitude toward marriage. The couple took refuge in the sanctuary of a church. Chilperic camped in front of it and entreated them to come out, swearing a holy oath that he would not try to separate two whom God had united. Knowing the proven perils of betraying vows, the couple believed him and came out of sanctuary. The king kissed them both and entertained them at dinner.

Then Chilperic left Rouen, taking Merovech with him, ostensibly requiring his help in the defense of Soissons, Chilperic's capital city. But Merovech was not allowed to participate in this engagement; his father took his arms away and ordered him closely guarded until he should decide what to do with him. The king settled, for once, on leniency: the unruly young man was to be tonsured, ordained a priest and sent to a monastery in Le Mans for instruction. (The ease with which disobedient young princes and princesses were punished by forcible commitment to holy orders is a trenchant comment on Merovingian cynicism.) Merovech did not take his consecration seriously. He escaped with the help of his loyal servant, Gailen, put his secular clothes back on and made his way to Tours. He walked into Saint Martin's church while Bishop Gregory himself was celebrating Mass, threatened to kill some of the congregation if he was not allowed to take communion, and demanded sanctuary. The bishop, who disapproved of him, had to give way in the face of these threats. By taking in the rebellious prince he brought down the wrath of King Chilperic, who threatened to "set your whole countryside alight" if the fugitive were not surrendered. Gregory stood his ground: he not only defied the king, he even entertained his guest at dinner, trying to bring Merovech into a more Christian frame of mind by reading the Scriptures aloud to him. " 'The eye that mocketh at his father,' " the good man read, " 'the ravens of the valley shall pick it out.' Merovech," the priest continued, "did not see the point of this."

Knowing his father was coming after him, Merovech did not dare stay in Tours. He made his way to Auxerre and took sanctuary in the church of Saint Germain. Purused there, he tried to return to Brunhild, but his own wife's people, the independent Austrasian nobles, refused to receive him. The fugitive then attempted to regain sanctuary at Tours, but his father had all the approaches to the church blocked by armed guards except one small door, through which the clergy were allowed to pass; no one could even go to church. Through trickery Merovech was lured to a country house near Rheims. The house was surrounded and Chilperic summoned.

Then the desperate prince decided that his only course was to take final vengeance out of his father's hands. He called his servant Gailen to him and said: "Until this day we two have always shared the same intent and the same thoughts. I beg you not to allow me to fall into the hands of my enemies. Take my sword and kill me." Gailen did not hesitate, and when Chilperic arrived his son was dead. Reprisal was taken out instead on the faithful Gailen, at the direction of Queen Fredegund: "They cut off his hands, and his feet, and his ears, and his nose, tortured him cruelly and then despatched him in the most revolting fashion."

That was the end of Brunhild's ill-conceived attempt to redesign her life. Henceforth she resolved to devote herself to the role of queen mother, and to work toward the security of her son's position as king of Austrasia. In the beginning she was helped by those very nobles who, having rescued her son, planned to rule the kingdom through him. Chilperic at the moment was down in Aquitaine trying to take some of the southern cities of his brother Guntram of Burgundy. For once Guntram happened to have at his command a brave and skillful general, Mummolus. Chilperic's army, thoroughly beaten, retreated in disorder, and Chilperic decided that his wisest course was to try to make allies of the family and followers of the brother his wife had had murdered. The Mayor of the Palace of Austrasia and his friends had requested that the queen mother be freed from her enforced exile at Rouen and returned to her court at Metz. Chilperic now acceded to their plea. The motivation of the Austrasian seigneurs is unclear: possibly they wanted to underline their loyalty to the Merovingian rulers. Obviously they misread the character of the pretty young widow whom they considerately proposed to reunite with her little son.

Brunhild, established at Metz, proceeded to rule as regent for her son with the same firm hand that had irritated the nobility in her husband. Her girlhood in Visigothic Spain, where Roman mores were still predominant, inclined her toward the orderly and despotic methods of late imperial Rome. She rebuilt the Roman roads—there are still roads in Belgium called *chaussées de Brunehaut*—and reconstructed many of the crumbling Roman edifices ignored or despoiled by the careless Franks. Traces of her restorations can be seen in corners of two of her capitals, Besançon and Metz, almost hidden among the modern buildings of these energetically industrial cities. One of Brunhild's favorite retreats, away from the troubles of the regency, was Autun.* The earlier ages are more visible in this gracious Renaissance town in central Burgundy: a stark, square Roman

---

*Among its other claims on ancient history Autun is thought to have been the home of the Nibelungs, the clan fatefully entwined with the destines of Siegfried and Brunhild—who may have been the poetic descendants of Sigibert and his queen.

gateway dominates a main street, and the museum displays sixth-century Christian sculptures—primitive little crowned heads, probably from a sarcophagus—found in the ruins of one of the two monasteries the queen mother built here.

Besides seeing to the physical tidiness of her realm Brunhild tried to inject autocratic principles into its political management. Specifically she sponsored a return to the Gallo-Roman system of taxation. Her attempts to assert the prerogatives of royalty outraged the Frankish nobility, inclined toward the proud independence of its German ancestry. The nobles would prefer to have no king at all; having one, they desired that he should be their creature.

In the contest with her hostile seigneury Brunhild had the friendship of her brother-in-law, Guntram of Burgundy, who had become disenchanted with Queen Fredegund. But his support was intermittent and unstable, and Brunhild had to rely mostly on her own enterprise until her son, still in his early teens, was considered old enough to assume a king's responsibilities.

Childebert II, under the aegis of his mother, was well educated and humane for his period, and he gave the promise of being a fair ruler. However he possessed both the greed and the precocious daring of his family. In 584, when he was only about fourteen, he accepted from Maurice, the Roman emperor at Constantinople, fifty thousand pieces of gold to attack the Lombards in northern Italy. Childebert marched across the Alps, and the Lombards, seeing themselves outnumbered, declined to fight and substituted gifts for combat. Enriched by both sides, Childebert returned to Gaul without having to lift his battle ax. Emperor Maurice asked for his money back, but the cocky young Frank did not even send an answer.

Scornful of a foe who would not fight, Childebert made several more sorties against the Lombards, the last in 590, when he marched at the head of twenty divisions led by twenty counts. For all its generals, it was an unruly horde; even before the soldiers left Metz they were spreading havoc in their leader's own capital. In northern Italy they succeeded only in capturing five castles. The Lombards easily held out against the undisciplined Franks, who then resorted to plundering to keep themselves alive. They retired at last, defeated by hunger and dysentery, like Guntram's troops in Spanish Gaul a few years earlier and Theudebert's in Ostrogothic Italy a generation before. The pride and expertise of Frankish armies had died with Clovis. The conscripted troops of Clovis's grandsons, and of the sixth century in general, were masses of untrained peasants. Led by incompetent officers, ill-equipped and badly paid, these hopeless armies were commanded by their king to engage in ambitious wars for unrealizable ideals. Before and after battle they had no recourse but to live off the land, and no defense against their most lethal enemies, famine and disease.

Aside from his covetous duplicity, a quality endemic in Frankish chiefs, and his lack of control over his armies, the domestic rule of Childebert II was both sane and strong. It was unfortunate for the future of his dynasty in Austrasia that he did not live long enough to assert his authority over the fractious aristocracy. In 595 he was poisoned in a conspiracy by Austrasian nobles who purposed to control the throne through their guardianship of his infant sons. Very little has come down to us about Childebert II's private life; he was only twenty-five at his death. By that time he was king of more than two-thirds of Frankish Gaul, having succeeded to his uncle's throne of Burgundy on King Guntram's death three years before.

The nobles failed in the objective of the assassination, for Brunhild at once took over the regency for her grandsons, Theudebert II and Theodoric II, the child-kings of Austrasia and Burgundy. But it was a continuous struggle to keep their kingdoms intact until they should come of age, and she had no male relative old enough to help her deal with the active antagonism of the Austrasian nobles. Although one of her enemies, Chilperic, had died, the Austrasian dowager queen had to contend with the unremitting hostility of his widow, Queen Fredegund, her lifelong foe, whose ways were those of the covert plot and the poisoned dagger. With age and tribulation Brunhild became increasingly hard, autocratic and, when driven beyond control, cruel.

We will leave until the next chapter the difficulties of the queen mother of Austrasia, and turn to her bête noire, the royal family of Neustria. Its king, Chilperic, was unpopular with the clergy. Therefore the portrait bequeathed to us by the clerical historians paints him as an unregenerate scoundrel—and, more damning, a scoundrel with laughable pretensions to culture. However, in surveying his involved machinations to embarrass his brothers and to acquire their property, he seems hardly more blameworthy than the upright Sigibert or "Good King" Guntram. In fact he was in some ways a progressive monarch, forecasting an ideal of kingship free from the ascendancy of the Church. He was also, unlike his brothers, literate. His essays into the world of poetry and philosophy may have been crude, but he at least made them, and this lifts him above his royal contemporaries. But for all the interesting complexity of his character, Chilperic's career was a typically Merovingian one, activated by cupidity and implemented with violence and deceit. In him these features were accentuated by his thralldom to Fredegund.

The years of his inimical engagements with his brothers comprise a tangled history of side changing. The first part of his career consisted of a determined effort to confound his brother, Sigibert, target of Chilperic's resentful jealousy, a sentiment intensified by his wife's hatred for Brunhild. He was foiled by Sigibert's superior military ability. After Sigibert's opportune murder, he aimed to gain the mastery of Austrasia by sequestering his widow and disposing of the five-year-old heir. But the inheritance was protected, for their own purposes, by the strong Austrasian aristocracy, and the would-be usurper was further balked by the queen mother's decisive assumption of power.

Thwarted in his attempt to win control of Austrasia, Chilperic turned to Sigibert's southern domain of Aquitaine. His career in this direction is a comedy of blunder. First he made an attempt on Tours through his deputy, Duke Roccolen, who truculently announced that he would burn the city to the ground if a certain fugitive, harbored in Saint Martin's church, were not released to him. Bishop Gregory refused disdainfully, and Roccolen contented himself with pulling apart a wooden church-house on the opposite bank of the Loire—his men, in the process, made off with all the nails. Roccolen again blustered to Bishop Gregory, but before he could carry out his threats he fell ill of jaundice and was so weakened that he was forced to withdraw. He set out for Poitiers, which he aimed to capture and mulct. But in spite of his illness, and even though it was the Lenten period, he stuffed himself continuously with baby rabbits and died in agony the day before he reached the city. "He was killed," wrote Gregory, "by the miraculous power of Saint Martin."

Then Chilperic sent his son Merovech to counter this futile exercise and complete the conquest of Poitiers. Merovech, as we have seen, disobediently turned and went the opposite direction, to Rouen, lured by the loneliness of his aunt Brunhild. After the fiasco of Merovech, Chilperic tried once more, with Merovech's brother, Clovis, the only surviving son of Queen Audovera. This prince was instructed at the same time to invade Burgundy—in defiance of the fact that its king, Guntram, had been Chilperic's ally all through the Austrasian undertakings. Clovis was handily defeated by Guntram's general, Mummolus.

Although his designs on his brothers' lands had been circumvented, Chilperic was still master of a large part of Gaul. He was a despotic master, oppressive in taxation and brutal with recalcitrants. His main target was the Church—so naturally he was regarded by the priestly chronicler, Gregory, as a public enemy. But Gregory has the grace, probably unconscious, to quote his adversary in a revealing passage: "My treasury is always empty. All our wealth has fallen into the hands of the Church. There is no one with any power left except the bishops. Nobody respects me as King: all respect has passed to the bishops in their cities."

From the year 503, when Clovis was converted, to the access of his grandsons fifty-eight years later, the Church in Gaul had developed a formidable strength. From archbishop down to parish priest the Church dealt with the people on their own levels, so its tentacles pervaded every crevice of life. In the area of government the administration was dominated by educated bishops who entered into all areas of politics. The power of the higher clergy was such that the system was in danger of becoming a theocracy. The Church was not only more influential than the monarchy, it was probably, as Chilperic complained, wealthier as well. Kings feared to levy taxes on the vast riches in land and gold that continued to come to the Church from inheritance and outright gifts, lest the saints should reach down out of heaven and paralyze them, send them up in smoke or visit mortal illnesses upon their children. Bishops, literate, experienced and secure behind the impenetrable walls of credulity, not only had no fear of kings, but freely counseled and scolded them.

In this atmosphere it was remarkable that Chilperic had the audacity to strike back, taxing church lands and tearing up wills that bequeathed new property to the Church. His motives are obscured by the prejudice of the chronicler but they are easy to guess. He saw through the cobweb of superstition that lay over all of sixth-century life, to the truth of the clergy's avidity underneath. Besides, as a singleminded despot, he resented the bishops' assumption of superior power. Whatever his reasoning, his actions were considered offensive and dangerous, and his spiritual judge retaliated—not by striking him blind or dumb, but by laying on him the curse of posterity. Chilperic, in Gregory's pages, is an unconditional monster.

But in the eyes of his people his curtailment of the Church's overgrown power was a popular move. Gregory cannot quite suppress the truth that Chilperic was appreciated by the laity. He thought about his people's welfare and their pleasure. In friendly contact with Emperor Tiberius, Chilperic probably took legal advice from him, because he made emendations to the Salic law: among them he decreed that a professional malefactor who evaded the normal legal recourses would himself be outside the law. As an outlaw he would be fair prey, and whoever attacked him would not be liable to legal reprisals. This high-handed defiance of constituted law could become dangerous; but Chilperic's people accepted it with gratitude and relief. On occasion he gave the right of inheritance to a woman, a foresighted departure from ancestral Frankish legal practice. In the area of public pleasure he built Roman-style amphitheaters at Soissons and Paris.

One quality was harder than all else for Gregory to forgive: Chilperic's pretensions to scholarship. The Church frowned on literacy in kings; it was healthier all around if education were left to the clergy (in the case of Queen Brunhild culture was forgiven—she was only a woman and, besides, an enthusiastic Catholic woman). Chilperic offended conspicuously in this direction. He had the effrontery to dispute on the Trinity, a subject which had been argued abstrusely by the most sophic of theologians since the third century. Further, he produced six books of poems in which, wrote Gregory, "the verses were feeble and had no feet to stand on: he put short syllables for long ones, and long syllables for short ones, not understanding what he was doing." There was one churchman, however, who had appreciative words for the poet-king. That was Fortunatus, who wrote an encomium to Chilperic and Fredegund. The praise was self-serving, but at least the versesmith acknowledged a confrère: "I must greatly admire the king whose vigor/Leads battles with excellence, and whose file/Polishes poems./Thou ruleth arms by means of laws and Thou/Directs laws by means of arms:/Thus a path is entered which at the same/Time makes use of different methods."[6]

In the field of the graphic arts, too, Chilperic showed a certain sensitivity. His interest, so far as we know, was confined to the work of the goldsmith and the jeweler. He took pride in fostering Frankish artisans, hoping that through his patronage they might come to rival the Byzantine. He ordered them to design and execute a gold salver weighing fifty pounds and encrusted with gems, telling Bishop

Gregory that this work was "for the greater glory and renown of the Frankish people," and that he proposed to have other objects made by native craftsmen.

His agent for the purchase of art works was a Jew named Priscus. The Catholic Church, strong as it was in Gaul, had not yet developed the intolerance that would darken it in the later Middle Ages. In Catholic Gaul Jews were neither persecuted nor quite accepted. They were allowed to practice their irritating faith, and they were almost equal under the law to other Frankish citizens. If a Jew was suspected of malice—and often the outrage was real, for the Jews were bold in their dislike of the Church—at worst he was compelled to convert. If he balked he was expected to emigrate. Some bishops tried to enforce mass conversion, and many Jews, not wishing to court trouble, made token submissions, continuing to practice their own religion in secret. King Chilperic vacillated, in the manner peculiar to him, between extreme barbarism and fatherly concern. He issued a capricious order that all the Jews of Paris who refused conversion should have their eyes gouged out. The decree was never implemented, but Chilperic himself went to church to stand godfather to some timid Jews who accepted the true faith. The king was personally distressed that his agent and friend Priscus refused to see the light. He considered the merchant his equal to the extent of holding a long discussion with him on the pros and cons of Christ's divinity. This argument, in which the Jew at least held his own, is recorded in full by Gregory, who has no special anti-Semitic axe to grind. The two naïve debaters threw texts at one another, missing the point, until Chilperic was finally silenced by Priscus's sensible question: "How could God be born of woman, or submit to stripes, or be condemned to death?" At this point Bishop Gregory, better trained in persuasion, entered the argument; if his resolution of it is unsubtle it is at least logical. He could not persuade Priscus, however. The merchant stubbornly continued to worship in his ancestral way until he was murdered by a converted Jew (one of those to whom King Chilperic had stood godfather). Priscus's relatives in turn murdered the murderer, and no legal action ensued. In the case of a Jew, it seemed, the slate was considered to be wiped clean.

Much of the popularity Chilperic gained by his attention to welfare he forfeited through heavy taxation. The decrees he continued to issue were so onerous that many people elected to leave their lands and move to a more lenient kingdom. Those who stayed sometimes rebelled: in Limoges the people gathered in protest and decided to kill the tax collector. The bishop saved him, but the mob seized his collection books and burned them. Chilperic reacted with fury: the soldiers he sent to the city were licensed to engage in indiscriminate torture and execution. The insurrection was suppressed and the taxes became even more burdensome. In Brittany, then under Chilperic's nominal control, the people rioted and burned property near Rennes, in revolt against punitive taxes. The forces Chilperic sent against them chastised them with further destruction of the land. This only made the people angrier, and the king was forced to give way.

Then came a natural disaster which, everyone knew, was God's retribution on the heartless king. In 580, after a series of ominous floods, earthquakes and fires from heaven, the plague of dysentery spread over the land. The king fell ill; although he recovered, his two little sons, Fredegund's children, the younger not yet baptized, were fatally infected. Fredegund, fierce in her mother love, reacted with a passionate renunciation: "God has endured our evil goings-on long enough. Now we are going to lose our children. It is the tears of paupers which are the cause of their death, the sighs of orphans, the widows' laments. Yet we still lay up treasures, we who have no one to whom we can leave them. Our riches live on after us, the fruits of rapine, hated and accursed. Now we are losing the most beautiful of our possessions! Come, then, I beg you! Let us set light to all these iniquitous tax-demands!" She consummated her words by throwing on the fire all the tax rolls of her own cities.* King Chilperic, ever compliant with his queen, followed her lead, burning his own tax files and sending messengers around his kingdom to announce the remission of taxes. He made further amends, for the rest of his life, by giving alms to churches and to the poor. The little boys died anyway.

Queen Fredegund's mercy did not outlive her children. She unleashed her malice against her stepson, Clovis, the only living son of Chilperic's first wife, inducing her husband to send him to Berny, where the plague of dysentery still raged. The prince did not oblige her by catching it, and she turned to guile, accusing him and his mistress of witchcraft against her and her dead children. She managed to persuade Chilperic of his guilt. The prince was captured, and while a prisoner he was stabbed to death. Messengers to Chilperic

*In accordance with Frankish custom Chilperic had endowed her with the cities as gifts, morgengabe, on the morning after their first wedded night together.

announced that the prince had slain himself. "In my opinion," wrote Gregory, "it was the king who had delivered Clovis up to death, and he wept no tear."

Chilperic now had no heir, but his line was not to die out. Fredegund, habitually disloyal to her husband, took a lover named Landeric, who was the Mayor of the Palace. That much was known in her lifetime. For the ensuing events we have only the word of the chronicler who wrote in the following century.[7] One morning Chilperic, experiencing a longing for his wife, returned unexpectedly from the hunt to his palace at Chelles (east of Paris), and went into her bedroom. He found her washing her hair, her head down in the water. He "came up behind her and whacked her on the buttocks with a stick. She, thinking that it was Landeric, said: 'Why do you do this, Landeric?' Then she looked up and saw that it was the king. Very much saddened, [Chilperic] went off to his hunt." Fredegund, not sure how far she could try the adoring patience of her husband, feared that it was his life or hers. She called her lover to her, according to this chronicle, and they decided to kill Chilperic. As the king dismounted from his horse at the end of that day he was stabbed in the belly by two assassins "sent by Fredegund and drunk on her wine." The killers at once blamed the king of Austrasia, Brunhild's son, Childebert II. The unending feud provided convenient excuses for a multitude of large and small transgressions. Fredegund was not accused. In fact there is some doubt as to whether the queen was implicated at all. Gregory of Tours, who detested her, would have been unsparing had he suspected her. But he writes only that Chilperic was stabbed after the hunt, and that he died "deserted by all." The dead king, the account goes on, lay where he had fallen until a bishop, waiting in vain for an audience, found the body, washed it, dressed it and took it in a boat to Paris, where it was buried in the church that is now Saint Germain des Prés. The year was 584, and Chilperic had reigned for twenty-three years.

Fredegund had a late son, named Lothair, born either shortly before or after Chilperic's death. For want of other living heirs Lothair II was the new king of Neustria. There was a question as to whose child he was. King Guntram, who was Fredegund's protector during the early period of her regency, asked her to present the child for baptism in Paris. Three times the king of Burgundy traveled there to stand godfather, and the baby was not produced. This made Guntram suspicious, and he ordered Fredegund to present "incontrovertible evidence" that Lothair was the son of Chilperic. The queen thereupon assembled a magnificent host of compurgators*—three bishops and three hundred important laymen—all of whom swore on the altar that Lothair was the legitimate son of the late king. King Guntram's suspicions were silenced. Chilperic had been responsible for the deaths of two of his three adult sons (the third had died in battle). Now his throne devolved on a dubious scion whom he had possibly never seen, who, as the sole heir of the Merovingian dynasty, would become king of all the Franks, and who inherited his mother's ferocity in full.

Following his brief account of the mean death of King Chilperic, Gregory of Tours appends a scathing obituary, ridiculing and excoriating the king at the same time. He was "the Nero and Herod of our time. He cared for no one, and he was loved by none." His poetry was wretched and his theology laughable; he was a glutton "and his god was in his belly." He was never happier than when he was devising ingenious new tortures for his much-afflicted subjects. Most reprehensible of all his moral defects, he openly despised the bishops, accusing them individually of being empty-headed, pompous, lightminded, sybaritic and lecherous. Gregory himself has much to say on the subject of delinquent bishops. But it was acceptable that a bishop should criticize his compeers, quite improper that a layman, even a king, should so presume.

However, King Chilperic was prepared to listen at least to this bishop—even on occasion to accept criticism flexibly—and to instill into their intercourse something of geniality. When they argued over the Trinity Gregory ended the discourse by saying flatly: "Anyone who is prepared to accept your proposals will not be a wise man but a fool." Chilperic "gnashed his teeth" but said no more, and a few days later he quietly changed his opinion. When the king and the bishop together had given up trying to convince the Jew Priscus of the divinity of Jesus, King Chilperic said to Bishop Gregory in a most friendly manner: "'I will not let thee go, except thou bless me.' We washed our hands, and I said a prayer. I then took bread, gave thanks

*Compurgators were men willing to swear a sacred oath in church to affirm a truth. Compurgation was a religious act, but it was used for legal purposes and performed on judicial order. Its validity was considered indisputable, because there were few souls brave enough to chance the retribution, right there at the altar, that would requite perjury.

to God, received it myself and gave it to the King. We drank the wine and parted, saying farewell to each other." In these and other passages Gregory belies his own valedictory denunciation: they do not display either a fiend or a fool.

Gregory's main quarrel with Chilperic was the king's attitude toward the Church. In his reign, complained the historian, "church-men were rarely elected to bishoprics." In fact Chilperic sold empty sees, often to laymen. Simony was rightly frowned upon; but in this way the king was sure of having bishops who would listen to him rather than to an archbishop who disapproved of him. The strength of the old-line bishops had been a vital aid to government when the Frankish rulers had still been primarily warrior chiefs. By the middle of the sixth century the Merovingian kings, no longer raw barbarians, were learning the business of government themselves. Chilperic in particular, admiring all things Roman, had acquired an informed knowledge of the rights and duties of kingship as his generation understood it. Aware of the trend toward a theocracy the king sowed the seeds for a strong secular state independent of the domination of the clergy.

Laying aside Gregory's opinion of Chilperic's shallow pretensions, this Merovingian king displayed a sagacity and a firmness of purpose superior to the other kings of his generation. He deserves the respect of posterity for his experimental pointer toward the future France.

CHAPTER SEVEN

FREDEGUND AND BRUNHILD

After the death of King Chilperic in 584, Dowager Queen Fredegund was the regent for her baby son, Lothair II.[1] She was a strong and successful ruler. Ambitious, unscrupulous and clever, she had made good use of her twenty years as Chilperic's queen, exerting a strong background influence on the political and military affairs of his kingdom. Unlike Brunhild, whose ways were too Roman for the proud Teutonic aristocracy of Austrasia, Fredegund had the Neustrian seigneurs on her side: though lowborn she was racially and temperamentally one of them. Her tastes, instincts and methods had a primitive cast which marked her as absolutely Teutonic, a throwback to an earlier age. But it is misleading to characterize Fredegund as an archetypal tribal woman, supportive of her husband in war, personally brave, a tigress in defense of her children. Her ruthlessness was motivated only in part by devotion to her family. Political expedience and an appetite for personal power dictated much of her action, and her cruelty was sadistic rather than barbaric. Within the narrow area of her dominance Fredegund exerted a vicious influence. Still her nobles liked her, and not only for their sympathy with her Teutonic grain. We must infer that she was beautiful; it is clear from all accounts that her sexual allure was irresistible to most men.

During her husband's lifetime she had continuously urged him into hostilities that would discomfit Brunhild. But Chilperic had habitually lost all his battles. Fredegund was astute enough to see that an effective military leader was essential if the quarrel was to be successfully resolved. Her lover, Landeric, Mayor of the Palace, was such a one, and with his help, Fredegund ran the contest until her son was mature enough and well trained enough in dislike of his Aunt Brunhild to take over the feud.

Fredegund's regency was one of brutal efficiency. She had the approval of most of her aristocracy, and she kept it by dealing ferociously with the occasional mutinous seigneur. One Leudast, a vicious and degenerate count who may have deserved what he got, led a plot against her. One of his followers was captured, his hands were tied behind his back by the queen's order, and he was hung thus from a tree for six hours. Then he was taken down and put on the rack with ropes and pulley, to be beaten with sticks and whips by anyone who passed by. Just before he died, incredibly still vocal, he confessed his part and gave the names of the other plotters.

Leudast himself eluded capture and managed to continue his seditious maneuvers. He was finally caught, and badly wounded in the attempt to get away. Fredegund ordered her doctors to treat him until he recovered sufficiently to die by torture. Then, "at the personal command of the Queen he was placed flat on his back on the ground, a block of wood was wedged behind his neck and they beat him on the throat with another piece of wood until he died." The sixth-century historian adds that Leudast "met a fitting end."

Like her late husband Fredegund did not truckle to the Church, and she had no patience with clerics who went counter to her interests. One of these was Bishop Praetextatus of Rouen, the churchman who had married the newly widowed Queen Brunhild to Chilperic's son, Merovech. Following this initial imprudence the bishop went on irritating the Neustrian royal family. Injudiciously critical of King Chilperic, he was accused of conspiring against him, tried in court, found guilty and exiled. (In the course of the trial Queen Fredegund offered Bishop Gregory of Tours two hundred pounds of silver if he would testify against the bishop of Rouen; the offer was indignantly refused.) After the king's death Praetextatus was restored to his bishopric. Unregenerate, he engaged in a bitter exchange with Queen Regent Fredegund, scolding her for her malicious disposition. The queen was so enraged that she sent an assassin into church while the bishop was celebrating the Easter Mass. Praetextatus was stabbed under the armpit. Mortally wounded, he continued the service, his lifted hands dripping with blood. After he had completed the rite he was carried to his bed. There Fredegund came to him to offer the services of her best doctors to heal his wound. Praetextatus answered, denouncing her with his last words: "God has decreed that I must be recalled from this world. As for you, as long as you live you will be accursed, for God will avenge my blood upon your head."

This time a holy curse, so often gruesomely fulfilled, did not affect the course of Queen Fredegund's life and fortunes. She continued to order the affairs of Neustria and to embarrass the royal family of Austrasia without serious hindrance.

Assassination, to Fredegund, was the most convenient way to dispose of awkward enemies. She made several unsuccessful attempts on Brunhild and her family, including a plot to dispatch Childebert II and his elder son, Theudebert. It was a clumsy conspiracy, involving twelve assassins. One of them lost his nerve just before he was to strike the young king down in his oratory; and he gave away all the others. They received varying punishments, of which the main ingredient was torture: "Some had their ears and noses cut off, and were then let out as a subject of ridicule." The sixth century had a gruesome sense of humor. "In one way or another," the historian continues, "the King certainly had his revenge." Fredegund had no monopoly on the routine use of torture.

Failing with the son and grandson, the Neustrian queen made a direct attempt on Brunhild. She sent a cleric of her entourage to Brunhild's court at Metz, with instructions to ingratiate himself as a fugitive from the Neustrian household, then to find opportunity to assassinate the dowager queen. Brunhild received him kindly, but he was a maladroit conspirator and his manner was suspicious. Finally she had him flogged until he confessed his errand, then she sent him back to his mistress. Fredegund scorned the chastisement of a mere beating. She had the unsatisfactory assassin's hands and feet cut off.

Near the end of her life Fredegund personally directed a battle which has a literary postcript. In 596 Childebert II, taking over his mother's running feud with Fredegund, invaded the area of Soissons. Fredegund summoned her lover and war leader, Landeric, who marched an army into Champagne to counter the Austrasian attack. Fredegund accompanied the army like an old-time Teutonic help-meet. The day before the battle she counseled the men thus: " 'Let us go against them at night with lights carried by our retainers, who will go in front of us with branches of trees in their hands and little bells tied on their horses [the horses were belled only when they were out to pasture] so that the enemy's guards cannot recognize us.' When the guards saw the tree branches in masses in front of the [enemy] line and heard the ringing of the bells, one man said to his companion: 'Yesterday was there not a field there? How is it then that we see a forest there now?' His companion said, laughing: 'But of course you have been drunk, that is how you blotted it out. Do you not hear the bells of our horses grazing next to that forest?' "[2] The attackers swept over the sleeping army with great slaughter. A thousand years later Shakespeare used Fredegund's ruse as an instrument in the resolution of Macbeth's fate.

Fredegund had one true loyalty in her later life: to her young son, Lothair II. Her active devotion to his interests and to the competent administration of his realm until he should be old enough to rule made her a patriot, even a heroine, to those who knew her only toward the end of her life. She died peacefully in 597, and was buried with honors at Saint Germain des Prés, beside her husband and his uncles. Her body, along with theirs, disappeared at the time of the Revolution, but her effigy lies beside the high altar at the cathedral of Saint Denis. It is a lovely twelfth-century Romanesque figure executed in copper in low relief. Colored mosaic rosettes decorate her three-pronged crown, her straight, simple gown and the edges of her rectangular plaque. She has an air of well-bred modesty.

The fate of our other queen presents an appalling contrast. While Queen Fredegund had the support of her aristocracy Brunhild had to cope with the obstinate hostility of hers. This relatively new order had arisen in the hundred years since Clovis had eradicated the old Teutonic aristocracy. It was heterogeneous, changeable and drawn from all classes. But wealth and position generate their own laws. By the time Brunhild took over the rule of Austrasia in 575 on behalf of her minor son, Childebert II, she had to confront an entrenched body of Austrasian seigneurs of proud Teutonic ancestry, who hated her for her non-Frankish birth and even more for her Roman type of autocracy. The new class was stronger in Austrasia than in the other Frankish kingdom of Neustria: the eastern realm was in immediate contact with Germany, and the Roman influence had never been as cogent there as in the western part of Gaul. In Neustria a nucleus of old Gallo-Roman families was favorable to the maintenance of central authority along traditional imperial lines. They moderated the stiff-necked independence of the Teutonic nobility.

Brunhild was committed to the idea of absolute monarchy on the imperial pattern. She was easily as obstinate as her Austrasian nobility; and she had the misfortune to operate in their realm. When her husband died the seigneurs thought they had their opportunity: with a woman as regent they might control the young Childebert II. They misread Brunhild, but her regency for her son was a continuing struggle to protect the Merovingian prerogative. Her difficulties were aggravated by the active enmity of her Neustrian relatives. For most of the course of their conflict Neustria, under the regency of Queen Fredegund, held the upper hand. The aristocracy, among other grievances, blamed Brunhild for the never-ending warfare—particularly since her side lost most of the battles.

But the seigneurs could not assail the Merovingian public image. Strange to a modern eye, the interminable backbiting of the two queens, on top of the youthful weakness of the male heirs, had no deleterious effect on the people's conservative loyalty to their immemorial ruling family. The contemporary truth was that the actions of Merovingian kings and queens were little different from those of other rulers of their time. Roman emperors, when they could stay in power, were just as cruel, conniving and despotic; and in Spain the Visigothic kings, hated by their people and disapproved of by the Catholic Church, could not keep their thrones more than a few years. "The Goths," wrote Gregory, who discountenanced everything about Spain, "had adopted the hateful custom of killing any king who displeased them and appointing the person on whom their fancy fell."[3]

The Merovingian dynasty, by the beginning of the seventh century, had been supreme in Gaul for a century, far longer than any other of the erstwhile barbarian royal families. They might murder one another, but there was always a member of the younger generation left to fill the gaps created by homicidal uncles and aunts; and one after another they enjoyed sustained popular favor. Beginning with Clovis they had the aim to please their majority population, the Catholic Gallo-Romans. The result was that the dynasty endured, in contrast with the unpopular Arian regimes of Italy and Spain. Frankish Gaul was the biggest and richest power in Europe; Frankish princesses were the most sought-after royal brides; and the Church, the cohesive power of Europe, supported the stability of this favored Catholic family. The people cherished their long-haired kings: so sturdy was the popularity of the Merovingian clan that even the most fanatical among the emerging seigneurial class realized that they could never get anywhere without the talisman of a Merovingian name.

Early in Brunhild's career as regent they found one—illegitimate, ignored by his presumptive father, and possibly spurious. It was a shaky choice, but the nobles needed a protégé, and the current Merovingian children were under the protection of their formidable mothers. This one, besides his alleged paternity, had a valuable asset: he was acknowledged and backed by the court of Emperor Maurice at Constantinople. He would do as a peg on which the insubordinate Austrasian seigneurs could hang their aspirations.

His name was Gundovald,[4] and he claimed to be a son of Lothair I, and thus half brother to the current kings. He had gone to his father, demanding recognition. Lothair, on seeing him, said, "This is no son of mine," and ordered his long hair to be shorn. Repudiated by his supposed father and lacking supporters, Gundovald was reduced to hiring himself out as a wall painter in order to eat, a lowly occupation that later brought scorn on his pretensions. After Lothair's death in 561, Gundovald let his hair grow out again and tried his fortune among the successors, backed by a dissentient group of aristocrats. Guntram of Burgundy would have none of him, declaring him to be the son of either a weaver or a miller (or both), one of the palace serfs. To emphasize his denial of the quasi-prince's pretensions, the king ordered decaying horse dung to be flung at the heads of Gundovald's noble envoys as they departed. King Sigibert was equally negative though not so petulant: he simply ordered the upstart's hair to be cut off again and sent him as a prisoner to Cologne. Gundovald escaped and made his way to Italy, where Justinian's general Narses received him favorably. About 565 he went to Constantinople and lived there, honored as a royal scion, for about fifteen years. In 582 the Frankish aristocracy, looking for a protégé to support their increasing dissatisfaction with the strong rule of Lothair's sons and later of their widows, took up Gundovald's cause. They were the more willing to adopt him because of the sizable treasure conferred on him by Emperor Maurice. The pretender was backed, not only by the seigneurs, but by the strong arm of Mummolus, Guntram's erstwhile general, who, after quarreling with his Burgundian employer, settled in Austrasian territory and became the willing tool of the factious aristocracy there. Some of the bishops also joined the conspiracy.

Besides the support of the seditious bishops, Gundovald felt that his success would be assured if he could gain possession of a certain relic said to be infallible in battle, the thumb of Saint Sergius the martyr.* Its owner, an eastern king, used to attach the thumb to his own right hand; when he raised it the enemy troops would turn and flee in midattack. This particular holy bone was not available, but Gundovald tracked down a duplicate to a Syrian merchant in Bordeaux, and sent General Mummolus to get it either legitimately or feloniously. The merchant, refusing to part with it, tried to buy off the emissary with gold, but Mummolus ignored his pleas and sent his aide up a ladder to the top of the wall where the casket hung. In it was a tiny finger bone of the saint. Mummolus, examining it, knocked it with his knife and it broke into three pieces which scattered out of sight on the floor. Everyone present, including the Syrian merchant, knelt in prayer, and the fragments were forthwith found. Mummolus took one of them, "but not with the approval of the martyr," remarks the historian, "as the remainder of the story has made clear." Gundovald, however, was now ready for war.

The object of the uprising, which occurred in 585, was to unseat the two remaining Merovingian kings, Guntram of Burgundy and his nephew and heir, Childebert II of Austrasia, son of Brunhild and Sigibert. (Lothair II, the infant son of Chilperic, was not considered a threat.) The decisive engagement took place in the hilltop town of Saint Bertrand de Comminges in the Pyrenees. This town was occupied by Gundovald and General Mummolus, and the forces of the two legitimate kings besieged it. As the attacking soldiers climbed the hill they taunted the pretender: "You are that painter fellow, aren't you, who used to slap whitewash on the walls and cellars of oratories?" Mummolus saw certain defeat ahead. Turning traitor, he tricked Gundovald into leaving the protection of the town walls and going down to the enemy's camp, where King Guntram, it was claimed, awaited him with forgiving clemency. The pretender was escorted on his way by his chief supporter, a greedy scoundrel named Guntram Boso, who had already appropriated most of Gundovald's eastern treasure. The double traitor pushed his charge over a ravine on the way down from the town, and threw rocks on him when he

*Sergius was a Gallo-Roman soldier of the late third century who refused to enter a temple of Jupiter, was led through the streets in women's garb, then scourged, tortured and beheaded.

tried to crawl up again. One rock hit the pretender on the head and killed him. A mob of the besiegers siezed his body, tied the feet together and dragged it through the army encampment, pulling out its hair and its beard, then leaving the corpse unburied where they dropped it. With King Guntram's approval, General Mummolus himself was put to death by the attacking soldiers—even though he had resumed his allegiance to the Burgundian king with his betrayal of the pretender.

Guntram Boso also met a gory end, though his retribution came only after another abortive uprising against the same two kings. He took refuge in the house of a bishop, threatening to kill the bishop if he were refused sanctuary. King Guntram countered that the bishop would lose his life anyway if he did not put the fugitive out, and he followed this up by having the house set on fire. Guntram Boso, running out through the smoke, was hit by a javelin as he stepped through the door. The mob closed in, thrusting so many spears into his body that it stood upright against the wall, too stiff to fall, a grisly monument to perfidy.

The fate of the town of Saint Bertrand de Comminges was even crueler than that of the protagonists. "When the besiegers had killed every living soul, so that there remained not one that pisseth against a wall, the troops burned the whole city, with all the churches and every single building, leaving there nothing but the bare earth." It would be seven hundred years before the town would rise again.

One is tempted to feel sorry for the pretender, Gundovald, used, ridiculed and duped, were he not himself such an unappealing character. His story throws a merciless light on the sixth-century blend of savagery and corruption, which was not confined to the royal house but permeated the Church and the aristocracy as well.

Queen Brunhild was not directly involved in the affair of the pretender, but it was symptomatic of the insurgence of the Austrasian nobility, and her behind-the-scenes power was one of the chief objects of their resentment. Another outbreak occurred, openly directed against her and supported in the wings by Queen Fredegund. Lupus, duke of Champagne, was a valiant and effective warrior against the Saxons. As a strong supporter of Queen Brunhild and her young son, he was the immediate object of harassment by a group of seditious seigneurs headed by two ringleaders, Ursio and Berthefried, protégés of Fredegund. After despoiling Duke Lupus's territory they sent an army against him with the sole aim of killing him. Queen

Brunhild donned a man's armor and went out before the attackers: " 'Warriors, I command you to stop this wicked behavior! Stop harassing this man who has done you no harm. Stop fighting each other and bringing disaster upon our country.' 'Stand back, woman!' answered Ursio. 'It should be enough that you held regal power when your husband was alive. Now your son is on the throne, and his kingdom is under our control, not yours. Stand back, I say, or you will be trodden into the ground by our horses' hoofs!' "[5] Despite Ursio's insolence the queen prevailed. The aggressors subsided into threats, contented themselves with looting some of Duke Lupus's houses, and departed. The duke, however, considered that his future would be more stable if he removed himself, and he took temporary refuge in the court of King Guntram. Brunhild had lost another strong friend.

A few years and several conspiracies later the two dissident leaders were trapped in a fortified house by troops of King Childebert II, by now old enough to take the field on his own behalf. His men prepared to force an entry, but before they could attack, Brunhild sent a messenger in to plead with Berthefried to withdraw his loyalty to Ursio and save his own life. The queen had stood sponsor to his daughter at her baptism, and this connection disposed her to mercy in spite of extreme provocation. Berthefried refused her pardon. In the ensuing attack Ursio died defending himself, while Berthefried fled and claimed the sanctuary of a church. The soldiers demanded his ejection but the bishop refused to hand him over. They then climbed on the roof, smashed a hole in it and dropped roof tiles down on the fugitive within, killing him. This was a new way of breaking sanctuary, and it illustrates the helplessness of even the more well-intentioned of the clergy in the face of the lawlessness of the time.

When Childebert II reached his majority he took on the conflict with the seigneurs, but he did not live long enough to assert the power of the throne against the encroachments of the aristocracy. Still, while he lived the combined kingdom of Austrasia and Burgundy was the strongest power of Frankish Gaul; and the efficient and harmonious combination of mother and son elevated that branch of the Merovingian family, in the beginning, to a seemingly unassailable dominance. Its strength did not outlive his reign.

Childebert died in 595 (two years before Fredegund), leaving his large kingdoms to his two minor sons. The older, Theudebert II, succeeded to the throne of Austrasia and his brother, Theodoric II, became king of Burgundy. Their grandmother administered the Austrasian kingdom from its capital of Metz, while the government of Burgundy she entrusted to those of the nobility at the moment friendly to her. Now cracks began to show in the unwieldy realm. Brunhild, fifty years old, was becoming an autocrat implacable in defense of the status quo. She was not as levelheaded in ruling for her grandsons as she had been in the years of her son's minority. Her stressful regency was hardening her sensibilities. She became imperious and willful, flaring into anger when her authority was flouted, on occasion provoked to inhumanity.

The queen regent's attitude toward the Church is an example of how different was this stony, middle-aged queen from the eager princess who had striven to please her new Frankish husband in every area of his life. She had adopted Sigibert's Catholic faith with graceful docility, becoming in her own right one of the most zealous supporters of the Gallic clerical establishment. The Gallic Church in the late sixth century was not entirely worthy of her ardent commitment.

Pope Gregory I, the Great, regarded Brunhild as his mainstay in Gaul, a champion he very much needed in the precarious state of the papacy. Gregory was faced with arduous difficulties in keeping alive a very shaky Church. He had been elected in 590, a time of extreme crisis for the Western Church. The invading Lombards prevailed over most of Italy, and peace had to be made and kept with these tough conquerors, whose kings followed the Arian heresy. Famine, floods and plague were devastating Europe; the dominant barbarian rulers were either pagan or Arian; much of the wretched, illiterate, superstitious population was out of reach of even the most well-disposed bishop. Compounding the pope's problems was the continued endeavor of distant Constantinople to enforce its ascendancy over the Rome-based Western Church.

The survival of the Church in Europe depended on Pope Gregory's ability to deal with these dissonant externals and to exact undeviating orthodoxy within the Church, from the bottom ranks up through the hierarchy. Practical, sagacious, statesmanlike, above all dedicated, Gregory succeeded brilliantly in all his aims. To him is due the impressive continuity of the Church through the years when everything else in Europe changed. We see him in the light of history as the first medieval pope, the earliest architect of the monolithic, inflexible

Church of the later Middle Ages. This development, deplorable or commendable depending on the angle of vision, was probably not quite intended by Pope Gregory I. In the early seventh century his authoritarianism was justified: the very existence of his Church was threatened. To ensure its continuance he needed to sustain the few viable Western establishments. He had to demand, in return, their unquestioning conformity.

Pope Gregory found in Queen Brunhild's Austrasia the sound episcopal continuity he needed, and he rewarded the queen's loyalty by supporting her Gallic establishment uncritically. This establishment included some immoderately worldly exponents, the rascals who inevitably thrive in a large power network. The Church was unavoidably tainted by the corruption around it. In imitation of their lay compeers a few members of the higher clergy were egregiously improper, openly indulging their appetites for sex and drink and other kinds of secular depravity. Bishop Eunius of Vannes, for example, fell to the ground excessively drunk and "neighing like a horse" while celebrating Mass one Sunday.[6] Theudulf, a deacon in Paris, while walking on the walls after too much wine at dinner, struck his servant with such force that he himself lost his balance, fell off the wall and died of his injuries "after vomiting blood and bile." Abbot Dagulf was found in bed with the wife of one of his parishioners, who killed them both on the spot with an axe. Bishop Bertram of Bordeaux was reputed to be the lover of Queen Fredegund and, on surer ground, was an accomplice of the pretender Gundovald in the theft of Saint Sergius's finger bone. Bishop Sagittarius of Gap paced the walls of the besieged town of Saint Bertrand de Comminges during the pretender's last stand, dropping rocks on the heads of the attackers below. When the town surrendered the invading soldiers captured him and cut off his head "and his hood with it." Sagittarius's dissolute brother, Bishop Salonius of Embrun, beat members of his own congregation with a wooden club when they disapproved too openly of his amours and his orgiastic feasting.

Other clerics yielded to political or monetary influence in allowing the violation of sanctuary; accepted bribes for aiding highborn miscreants; closed their eyes to simony; enjoyed conspicuous pomp and luxury in their overstaffed urban palaces; looked the other way when their uneducated country priests resorted to pagan practices— such as reading the entrails of birds—to please their backward congregations.

Pope Gregory was well informed on the flawed bishops of Frankish Gaul. He also understood that without the higher clergy Merovingian authority would crumble and his main support in Europe would fail. The scoundrels were a small minority; most of the Gallic clergy were well-intentioned men, hardworking and reasonably pious. In a few, statesmanship was conjoined with genuine qualities of saintliness. The general level of education, even in the priesthood, had fallen below even late imperial standards. But the higher clergy had political expertise, their heritage from traditional family service to the Roman Empire, and they were committed to the maintenance of order in the realm. They helped to humanize and organize a despotic, neo-barbaric regnancy; they were the only champions of the downtrod-den and the only succor of the destitute. They soothed ferocious counts, chastised delinquent princes and talked back to capricious monarchs. They were the pillars—cracked in places but still funda-mentally sound—of Francia.

Gregory of Tours is a fine example of the good side of the Frankish episcopacy. He was born at Clermont-Ferrand in 540, of a Gallo-Roman family prominent in status, wealth, service to the state and dedication to the Church. He was committed from an early age to following the family tradition of entering the Church, and his education was tailored to this purpose. Aspirants to the higher clergy were not intended to be overscholarly. Gregory had a grounding in sacred literature, wide but not profound; a smattering of classical writers (including Virgil and Sallust but not Cicero or Pliny) and a touch of astronomy. Philosophy, logic, rhetoric and the sciences were unknown to him: these abstract disciplines were considered unneces-sary to ecclesiastical advancement. More important than book learn-ing was the practical knowledge he gained as deacon at the cathedral school of his great-uncle Nicetius, bishop of Lyon. Observing and assisting this strong, practical bishop, Gregory received training invaluable to his own episcopal career.

Gregory's background, his connections and his education destined him for a high position in the Church, and he waited for the bishopric he wanted most—Tours. This see became vacant on the death of Gregory's relative, Bishop Eufronius, in 573, when Gregory was thirty-three years old. The episcopacy of Tours, one of the chief cities of Frankish Gaul, was a plum in those years. The see was under the protection of Sigibert, the reigning monarch of Aquitaine and the most stable of the sons of Lothair I. King Sigibert's wife, Brunhild,

intelligent and humanitarian and a devoted Catholic convert, was a
benison to bishops. With his long family tradition of public service
Gregory found the ideal niche at Tours. A bishop in sixth-century
Gaul was in an almost impregnable position, with a sustained
influence even more secure than that of the king's most trusted
officers, who could be dismissed at the royal whim. But a king could
not get rid of his bishop even if he disliked him—only an ecclesiastical
council could unseat him—and if relations were pleasant the churchman could profitably advise his monarch in all areas, moral, political
and religious. Gregory's association with the steady and sensible king
and the sympathetic queen were the ideal of Merovingian-ecclesiasti-
cal cooperation: the spirit of compromise on both sides assured a
smooth working partnership in all matters that concerned them
both.

It did not last. Less than two years after Gregory's election King
Sigibert was murdered and Touraine was taken over by that overt
enemy of the clergy, Chilperic. For the next ten years, until
Chilperic's murder in 584, the bishop of Tours had to administer his
see with the active noncollaboration of his king. Not only had he to
withstand an inimical ruler, but he was harassed by the vindictive
interference of Queen Fredegund. He had incurred her energetic
annoyance: first with his unwilling succor of Prince Merovech,
Chilperic's disobedient son; later with his defense of Bishop Praetextatus and his repulse of the queen's attempt to bribe him.

When Chilperic died Touraine reverted to the Austrasian throne in
the person of Sigibert's son, the minor heir Childebert II, and it was
ruled for him by his foster father, Guntram, king of Burgundy. Bishop
Gregory's course became smoother: the congenial Guntram had been
his friend since Gregory had spent some youthful years in Burgundy.
Gregory's last decade was comparatively tranquil. His harmonious
relations with King Guntram were succeeded by an equally reciprocal
accord with Childebert II, who came to his throne in 587.

Gregory died in 594, and he was soon canonized. But he had been
a practical leader, not a spiritual one: he was sainted for his good
works in a turbulent period, rather than for transcendent holiness.
Actually he was quite worldly, taking pleasure in good food and wine,
and enjoying cheerful company. But he did not live in the luxury of a
palace, like some of his contemporaries. His house, which adjoined
the church, amounted to a public thoroughfare, and his private life
was nonexistent. Occasionally he retired to a cell in Marmoutier,

Saint Martin's monastery outside Tours, but even here he practiced
no forbidding austerities. He was accessible and democratic, talking
easily to fishermen and farmers, generally about the miracles of his
personal sage, Saint Martin—rejoicing with them over the cures
effected by that saint's resident spirit, of common illnesses, sores and
broken bones. His humanitarian feelings were sensitive: though he
rarely speaks of himself in his writing, he occasionally voices tenderness in other connections, as in his lament over the toll of dysentery
among children: "And we lost our little ones, who were so dear to us
and sweet, whom we had cherished in our bosoms and dandled in
our arms. As I write I wipe away my tears."[7] He also had an
inconvenient saintly penchant for setting prisoners free no matter
how disorderly their conduct. He always exulted when Saint Martin
or other efficacious ghosts caused prison gates to fly open and chains
to drop from legs and arms. His credulity was unending: if this seems
simpleminded in an educated churchman we must recognize Gregory
as a true child of his age. In sixth-century Europe the scientific
knowledge of classical times was all but forgotten and intellectual
curiosity was a tool of the devil. Gregory, frail from childhood and on
occasion almost mortally ill, scorned the attentions of physicians and
relied absolutely on the touch of the saints. His faith was so true and
his spirit for life so strong that his belief was, in appearance, justified.

   In his dealings with kings and counts Gregory tactfully tried to
avoid altercation except when the inviolability of the Church was
threatened, but he had a practical interest in maintaining the
strength of royalty against the presumption of the aristocracy. The
latter, in Gregory's time, was self-seeking and anarchic, whereas kings
could preserve some sort of public order—with the counsel of earnest
clerics. Gregory's aim was a close alliance of crown and Church. This
was the concept that would prevail in Frankish Gaul for two and a
half centuries, from the conversion of Clovis in 496 until the year
751, when Pepin the Short would dethrone the last of the long-haired
kings. It was the ideal that would help to maintain the Merovingian
dynasty until it would fall of its own rot; and it would become the
central tenet of the Carolingian rule.

   Gregory strove against unequal odds to support order and moral
goodness. In his *History of the Franks*, he depicted with literal
emphasis the delinquency of the clergy and the iniquity of dukes and
counts, not because he relished ghoulish detail but because he wanted
to drive home a moral by presenting horrible examples. He was

deeply distressed at the destructive quarreling of his kings and queens, and tried to broaden their vision with reasoned advice and good-natured scolding. Yet throughout the stormy years he was ever optimistic. Although not an abstract thinker Gregory was almost a social philosopher. Observing the resilient quality of the Franks, he recognized that they had a capacity for national development lacked by the other Teutonic conquerors. The rulers of Italy and Spain had no rapport with their subject peoples and would never succeed in adapting their outlook to suit their conquered lands. The Franks, individually ferocious and arbitrary, were in the aggregate a responsive people: they mingled easily with their subject Gallo-Romans, learning from them even as they imposed their own mores. The mutual education was not all good—the Franks absorbed the ways of corruption from their late-Empire subjects, while the Gallo-Romans coarsened. But in the long run a robust new people evolved, with pride in the country they had made their own. By the time of Charlemagne they were a nascent French nationality: Gaul was ready to become France. Gregory, from the darkness of the sixth century, saw the root vitality of his people, and he was hopeful.

Gregory is the prototype of the good Merovingian bishop: the sagacious voice of educated moderation, the counsellor and the conscience of kings. Though genuinely pious he was on the worldly side of the dualistic Church of Frankish Gaul. On the spiritual side were the monasteries. In our period these tended to be harbors for the elite escapist as much as sanctuaries for the authentic religious. Their abbots and abbesses ministered tactfully to the souls of their charges and ignored the noisy contention outside the convent walls. Some of the monasteries, as we have seen at Radegund's Holy Cross, reflected the pervasive corrosion of the times. At others reaction against materialism reached an extreme of pointless and repulsive asceticism. The monastic movement was failing with the sickness of its century.

In the realm of Queen Regent Brunhild there was one monastery that brought the light of sanity and integrity back into the Frankish monasticism. Its abbot, an opinionated and high-minded missionary monk from Ireland named Columbanus, had the vision to look back to the pure spirituality of early Christianity and forward to a day when European monasteries would be the centers of medieval progress. Abbot Columbanus was the spiritual counterpart of the more practical Bishop Gregory in the religious life of Frankish Gaul.

Columbanus was a product of Ireland's intellectual golden age, the four or five centuries when that little country, on the edge of Europe and untouched by the barbarian invasions, led the world in scholasticism, art and literature. The era had begun in the fourth century, when Ireland was converted to Christianity. The Celts, an emotionally receptive people, had embraced the new religion wholeheartedly. Almost at once there began to grow the institution of Celtic monasticism, an anticlerical, indomitably independent movement that could only have matured in a country secure from the riptides of European politics. The Celtic people were also traditionally imbued with the love of learning and in the fifth century Ireland was to become a haven for continental scholars fleeing the barbarians. Bringing nothing but their precious books, they found in the outer island an atmosphere of agreeable tolerance, and they gave their learning in return. Much of Europe's classical and Christian lore thus found a home in the Irish monasteries, where Gallic sages taught young Irish monks, who in turn transmitted their knowledge to the following generations. In the late sixth century Irish missionaries and scholars began to spread out of their own land and to take back to the Continent the learning that had been lost in postimperial disorder. Along with knowledge these evangelists brought back the pure fire of early Christian faith to a torn and materialistic country that had long since lost contact with the roots of its religion.

Columbanus was one of the earliest of the Irish apostles. He had received a fine education, and was well versed, not only in the writings of the Church Fathers, but in the pagan Latin and Greek classics regarded by continental churchmen as morally dangerous. He had been a revered teacher at Bangor, one of Ireland's great monastery schools. He was past forty-five when, in 590, he decided that he could better serve God by exiling himself from his too-serene cloister, to bring faith and hope to the peasantry of a harsher land. He left Ireland with twelve companions in his search for the most inhospitable territory, with the most disadvantaged inhabitants, that he could find. This was a quest typical of those generations of Irish monks, who did everything the hard way, with the sure knowledge that only thus could they find God.

Landing in Brittany, Columbanus made his way across Gaul to the court of Childebert II at Metz in Austrasia.[8] Advance word of his learning and eloquence had reached the young king and he invited the Irish missionary to lecture to the court. Columbanus was a poet as well as a teacher and words came happily to him. He acquitted himself in Latin so felicitously that Childebert and, even more so, his enlightened mother, Dowager Queen Brunhild, were enchanted. Columbanus was invited to make his home at Metz, to be a teacher and an ornament to Childebert's court.

But the missionary looked for a sterner challenge. With royal permission he traveled east and south until he found what he sought in the deeply forested, robber-infested valleys of the Vosges Mountains (today's Franche-Comté, near the Swiss and German borders). He chose an abandoned Roman fort at Annegray, a green hollow in the foothills. The inhabitants of the region were more than adequately benighted for the eager proselytizer. They were Suevians— descendants of the Teutonic tribes who, under the leadership of Ariovistus, had been defeated by Caesar five centuries before and had retreated to central Germany, never to feel the gentling touch either of Rome or of Christianity. They subsisted on primitive farming, and they pieced out a living by robbing travelers through the mountain passes. In the wintertime they starved.

The Suevians looked on the newcomers, with their unprotected monastic village and their virtuous scorn of weapons, as easy prey. But the monks had as little as they, sometimes going for weeks with nothing to eat but wild herbs and the bark of trees. Withal they were freehanded with their meager supplies. And for all their apparent mildness, they were at least as tough as their neighbors, and a good deal more efficient. When spring came they began to clear the rocky hillsides, the abbot working alongside his monks. The natives saw the corn come up, and they saw it harvested and threshed and stored against the winter. Soon the local populace was streaming in to Columbanus's village for food, for healing (he was one of those fortunate saints, familiar in Irish hagiography, who could cure wounds with his spittle), for advice, and finally for baptism.

Columbanus, starting with these destitute peasants, brought to Frankish Gaul a spirit that had long been absent in continental Christianity: the appeal, originated by Jesus, to the lowly country people. The Irish monastic system was close to the teachings of Jesus: it had the simplicity of primitive Christianity and of the Egyptian desert hermitages. Out of Ireland came a breed at once pragmatic and visionary. The Irish monks, transcendently devoted to the worship of God, were at the same time clearminded, hardworking and competent. Their philosophy of life aroused an enthusiastic response in

Merovingian Gaul. Within a few years not only the local farmers but the sons of nobles were coming to Annegray for help and counsel. Columbanus's foundation outgrew his first settlement and he founded another monastery at nearby Luxeuil, in a broad vale below the Vosges foothills. Many of his suppliants stayed on as monks. Many more were turned away from enrollment, for Columbanus's discipline was too rigorous for any except the strongest souls; he did not want fugitives from life looking for easy sanctuary.

Those who stayed were subject to a discipline that seems ruthless to us. The Irish abbot saw no painless road to salvation: the brothers were punished with the rod for an exasperating array of very minor delinquencies. As a general rule they must observe silence except at prayer times; they must work unremittingly, eat sparingly, sleep as little as possible; above all they must obey their superiors immediately and without qualification. Columbanus's strictures, harsh today, were welcome in his time. The farmers were used to hard work and privation, and the sons of noblemen welcomed the stern simplicity of the monastery, with its attendant wholesome tranquillity. Above all, everyone loved Columbanus himself, that ever-responsive spirit from whose genius flowed the ordered harmony of his institutions.

Luxeuil and its multiplying daughter houses were a vital spark in Merovingian Gaul, but to the upper clergy they and their strong-willed abbot were a nuisance. Gallic monasteries were supposed to be under the direct control of the bishops. The nonconformist Irish abbot paid no attention to their strictures, and there was no rule in the episcopal establishment that he did not break. In Ireland bishops were but adjuncts to the autonomous monasteries subservient only to their sovereign abbots. The pope himself was no more than a somewhat loftier bishop—in fact the Irish customarily referred to him as the Bishop of Rome.

The Gallic clerics thought that the upstart monk from simple, rural Ireland could easily be brought to heel. There were two obstacles: the first was the affection in which Columbanus was held by the king and the queen mother, for whom the charismatic Irishman could, at the moment, do no wrong. The second was Columbanus himself. Coming from a large and complex institution, where he had been the chief teacher and advisor to the abbot, he was no stranger to political maneuvering. He welcomed battles of words and he gave as good as he got.

Since Columbanus enjoyed royal favor the bishops could not get rid of him on the grounds of insubordination. They resorted to technical tactics, charging him with heresy in the Irish reckoning of the date of Easter.* Columbanus answered this challenge by writing directly to Pope Gregory I. The letter was a passionate, discursive appeal, warmly expressive of its writer's personality. It touched a chord in Pope Gregory, who had been abbot of his own monastery— an institution as austere as Luxeuil—and whose personal sympathies were on the side of the monasteries as against the materialistic episcopacy. But the pope could not afford to alienate the Gallic establishment, his chief support in Catholic Europe, simply to indulge his rapport with an appealing but stubborn and hot-tempered Irish monk. He had to settle the quarrel in Gaul and at the same time to heed his own conscience. He acted with finesse: he did not answer Columbanus's letter, as this would have emphasized the importance of the dispute. But he put the abbot of Luxeuil under the protection of the abbot of prestigious Lérins.

The bishops could no longer touch Columbanus. As it turned out they did not need to. The tactless abbot was setting about to undermine himself. In 595 King Childebert II, Columbanus's protector, died, and his minor sons, Theudebert II and Theodoric II, succeeded to the thrones of Austrasia and Burgundy under the regency of their grandmother. Brunhild was resident in Metz, where, as we have seen, she was an unending source of vexation to her nobility. The seigneurs sought to exert their influence through their representative, the Mayor of the Palace, and this personage finally, in 599, induced the weak-willed young king, Theudebert II, to banish his grandmother from the kingdom.

Brunhild did not go unwillingly. She had had to endure the acerbic rivalry of her grandson's queen, Bilichild. This girl was an ex-servant whom Brunhild had bought from a slave merchant, and who had risen through the position of king's concubine to that of king's wife. Bilichild "was much loved by all the Austrasians because she bore with nobility the simplemindedness of Theudebert."[9] For this reason, among others, she was a threat to the queen mother. Brunhild could only retain her influence over royal policy if she were the paramount

*The Irish religious establishment, separated from close communication with Rome and dispositionally unresponsive to papal authority anyway, followed the tradition in effect before 525, in which year the calculation of Easter Day had been changed by papal decree.

woman in the court; at her age she could not tolerate female rivalry. She tried to undermine Bilichild's position by disparaging her low origin. The young queen responded with spirit, and lost no opportunity for insulting the aging amazon. The two queens provoked one another to the extent that Brunhild was quite ready to remove herself to the court of her other grandson at Besançon in Burgundy.

King Theodoric II received her warmly. As pliable as his brother, but still without a wife to direct his feathery inclinations, he was cheerfully amenable to his grandmother's experienced authority. But he was also under the influence of the equally domineering abbot of Luxeuil. Through Brunhild herself, Columbanus's patroness, her grandson had learned to love the Irish monk. The monastery was not far from Besançon and intercourse between court and the cloister was frequent and friendly. At this moment, critical in all three lives, the righteous abbot made an inconvenient display of moral severity. The young king had four concubines, by whom he had had four children. This domestic arrangement was encouraged by Brunhild, who saw no menace in multiple nonlicit liaisons. It was stringently opposed by Columbanus, who admonished the king almost daily to give up his sinful affiliations and settle down with a legal, churchgoing wife. Easygoing Theodoric listened to his mentor and chose a Spanish princess, Ermenberta. The Gothic court in Spain was still, as in the time of Brunhild's girlhood, the most civilized in Europe, and the young woman's good upbringing was combined with the highest moral standards. She was even a Catholic, her father, the Visigothic king Reccared, having elected to be converted, along with all his court, from the Arian heresy.

Brunhild, a product of the same background, saw Ermenberta as a primary threat. With a new queen in Burgundy, no matter how well intentioned, the old queen would be superfluous. Brunhild had reached a state of frozen imperiousness where she could not countenance the loss of any of her prerogatives. She set about to rid her grandson's kingdom both of the dangerous bride and of the man who had inspired the choice, Brunhild's old protégé, Columbanus. She so effectively poisoned Theodoric's mind against his young wife that a year after his marriage he sent Ermenberta back to Spain—without her dowry—and took back his concubines.

Then the dowager queen turned to the abbot of Luxeuil. She had warmly admired Columbanus for his spiritual fire when he had first come to her son's court in Metz. Recognizing his purifying influence on the decadent Frankish establishment, she had protected him for years against her indignant bishops. Now her old friend was her open enemy. To Brunhild Columbanus had become a meddling monk dipping his fingers into politics when he should be attending to his prayers. On his side Columbanus saw his first patroness as a Jezebel pretending piety while she plotted to undermine the very foundations of the faith. As both had aged their perspectives had narrowed. There could be no compromise between their opposing and petrified prejudices.

Brunhild's enmity was activated by more than personal pique. The Irish abbot's flouting of the bishops had become a problem. The established church was indispensable to Brunhild's role as virtual monarch. The bishops valued her secular backing and her influence with the pope; she in turn needed their support in her struggle against the rebellious seigneurs. Columbanus had no sympathy for these worldly requirements. His aims were ethereal.

Brunhild took two of her grandson's bastard children to Columbanus and requested that he baptize them. As she had foreseen, this was a torch to the volcanic old man: he refused angrily, calling them "children of a brothel," and following his outburst with a letter to Theodoric threatening him with excommunication if he did not mend his depraved ways. Theodoric retaliated with the threat to cut off the monastery's alms, on which its continued existence depended. Columbanus replied that he did not want alms from sinners. He punctuated this unwise declaration with a rather silly miracle in which the dishes and flasks of a meal sent to him by Theodoric flew out of the servants' hands, scattering food and wine all over the courtyard. Theodoric, now exasperated, had Columbanus thrown into jail at Besançon. There the saint engaged himself in striking the chains from the prisoners' legs, causing the doors to fly open and leading the whole company to church, where a startled jailer found them praying for forgiveness for their sins. The officer herded his charges back into prison and quietly allowed the abbot to go home. Theodoric, understanding that heaven was temporarily against him, went to Luxeuil to try to appease his old mentor. But tempers ran high again. Theodoric demanded entry to the inner monastery, which he claimed was kept illegally secret, and Columbanus refused, calling his ex-protégé an enemy of religion and threatening him with a curse if he crossed the threshold. Theodoric, ignoring him, put his foot over the forbidden sill. Then, "All saw the power of God burst

into flame within him," as Columbanus uttered his curse: "Your
kingdom will be destroyed together with all your royal family."

Theodoric stepped back, shocked. He recovered himself sufficiently
to warn the saint that he would not honor him with "the crown of
martyrdom," but would follow the wiser course of banishing him from
the kingdom. Columbanus was forcibly expelled with all his Irish
monks, and in 610, nearly seventy years old, he set out on his
wanderings again, typically singing as he went, songs of his own
composition, to keep up the spirits of his equally aged companions.
The long journey took him finally, four years later, over the Alps in
midwinter to the foothills of the Apennines, country as wild as his
first retreat at Annegray in the Vosges. There, in a narrow curved
valley at the confluence of two rushing rivers, he founded his last
monastery, Bobbio, which would exert a potent influence on north
Italian monasticism, and would house one of the greatest libraries in
Europe. In 615, a year after the founding, Columbanus died.

Though flagrant self-interest had expelled the Irish monks from
Gaul no action in high places could dissipate the Irish influence.
Luxeuil continued to thrive under Gallic monks trained by Columbanus and committed to his brand of austere spirituality; and the
teaching of the Irish saint spread throughout Frankish Gaul. At the
time of Columbanus's death there were forty daughter houses, and
less than a hundred years later ninety-four monasteries for both men
and women, patterned after Luxeuil and based on the Irish rule.
Luxeuil itself, leveled by Arabs early in the eighth century, then again
by repeated Viking raids in the ninth and tenth, finally lost its power
of recovery. No trace remains in the present-day prosperous health
resort of the great sixth-century monastic center. The memory of its
founder lingers: outside the big dim thirteenth-century Gothic
church stands a bronze figure cast in 1945 by the sculptor, Claude
Granges. The piece has a windblown excitement, long hair streaming
back from the tonsured forehead, monk's habit flying, face grimly set
against wickedness, right arm raised in a gesture of vehement
indignation. The figure well expresses the words inscribed on the
pedestal: "Tous voyaient éclater en lui la puissance de Dieu."

Though Luxeuil is only a memory a few others of the Columbanian
institutions still exist, in much altered form, and here and there a
seventh-century chapel or crypt survives. One such is at Jouarre,
about forty miles east of Paris, a crypt with an extraordinary display

of Frankish Christian art. A double monastery was founded there in 635 by Adon, a monk from Luxeuil who had known Columbanus. Its backers and several of its abbesses were members of a family high in the court of King Dagobert, the last strong Merovingian. The enthusiasm of such consequential families, and the survival of Jouarre and other Columbanian houses long after the departure and death of their founder, give testimony to the enduring Irish genius.

The breath of fresh air that the Irish monks had brought to Gaul infused all facets of monastic life: besides the healing spiritual purity of the Irish outlook the new monasticism was sane and productive. It reached outward, in contrast to many of the reclusive Gallic monasteries. In the first place Columbanus did not share the prevailing ecclesiastical view of the impurity of women. Though an ascetic, he had no horror of the opposite sex;* he founded double monasteries and acted as spiritual adviser to married women. Many of his women friends became warm supporters of the monastic life and looked with favor on religious vocation in their children.

In another direction Columbanus's tolerance had a profound impact. He had never been suspicious of the seduction of pagan literature and alien philosophies; on the contrary the Latin and Greek studies of his youth had fostered in him an appreciation of the elegance and wisdom of the classical mind. It is partly due to him, through the schools and libraries he founded, that the classical poets and thinkers were given an honored place in the medieval curriculum. Though his mission was primarily evangelical Columbanus was the first in a long line of Irish scholars who would bring back to Europe its lost legacy of classical knowledge.

In his monastic discipline Columbanus harked back to John Cassian's conception of the eremitic life, in which idleness was to be avoided above all, as leading to the sin of acedia, and through it to all of human waywardness. Columbanus's motivation was more far-sighted than Cassian's. The poet-scholar, with his classical education and his background as a teacher, knew that an athletic spirituality was only half the purpose of the religious life. The other half was recognition of the diversified beauty of God's creation in all its human manifestations. Without cultivation of the mind the strength of the soul is arid and pointless. Columbanus did not advocate labor

---

*In his youth Columbanus had been neurotically shy of girls, but maturity had cured his fear.

simply for the purpose of keeping his monks out of trouble; work must be constructive and creative as well, in all areas from digging in the earth to the erudition of the scriptorium. His monks tilled the fields with the skills of contemporary agricultural science—not for therapy but so that they could feed themselves and their indigent neighbors in the inclement Vosges winters. They labored with their pens and inks in the cloister—not to keep their fingers busy but to transcribe on parchment in illuminated script the perishable words of the masters. Their fields were models of efficiency, their libraries are still famous today.

The Irish foundations in Gaul brought monasticism far on the way to its medieval position as the central force of industry and culture in Europe. Under the guidance of Columbanus and his followers the dark ages of Western education began to give way to ramified institutions of higher learning. The simple farming of peasants who still turned the earth with a single-stick hand plow inadequate for the heavy soil of northern Europe started to yield to revolutionary techniques evolved on the big monastic farms. Medieval farmer-monks developed the deep-furrow plow drawn by draft animals, the windmill, the stiff horse-collar, the horseshoe, the water wheel and other practical and radical innovations.

With all their beneficent influence, why then did the Irish fail in Gaul? Two reasons—their singleminded faith and their popularity—appear at first sight conflicting. The Irish missionaries, adamantly holy, had an ecstatic commitment to the attainment of grace. They were dedicated to conveying this to all the unsaved sinners of their new land. They succeeded to a remarkable extent: not only did they convert heathens and reclaim backsliders, they exerted a potent influence on wealthy and highborn Christians as well. But their unyielding self-denial was in the long run too rigorous for the Gallic temperament. A milder form of monastic discipline, that did not demand of its converts the equivalent of early Christian martyrdom, would ultimately fare better.

Still, the Irish monks, fervent, compassionate and humanitarian, were beloved to an extent that became both embarrassing and dangerous to the episcopal status quo. They offered too attractive an alternative to the hegemony of the established Church. It came down to a fundamental choice: should the Church, as in Saint Augustine's concept, encompass all of society? Or should it, following the purest monastic ideal, separate itself from the secular world? The latter was the end product of Celtic monasticism: Columbanus had pointed the way early in his Gallic abbacy by defying the authority of the bishops. The episcopacy was the vital network of Church authority. A threat to it as lively as Columbanus's dynamism endangered the continued existence of the centralized Catholic Church.

The pope himself was finally constrained to counteract. For all his sympathy Gregory I understood that the Celtic monastic movement had to be contained if fatal cleavage between the secular and ecclesiastical worlds was to be avoided. He found the answer in the Benedictine rule. Sixty years before Columbanus came to Gaul the discreet and gentle Saint Benedict of Nursia had founded a monastery at Monte Cassino in southern Italy, an institution distinguished by moderation and calm. Asceticism was temperate: Benedict's monks did not starve themselves to achieve grace; they slept normal hours with a pillow, not a stone, under their heads; minor disobedience was not punished with flogging. Work was mandatory simply as a foil to idleness: the brothers were not expected to strive for an ever higher plane. Benedict's rule was not importunate. It allowed for individual weaknesses and its main emphasis was on peace. If it appears a negative rule, it was by far more practicable in the seventh century than the strenuous aspiration of the Celtic rule. For Pope Gregory's purpose it was peculiarly useful: flexible, prudent and low key, easily lending itself to control from Rome. For the common run of novices it was a comfortable alternative to Columbanus's otherworldly ardor. The Irish abbot was too extreme for history. His movement, loftily self-determining, antiepiscopate, disdainful of worldly concerns, could not sustain its transcendental intensity amid the dislocation of the seventh century—nor, probably, could it have in any other epoch. It would fail in England, and ultimately even in Ireland, its cradle.

Pope Gregory gave the Benedictine order his blessing, and under the patronage of successive popes the rule spread over Europe. By the middle of the eighth century, two hundred years after its founding, the Benedictine discipline had become the principal monastic code, absorbing all other continental rules. But there was never any friction; in Gaul the two orders existed amicably side by side for many years.

The difficult, impractical Irish were gone, and the Gallic Church was the better for their having been there. But for Queen Brunhild, who had pushed them out, the bettering or worsening of the Church had little more moment. The point had come in the life of the old queen when she was as unwelcome to the political establishment as Columbanus to the episcopal, and the malevolence she aroused was more deadly than the disapprobation of a few bishops.

Brunhild's final years were dominated by the relentless opposition of her seigneurs. When the death of King Sigibert in 575 had given the Austrasian nobles a chance, they thought, to control the throne through the minor king, Childebert II, they had been, as a class, too irresponsible to offer anything but anarchy in its place. Brunhild's regency had then been a more attractive alternative. Twenty years later, by the time of the accession of Brunhild's grandsons, the queen had lost much of her early magnetism, and her imperial posture was out of date. At the same time her opponents had developed from a highborn rabble of raw dissenters to a class with a valid structure. A few had arisen within it who were accountable citizens with an honest concern for the welfare of their country.

Two of these conscientious seigneurs took the lead in the struggle of the Austrasian nobles against Brunhild. Though they were not personally responsible for the climate of hatred surrounding her, it was their prowess as warriors, combined with superior statesmanship, which created for this branch of the Merovingians the conditions of defeat.

One was Arnulf, an Austrasian of noble parentage who had risen high in the court of Brunhild's grandson, Theudebert II of Austrasia, and who would later become adviser to Brunhild's foremost enemy, Lothair II, the king of Neustria. Though Arnulf's early years were devoted to the services of various Merovingian kings his bent was toward the religious life. His opportunity arose when his wife became a nun; Arnulf thereupon decided to retire to the monastery of Lérins as a simple monk. But his services were too valuable to permit him the life of a hermit, and against his will he was made bishop of Metz by King Lothair II in 610. He fulfilled his position honorably, continuing to play a prominent role in state affairs, until he was finally allowed to retire in 626. His place of retreat was Remiremont, an abbey founded by one of Columbanus's companions (to become, in the eleventh century, a wealthy and powerful convent for highborn ladies of France and Germany), and there, in 643, he died. Remiremont, north of Besançon, is in the foothills of the Vosges, rolling country of fields and woods, gracious to the eye and extremely lush.

Nothing remains of the seventh-century foundation and very little of the eleventh, but the town, sheltered in a corner of the valley of the Moselle, has a pretty, old-fashioned tranquillity.

The other effective leader was Pepin of Landen (later to be known as Pepin the Old), an Austrasian noble of obscure descent. His sobriquet indicates an origin in Toxandria (eastern Belgium), the area of the first Frankish settlements in Roman Gaul. From the beginning of his career Pepin was actively opposed to Brunhild's hegemony in the kingdoms of Austrasia and Burgundy, and he would take a prominent part in the revolution of 613 that would cause her downfall. Pepin had a daughter, Begga, who married Ansegisal, a son of Arnulf: these two were the progenitors of the Arnulfings—the house of Pepin—a family which would produce, over the next hundred years, a succession of exceptionally able men, rulers of Francia in fact, later also in name—the last one being Charlemagne. In our period, the early seventh century, they represented the best of the Austrasian aristocracy. They aimed to abrogate Queen Brunhild's supremacy—not to aggrandize themselves or to indulge a lust for crude power, but because they considered her brand of absolutism anachronistic. In a seventh-century way they were prophets of a constitutional monarchy.

To Brunhild inalienable authority was implicit in kingship, and any frame of reference that entailed the shrinkage of the king's supreme dominion was anathema. Her upbringing and her years of practice in the habits of power had made her an unyielding absolutist. The Austrasian aristocracy, disliking her Roman perspective, had connived at her expulsion from Metz. After her establishment in Burgundy she acted with impetuous unwisdom to quell its contumacy and to crush its creature, her own grandson Theudebert.

First there was an immediate threat which needed the temporary cooperation of the two brother kings: the trespassing enterprise of young King Lothair II of Neustria. Fredegund's son, whatever his real parentage, had grown up to be an authentic sharkish Merovingian. Under the correct impression that his cousin of Burgundy was too weak to defend himself, Lothair had been appropriating pieces of the neighboring kingdom, but the joint action of the brothers under their grandmother's veteran pilotage was so successful that Lothair was not only thrown out of Burgundy, he lost much of his own kingdom as well.

Now would have been the ideal moment for the brothers to cement

their unity and push Lothair right to the Atlantic, making themselves joint rulers of all Francia. In the wonted usage of Merovingian
siblings they turned on each other instead; and their fratricidal
inclination was ignobly furthered by their grandmother. Brunhild
encouraged her Burgundian grandson, Theodoric, to attack his
Austrasian sibling, whose elimination seemed necessary to her maintenance of power. In 612 the two battled near Zülpich (where Clovis,
in alliance with the Christian God, had defeated the Allemans in
496) with surpassing viciousness: "The carnage on both sides was
such that in the fighting line there was no room for the slain to fall
down. They stood upright in their ranks, corpse supporting corpse, as
if they still lived."[10] The Burgundians prevailed in the end. Theudebert of Austrasia was captured and paraded in chains before his
brother; then his head was cut off and displayed on the wall of the
city of Cologne.

Theodoric was now ruler of combined Austrasia and Burgundy as
well as a good part of Neustria. He lived less than a year to enjoy his
magnified kingdom. In 613 he died of dysentery, aged twenty-six. A
chronicler of the late seventh century[11] declared that Brunhild herself
poisoned her second grandson because he drew his sword against her
in anger at her evil counsel, and that she then went on to murder his
young sons. There is no corroboratory evidence for this account. The
anonymous historian was probably attached to the court of the
Neustrian king, and his bias against Brunhild and her family was
based on provincial chauvinism.

Now the last of Saint Columbanus's prophesy was fulfilled.
Brunhild had four great-grandsons, all under eleven, and the indomi-
table queen proposed once more to assume the regnancy on their
behalf. Her imperial proclivity led her to go counter to the customary
Frankish practice of dividing the kingdoms equally among the heirs.
She saw the rule of one as more practicable, and she chose Sigibert,
son of Theodoric of Burgundy, as the sole ruler of the realm. Little
Sigibert II lasted but a few months. The Austrasian seigneurs were
not to be thwarted again. They authorized their leaders, Arnulf and
Pepin, to offer the combined thrones of Austrasia and Burgundy to
the Neustrian king, Lothair II. This time the insurgents had the
bishops on their side. The clear-sighted Gallo-Romans could read the
shape of the future better than most: they observed that the day of
their old-line royal ally was done, and that their continued well-being

required their active conversion to the cause of Francia's coming masters. On his side the new champion, Lothair II, needed no urging: still galled at his humiliating defeat by Brunhild's grandsons, he was glad to march against their detested grandmother. He apparently did not perceive that as king of all the Franks he would be little more than a figurehead subject to the de facto jurisdiction of the Austrasian leaders, Arnulf and Pepin.

The revolution of 613 took place without a battle. Lothair bought off Brunhild's generals, so that when the Neustrian army advanced against them the Burgundian forces fell back without resistance and the soldiers calmly went home. Three of the young princes were captured and two of them, Sigibert II and a younger brother, were immediately executed. A third was spared because Lothair had sponsored him at his baptism, and Christian superstition was, in this minor case, stronger than barbarian blood feud. The fourth child escaped. Neither made his way into subsequent Merovingian history.

Following his bloodless triumph Lothair II called Brunhild to him, ostensibly to make peace. She had no choice. Dressed in her royal robes she presented herself with formal courage before her enemy. When she appeared Lothair's army shouted for her death. Lothair, affecting to defer to popular outcry, reviled her for her general wickedness and then accused her of causing the deaths of ten Frankish kings. He decreed three days of diverse torture, after which the old woman (she was near seventy) was "led through the ranks on a camel. Finally she was tied by her hair, one arm and one leg to the tail of an unbroken horse, and she was cut to shreds by its hoofs at the pace it went."[12] Her corpse was burned, even the bones, and the ashes scattered. Queen Brunhild has no grave.

The fury that compassed Brunhild's end is out of proportion to her sin—intrinsically that of outliving her era. The Gothic princess had come to Gaul from a background of Roman education. Her husband, Sigibert, had a similar predilection toward the ancient Roman values—as, indeed, had all the four reigning grandsons of Clovis. In the sixth century an ineffable awe still surrounded the old imperial ideals. Rome's authority was discountenanced all over Europe, and even with Emperor Justinian's doomed experiment in Italy the western Empire was effectively dismantled. But the prestige of old Rome still lingered, and Brunhild tried to instill the imperial ethos in a German realm that had no such tradition. Oblivious to the rising currents of seventh-century Austrasia, she carried the lessons of her

youth right through to her last calamitous regency. She died exe-
crated.

She was an extraordinary woman for her time—for any time. Her
high courage, her able statesmanship and her capacity for the
arduous work of administration were combined with a natural
compassion very rare in the sixth century, outside of monasteries. She
had the misfortune to rule at the wrong time and in the wrong place:
to try to uphold by old-fashioned tenets a dynasty already entering
decrepitude, in the face of a social movement that was young and
dynamic.

Looked at from a distant perspective Brunhild represents the dying
breath of the Roman Empire in Gaul. In a more immediate context
her destruction marks the beginning of the end of the Merovingian
epoch: not far in the future is the glimmer of the Middle Ages. It was
an ugly beginning to a new era.

PART III  THE TRANSITION

CHAPTER EIGHT

THE MAYORS OF THE PALACE

Brunhild had been the victim of the thrusting power of the aristocracy under newly able leadership. Her death was a divide: on the far
side are one hundred and thirty-two years of generally strong and
warlike Merovingian kings. On the hither side five remarkable leaders
from the evolving upper class dominate the kingdom for the next
hundred and fifty-five years. The Merovingian dynasty, in these
years, sinks into the condition of "lesser beasts." The later Merovingians, continuing to wield the scepter and, incredibly, to hold the
loyalty—by this time largely ritualistic—of their subjects, are known
as *rois fainéants*, sluggard kings. The royal youths (few lived to
manhood) were, most of them, dissolute, weak willed and indolent.
Yet they were kept on the throne generation after generation by their
masters, the Mayors of the Palace. These noblemen, Francia's actual
rulers, propped up the useless incumbents of the throne because they
themselves were not yet ready to challenge the entrenched fidelity
still elicited by the descendants of Clovis.

The outstanding representatives of the new social and political
power were scions of the rising house of Pepin. Through the course of
a century and a half, five generations of this house held the office of
Mayor of the Palace, a position which had grown into ascendancy
since the death of Sigibert I in 575 and the accession of his minor
son.

The origin of the post of *majorus-domus*, Mayor of the Palace, was in the workaday area of domestic management, a sphere uncongenial to the conquering Franks. The Teutonic warriors, from a background of alternating battle and carousal, found themselves, in Gaul, metamorphosed into large landowners in a fertile and well-populated country. They were averse to the moil of plowing and sowing, and untrained to manage the wealth that came from it. The acquisition of landed riches with its accompanying civil authority complicated their lives immeasurably. The organizing of their new splendor and of their swelling flood of dependents required a domestic expertise not only beneath them, but also beyond them. The solution was the creation of the office of Mayor of the Palace, the summit of the domestic pyramid of the royal household.

Along with its domestic convenience the position of Mayor of the Palace came to include an intrinsic ascendancy in the administration of government. When the Franks had still been tribal chieftains whose main business was war, they had been subject to the *campus martius*, the periodic assembly of their warriors, who would counsel them, support them or reject them depending on their martial success and personal popularity. Now that they were kings they saw the *campus martius* as dangerously democratic. They did not want a group of independent stalwarts interfering with their despotic control of large and fruitful realms, and they discontinued the assembly. Instead, to help them manage the government, they came to rely on a council that included generals, antrustions, provincial dignitaries, bishops and a selection of the king's upper servants, known as courtiers. At the head of the palace courtiers was the Mayor of the Palace, who, if he were an able man, was the most influential figure in the royal cabinet, and usually its presiding member. Another quality was required of him: in those embattled times no secular official could rise high without military skill. Most of the men who held the position of Mayor of the Palace had to have been warriors before they became statesmen. The king depended on his top administrator to aid him in the frequent contests with the belligerent aristocracy. Up to the death of Sigibert I, the Mayor of the Palace discharged this duty loyally along with his domestic and administrative obligations.

Such was the commanding position of this personage that he became *ex officio* the king's deputy, and when the king was a minor he evolved into the executor of royal power. There were minor kings in Austrasia, as we have seen, from the death of Sigibert in 575 until the death of Brunhild's great-grandson Sigibert II, in 613. In this thirty-eight-year period, when the Austrasian seigneurs eyed the throne wolfishly, the position of Mayor of the Palace changed from that of the king's chosen surrogate to that of aristocracy's instrument. He was elected by the seigneurs as one of their own, to further their interests at court rather than, as had been his initial function, to protect the king against their importunities.

The same thing was happening in Neustria. Young Lothair II, not yet thirty when he became king of all the Franks, was by no means the potentate he had seen himself when he annihilated Brunhild and her line and took over the thrones of Austrasia and Burgundy. Though the growth of Neustria's powerful aristocracy was slower and less complete than in Austrasia, Neustria was in the same historical drift. In all of Francia the day of the warrior despot was over. Lothair II, for all his inherited belief in the implicit supremacy of the Merovingian dynasty, was in everyday practice the creature of the power elite. And the ruling circle itself, in all three northern kingdoms, was dominated by its chosen dean, first among equals, the Mayor of the Palace.

In 615, a year after his accession to the combined kingdoms, Lothair II called a council of seventy-nine bishops at Paris. Through them he promulgated the Edict of Paris, a remarkably reformist program for its time (it has been called the French Magna Carta), limiting the powers of royal taxation and administration. So far as we can read between the lines of contemporary history, the measures of the Council of Paris were not imposed by an assertive aristocracy upon an unwilling and capricious monarch. On the contrary the king appears to have called the council of his own volition, and the liberality of its directives was instigated by Lothair's sense of obligation to the seigneurs who had supported him.

In Lothair's final years, as king of all the Franks, an entirely different character emerges from that which he displayed in his sadistic destruction of Brunhild. He had reacted to the threat of the rival house with desperate, almost psychotic violence. But once he was secure in his supreme position he exhibited an amenability to reason, even a good humor, quite at variance with the monstrous steps he had taken to get there. We have to make allowances, in our view of Lothair II, for the prejudice of the seventh-century historian, "Fredegar," whose *Chronicle* is the only adequate source for the history of this period.[1] "Fredegar" is one of several authors who wrote under that name, almost certainly members of the clergy, since that was the only literate class. The first part of the chronicle is written by one who reported events firsthand from 603 until 642 from his base in Burgundy. His dislike of Brunhild is fanatical, and his approval unqualified of her enemies, the Austrasian Mayors of the Palace and the Neustrian royal house which backed them. Lothair II was king of all the Franks, he wrote, "for sixteen happy years, during which he kept peace with all the neighboring peoples." He was also an openhanded patron of churches and monasteries, and "patient"—an improbable characterization. His only flaws were gregarious ones: he was an enthusiastic and successful card player, he was excessively devoted to the chase and "he took too much notice of the views of women young and old."

Fredegar praises the king's friendly relations with the Mayors of the Palace and his ready cooperation with their wishes. The Austrasian seigneurs, who had in 613 successfully rebelled against their own monarchy, were developing a sense almost of separate nationality from the Neustrian Franks of the Seine basin. To keep them within the Frankish family and to preserve their loyalty to the Merovingian dynasty Lothair, in 623, relinquished his personal governance of Austrasia and gave the nobles his young son, Dagobert, for their own king. Dagobert, though recently come of age, was not to be an old-fashioned independent king: his Mayor of the Palace was Pepin of Landen, chief actor in the revolution of 613. Pepin's coleader, Arnulf, was still bishop of Metz, and these two industrious lords ordered the administration of the eastern kingdom.

But Dagobert, while cheerfully accepting the direction of his surrogates, had the trappings of an imperious, even a magnificent, monarch. In his era the legend was first recorded of the procreation of the eponymous ancestor, Merovech, by a sea monster. The story, recounted in the *Chronicle of Fredegar*, sprang into life full blown with no popular folk myth behind it, and it is likely that it was devised, by someone close to Dagobert's court, to glorify the royal name. Like his father Dagobert was freehanded, sociable, addicted to the chase and to women (he had at least three wives and "mistresses without number"). When Lothair II died in 629 Dagobert became king of all the Franks. He moved his court from the rough-textured environment of Austrasia and established it in Paris, where the neo-Gallo-Roman civilization was at its most corrupt. There he abandoned himself to uncontrolled debauch, indulging in countless mistresses and in such extravagance that arbitrary exactions had to be imposed to support the immoderate luxury of his court. He even stopped giving alms. Dagobert's last years were a sinister foretaste of the sick depravity of succeeding Merovingians.

While he lived in Paris Dagobert became a converted Neustrian, to the disgust of his Austrasian supporters; he ceased to listen to the counsels of the wise and strong Pepin, and appointed a more flexible Neustrian as Mayor of the Palace. The seigneurs became dangerously disaffected: battles against the Wends, trespassers on the eastern edge of the country, were consistently lost because Austrasian commanders refused to lead their men to war beside Neustrian troops. Even sunk in voluptuous debauch, Dagobert finally understood that his eastern kingdom was slipping away from him. The Austrasian nobles would not tolerate a Neustrian-slanted king, and to regain their fealty there had to be a new Merovingian on that throne. In 632 the king summoned bishops and nobles to Metz and presented to them as their future king his three-year-old son, Sigibert. Royal authority reverted to the hands of the aristocracy which, satisfied, once again became suitably warlike—and the Merovingian dynasty began its final downhill slide. Pepin of Landen was not made Mayor of the Palace for little Sigibert III. Dagobert no longer trusted the leading Austrasian insurrectionist, and appointed a bishop in his stead. The old warhorse was detained at the court in Paris as a sort of hostage. Pepin was eventually reinstated, and ruled until his natural death in 640.

Following the accession of Sigibert III the Neustrians sought to strengthen their hand in order to counteract the resurgent energy of the rival Austrasians. Aiming to unite the two kingdoms of Neustria and Burgundy, they persuaded King Dagobert to bequeath these kingdoms to another Merovingian child, Clovis. The new king, aged five, and the younger brother of Sigibert III, was Dagobert's son by Nanthild, a "maiden of the bedchamber" whom he had elevated to queen.

Before Dagobert surrendered to intemperate sensuality he was a strong and diligent king. He was the last Merovingian to direct his own armies: the final legatee of the barbarian convention of fighting as a requisite of kingly activity. Unlike those of his ancestors,

Dagobert's fights were planned campaigns in response to aggression on his borders.

His eastern kingdom was harassed by the Wends, an independent Slavic tribe which had been impelled west in flight from the freebooting Avars. But after Dagobert gave the Austrasians his son Sigibert as their personal king, they competently pushed the Wends back.

In the south Dagobert's army interfered in Spanish politics, helping the magnates there to rid themselves of a king they particularly disliked. He put down a revolt in the Pyrenees region by the Gascons, a people who had never lost their hostility to Frankish rule. Then he removed this same army, with remarkable speed, to overawe his perennially reluctant tribute people, the Bretons.

Between campaigns the active monarch found time, with the accomplished help of his council, to attend to the manifold business of administration, the disposal of land, appointments to offices, taxes, the dispensing of justice, all the complexities of his enormous realm. He also gave himself leisure to appreciate the arts, an indulgence unfamiliar to most of his undereducated family. The aesthetic fringe of his life is one of the most attractive facets of this last creditable Merovingian. Following the precedent of his grandfather, Chilperic, Dagobert supported ecclesiastical scholars and encouraged the growth of native Frankish art. His personal goldsmith, Eligius, or Éloi, was an energetic and greatly beloved man, later canonized. As bishop of Noyon and Tournai, Éloi evangelized Flanders. He also helped to ameliorate the lot of slaves, being instrumental in forbidding their sale out of the country and in giving them freedom to rest on Sundays. He had been a friend to Dagobert's father, Lothair II, who had made him master of the mint. Dagobert employed him to make exquisitely crafted gold objects—chalices, crosses and plaques, and to decorate tombs and shrines. Saint Éloi was distinguished not only for his beautiful designs but for his admirable economy: he made two gold thrones out of the metal allocated for one. He is the patron saint of metalworkers: in a fourteenth-century representation he shoes a horse whose leg he removes for the purpose, then replaces.

As a popular and emphatic preacher Éloi specifically anathematized superstition, which he viewed as a survival of pagan ritual—this was a boldly progressive stance in his day. On the secular side, as one of Dagobert's chief counsellors, he led a mission to the Breton king: in 636 he convinced that recalcitrant monarch to acknowledge Frankish authority without military inducement. (The success of this mission was insured by the persuasive presence of Dagobert's army encamped just over the border.)

Besides Dagobert's enthusiastic patronage of Saint Éloi the king was generous to the Church. Even during his extravagantly greedy days in Paris, when he used the Church as a luxuriant source of revenue, he also laid the foundation for the later wealth and renown of the abbey and church of Saint Denis. In his youth, while hunting north of Paris, Dagobert had followed a deer to a small village, Catolacus, where the animal fled up the main street and took refuge in an ancient chapel. This was the neglected church built in 475 by Saint Geneviève on the spot where Saint Denis had finally laid down his severed head and surrendered his soul. Later King Dagobert returned to this place, fleeing in his turn from the temporary anger of his father. He fell asleep in the shelter of the little church and dreamed of its martyr-saint. Thankful for the night's sanctuary, and for the comforting vision, he subsequently, about 630, had the church enlarged and embellished with gold and gems, "in the hope of ensuring the precious patronage of the saint." Among the decorations was an altar plaque by the goldsmith Éloi.

A miracle accompanied the opening of Dagobert's reconstructed church. On the eve of its consecration, when everyone had been ordered to leave, a leper hid himself in an alcove and went to sleep. He was awakened in the night by a shining light, and beheld Christ surrounded by the apostles, a crowd of angels, and Saint Denis. The heavenly host proceeded to consecrate the church. At the end Christ instructed the leper to tell King Dagobert the next day what he had witnessed. As proof of His presence Christ then removed the leper's diseased skin and threw it against the wall. Starting the next morning at the official ceremonies, the grisly memento became a holy relic.

The later history of Saint Denis is the story of the growth of a medieval city around a repository of holy relics. By the seventh century, unthinking piety had filled the intellectual gap left by the dissolution of the Western Empire and the fading of the classical tradition; and the cult of relics had become the dominant attribute of Gallic religious life. Besides the bones of its patron saint and the skin of the leper, the church of Saint Denis accumulated many blessed trifles and the collection attracted crowds of the sick or indigent faithful. Saint Denis and similar shrines around the country became the nucleus of towns and the focal point of economic and artistic activity. King Dagobert, recognizing the potential, made a large gift of land for the founding of a Benedictine monastery attached to the church of Saint Denis. He further enriched the growing village by establishing, about 635, the Fair of Saint Denis on October ninth, the saint's feast day.

When Dagobert died in 639 he was interred in the church, the first reigning monarch to be buried there. There had been two previous royal burials: Arnegund, the second wife of Lothair I, who died about 570, and whose exquisitely clothed and jeweled skeleton was found intact in her tomb beneath the present altar; and Dagobert the Young, the little son of Chilperic and Fredegund, who died of dysentery in 580. Subsequently the church became the necropolis of French kings from the Merovingians to the Revolution.

The present-day cathedral of Saint Denis is a magnificent twelfth-century structure, the first great Gothic church in France, prototype for Chartres. Dagobert's tomb, importantly placed beside the altar, is an elaborate thirteenth-century marble tabernacle with a pious drama carved on its panels. In the lowest panel, Saint John the Baptist views the soul of the Frankish king carried in a boat by demons down the river to hell. In the middle one he is wrested from their grasp through the grace of saints Denis, Maurice and Martin. In the top panel these three transport the child-sized naked spirit to be presented in heaven.

Dagobert reigned for sixteen years, and his death in 639 was the end of sustained Merovingian rule. A few individuals after him were self-respecting monarchs with a genuine interest in affairs of government. But they did not rule long, and they were preceded and followed by feeble princes with no desires beyond self-gratification. The picture is a sad one, of pampered, unschooled royal children hidden away in palace nurseries, allowed indulgence in every sort of vice while they grew into diseased or imbecilic adulthood. The accounts are exaggerated, but the decline of the royal line is real. However, it owed its eclipse as much to the new social forces as to its inherent defects.

The failing of the old line was gradual and the upthrust of the new power erratic. For nearly half a century the Mayors of the Palace quarreled among themselves bloodily and often fatally, much as had the fratricidal Merovingians of the century before. But the unruly seigneurs had not the authority of royal descent behind their bids for power, with the result that not even the victors could realize a united kingdom. The history of these destructive quarrels is so tangled that we will sketch it only briefly. Dagobert left only children on the thrones: Clovis II, king of Burgundy, and Sigibert III, king of Austrasia. Sigibert III was the first Merovingian who was veritably a puppet king. The real ruler, as we have seen, was the Mayor of the Palace, the hero Pepin the Old, who had already been administering the government for some years as deputy for King Dagobert. But Pepin died a year after Dagobert, and the Austrasian office devolved on his son, Grimoald, a strong, generous and initially sensible official. While Sigibert lived Grimoald honored him as a genuine king. In evidence of this the young king himself, at the age of eleven, was allowed to lead his troops into battle against the revolting Thuringians. The Frankish army was defeated, and we are presented with a pitiful sight: the little boy, "seized with wildest grief, sat on his horse weeping unrestrainedly for those he had lost." The child then had to ask permission from the enemy to find his way home; on the journey he was guarded and assisted by his mentor, Grimoald. Sigibert's ancestor, Clovis, still in his teens when he fought his first battle, would not have recognized this pathetic descendant.

Sigibert III died in 656, at twenty-seven, and Grimoald now became more ambitious than sensible. As Mayor of the Palace he had been ruler in fact. The death of the puppet king and the accession of his very young son appeared a propitious time for him to present himself with the name as well. He caused the royal child, Dagobert II, to be spirited away to Ireland, where he was shorn and consecrated as an eight-year-old monk. Grimoald had a son with the convenient Merovingian name of Childebert. Giving out that the true heir had died and that this youth had been adopted by Sigibert III, he persuaded his partisans to elevate Childebert on the shield as king of Austrasia.

But Grimoald anticipated history. The majority of Franks was not yet ready to reject the family of Clovis. More disastrously, Grimoald's action incurred the jealous opposition of the magnates of Neustria and Burgundy, angry at the Austrasian's assumption of supreme power. In trying to elevate his own house to the royal name, Grimoald exacerbated the conflict between Neustria and Austrasia that would nearly destroy Francia. His son Childebert was king for only a few days. Some of the disaffected Austrasian seigneurs, in league with the Neustrians, seized him and his father and transported them to the court of Clovis II in Burgundy. Clovis threw Grimoald into prison "tightly bound with chains. His death came with a great deal of torture."[2] The unfortunate young usurper was killed at the same time.

This Clovis, who had been made king of Burgundy by his father, Dagobert, when he was only five and who had assumed actual rule at age seven, had grown up to be a bestial libertine. "He had every kind of filthy habit. He was a seducer and a debaser of women, a glutton and a drunk. His mind became affected."[3] Legend links his madness with the tomb of Saint Denis in the church restored by his father. He was said to have had the reliquary opened to remove one of the saint's arms, which he wanted in his private chapel. On the instant the church was filled with a dark fog, and within an hour the young king had lost his mind. Clovis did in actuality succumb to insanity. But the origin of this tale is more prosaic: the king's order to remove the relic occurred in one of his sane periods, and included the requisition of gold and silver from church reliquaries for the relief of the poor during a famine.

Clovis II had one asset in his childhood, another in his manhood. The first was his mother, Nanthild, the servant girl his father had sensibly married. She chose an efficient and relatively just Mayor of the Palace and ruled with him until her son became titular king. The second was his wife, Balthild. In his warped life the prince had accomplished one praiseworthy act: he chose to marry a rational and attractive woman, an Anglo-Saxon slave girl. Balthild ruled as regent in her husband's periods of insanity, with a good Mayor of the Palace. These two forceful and intelligent people were more attracted toward making peace than war, and unwonted serenity attended the eighteen years of the mad king's reign. Balthild never forgot that she had come to authority through slavery: while she was queen she saw to it that the sale of Christian slaves was prohibited, and she herself purchased the freedom of many. With the death of her husband she turned to the religious life, which had always beckoned, and founded the double monastery of Chelles (site of the palace where Chilperic was murdered).

Clovis II died in 657, a few months after he had destroyed the overambitious Grimoald. Clovis's infant son, Lothair III, succeeded, and Francia was once more nominally united under a single ruler. The little king of all the Franks did not live to manhood; he died four years after his father and was succeeded by two inconsiderable brothers. But except for their precious name the Merovingians no longer mattered. For a few years two strong and compassionate women had borne much of the responsibility for propping up these cipher kings. With the retirement of Balthild the Mayors of the Palace became the actual rulers, and their ruinous wrangling the determinant of Francia's temporary destiny. Grimoald, of the line of Pepin, had been cut down because he prematurely reached too high. Savagery and chaos followed his death, and until the house of Pepin emerged from its eclipse some thirty years later the governance of the country was brought to virtual paralysis by the destructive machinations of rapacious seigneurs. Some tried to consolidate their power by backing the figurehead Merovingian children, others sought openly for self-aggrandizement.

Among these the most notorious and long lasting was Ebroin, who became Mayor of the Palace of Neustria in 657. Ebroin's manipulations, and the retaliations of his enemies, resolved basically into a mortal rivalry between the kingdoms of Austrasia and Neustria-Burgundy, the conflict that had begun with the feud of the two queens a century before. Ebroin, vindictive and greedy, used the Merovingian puppet kings as his tools, making and unmaking them. One of those he tried to exploit was Dagobert II, the son of Sigibert III—the child who had been sent to be a monk in Ireland. The Austrasians now, in 674, reclaimed him, but the moral ex-monk refused to be a *roi fainéant* and began actually ruling. An active Merovingian king in Austrasia was inconvenient for Ebroin, who preferred to deal with the less popular seigneurs—so he murdered Dagobert. Ebroin's twenty-four-year term as Mayor was a misrule of oppression and cruelty, during which he variously tortured, blinded and beheaded his opponents. In 681 he himself was murdered by a disaffected Neustrian. Through all these years, such was the disarray in the Frankish kingdoms that no one arose who could permanently unseat him: his rivals, while equally venal, were not nearly so agile. One time they nearly succeeded: Ebroin was captured in a revolt and sent as an involuntary monk to Luxeuil, but he slid out by intrigue, to enjoy several more years of iniquity.

Finally a scion of the house of Pepin came of age in Austrasia— Pepin the Younger, grandson of Bishop (now Saint) Arnulf and Pepin the Old. His mother was Begga (also sainted), daughter of Pepin the Old, a strong and virtuous woman, a beacon of light in her dark century—like some of the earlier Merovingian queens, whose selfless devotion to family and deep religious commitment redeemed the barbarity of their era. Sainthood would also be claimed for her son, Pepin the Younger,* who inherited her strength and something of her goodness. A man who combined military skill with wisdom and patience, Pepin inspired in his followers loyalty, not fear. For the first time since the deaths of his two exceptional grandfathers there would be a leader in the Frankish lands who might bring unity and hope to the torn country.

Though Pepin had the Austrasian aristocracy behind him, as well as the great landed wealth of his inheritance, he was not at once successful against the Neustrian tyrant. He met a military reverse at the hands of Ebroin, following which the Neustrian acted with typical ambidexterity. Pepin's ally, Duke Martin, had fled to a place of safety in Laon. Ebroin suborned the bishops of Paris and Rheims, who swore on a coffer which they claimed contained holy relics that the fugitive would not be harmed if he gave himself up. The duke believed the oaths, but he did not know that the reliquary was empty—and so he died.

Soon after, Ebroin was killed and his place taken by a series of inferior and conniving officials, the last one "a little fellow of small ability, light-minded and impetuous," whose incompetency so irritated the Neustrian nobles that in 687 they begged Pepin of Austrasia to help them dislodge him. Pepin assembled his army and sped west to meet the opposing forces at Tertry on the Somme (near Saint Quentin). Pepin sent emissaries to the Neustrian Mayor of the Palace and the Merovingian boy-king, Theodoric III, suggesting a course of peaceful negotiation to avoid bloodshed. Interpreting Pepin's overtures as the product of fear because his army was smaller, the Neustrians returned a scornful negative. Before dawn the next morning Pepin crossed the river and drew up his army to the east of the Neustrian camp so the enemy would be blinded by the rising sun. Spies brought word to the Neustrian leaders that the Austrasian camp was empty. They sent their men to pursue the supposedly fleeing foe, and Pepin attacked and easily overwhelmed them.

The victory at Tertry decisively established Pepin as a leader to whom the Franks could look with confidence. The day of disruptive

---

*Pepin the Younger was never formally canonized, but he is listed as a saint in some of the old martyrologies. The wholesale sainting of the house of Pepin was probably, in part, the grateful contribution of the Church to the renown of its supreme champion, Charlemagne.

cross-purposes among rival mayors was over: there was but one Mayor of the Palace now, and he was a man who would delegate but who would permit no disaccord with the central authority. More significant in a historic sense, Pepin's emergence marked the real end of the Merovingian dynasty. *Rois fainéants* would occupy the throne for another two generations of the house of Pepin, but the country had, in all but name, a new ruling dynasty.

Pepin was Mayor of the Palace of Austrasia, and he now controlled the same offices in Neustria and Burgundy. Since one man alone could not handle the sprawling administration, Pepin divided the governments between two of his sons, Drogo and Grimoald. Drogo became Mayor of the Palace of Burgundy and Grimoald of Neustria.

Francia prospered: taxes were fair and the aristocracy was kept firmly, if unwillingly, within bounds. Pepin was loved and trusted nationally to the extent that he decided he could safely reestablish the ancient German institution of the *campus martius*, which had been abolished by the Merovingian kings as too inviting a stage for potential insurrectionists. Its reinstitution was a measure in the direction of democracy.

As supreme commander of the armies Pepin repaired Francia's boundaries, eroded by subject and tributary peoples who had taken advantage of the near chaos of the past thirty years to assert their independence. On the east he pushed back and subjugated Frisians and Swabians and aroused respectful awe in Saxons, the most unmanageable of the encroaching German barbarians. On the west and south he mastered the perennially unsubmissive tributary Bretons and Gascons. In consolidating his borders and restoring hegemony over the tribes beyond them, Pepin was preparing the way for the Frankish empire to come.

Pepin had a further aspiration: throughout his twenty years of border warfare he tried to make Christianity a condition of peace for the subjugated tribes. He tended to be merciful in victory, and some of the conquered barbarians accepted conversion in token of their gratitude. Among those who still held out, the Frisians and the Saxons were the most stubborn. Besides being primitive in their mores they were resistant to the heavy Frankish taxes that inevitably followed submission. Frankish soldiers carrying crosses signified little to warriors still respectful to the hammer of Thor. The temperate preaching of Irish and English missionaries touched the rude fighters

with greater effect. Pepin supported these dedicated apostles, recognizing that they were in their way as undauntable as the savages they
intended to gentle.

Some of the saintly teachers were martyrs, others lived long but
dangerous lives. Among the martyrs were two English missionaries,
Hewald the Black and Hewald the White (their bynames referred to
the color of their hair). While waiting in the Saxon countryside to be
taken to the local chieftain the evangelists set up an altar and began
singing psalms. The peasants, seeing that the aliens were of a different
religion, and afraid that their lord would turn away from the ancestral
gods, seized them. Hewald the White they slew quickly by the sword,
while Hewald the Black suffered lingering torture and was torn limb
from limb. The bodies were thrown into the Rhine, and during the
night they floated (wrote the chronicler) forty miles upstream against
the current until they reached the place where their companions
rested. A great ray of light shone all night above the spot where the
bodies came to land. It was seen by the frightened heathens who had
murdered them—and they then saw the light figuratively as well,
accepting baptism. When Pepin heard of the deaths he had the bodies
of the martyrs brought to him and arranged splendid funerals for
them in his church at Cologne.[4]

Among the outstanding evangelical successes was the Anglo-Saxon
Willibrord, "Apostle to the Frisians."[5] He was born in Yorkshire in
658, the son of a holy hermit, educated at Ripon under its renowned
abbot Wilfred and sent thence to Ireland, still the headquarters of
learning in western Europe. About 690 Willibrord went with twelve
companions to Frisia at the mouth of the Rhine, a province recently
reduced by Pepin to tributary status. Its king, Rathbod, was still a
pagan and his allegiance to the Franks was reluctant. Despite his
restive host Willibrord had great success among the peasants, who
loved him. In 696 he was sent by Pepin to Rome, where the pope
consecrated him archbishop, renamed him Clement and designated
him, on Pepin's urging, archbishop of Utrecht. From this center he
continued his missionary work until 714, founding churches and
monasteries and evangelizing among the farmers. In that year King
Rathbod revolted against his Frankish masters, burned churches and
killed priests. Willibrord, his work destroyed, was driven from the
country. When Rathbod died five years later, the evangelist returned
to rebuild his churches and to preach in heathen country farther east.
In his old age, feeling that his mission in Frisia was accomplished,

Willibrord went to Denmark and started converting heathens all over again. Among other deeds the old priest bought thirty slave boys and educated them as Christians; killed some sacred cows to feed his starving followers; and personally smashed an idol in the face of death threats from its pagan worshippers. He lived to be eighty-one, having preached to the heathens for forty-nine years, and he was sainted almost immediately after his death in 739. His success among the Frisians was the beginning of a hundred years of English Christian influence on the Continent.

Successful as he was in all areas of government, Pepin never had the pride that can come with ascendancy: he had no wish for the name of king. He was perspicacious; the vestige of reverence for the Merovingian family lurked in the hearts of the populace. Further, if Pepin had usurped the all-but-empty throne he would have had to contend with the jealous seigneurs of Austrasia, his home kingdom, still arrogant if temporarily quiescent. Pepin had the substance of power and he had the love of the people. Apparently, he was content.

He died of a fever in 714, after twenty-seven years of governing. But with all his strength, sagacity and ability it was predestined that the integration of Pepin's Francia would dissipate with his death. The cohesion of his country depended directly on his presence. The idea had not yet been conceived of consolidating and bequeathing organic unity in government—the spirit of nationhood was still far in Europe's future. Pepin had made his office hereditary. But his only living son, Grimoald, was murdered while Pepin lay dying, victim of a plot by the Austrasian nobility, who were rebellious at Pepin's attempted perpetuation of his power. Pepin arose from his deathbed to avenge the murder. He returned to die, and with his last breath to name Grimoald's bastard son, Theudoald, his heir. This promised to bring on the Merovingian convulsions all over again. Little Theudoald was Mayor of the Palace to little Dagobert III, the latest of the Merovingian shadow-kings, and the two children were managed by Theudoald's grandmother, Pepin's widow Plectrudis. This lady now became the actual ruler of the kingdoms, which she administered from Cologne, the Austrasian capital.

At once rivalry between east and west flared into turmoil. The Neustrians (the Romance people) resented being under the Austrasian (German) yoke. In addition they refused to obey a female regent, remembering too well the ruinous feud of the regent queens Fredegund and Brunhild. There was a confused battle near Compiègne, north of Paris, during which Plectrudis's forces were defeated and Neustrian authority was extended to Austrasia. The only use the Neustrians made of their victory was to lay waste Austrasian territory all the way east to the Meuse River. In the virulence of their anger they even allied themselves with the pagan King Rathbod of the Frisians, whom we last met killing priests.

A contradictory factor further snarled the already anarchic situation. Besides his first sons, Drogo and Grimoald, Pepin had a bastard younger son by his concubine, Alpaida; this was Charles (later called Martel): "And the child grew, and a proper child he undoubtedly was." Charles was the young hero of the Austrasians, who regarded him as their natural chief. Thus he presented a threat to his stepmother, Plectrudis, in her regency for her grandson. When she took over the government of Austrasia she had Charles imprisoned. This put the Austrasians in a quandary. Theudoald and his guardian, Plectrudis, were their rulers by the choice of Pepin, and the nobles were obliged to be loyal for the sake of their own defense against Neustria. On the other hand Pepin's son Charles was their preferred champion.

After the defeat at Compiègne, however, the knots began to untangle. Little Theudoald fled before the Neustrian advance, leaving the Austrasian mayoralty chair untenanted. Shortly after this the Merovingian puppet king, Dagobert III, died. The Neustrians chose another Merovingian relative as King of all the Franks. This time they had sought for and found one who was not infantile, imbecilic or degenerate: a priest named Daniel, reputed to be a genuine Merovingian descendant, and renamed Chilperic II. At about the same time the scion of the house of Pepin, Charles, escaped from prison "by God's help"—implemented by his Austrasian followers.

Two strong men now faced each other across the border of Austrasia and Neustria. Charles received the homage of Plectrudis's defeated forces as well as his father's treasure, at the hands of his now compliant stepmother. But with a much smaller army at his command he was not immediately successful against the Neustrians and their new, energetic king. Besides their barbaric Frisian ally, King Rathbod, the Neustrians had the aid of Duke Eudo, ruler of semi-independent Aquitaine. The great Gallo-Roman land between the Pyrenees and the Loire, wealthy and superior in civilization, had only reluctantly accepted the suzerainty of the Franks. Aquitaine was at this time virtually a separate realm and its duke elected to ally himself with the more Latin Neustrians against the cruder Austrasians. Charles met a reverse at the hands of this formidable opposition before he succeeded in restructuring Plectrudis's Austrasian forces.

Like his father Charles was a keen military strategist. He knew the value of combined moderation and discipline, and before long he commanded a skilled, flexible and devoted force. With his little army he met the Neustrians at Vincy, near Cambrai. Again in imitation of Pepin, Charles offered to negotiate in order to spare the lives of courageous men on both sides. The Merovingian king, with his far larger army—but the dregs of society, raggedly trained—refused. The ensuing battle was an unequivocal victory for Charles, who pursued the demoralized Neustrians to the gates of Paris. He was not yet strong enough to take over the reins of defeated Neustria, so he left the ex-priest, Chilperic II, to his throne. Returning to Cologne he began the task of trying to restore the vitality of his own disordered realm.

But peace for reconstruction was not yet allowed to Charles. Chilperic II still refused to be a cipher king and he had the injudicious backing of his Mayor of the Palace. Two years after the defeat at Vincy, Chilperic asked Duke Eudo to help him renew the war against Austrasia, promising in return the complete independence of Aquitaine. Eudo agreed, and in 719 he brought his army of Gascons to Paris. Efficient fighters as the Gascons were, they were not prepared for the swiftness of Charles's small army, which jumped on them before they were ready, defeating them roundly. Eudo fled back to Aquitaine, taking the Merovingian king with him, and Charles was left to be, if he wished, undisputed master of Neustria. But again the victor chose moderation: he offered Eudo terms of peace if he gave up Chilperic and acknowledged the suzerainty of the north. Charles attached another condition to his mercy: he promised to acknowledge Chilperic as king of all the Franks if he himself were recognized as mayor of the united kingdoms of Austrasia, Neustria and Burgundy. Eudo and Chilperic had no choice but to accept. The following year, in 720, Chilperic died. The next Merovingian to ascend the throne, Theodoric IV, was a child of seven. Charles was uncrowned king of the Frankish kingdoms. But Duke Eudo, nominally subject to the Franks, retained his autonomy as well as his rebellious spirit, and Charles was momentarily unable to conciliate him.

In order to consolidate his supremacy and strengthen the unity of his country Charles still had to deal with the threats on his northern and eastern boundaries. With the death of King Rathbod of Frisia in 719 Charles regained control of that kingdom. At about the same time he drove back Saxon intruders on the right bank of the Rhine, and in the following few years contended successfully with Allemans and Bavarians. The contemporary accounts have him triumphant in every engagement—but there were so many of them, always against the same groups of combative barbarians, that Charles had a strenuous ten or twelve years before his country was safe enough along its edges so that he could turn to its internal well-being.

The years of weakling kings and warring seigneurs had made chaos of the Frankish empire. There was no central government, law could not be enforced, military conscription was ignored or circumvented, those who were in power spent their energies feuding with one another. Pepin the Younger had made a start at strengthening the central government and checking the lawless arrogance of the aristocracy, but he could not accomplish a complete reform, and on his death the country fell again into demoralized anarchy. Now Charles took up the intention of his father and carried it to a transformation: under his rule the shape of medieval France was first drawn.

We have seen how a new landed aristocracy rose during the century and a half of Merovingian strength. By the time of the Merovingian decline, before the house of Pepin had decisively asserted its ascendancy, this class had come to constitute an oligarchy, small, powerful and irresponsible. Its wealth was based on the amassing of land and the consequent increase in dependents, freemen like their masters, but landless and hopelessly in bondage. With the largest percentage of the population in servitude to the smallest there could be no public freedom, no law and no justice. Petty tyrants exercised absolute control in their demesnes. Oppression of their dependents, disobedience to the law and outright treason was the *modus vivendi*.

Charles could not destroy the aristocracy—nor would he have if he could, being himself a product of it—but he could instill in it a rationale of responsibility and of subservience to the higher authority of the state. First he forcibly quelled the insubordination of the most lawless, and obligated every landowner to supply and equip a proportionate number of men for the army. But he could not bind the seigneurs to him by intimidation. To create an incentive for loyalty, he had to strengthen rather than emasculate this class. The Merovingian kings had rewarded their favorites with free and unconditional deeds of land, but by the time of Charles these lords had become land engorged. Instead, Charles imitated the Church's system of benefices: nonhereditary land was granted that was revocable at the will of the grantor and ended with the death of the lessee. Under Charles's administration the benefice could be terminated only for treason or disloyalty, but it still reverted to the state when the lessee died. The system was a great success with the seigneurs, who gained in wealth and in dependents. As long as the ruler was a strong man it was a success for him, too. He had the fealty, capricious no longer, of the puissant seigneury, bound to him for their profit as well as their honor. They vied for his favor, aided him readily in times of war and subjected themselves to his law in peacetime. The system—a forerunner of the feudal fief—was a powerful machine which Charles, and his son and grandson after him, could control. Under weaker rulers the machine would become unmanageable: Charlemagne's successors would be as helpless against the medieval noblesse as the *rois fainéants* had been against its predecessors. But at the time of Charles the system worked a miracle in the shattered country.

Another institution in Francia had grown to dinosaur proportions of wealth, presumption and immorality: the Church. From the licentious and factious parish priest to the imperious, intriguing bishop, its personnel was immune to civil law, safe from conscription and free of taxes. This protected class was far harder to restrain than the wayward seigneury. What the Frankish Church needed most was internal reform, but Charles, not overly religious, was more interested in secular constraint. From his viewpoint the Church was an agent erosive to the central authority. It was also a huge potential war chest. His first measure of control was to require the great landowning ecclesiastics to provide men for war, even to lead them to battle as did their lay compatriots. The second operation, initiated by Charles in his need and formalized later, was less healthy for the Church. With no superstitious awe in his makeup, Charles viewed the wealthy, worldly bishop in the same way that an executive sees his disloyal or refractory employee. There was one sure way to curb the troublemaker: replace him. Charles granted bishoprics freely to his generals and faithful servants, without concern that most of them were baldly unspiritual. Sword-wielding bishops easy in their morals and illiterate in ecclesiastical and most other fields were detrimental to a Church already in moral disrepair. This secularization of the Church, potentially pernicious, was, in Charles's time, critical to the centralization of authority. Further, it enabled Charles, through his lay-episcopal friends, to redistribute some of the excessive ecclesiastical wealth for the benefit of the state.

Charles compensated for creating bristly bishops by endowing religious houses, by backing missionaries to the pagan Germans and by defending the pope against the Lombards. The Church gave him its polite approval while he was still alive. His contemporaries recognized that, while not noticeably devout, neither was he hostile to the religious establishment. With the money he liberated, he led his armies successfully against pagans in the north and infidels in the south.

But after his death ecclesiastical writers began to censure him: he had died a horrible death, they maintained, for the sin of appropriating Church property. In the ninth century a tale was circulated of the vision of Saint Eucherius. This holy man, bishop of Orléans, ran the story, was transported in a dream to the other world, and there he saw Charles burning in hell. When he returned to earth he told of his vision to Boniface, apostle to the Germans, and Fulrad, abbot of Saint Denis, and the three went to Charles's tomb. Upon opening the grave they found the corpse was absent; in its place was a dragon which flew out, emitting a horrible smell.[6]

Charles gave Frankish Gaul the outline of medieval France. He both strengthened and subdued the aristocracy; he pruned the immoderate privilege of the Church and he created a loyal and efficient military machine. In civil affairs he was superlatively practical; in character, a just and moderate ruler loved by his people and respected by his tributary states.

But to posterity all Charles's actions and assets fade before the milestone event of his reign: his victory over the Moslems. In popular history he is Charles Martel, the Hammer, who arrested the infidels' advance and saved Christian Europe from extinction.

In 622 Mohammed, driven out of Mecca, had built his model theocratic state at Yathrib (now Medina). Mohammed regarded himself as the latest prophet, and his beliefs as the culmination of the worship of the single, unknowable God—the ultimate perfection for pagans, Jews and Christians alike. With the help of his fervent followers, Mohammed's mission was to bring his ideal to all peoples. If any would not accept it willingly they must, like children, be forced for the good of their souls to submit—a psychology hardly alien to those Christian soldiers, Constantine and Clovis. By 629 pagan Arabia was converted, and Mohammed's bands of light horse, accompanied by a few camels bearing their modest equipage, were conquering east and west through Persia and Syria. Ninety years after Mohammed had founded his holy state, Islam was in control of all of Asia Minor from the mouths of the Indus through Kabul to Bukhara and Samarkand; of most of North Africa from the Nile to the Atlantic, and of part of India.

In 710 Musa ibn Nusayr, the Moslem governor of North Africa and Caliph Walid I's chief general, looked north across the Straits of Gibraltar to untapped Europe. He tried to take Ceuta (one of the Pillars of Hercules), the last European stronghold in Africa, fourteen miles across from Spain. The attack was ably repulsed by the Spanish defender, Count Julian. The following year Julian turned defector—for the familiar Spanish reason of disaffection with his sovereign (who may have molested Julian's daughter)—and opened the gates to the Moslems. Musa sent Tarik,* his freed Berber slave, over the strait with a few hundred soldiers, to be welcomed at Algeciras by the recreant Julian. The rest of Spain was an easy conquest for the Moslems, who found little resistance among the Visigoths, debilitated by many generations of wealth, safety and easy living. A few, with a remaining trace of valiance, escaped into the mountains of Asturias, where they found a small Christian enclave, gradually regained their ancestral strength and became the spearhead for the eventual Christian reclamation of Spain.

In 718 the Moslems crossed the Pyrenees and conquered Narbonne, killing all its young male inhabitants and sending the women and children into slavery in the East. Then they went on to Aquitaine which was, as we have noted, a semi-independent state, tributary to the Franks, under Count Eudo. In 721 Eudo defeated the Moslems at Toulouse, but later he made peace with them, perhaps partly out of fear of their continued aggression. His chief motive, however, was to make trouble for the Franks: he had broken his treaty with Charles, and the Frankish leader had defeated him a second time so that he

*Gibraltar is named for Tarik: Gebel-al-Tarik.

was "an object of scorn." Eudo went so far as to give his daughter in marriage to the Moorish governor of Spanish Gaul, an act sure to be even more abhorrent to Moslems than to Christians. Capping his overtures of peace he invited the infidels to send some small bands north to embarrass Charles.

The Aquitanian repented when the small bands of Moslems became hordes. In 725 a large Moslem army crossed the Pyrenees, captured Carcassonne and Nîmes and occupied most of Septimania, Spanish Gaul. Their intention was to push north into the rich Catholic realm of Frankish Gaul. At this point in Moslem history, the undefended wealth of churches and monasteries was a more potent inducement to battle than missionary ardor. They made a raid into Burgundy, destroying Brunhild's city of Autun and Columbanus's Luxeuil. But their military zeal was weakened by internal strife among rival sects, and their offensive crumbled. A few years later, in 731, the dynamic and well-liked governor of Moorish Spain, Abd ar-Rahman, pulled the attack together again. He crossed the Pyrenees with four hundred thousand men and overran Aquitaine with ease. In his triumphant advance the Moslem leader paused to punish the recreant who had married the Christian heiress, sending the Moor's head, along with the lady, to the caliph in Syria. He went on to capture and burn Bordeaux, and defeated Eudo decisively between the Garonne and Dordogne rivers. Then he advanced along the old Roman road which led from Bordeaux through Poitiers to Orléans. He took Poitiers in 732, burning Saint Hilary's church, and continued north along the Clain River toward the major city of Tours. He did not reach Tours because in the wide valley between the Clain and the Vienne he came face to face with Charles.

The Frankish leader had been up to now neither dilatory nor cowardly; he had been busy. The Frisians, Swabians, Bavarians and Saxons on his northeastern borders—heathens just as belligerent and anti-Christian as the Moslems—required his constant military attention. He did not dare to leave his northern flank insecure before bringing all his forces to bear on the menace to the south. But the collapse of Eudo, the capture of Poitiers and the immediate threat to Tours brought him finally to the inevitable confrontation.

The armies faced one another for seven days in the plain between the villages of Vieux-Poitiers and Moussais-la-Bataille. Charles, with his much smaller army, could not initiate the attack but took up a tight defensive position. When the Arabs at last attacked, their light cavalry broke before the impregnable wall of Franks. The Arabs were thrown back and Charles took the offensive, coming upon the enemy "like a mighty man of war. With Christ's help he overran their tents, following hard after them in the battle to grind them small. And when Abd ar-Rahman perished in the battle he utterly destroyed their armies, scattering them like stubble before the fury of his onslaught." The large and bloody battle lasted until nightfall. The next morning the Franks, ready to resume the fighting, found the Arab tents deserted: the infidel had fled "the power of Christ." Besides the Moorish leader three hundred thousand Moslems, writes the chronicler, lay dead on the field, as against only fifteen hundred Franks. The hero of the spectacular victory was henceforth known as Charles Martel, the Hammer.

It is not clear from contemporary accounts why the Arabs were so easily routed. Perhaps their morale was low: they had lost the irresistible fanaticism that had propelled them across the deserts and mountains to vulnerable Europe. Perhaps, on the Frankish side, Teutonic heroism regenerated in this contingency. As far as battle technique is concerned the Franks and the Moslems were equally skilled in contemporary methods. It is not provable, as scholars sometimes maintain, that Charles initiated a military revolution with his victory at Tours, being the first to make use of mounted, armored shock troops with long lances. The stirrup, essential to this type of warfare, was an innovation learned by Charles and his contemporaries from the Arabs themselves.* Although the device was known in western Europe it was not yet in general use by the time of the Battle of Tours, and it is unlikely that Charles suddenly introduced it then. Even at the Battle of Hastings, over three centuries later, traditionally the first engagement won by the employment of armored knights, this force was not the determining element.

The Carolingian chroniclers understandably overrated the consequence of the Battle of Tours. Even making allowance for exaggeration it was a crucial event: it was the first time the Arabs had been decisively defeated in the West, and it was the beginning of the end of their European advance. But it was not only Charles who turned them around; a cogent factor was the revolt of the Berbers in North

---

*The stirrup was not an Arabian invention: its use had been introduced to Byzantium over a century earlier by the Avars. The Moslems learned it from the Byzantines and brought it west when they invaded Africa and Spain.

Africa, which required undivided Moslem attention. And the Arabs were not yet finished in Europe. They had known reverses before their defeat at Tours, and they were not likely to be demoralized to the point of absolutely abandoning their ambitions in Gaul. Opportunity came to them again a few years later. Count Eudo had died in 735. His successors ignored their debts to Charles, and in 737 the then count of Provence imprudently invited the Arabs back, handing them the city of Avignon for headquarters. The Provençal mistakenly thought that with Arab help he could free himself from the Austrasian hegemony. He was backed by dissident Neustrian seigneurs with no experience of Arabs, who hated the sovereign Austrasian mayor and wanted to see him in trouble.

From Avignon the Moslem leader made a swift attack into Burgundy, leaving fire and blood in his wake. He took Vienne and got as far as Lyon before a surprised Charles could collect his forces. Involved with Saxon inroads in the north, Charles sent his younger brother, Hildebrand, with as many men as he could spare, to halt the Moorish advance. The Arabs were driven back to Avignon, where they entrenched themselves until Charles himself came south, took the city and killed the Moslem garrison. He and his Franks then followed the fleeing Arabs across the Rhône and through Spanish Septimania, retaking all the Moslem-held towns except Narbonne, and attaching a great part of the territory of Spanish Gaul to the Frankish empire.

Charles was now the Christian savior of Europe. As such he had become, not entirely intentionally, the champion on whom the pope found it politic to rely as the secular defender of his spiritual empire. Even before the rout of the infidel, Charles had on occasion demonstrated a militant Christian zeal in his transactions with defeated heathens in the north, offering them (after the manner of the Moslem foe) the choice of baptism or death. His Christian overtures were not always successful. He persuaded King Rathbod of the Frisians to undergo baptism. The pagan was agreeable, but with one foot in the font he paused to ask. "Where are my ancestors who have gone before me?" "They are in hell," answered the officiating priest, "with other infidels." "I had rather feast with my forefathers in the halls of Wotan," said Rathbod, withdrawing his baptized foot, "than live in heaven with those fasting little Christians of yours."[7]

In the eighth century the Church at Rome was at a crossroads, and neither way was attractive. The pope could retain his obeisance to the Byzantine emperor, conveniently far away and tolerant of the Italian's sovereign control of Rome because it represented one of Byzantium's few viable contacts with Italy. But the Roman emperor in the East could offer only gestures of support. On the other hand the pope could ally himself with the Lombards, who owned all of Italy except Rome, Ravenna and a few ports on the Adriatic. Earlier in the century the Lombards had been converted from the Arian heresy, and were now stalwart Catholics. But this alliance had a substantial flaw: the Lombards saw the pope as an obstacle to their complete subjugation of Italy. As well as being the spiritual leader of the West he was the virtual ruler of the duchy of Rome, with the great temporal wealth of the Eternal City under his dominion.

The pope chose allegiance to Byzantium as the course that would leave him the widest latitude. But in 726, a fierce controversy over iconoclasm started when Emperor Leo III issued an edict ordering the destruction of all icons. His spiritual mentors had convinced him that painted images emphasized the human side of the Incarnation as against its eternal immaterial truth—therefore they were essentially idols, leading to apostasy. Not only did icons pervert Christians, the Byzantine emperor's advisers maintained, but their excessive use discouraged the conversion of Jews and Moslems, whose creeds forbade all human representation. Under Leo III and his successor, Constantine V, there was widespread persecution of monks, the most zealous defenders of icons. The rebellious monks were joined by several of the important eastern patriarchs—and by Pope Gregory III, who, in 731, held two synods at Rome condemning the Byzantine decree and refusing, on behalf of the entire Western Church, to comply.

This action effectively cut the pope off from Byzantine support and forced him back to the Lombards. Although Rome had great wealth in addition to her spiritual ascendancy she was not yet a political state, and her autonomy within the Lombard kingdom was uncertain. The Lombard king, Liutprand, venerated the pope as the religious leader of the West, but in temporal matters he regarded him as a subject, not as the ruler of an independent state within his own kingdom. Seeking the unification of all Italy under his rule Liutprand first marched on Ravenna, Italy's other great nonaligned city. The city, under the impotent rule of the Byzantine exarch, fell easily before his army. In 729 he advanced on Rome, but the pope deflected the Lombard leader for a time with a combination of diplomacy and silver.

In 739 Liutprand marched again on Rome. This time he got all the way to the gates of the inner city, robbing the Church of Saint Peter on the way (it was outside the walls) of its candlesticks. The pope was in a plight, afraid he would soon be demoted to but another western bishop. In this strait Gregory III turned to his third alternative for protection, the new Christian champion of the West, Charles Martel. Charles was between battles, recovering from his operations against the Arabs in Burgundy, and his forces were in no condition to march south on a fresh campaign. Besides, he had a fraternal sympathy with King Liutprand, a leader, like himself, bent on strengthening his country through unity, and whose military and political alliance he valued. In any case war was not a temperamental necessity to Charles but a last expedient when negotiation no longer availed.

In this case negotiation worked temporarily. Liutprand agreed to Charles's suggestion that he spare papal territory; on the other side, the Romans should cease to interfere between the Lombard King and his rebellious subjects. But the following year Liutprand brought his armed troops again to the gates of Rome. This time Pope Gregory III appealed more trenchantly to the Frank. He sent ecclesiastical dignitaries to Charles bearing a special honor: the title and dignity of Roman Patrician, a rank of the Roman Empire which the pope was not authorized to bestow. Gregory's citation, given in his extremity, had a far-reaching significance: it marked the end of the dependence of the Western Church on Byzantium. With his action the pope cast off his allegiance to the Roman Empire at Constantinople and placed himself under the "invincible clemency" of the Frankish ruler. As well as the end of the spiritual union of East and West, Gregory's gift betokened the beginning of the alliance of the papal state with the kingdom of the Franks.

The prime movers of this historic action had no time to see its results. It took place in 741, and by the next year all three of them were dead. Charles Martel and Gregory III died in 741, Liutprand in 742. Their successors, with the same motivations and similar strengths, would carry the course of events undeviatingly forward.

The contour of France to come shows through eighth-century war and peace, but the shape of Charles Martel, its latest architect, is lacking. The biography of the historic mayor of Austrasia is no more than a busy chronicle of deeds. Charles Martel lacked a Gregory of Tours to recount his conversations and detail his petty vices, or a Fortunatus to record in clever Latin verse what he had for dinner. Even his thirteenth-century memorial effigy at the Cathedral of Saint Denis is featureless: an idealized robed figure with a crown upon its head—although he never wore one—and a disconcerting similarity to the figure that lies beside him, the mad, depraved King Clovis II. Charles Martel's character can be implied through his actions: his straightforward honesty in his dealings with his aristocratic peers; his gentleness with defeated enemies; his bravery in war in the face of daunting odds; his preference for negotiation over bloodshed. And a certain keenness of intellect is evidenced in his disdain for superstition and ecclesiastical hypocrisy.

Charles had a historic aim: the unification of Frankish Gaul. His predecessor, Clovis, had had the same laudable ambition, but his methods and his perspective were contrapositive. Clovis was the heir of northern warriors untouched by the civilization of Rome or the teachings of Christ. Murder and treachery were his tools and unalloyed might his goal. But without the fighting Frank, Charles Martel would not have been possible, nor would the emerging nation of France.

Charles Martel's two sons by his first wife, Pepin and Carloman, were his designated heirs. Pepin became mayor of Neustria and Burgundy, Carloman mayor of Austrasia and the German duchies. Charles had married a second time, a Saxon princess named Sunehild whom he had taken captive in war. She had borne him a third son, Gripho. Such was Charles's love for his beautiful young wife that he let her persuade him to leave a portion of each of his elder sons' inheritance to the younger. This made for trouble at the very beginning of the new reigns. Neither the Saxon Sunehild nor her son were popular with the Franks. They mistrusted the influence of the hated foreign woman over their hero Charles Martel, and they disliked even more, after his death, the arbitrary cession of part of their lands to the half-Saxon. Gripho aggravated their hostility by coveting more than the share allotted to him, and by calling on the tributary chieftains along the edges of the kingdom for help in confounding his half brothers. As a focus of disaffection he was useful to the border tribes, who thought the opportunity had come to reassert their independence. It looked easy: the kingdom was once again divided between brothers, who at first sight did not appear as martial as their father and who, all were sure, would retrogress into the customary fratricidal bickering. The border chieftains were wrong in both suppositions. Pepin and Carloman worked as a harmonious team, and if they did not at once exhibit the consummate military genius of their father, their talents were adequate for the challenges that faced them.

Gripho's chances were extinguished when his sister ran away and secretly married Duke Odilo of Bavaria, chief of one of the border lands subdued by Charles Martel and now in hopeful revolt against his successors. Gripho and his mother, blamed for the ill-considered elopement, shut themselves into the fortress at Laon. When Pepin and Carloman appeared at the gates the two refugees surrendered at once. Sunehild was sent into a nunnery and Gripho imprisoned.

The brothers, their authority temporarily safe, now cooperated in subduing the rebellious tributaries. These ranged from the Saxons and Swabians, marauders along the northeast boundaries, to the Bavarians under Duke Odilo, and the Aquitanians in the south, who had never gracefully accepted Frankish rule. Pepin and Carloman were successful in all their campaigns. For the most part their treatment of the vanquished rebels was humane, but Carloman committed one act of treachery. In 746 the leader of the Swabians, Theobald, was thought to be considering a new revolt. Carloman crossed the Rhine with his army to prevent the incipient uprising, and ordered Theobald to join him, along with his entire army, to discuss terms of peace. Theobald trustingly complied; he and all his soldiers were seized and bound, then he was executed.

Shortly after this Carloman abruptly gave up his office and took the vows of a monk. It is not known whether his renunciation was due to remorse or was the fruit of growing religious conviction. He founded a monastery for himself just below the summit of Monte Soratte, an isolated limestone ridge north of Rome. But the retreat of the celebrated Frankish mayor became too popular with sightseers, and the penitent sought anonymity in the Benedictine foundation at Monte Cassino, where he enrolled as a simple monk.

Pepin now ruled the Frankish empire alone. His half brother Gripho still lurked enviously in the background brooding over his lost inheritance and Pepin, in this instance more generous than wise, thought to mollify him by ending his imprisonment. Gripho at once

gathered around himself a few younger dissidents among the seigneury and went to the Saxons to enlist their patronage in realizing
his pretensions to sovereignty. Pepin quelled the uprising with swift
competence, and Gripho fled to Bavaria, where his sister, since the
death of her husband, Duke Odilo, ruled in the name of their son.
Gripho heartlessly unseated these two, declared himself ruler of the
duchy and gathered as allies a group of Bavarian and Swabian local
chiefs. Pepin marched again, and the allies surrendered without a
fight, awed in advance by the Frank's military reputation. Again
Pepin was lenient to the foe; he even granted his traitorous half
brother a full pardon and instated him as ruler of the area of Le
Mans. Gripho, thwarted but not chastened, tried to foster dissension
again, but he was not even partially successful. About 750 he was
killed by a Frankish duke loyal to Pepin as he was on his way to
northern Italy to try to gain the support of the king of the Lombards.

Pepin's easy success against Gripho and the allied oppositionists
within his kingdom and among his tributaries is evidence of his
unchallengeable supremacy. His father and his grandfather had
justified themselves as rulers of the Frankish empire by their military
skill and their moderation in peace. The Frankish seigneury had at
last been brought around to acceptance of superior control, the
borders were nearly secure and the country was as much at peace as
was achievable in the unsettled eighth century. Pepin, heir to the
accomplishments of his predecessors, added his own strength and
sagacity to his birthright. It says much for the inner vitality of the
Franks, that throughout a century of insubstantial kings, lawless
seigneurs, oppression, misrule and unceasing warfare, with a
wretched, superstitious populace and an illiterate, irresponsible aristocracy—somehow the life force endured to bring into the foreground
one fine man after another of the extraordinary Arnulfing clan.
There was a nascent genius in this country, which would come into a
time of bloom under Pepin's son Charlemagne.

Since 737, before the death of Charles Martel, Frankish Gaul
had had no king at all, even hidden away in an obscure Merovingian palace. Pepin and Carloman were still, like their father, titled
Mayor of the Palace. Early in their reigns, when tributary chiefs
were rising all along the borders, the Frankish brothers considered
that it would be politic to bring forth another Merovingian king,
since the descendants of Clovis still commanded the superstitious

loyalty of the mass of the people. They feared that otherwise the rebellious tributaries might try to attach their own aspirations to the name of a legitimate heir. In 743 the mayors found a royal relative in a monastery and placed him, as Childeric II, on the throne. He was no more than a convenient figurehead. The brothers continued to rule the country, to dispense justice, to decide on war when necessary, to convoke Church councils, even to live in the royal palaces.

There was nothing reportedly the matter with Childeric II. The only manner in which his name enters the annals is as the last Merovingian king. Charlemagne's biographer, disdaining to name him, draws a scornful picture of his pathetic existence: "There was nothing left the King to do but to be content with his name of King, his flowing hair, and long beard, to sit on his throne and play the ruler. He had nothing left that he could call his own, except a single country seat, that brought him but a very small income. There was a dwelling house upon this, and a small number of servants attached to it, sufficient to perform the necessary offices. When he had to go abroad, he used to ride in a cart, driven peasant-fashion, by a ploughman; he rode in this way to the palace and to the general assembly of the people, that met once a year for the welfare of the kingdom, and he returned in like manner."[8]

One must make allowances for the biographer's predisposition to ridicule the old house in order better to extol the new. But even without overstatement the last days of eighth-century Childeric II are a sad and sordid substantiation of the dream of the first Childeric in the fifth century.

After the abdication of Carloman and the declawing of Gripho, Pepin, at age thirty-five sole ruler of an empire larger and more coherent than ever before in its history, decided it was both safe and politic to go one step further and have himself endowed with the name as well as the actuality of king. The final step was small but audacious. To dislodge the Merovingian king physically from his throne was a lesser matter than to uproot the Merovingian myth from the Frankish soul. The Mayors of the Palace were still, in the public eye, glorified servants of the king. The replacement of a royal descendant required elaborate preparation, and Pepin could not have undertaken it without the full cooperation of the Frankish Church and the blessing of the pope.

In 750 a delegation of Frankish clergy went to the papal court to make a legal deposition before Pope Zachary: "Whether it was expedient that one who was possessed of no authority in the land should continue to retain the name of king, or whether it should be transferred to him who really exercised the royal power." Zachary gave his expected and prepared reply: "He who really governed should also bear the royal name."[9]

In 751 Childeric II was formally deposed by order of the pope, not for moral, mental or physical blemish but *quia non erat utilis*—because he was not useful.[10] A long-haired king was shorn for the last time and sent, in the conventional routine, to live out the rest of his days in a monastary. Pepin was named king in a splendid religious ceremony at the cathedral of Saint Médard in Soissons, burial place of early Merovingian giants. The new monarch was anointed with holy oil by the most influential ecclesiastic of the period, his good friend Boniface, apostle to the Germans and archbishop of Mainz. After the Christian ceremony, honor was paid to a more ancient Frankish tradition as Pepin was raised on a shield by his warriors and borne three times around the city. No hand was lifted to bring back the shorn Merovingian king or his living son; no whisper was heard that the new ruler usurped a throne whose origins lay, in the Frankish mind, in mythical antiquity. The solemn and gorgeous ecclesiastical coronation substituted the sacred drama of Christian ritual for the magic of Merovingian legend. The new king was *Gratia Dei rex Francorum*, king of the Franks by the grace of God.

Pepin's relations with the Gallic Church seem at first sight ambivalent. Like his father he was realistic about the Church's absorption of most of the national wealth vis-à-vis his own constant need for funds for his expensive wars. However, he saw that if he tapped the Church's wealth he had to display corresponding deference in his treatment of its senior ministry. He was well aware that battling seigneurs make inferior bishops, but he was equally cognizant of the disgraceful self-interest of the legitimate hierarchy. He consulted with his friend and mentor, Boniface, and decided to call a synod, the first Frankish church council in eighty years.

Boniface was the most consequential churchman of Pepin's reign. He began his religious life as Winfrith, an Anglo-Saxon monk in Devon, and he was ordained a priest about 706, when he was thirty. A politic man with a ready tongue, a natural teaching ability and a tolerably good education—he had enough Latin to produce the first

Latin grammar in England—he received the favorable notice of the king of Wessex, who appointed him envoy to the archbishop of Canterbury. With a successful future assured, the Wessex priest elected in 716 to throw overboard his fair prospects and engage in missionary work among the heathens of Germany. Despite daunting setbacks, he was successful enough to earn the title of "Apostle to the Germans": he personally destroyed idols and baptized the overawed peasantry to the number, it is claimed, of one hundred thousand; he organized the Church in Bavaria into four bishoprics; and he founded monasteries all over Germany, of which the most renowned was Fulda, in central Germany (today's Hessen-Nassau). Already in Boniface's time Fulda was the missionary headquarters of Germany, and by a century later it had become a center of theological learning.

Boniface himself, although he fostered education in his monasteries, was an indifferent scholar. He was much irritated by the threatening popularity of an Irish rival in Germany, Virgil (the Celtic Fergal). Boniface, a firm believer in the ecclesiastical establishment which backed him, distrusted Virgil for his obstinate Irish independence—the Celtic priest acknowledged no hieratical superior but God—and he was outraged that the charismatic Irish missionary received the enthusiastic patronage of his own personal sponsor, Pepin, and, further, was backed by the pope to the extent of being made bishop of Salzburg. Virgil, a thinking scholar somewhat advanced for eighth-century Teutonic Europe, audaciously drew fire on himself by teaching that the earth was round, and that, a posteriori, there were people living at the antipodes. Boniface seized the opportunity to oust Virgil by having him denounced for heresy. If creatures existed on the other side of the earth, he held, whatever its shape, they must be walking around head downward. They could not, therefore, belong to the human race, or have been created by God or saved by Christ. Whoever postulated their existence offended against the true Church. Boniface was a letter-perfect child of the early medieval Church, which regarded scientific study as unscriptural and therefore heretical. The sphericity of the earth belonged in the area of a classical learning not so much lost as suppressed. The conformist Anglo-Saxon missionary, unaware that Virgil was not alone in his daring hypothesis, failed to prevail against the Irish savant. Even after death Virgil outdistanced his rival: he was sainted, as Boniface was not, even though the Apostle to the Germans died a martyr, his skull cleft with an ax by an unregenerate Frisian pagan.

Boniface had been a strong believer in the ecclesiastical hierarchy and the supreme authority at Rome. He did not aim solely to evangelize, but envisioned a Christian Germany solidly embedded in the network of the Roman organization. He assiduously cultivated the patronage of the pope, who created him archbishop of Mainz in 732, and that of the Frankish rulers, the pope's secular allies, who held tributary dominion over Boniface's missionary areas. He could not, he himself admitted, have accomplished anything in Germany without the pope's official blessing or the supportive friendliness of Charles Martel and Pepin.

It was his friendship with the Mayors of the Palace that motivated Boniface to turn his attention to the reform of the Frankish Church. In 742, secure in the approval of his Frankish allies, he dared to write openly to the pope of the priestly ungodliness in Francia: "Discipline has been despoiled and trampled upon. The episcopal sees in cities are in the hands of greedy laymen or are exploited by adulterous and vicious clergymen. I find among these men certain so-called deacons who have spent their lives since boyhood in debauch, adultery, and every kind of filthiness. Entering upon the priesthood, they continue in the same vices. And certain bishops are drunkards and shiftless men, given to hunting and to fighting in the army like soldiers."[11] Pepin, and even more so his pious brother Carloman, who was still ruler of the eastern part of Frankish Gaul, agreed with the forthright archbishop that reform was in order.

In 743 they called a synod at Lestines, near Cambrai in the northwest. There secularization, begun by Charles Martel, was regularized and brought under the supervision of the Church. In a rational compromise the bishops consented to the voluntary surrender to the State of a portion of Church funds. In return the civil rulers were not to interfere with ecclesiastical discipline, nor to lay unauthorized hands on Church property. Francia's secular rulers no longer needed to hand out bishoprics to friendly seigneurs in order to free Church money for martial use. In the future illiterate, profligate and militaristic bishops would be weeded out. The clergy was prohibited from war, hunting and sexual intercourse and other secular pursuits (among these was the clerical diet, from which were banned jackdaws, crows, storks, beavers and wild horses). Not only the urban episcopate but the monasteries came in for reform: the temperate Benedictine discipline was to be the basic code for all Frankish religious houses.

The Act of Secularization—concluded at Lestines, amicably arranged and ostensibly a compromise—still evidences the absolute dominance of the State over the Church. Pepin and Carloman dictated its terms, and it was due only to their graceful Christian respect, not to ecclesiastical influence, that the Church retained its security and a great part of its landed wealth. Boniface was as aware of their power as of their generosity; he himself had helped to draft the compromise that made the act palatable to the lords of the Church. When the time came, nine years later, it was as much an act of gratitude as of policy on Boniface's part to anoint the self-made king Pepin with holy oil and place the crown upon his head.

The house of Pepin had not only moved onto the royal throne perforce vacated by the Merovingians, but had also inherited along with it the fealty of the Frankish Church. In earlier years this Church had been, next to the Merovingian force of arms, the most potent asset of the primal house. The new rulers arrogated to themselves the holy scrap of Saint Martin's *chape*, the Merovingians' cherished talisman. Pepin's son, Charlemagne, would carry its blue likeness on his battle standard. Saint Denis, whose church had been rebuilt and whose cult had received its initial impetus from Dagobert, the last strong Merovingian king, became the patron saint of the new house.

The transfer of Clovis's Church into the orbit of the house of Pepin was quiet, inevitable and long in the process. It had started during the Austrasian revolution of 613 against Queen Brunhild. At that time her bishops deserted her cause and moved into the inexorable stream of history, backing the insurgent leaders, Arnulf and the first Pepin. Now, one hundred and thirty-eight years later, the shift was completed as Pepin was crowned king of the Franks with the blessing of the Frankish Church.

In one direction the Church of Pepin's era differed from that of the Merovingians': in its close ties with the papacy. The Frankish Church of the sixth and seventh centuries had been practically independent of Rome, its powerful bishops ruling their huge dioceses in virtual autonomy. Though Pope Gregory I made strong efforts to channel influence up the hierarchical ladder to himself, in general the popes did not interfere. They made sure to stay on the right side of the cardinal ruling house of Europe. But the papacy had still been under the shield of the emperor at Constantinople, and the pope did not need European friends as desperately as he would in the eighth century.

In 749 the Lombards under their cruel and militant king, Aistulf, marched on Rome. The new pope, Stephen II, temporarily bought immunity. But Aistulf wanted ever more gold to keep his acquisitive soldiers out of Rome. Stephen appealed in vain to the uncaring emperor at Constantinople. In 753, with the enemy scowling on his doorstep, he decided to journey to Francia to plead his exigency with the newly crowned king. He was prepared to appear both as suppliant and as patron: in the course of his visit he would recrown Pepin as a kind of bribe, or earnest of his shifted allegiance.

Pepin needed the heavenly authority of the pope as much as Stephen needed his terrestrial. The house of Pepin had held its own for nearly one hundred and fifty years only through the individual genius of its remarkable progeny. The family had no claim on the throne either hereditary or spiritual, and when Pepin assumed the regal title in 751 he had need of a higher proponent than the strength of his right arm, his superior mental powers or even the sanction of the Frankish bishops. The new dynasty required a basis for durability at least as strong as the Merovingian claim of descent through the legendary mist of the past. Though Pepin had already been anointed by Boniface, only the highest Christian authority in the western world could give his house the luster of the chosen that had haloed its predecessor.

In midwinter of 753 the aging pope crossed the Alps and was greeted at the Frankish border by ecclesiastical and lay dignitaries. Seventy miles east of Pepin's palace of Pontyon, near Chalon-sur-Saône in Burgundy, he was met by an eight-year-old boy, Pepin's son, Prince Charles, the future Charlemagne, making his first entrance into history; and three miles outside the palace King Pepin himself came on foot to escort his guest. The two primary spiritual and secular leaders of Europe met in humility, Pepin in the guise of the pope's marshal, walking by the side of his palfrey, Stephen in the simple dress of a pilgrim. In the course of his year of residence at the monastery of Saint Denis in Paris, Pope Stephen consecrated Pepin once more, in the church of Saint Denis. He also conferred on the new king the Roman title of Patricius, the same that his predecessor, Gregory III, had given Charles Martel, and with the same motive: to proclaim the pope's independence of the emperor at Constantinople.

This alliance would mutually strengthen the papacy and the Frankish empire, and would lead to the spiritual and temporal supremacy of Charlemagne's Holy Roman Empire, the closest approach that history would make to Saint Augustine's City of God.

King Pepin had got what he needed; now, in honor, he had to repay his benefactor by subduing the Lombards who continued to menace Rome. This required that at the very outset of his legitimate reign, Pepin had to engage in a distant and expensive campaign with reluctant troops and unwilling vassals. Initially he tried peaceful means with the Lombard king, styling himself in his letter "Defender of the Holy Roman Church by Divine appointment."[12] It is an interesting point that Pepin demanded that the towns and lands captured by Aistulf, including Byzantine Ravenna, be restored, not to the emperor at Constantinople, but to the Church of Saint Peter at Rome. Aistulf refused to grant any of his stipulations except to allow the unmolested return of Pope Stephen to Rome.

Pepin had no alternative to war. In 755, with the pope in his train, he crossed the Alps by the seven-thousand-foot Mont Cenis Pass (the same used by Constantine when he crossed from Gaul to Italy to engage in the Battle of the Milvian Bridge), and began the descent to the high Valley of Susa, where King Aistulf had come to meet him. Pepin's army ran into difficulties negotiating the narrow rocky pass and only a few of his men reached the valley. There Aistulf pounced confidently with his whole force. The Franks called upon God, and with the ferocity of desperation they defeated the Lombards, scattering Aistulf's army and inflicting large casualties. They followed the fleeing enemy to Pavia, ravaging, burning and pillaging as they went, in the style made traditional by Merovingian predecessors. The Lombard king begged for terms, promising hostages, the cession of Ravenna and other towns to the Holy See, and permanent tribute to Pepin as his overlord. The pope added his pleas: not eager to substitute one aggressive overlord for another, Stephen preferred his enthusiastic champions, now that they had saved him, back over the Alps. Pepin always favored negotiation to battle. Happy to yield, he allowed Aistulf to keep both his life and his crown. After seeing Pope Stephen reinstated on the papal throne, the Frankish king "with God's help returned home with his army, laden with great treasure." Pepin's punitive expedition differed only in its honorable motivation from earlier profitable Italian forays of Merovingian kings.

Also following precedent, King Aistulf failed to honor his oaths. In the following year, 756, he began marauding in the area of Rome, burning houses around Saint Peter's church. Pepin, still concerned over the solidity of his royal claim, had no choice but to promise his intervention on the pope's behalf once more. He led his troops, as before, to the Pass of Mont Cenis, but there they balked. The near-disastrous first expedition had disturbed his vassals to the extent that they threatened to desert. Somehow Pepin persuaded them to go on; once again they met Aistulf in the Valley of Susa and once again the Lombard was routed, his men retreating in confusion. He sued for peace, which was granted. This time he had no opportunity to break his word: soon afterward he was killed in a hunting accident. His successor, a friend of the pope, and chosen by him, showed no ardor to challenge the indestructible Frank.

The pope was safe, and so was Pepin's claim to the throne. But there was one more step to take to secure the pope's supremacy and to bind the papal-Frankish alliance indissolubly. The pope had to be freed from vassalage to the emperor at Constantinople. Throughout the Lombard vicissitudes he had never formally relinquished his tie to Byzantium. The ownership of Church lands in Italy was a foggy province. The Lombards had captured them and the Franks had seized them in turn. By now it was not clear to whom they legally belonged. The Frankish king was good at cutting knots. Since the conquered towns were in practice the victor's to dispose of as he wished, Pepin forthrightly "restored" them to the papacy. But the papacy only had a vassal's claim on them: the pope's fealty was to his historic overlord, the emperor of Rome, who lived in Constantinople. The emperor would not easily lose his only remaining—and very valuable—realty in the West. He sent ambassadors to Pepin to plead for the restoration to the empire of Ravenna and other exarchate towns. But Pepin refused, asserting that he had freed those towns for the sake of the Roman chair, and under the aegis of the Roman chair they would remain. He implemented his declaration by sending deputations to the disputed towns, to receive their formal surrender. His envoys returned with some of the responsible local citizens, who carried the keys of their cities to Rome and laid them in Saint Peter's grave in symbolic gift to the Holy See.

This act, known as the Donation of Pepin, freed the pope from the Byzantine connection. Thanks to his bold ally the pope was now the indisputable lord of his own territories, and henceforth could take his place among Europe's sovereigns. Pepin was the creator of the Papal State.

Although Pepin had confirmed his dynastic claim on the Frankish throne his wars were not over. After four years of respite there began a bitter and tiresome campaign which lasted the rest of his life, from 760 to 768. This was the conflict with Aquitaine, waged with the rancor of a civil war. Historically Aquitanians and Franks despised one another—brash Teutons versus overbred Gallo-Romans. The mutual dislike that had led to clashes starting with Clovis and his rampaging son, Theodoric, in 507, had been inherited by their Merovingian descendants and was shared to the full by the German-oriented house of Pepin. In this war we see a side of Pepin discordant with his magnanimity to defeated enemies. Vengeful hostility marks every stage of his endeavor to render Aquitaine an inalienable part of the Frankish empire.

The present lord of Aquitaine was Duke Waifar. Besides his contumacious attitude to his Frankish neighbor and liege lord, Waifar had the potentially dangerous background of collateral Merovingian descent. The Aquitanian indulged riskily in border inroads, so arousing Pepin's exasperation that in 760 he issued a series of ultimatums. If Waifar obeyed them all he would be rendered entirely subordinate to the Frankish king. The alternative, which the duke invited, was wholesale war. Pepin's initial attacks were petty marauding raids in which his men fired and devastated Auvergne until Waifar cried for quarter. After exacting promises, Pepin "returned home, by God's help unscathed, laden with much plunder."

Waifar had no intention of honoring his enforced pledges, and the next year he took the initiative, invading Burgundy and plundering and burning north to Chalon-sur-Saône. Pepin reacted with fury: following his victory over the invaders he stormed after them into Auvergne, where he put all his prisoners to death, burned towns along with their helpless inhabitants and "tore up all the vineyards from which almost all Aquitaine, rich and poor, used to obtain wine." Such was the virulence of the fighting that even monks took up arms: one of Waifar's vassals, the count of Poitiers, "who had gone plundering in Touraine, was killed by the men of Abbot Wulfard of the monastery of the blessed Martin."

By 764 both sides were exhausted and Pepin's forces refused to move. There was a year of rest; then the Aquitanians, persistent as hornets from a disturbed nest, began raiding the borders again. Pepin's vassals were aggravated into action, and in 766 they voted to end the Aquitanian nuisance decisively. Pepin threw all his strength into this last campaign. The Aquitanians, though they could not equal the Franks in fighting ability, defended their homeland with hopeless courage for two years. Finally exhausted, they had to beg mercy from their conquerors.

But there was no mercy for Waifar. His wife and children captured, his chief supporters caught and hanged, he himself deserted by his soldiers, the duke hid out in the Forêt de Ver (near Périgueux in Dordogne). There he wandered like a wild animal until his own followers assassinated him "allegedly with the king's connivance." With the death of Waifar the independence of Aquitaine was extinguished. This intractable corner of France, whose inhabitants had defied conquerors with stubborn valor as far back as Caesar, finally succumbed. "And all came to [Pepin] to become his men." From 768 Aquitaine was part of the Frankish empire, governed by vassals of the king of the Franks.

Pepin barely outlived his southern enemy. Following his last victory he was at the height of success: the kingdom was finally at peace, its borders secure, its tributary states subdued or friendly. The Frankish empire was bigger and stronger than ever before: on the north it bordered the North Sea (although the Saxons had yet to be subordinated), on the east it abutted Bohemia and Carinthia, and it reached south to the Pyrenees and the Italian Alps. This includes today—besides all of France—western Germany, Switzerland and western Austria. But before he could apply the wisdom of age and experience to the consummation of his military and political accomplishments, Pepin, at the age of fifty-three, was struck ill with fever at Saintes. The king went to Tours to pray at Saint Martin's shrine, thence to that of Saint Denis in Paris. But the saints withheld their favor, and Pepin, accepting his end, went to die at Heristal, his ancestral home. He called his vassals to him there and received their agreement to the division of the kingdom between his sons, Charles and Carloman.

His tomb is near that of his father, Charles Martel, in the cathedral of Saint Denis. The only inscription at the foot of the dignified thirteenth-century reclining stone effigy is: *Pater Caroli Magni.*

The father of Charlemagne and the son of Charles Martel deserves more than tangential fame. Pepin had no opportunity for the spectacular military coup which gave his father an eternal niche in history. He was not, like his son, the creator of a bona fide Christian empire. But in his twenty-seven-year reign he consolidated his father's successes: he completed Charles's partial conquest of Septimania from the Arabs; he achieved the subjugation of the Bavarians and the Swabians to Frankish control; he drove the Saxons back from his borders and contained them in the north; he defeated the Lombards, extending Frankish influence through northern Italy to Rome. These first steps—the confining of the Saxons and the routing of the Lombards—would be carried by his son to outright conquest. But conquest was made ready for Charlemagne. So also was the title of emperor, the logical upward move from Pepin's daring usurpation of the name king of the Franks. Pepin's moderation and wisdom in peace made possible a unified Francia from which his son could step forth as the first emperor in western Europe since the deposition of Romulus Augustulus.

Of Pepin's personal life, character and appearance we have little knowledge. Like his father he suffered from the lack of firsthand reportage. All we have are a few generalized compliments: "energetic, honorable prince distinguished alike by his victories and virtues,"[13] and the epithet "the Short," which was not bestowed on him until three centuries after his death. The scanty facts about his personal life indicate that it was morally uneventful. He was more sincerely religious than his father: ecclesiastical writers of the period refer to him with enthusiasm lacking in their cool praise of Charles Martel. He kept a firm dominance over the ecclesiastical affairs of the realm, and did not scruple to avail himself of the overweight wealth of the Church. Yet the lords of the Church appreciated him, not so much as their master as their champion. He earned the eternal gratitude of the papacy, for he made possible the terrestrial power of the Church in Rome.

In internal civil affairs Pepin was a just and capable administrator, knowing how to delegate yet holding a tight rein. He advanced the strength of the seigneury by continuing his father's policy of benefices, but while he was ruler their presumption was held in check.

In only one instance have we a glimpse of ferocity: in Pepin's obsessive hatred of Waifar and the insubordinate Aquitanians. The southern province, to be sure, gave him cause for irritation. Its Gallo-Roman population was impudent and condescending; to Pepin, with his inborn Germanness, it was also overcivilized to the point of effeteness. Aside from his pitiless resentment in this one case, Pepin was a fair conqueror and ruler. In one area at least, he was aware of the racial skew in his otherwise well-tuned character. He understood that his Neustrian and Burgundian citizens chafed at the haughtiness of the Austrasians, and found their king's overriding Teutonism unpalatable. Pepin's extended hospitality to Pope Stephen II was intended to placate this sector of the people. His friendly concordance with the pope and the incidence of the second crowning in Paris gained him the respect of these mixed populations.

Pepin bequeathed to his sons a realm on the verge of realizing itself as a nation. Since the grip of Rome had slipped from Gaul the consciousness had been slowly evolving. The Merovingian dynasty, heirs of the barbarian invaders—truculent, greedy and unscrupulous—had in their rude way been the first builders. As they enfeebled their own strain with intemperance they gave place to the new type of ruler embodied in the Arnulfings, strong, warlike men, generous in outlook, of higher moral stature than their predecessors, and with a warmer regard for culture. The house of Pepin and all it represented was the organic product of three centuries of the melding of two civilizations, under the sustained mediation of Christianity.

But nothing could have been done without the terrible Merovingians, the only successful barbarians of Europe. Theirs is a cruel history but it is a constructive one: it does not head into the downward spiral of degeneracy as did the later Roman Empire, but upward toward the brief and beautiful flowering of the Carolingian renaissance. With all its vicissitudes and its evils, Merovingian Gaul expressed the arrogant health of youth.

CHAPTER NINE

THE
MEROVINGIAN
LEGACY

The label Dark Ages has the connotation of the end of a world: the overwhelming by ignorant and uncouth northmen of the antique grace of the Mediterranean civilizations. A truer appellation would be the Age of Change. The quality of lightlessness in those centuries was not the darkness of a nether world but the darkness of predawn. The German barbarians who filled the vacuum after the dissolution of the Roman Empire in the West had, at the time of their invasions, small sensitivity to the nuances of classical culture. Despite their crudeness, and partly because of it, the esthetic fringes of life in Frankish Gaul took on a new cast during their centuries. The Franks were flexible masters, and their hand lay lightly on post-Roman Gaul. They allowed latitude to their subject peoples, and the result was a happy fusion of the older and the younger civilizations in the area of art and literature. In some aspects the culture of the transitional period was as revolutionary as the rude northerners who brought youth to the enervated Roman province. In others it traced descent from the ancient world as filtered through Byzantium.

In one direction the classical tradition took the lead: language. The Gallo-Roman population, in the Merovingian centuries, far outnumbered the Frankish. In the end, despite the political mastery of the German sector, the Latin complexion prevailed over the Teutonic, and the Gallo-Franks became a Romance people—unlike their neighbors to the north and east, Britain and Germany, lands only casually touched by Rome. The main implement of the ascendancy of Gallo-Roman culture was the Latin language. The victory of Latin over German was a phenomenon of lasting benefit to the Frankish conquerors. Latin was the language of education, of commerce and the law, of military service, of the Church. It was the prevailing speech of the court, where the Frankish kings surrounded themselves with the useful representatives of the highest Gallo-Roman families. Many of the common people must also have understood it, for kingly edicts were promulgated in Latin, justice was administered in Latin in the provincial courts, the ritual and the sermons of the Church were in Latin. It was the tongue of organization, and its wide acceptance went far toward putting order into what might have been, following the dissipation of Roman centrality, incorrigible confusion.

Following Caesar's conquest the Celtic language too had vanished before the superior utility of Latin. But in some intangible ways the Celtic influence lingered right through the time of Roman Gaul into the era of Frankish dominance. The Celtic spirit had been the chief agent in raising the educational standards of Roman Gaul to the status of the finest in the empire. The touch of these people is still discernible in the language: modern French differs from Italian and Spanish, also direct derivatives of Latin—but its differences are not Teutonic. Filtered through the overlay of centuries, traces of the Celtic tongue live on—the speech of a people who had no written language. Besides some Celtic words, the distinctiveness of French construction and pronunciation has, philologists believe, a Celtic origin. Long after Latin had taken a firm hold of the urban intellectual centers of Frankish Gaul the older language persisted in areas more remote from the Roman ambit. It was in these regions, where the Celts had most obstinately resisted Caesar, that the precursor of modern French first evolved. Well into the fifth century, Celtic was the prevailing speech in these rural areas, even in the class most closely associated with Latin, the clerical. Sulpicius Severus writes of a disciple of Saint Martin who, apologizing for his inexact Latin, is advised to "speak in Celtic, if you prefer it, provided that you speak of Martin."[1] The Celts have always been loath to resign their identity.

The influence of the fading Roman civilization on the rising Gallo-Frankish was almost undiluted in the field of education, an area where the illiterate barbarian conquerors had nothing to offer. We have seen that the Roman schools established in the main Gallic cities reached a level of excellence unequaled in the empire. The curriculum was based on the classic Greco-Roman faculties of grammar, rhetoric and logic—a system of broad scope that included the study of the pagan philosophers and poets. Its classical alignment was uncongenial to the Western Church, but in the time of Roman Gaul the Christians of Europe had not yet a tradition of learning with which to replace it. Toward the end of Rome's supremacy in the West education, along with most other facets of a gracious life, was crumbling in the wake of social unrest and political anarchy. The Church was faced with the need to reactivate the foundering schools at least to the extent of providing a minimal literacy for her higher clergy. The basis of Christian schooling was necessarily the traditional Roman curriculum, but the writings of the Church Fathers were substituted for those of the heathen philosophers. By the fifth century there were in the West enough Christian-oriented thinkers to provide a respectable alternative to the pagans, whose prose was considered to lead too attractively downhill. In the sixth century three brilliant scholars put form and body into the fledgling Christian educational system: Cassiodorus and Boethius in Italy and Isidore in Spain. A fourth master, the Venerable Bede, brought the scholastic renascence to Britain in the seventh century. These teachers went straight back to the feared classics, establishing their educational system firmly on the foundation of the classical disciplines, and encouraging the study of Greek and Roman literature— along with, of course, the works of Christian theologians. The method of study included the copying of classical texts: to these wise masters we owe their preservation through centuries of combined ignorance and moral reprehension.

From their work emerged the medieval curriculum, the seven liberal arts, divided into the trivium and the quadrivium, which survived into the Renaissance in European universities. The trivium—grammar, dialectic and rhetoric—included the study of literature, logic, law and composition in prose and verse. The quadrivium, comprising geometry, arithmetic, music and astronomy, trained the higher scholars in geography, natural history, the medicinal properties of plants, calendar computations, Church plainsong, the theory of sound and the science of harmony, and the courses of the heavenly bodies (the latter subject strongly tinged with astrology). The early medieval curriculum, instituted by these tolerant sages and enlarged by their successors, reached back to Socrates and survived into the Renaissance. It ensured the preservation of the lustrous intellectuality of antiquity through the dark and martial years when little store was set by the cultural relics of an age long dead.

But in our period that continuity ran very thin. The courses in the seven liberal arts existed in theory, but in most Gallic schools the prevalence of undereducated teachers and backward pupils obliged that they shrank to two: grammar and rhetoric, that is, linguistics and letters. The scholar of the sixth and later centuries received no mathematics or science and very little history, geography or philosophy. Even in letters his field of learning, outside the study of the Church Fathers, narrowed to a few of the Latin classics of Virgil, Terence, Sallust and Cicero. Greek learning was in the main lost.

Despite the ecclesiastical orientation of education the Church did not monopolize either the endowment or the student body of institutes of learning. Long before the Franks had become the dominant power in Gaul the Roman administration had instituted schools for the education of the sons of chieftains—those barbarian infiltrators who had lived long enough within the Roman orbit to have become *foederati*. The most famous schools were those at Autun and Marseilles, where the princelings underwent a thorough Roman programming. When the Franks became the sovereign race their kings understood the value of this indoctrination for dealing with their majority subject population. The royal children, along with sons of the courtiers, were exposed to a Roman schooling that at least partially prepared them for their future responsibilities. The first Frankish ruler to see the advantage of the Roman legacy was Clovis: after his conversion he instituted a chapel* and school, where highborn boys pursued a kind of page's course designed to lubricate their entry into public life. Besides the obligatory if perfunctory religious education, the children received instruction in the decadent literature of the later empire, and in the arts of the courtier. To make sure that they did not forget their birthright of German masculinity, the boys were also trained in the practice of arms.

The schooling of upper-class girls, during the few years allowed to

---

*The present-day meaning of the word "chapel" probably came into the language at about this time: it is derived from the Latin *capella*, a short cloak, and it refers to the relic of Saint Martin's torn cape, enshrined in a small building that attracted local worshippers and pilgrims.

them before marriage, was generally in the hands of the only Frankish women to receive a higher education, the nuns. Convent education specialized in religious studies, knowledge of the rituals of the ceremony, copying and illuminating religious manuscripts and spinning, weaving and needlework.

The growth of Christian scholarship did not include a parallel flowering of original prose and poetry. Literature in the Merovingian era was at a low ebb. The Roman tradition of letters could not survive into a rougher and simpler age—nor should it have. Long before the barbarians became the masters of Europe the Roman genius had been drying out. The secular prose and poetry of the later Roman Empire, formal, elaborate and vapid, gave evidence of the desiccation. Even religious writing lost its immediacy: with a few exceptions the output of the fifth-century theologians was stereotyped and technical, with no elasticity of mind or freedom of ideas. The literature that grew up outside the lingering scholasticism was for the most part primitive and artless; its main virtue was unpretentiousness.

Roman Gaul, at the edge of the empire and with a population still livened by the Celtic blend, suffered the creeping aridity to a lesser extent than the older Mediterranean culture. But even here the literature tended to sterility and the poets preferred to look backward. We have seen how Ausonius cushioned himself within his pretty country estate, his face firmly turned away from the black clouds gathering on all his horizons. And how even Sidonius who, as bishop of Clermont, helped to defend his beleaguered town against the Visigothic King Euric, contrived in the verse and letters of his few peaceful moments to create an idyllic oasis of humor and pastoral bliss in the midst of storms.

By the sixth century there was no longer any place in Gaul for an Ausonius and a Sidonius—nor, toward the end of the century, anywhere in western Europe. The atmosphere was becoming increasingly anti-intellectual. Italy had her Cassiodorus and her Boethius, the last great exponents of the classical tradition, who ennobled the literature of the first half of the century. But Gregory I, who became pope in 590, fostered a counter spirit. No good religious purpose, he believed, was served by the trivialities of grammar, rhetoric and logic. He regarded culture in general as obstructive to the unquestioning, submissive faith he had to encourage in order to realize the formation of a monolithic Church. His attitude was explainable in view of his contemporary needs, but it was responsible for the obscurantism, parent of prejudice, that engulfed the Church all through the Middle Ages, and that would lead at last to the atrocities of the Inquisition.

The influence of Gregory I was not at once felt in Gaul, where the pope was hardly more than a distant friend and the urban bishops ruled their sees without the attention of Rome. The great Gallo-Roman families still survived, and their day-to-day lives retained an archaic gentility. But the scions of the old families had a different temper in the sixth century: for one thing education in Frankish Gaul had fallen far below even late imperial standards. The Latin that was spoken and written was no longer the clean elegant tongue of Virgil and Horace but an imprecise descendant already being vulgarized to fit the simpler needs of the German conquerors. For another, while the remnants of Roman tradition still clung to the older intellectual aristocracy, its exponents were perforce involved in the affairs of the uneducated barbarians, if they wanted to keep their lives safe and their estates intact. The writers of the sixth and seventh centuries composed for a different audience from that of their nostalgic predecessors.

Fortunatus is a conspicuous example: the poet-scholar, trained in the classical tradition of Byzantine Ravenna, trimmed his sails to the more blustery winds of Frankish Gaul, and succeeded in making himself the literary pet both of royalty and the upper clergy. Much of the figured elegance of his rhetorical verse is lost in translation; but in the sixth century it was considered the acme of distinction to receive an encomium from the pen of the witty priest. Fortunatus's scintillating conceits appealed, as their author intended, to the snobbish neo-Romanism of his highborn ex-barbarian clientele.

Fortunatus came to terms with a world that was not originally his. Gregory of Tours, born into it, was the first practitioner of a genuine and exciting literary departure. Without consciously intending it he broke new ground: in his person and in his writing he represents a synthesis between the Mediterranean tradition that was withering in the West and the brash, impressionable spirit of the conquering northerners. Though the scion of a wealthy and public-spirited Gallo-Roman family of Auvergne, Gregory never acquired the mannered gloss of Fortunatus. As a young patrician destined by background and by personal choice for the Church, Gregory had the best schooling that southern Gaul could offer; but the best was much scantier than it had been a century earlier. Though, as we have seen,

Gregory's basic education was sketchy, it fit him better in sixth-century Gaul than a deeper philosophical schooling would have. In his dual role as metropolitan bishop and historian Gregory had no need to bend his mind toward the disciplines of logical speculation. Nor was he inclined this way. Like most of his better-educated contemporaries he was a doer, not a thinker. His *History of the Franks* reflects both his times and his character.

Under the influence of Christian teaching fourth- and fifth-century chroniclers had inaugurated a fresh method of historical narrative which slotted local history into biblical history. Whatever their final goal in contemporary events they all started with Adam. This style of chronicle was still fashionable when Gregory began his *History of the Franks* with the creation of the world, skimmed rapidly through the Old and New Testaments and dovetailed into his précis, after not too many pages, the rise of the early Franks, their warriors and their saints.

Gregory was humbly aware of his faulty Latin: "I apologize to my readers," he writes in his opening preface, "lest by syllable or even letter I offend against grammatical usage," and again at the end of the last book: "I know very well that my style is lacking in polish." Nevertheless he concludes with the plea that his work not be gelded: "If what I have written seems uncouth to you, do not, I beg you, do violence to my Books. . . . Keep them intact!"[2]

However sincerely he deplored his stylistic and linguistic defects, Gregory's simple and inexact Latin made his history approachable to readers who had less schooling than he. Fortunately Gregory did not know the classical writers well enough to imitate them; had he attempted to write in the turgid style of the later empire his audience would have melted away. The sixth-century reading public—the minute segment that had even enough education for Gregory's crude Latin—was a rough-textured, aspiring ruling elite whose fathers had been unlettered warriors. Gregory's history appealed to them as it appeals to us, and for similar reasons: although it is naïve and nonanalytical, and often illogical and unstructured, it is full of zest. Above all it is genuine history. Its author neither embroiders nor fabricates, and he makes an effort to preserve chronological unity. To a modern reader he has a penchant for excusing the most blatant savagery—the sinner is treated leniently on a scale with the size of his ecclesiastical donations—but the motivation is understandable. For the most part Gregory is honest, courageous and sincere. He is also sharply humorous, and he has no fear of admonishing royalty. Clovis's bloodthirsty grandsons, Gregory's kings, cannot have been quite so ferocious as posterity has claimed: they reacted with remarkably good temper to Gregory's barbed scolding.

The History of the Franks is the outstanding literary opus of the period. In the two centuries after Gregory wrote there were several chroniclers whose work is instructive for the modern historian. But they were annalists, not historians. In its honesty and its many-colored detail Gregory's work bears direct comparison with the Histories of Herodotus. In Europe of his own day he can be compared with Bede. But Gregory's history has more immediacy than that of the cloistered English monk, because he himself, as a man of the world, was an actor in many of the events he describes with such piquant detail.

At this same time another kind of literature was developing in the West: hagiography. This genre was native to its time and place, and was designed to appeal to a vast, humble audience, the majority of which could not read at all. The lives of saints, inspirational lessons and at the same time appealing tales of romance and magic, have a kinship with the pictorial art of the period. Meant to be read aloud, they were at the same time hortatory and dramatic and, like literature for children, purposefully simple and repetitive.

Hagiography in the West went back to the fourth century when Athanasius's Life of St. Anthony achieved a tremendous popularity in western Europe, becoming the bible of the early hermits and the well-head of the monastic movement in Gaul. Soon after Athanasius's biography was circulated an imitative native literature arose that had a chauvinistic bias: our western saints are just as holy as yours, and what is better, they are not Greek and Roman. The outstanding and most popular example of this nationalistic, mildly revolutionary literature was Sulpicius Severus's blithe and graceful Life of St. Martin.

Sulpicius was a highborn Aquitanian youth who, attracted by the gentle bishop of Tours, became a monk at Martin's Marmoutier. Later he donated all his estates to the Church but one villa; this he converted to a monastery where his slaves became his brothers. Sulpicius had the biographer's advantage of knowing his subject personally; his biography was completed before Martin's death in 397. Further, his work is rich in apposite detail, giving the modern reader an authentic picture of religion in fourth-century Gaul: the struggles of the ascetic movement against the disapproving bishops, the brisk clash of fire-eating missionaries with idol worshippers. Acquainted with many of the leading lights of his day, Sulpicius is also well informed on the state of Christianity outside of Gaul: the ecclesiastical bickering in Alexandria, the ascetic movement in the deserts of Egypt and Palestine, the controversial personality of Saint Jerome. The *Life of St. Martin*, intended as a reverent portrait of an authentic Gallic saint with a miracle-studded halo, is almost—but not quite—genuine history. Sulpicius's successors and imitators in following centuries went much further: they deliberately eschewed the historical man, concentrating exclusively on a devoutly minute depiction of his halo.

Through the fifth century, while genuine Gallic saints were close at hand and facts were available to their near contemporaries, blurred, of course, by "eye-witness" miracles, the narrative style of Sulpicius prevailed. Two charming examples of fifth-century hagiography are *A Discourse on the Life of St. Honoratus* by Hilary, bishop of Arles, a touching eulogy to a happy saint, and the *Life of St. Germanus of Auxerre* by Constantius, a monk of Lyon, a spirited, unvarnished account, with only minor attention given to miracle working, of an ascetic activist. Both these works were written near the time of their subjects' deaths—Hilary's the year after Honoratus died and Constantius's thirty-two years after Germain. Firsthand evidence gave them objectivity.

By the sixth century the emphasis had changed: hagiographers were going further back in time for their subjects, and, since they relied on oral tradition and local legend, their hold on authenticity grew tenuous. It was a purposeful deviation. By that time factual truth was not the intention; inspiration and awe had taken its place. The saints no longer lived mortal lives, but came to resemble images in stained glass, each, surrounded by his familiar symbols, engaging with hieratic stiffness in his time-honored activities. It was literature for the faithful illiterate, and it was what the period demanded. Through the sixth and succeeding centuries, hagiography was almost the only literary form, taking the place of history, poetry and philosophy. It was also a substitute for public entertainment, which had died out with the Roman retreat. The common people could no longer forget their dreary and fearful existences at the theater or the circus; they escaped vicariously through these pious romances. For the lives of the saints were not only morally uplifting, they were by turns tender and terrifying, mysterious and luminous. They had a further virtue in those stormy centuries: without exception their heroes were the defenders of the oppressed against the brutal arrogance of kings and noblemen. The cowled knights-errant magically opened the gates of prisons and caused the chains to drop off pinioned limbs. They paralyzed the upraised sword arms of local tyrants. They afflicted the secret thief, adulterer or extortioner with lightning strikes or paroxysms. Retribution was inflicted, fittingly, in church, through the agency of its long-dead patron saint. They laid curses on provoking royalty, and their destructive maledictions tended to come distressingly true.

In another aspect these holy brothers appealed to people looking for the pity and tenderness that did not exist in their own hard lives. The saints preferred to live in solitude in gothically gloomy forests; there they held amicable concourse with wild beasts and held off the hunter and the robber. Many were the dogs whose baying pursuit was halted suddenly at the entrance to the cave within which the trembling hare sought refuge; many the horses immobilized under their noble riders before the saint with his arms around the wounded deer. Wolves, bears and boars were gentled into obedience by the friendly voices of the hermits, birds lit on their shoulders and fish leaped in the streams to do them honor.

A few examples illustrate the engaging credulity both of the saints and their chroniclers. Saint Carileffus (after whose monastery Calais was named) started his religious career as a forest solitary.[3] In his retreat he made friends with an aurochs (the European bison, rare then, now almost extinct), which he petted and fed. King Childebert, one of Clovis's sons, hearing of the marvelous size and fierceness of the aurochs, determined to hunt it. He found its tracks and followed them to the bough-roofed refuge of the hermit, who stood protectively beside the animal. The king accused Carileffus of trespassing on the royal hunting preserve. The hermit replied mildly that he was there only to pray, not to flout royal authority. Childebert bade him leave at once, but when the king advanced to implement his order with force, his horse balked. Childebert, realizing that he could not defy the power of heaven—obeyed even by dumb animals—dismounted and knelt before the holy man. Carileffus not only blessed him but gave him wine from his own little vineyard. Though the wine was sour the king's heart was touched, and he offered the saint all the lands thereabout for a monastery. Carileffus demurred, but finally agreed to take as much land as he could ride around in a day on his donkey. Later Childebert's queen expressed a wish to visit the anchorite, but Carileffus refused: "As long as I live I shall never see the face of a woman, and no woman shall enter my monastery. And why should this queen be so desirous of seeing a man disfigured by fasts and rural labors, soiled and covered with stains like a chameleon?"

Saint Columbanus similarly numbered the beasts of the forest among his friends and, ever the teacher, chided, comforted and educated them as if they were children. On one of his ambles through the Vosges foothills he came on a bear about to devour the carcass of a stag recently killed by a wolf. He begged the bear not to injure the hide in the course of its feast, because the monks needed it for shoes. "Then the beast, forgetting its ferocity, became gentle, and drooping its head left the body without a murmur."[4] Another time, when Columbanus was working in the field beside his monks, his work gloves disappeared. The saint knew that the only animal which would have stolen them was the raven, "the bird which was sent out by Noah and did not return to the ark." While the monks looked for the thief their abbot stood quietly. Soon a raven flew down and laid the gloves at his feet and "humbly awaited its punishment." There was none. Columbanus merely told it to go. When he and the Irish brethren had been forced out of Luxeuil they halted their wanderings briefly in eastern Gaul, at a place where there was nothing to eat but little wild apples. In the morning they found a bear foraging among the fruit. Columbanus, respecting the animal's hunger, "set aside a part of the fruit trees for the bear, and ordered it to leave the others for himself." Thereafter the bear took only its assigned portion.

Sulpicius Severus's *Life of St. Martin*, for all its relative authenticity, has its share of small miracles. When Martin, at the end of his life, was on his way to the village of Candes, he paused by the river Loire. There his eye was caught by the sight of kingfishers darting after fish. The saint exclaimed: "This is a picture of how the demons act: they lie in wait for the unwary and capture them before they know it, and they can never be satisfied." He then commanded the birds to leave the water and to "betake themselves to dry and desert regions. Accordingly all those birds formed a single body and made for the mountains."[5] Sulpicius's parable is remembered in the birds' popular name, *martin-pêcheurs*.

One can too readily ridicule the simpleminded piety of these tales, their repetitions, their vacuity. The fact was that by the sixth century there was no class in Gaul capable of developing a sophisticated literature. Southern Gaul no longer had literati; the inadequacy of education affected even Gallo-Romans, who by now shared the ignorance and superstition that clouded every aspect of life. The lives of the saints were universally popular partly because there was no other literature available.

Judged objectively the stories have a winning naturalness. Their authors apologized for their clumsy Latin and their want of artistic skill. They probably failed to recognize the appeal of this very artlessness. Not quite so uneducated as their reading and listening public, the writers still had an ingenuous faith mirroring that of their audience. The literary art of the premedieval period, like its sculpture, has a shining religious simplicity. Though it flourished in a transitional period it is *sui generis*: it comes close to being folk art.

An authentic folk literature whose origins were far older existed alongside premedieval hagiography. When the Franks came to Gaul they brought with them the stories of their past, preserved in oral tradition—the only kind of record of their antecedents the nomadic Teutonic tribes could keep. Much of the material of Teutonic lore was a product of the period of the great migrations, from the time of Ariovistus to that of Charlemagne. This era lent itself easily to the growth of legendary history: the amorphous and momentous movements of peoples, the rise of charismatic, doomed warrior chiefs, the pervasive credulity of the northern Europeans, heathen and Christian alike, the confusion attendant on the withdrawal of the Roman organization from the fabric of the West.

Tacitus recognized the germ of history in the legends of an earthborn god and his children, whose names were those of Teutonic tribes. Later the Merovingian fighting kings of Gaul entered the heroic sagas, their doings blended into the mortal conflicts of the gods. There is evidence that a large body of oral literature peculiar to Frankish Gaul existed up until the time of Charlemagne. Only fragments of this semihistorical lore live on today in the *Nibelungenlied* and the *Völsungasaga*, whose settings are Burgundy, Belgium and Austria.

A few of the heroic men and women of the German songs are cloudily recognizable. The mythical Siegfried is a fusion of several historical figures with an earlier Teutonic demigod. Among his human prototypes are Hermann and Civilis, the earliest proponents of Teutonic unity in Gaul; and Sigibert, son of Lothair I, the Merovingian king slain young by a woman's treachery. Brunhild of the sagas can be equated with some aspects of Queen Brunhild, whose bitter feud with her rival led to the catastrophic destruction of all her line. Other characters involved in Frankish history are Attila the Hun, in an unlikely amiable version named Etzel or Atli; Theodoric the Ostrogoth as the hero Dietrich of Bern (Verona); and Gundahar of Burgundy, the Gunther of the *Nibelungenlied* who wooed and won Brunhild. (The heroic queen, angry at being wed to the wrong man, vented her resentment on their bridal night by tying Gunther in a knot and hanging him on the wall—a performance of which the sixth-century Brunhild might have been capable.)

The oral literature of Frankish Gaul was the only lore universally available and comprehensible. Yet these few remnants, in the literature of another nation, are all that survive. Even when cloistered scribes were copying Roman and Greek texts and biographers were recording the sayings and miracles of the native saints, no one of the literate class saw fit to record the new-old poetry that was the only genuine Frankish literature. The Christian literati looked on the popular tales as barbaric and potentially sinful. Gregory of Tours, though he used some of the legends in his narration of early Frankish history, generally ignored the indigenous mythology as a pagan aberration. Frankish Gaul had no great native poet like the anonymous eighth-century Anglo-Saxon compiler of the Danish *Beowulf* legends, or the medieval Icelandic scholars who cast the Norse mythology of the origin of the world into the prose and poetry of the *Eddas*, or the unknown German poets who transformed a patchwork group of western European folk tales into the *Nibelungenlied*, or the unnamed scribes, products of the great monastic schools of Ireland, who recorded the oral lore of the Celts.

There may have been an effort to keep the Frankish songs alive: Charlemagne, proud of his Teutonic heritage, ordered the oral tales to be collected and written down. But the collection was destroyed, it is said, by order of his sanctimonious son, Louis the Pious, who was afraid of its heathen allure. The barbaric lays are gone, and the world is poorer.

Music was the one field of artistic expression in which the classical tradition survived the barbarian conquests almost intact. The Franks liked the music they found in Roman Gaul. Aristocratic children were taught the psalms in Gallo-Roman church schools so they could take part in choral services, and Merovingian kings ordered fine instruments to be sent them from Byzantium and Italy. But although the Teutonic conquerors were reputed music lovers, teachers from the south complained of the guttural voices of their Frankish pupils and were unenthusiastic about their performances.

The only European music of this period of which we have evidential knowledge is church music. Not until the troubadours and minnesingers of the twelfth to the fourteenth centuries is there any authentic record of secular music in western Europe. Naturally the laity of the Dark Ages had dances and songs, but their provenance has vanished.

The music of the early Christian service, and consequently much of our music today, was the lineal heir to that of Greek antiquity, with a few elements from the Hebrew temple ritual. In the first three centuries of Christianity, when it was still a forbidden religion, the service was a mutual, informally organized exercise. The music, as part of the service, was adapted to each group according to its taste, and sung by the worshippers. They sang the music they knew: that of classical Greece, overlaid by elements of the Hebrew service and filtered through the Roman imperial structure. It had lost the science and subtlety of its antecedents, but its basis had not changed. Though most of the arts and learning of the classical era withered or were irretrievably changed as Rome's hold weakened in the West, music, through its spontaneous inclusion in early Christian worship, sustained an almost unbroken continuity from classic antiquity to the Middle Ages.

The early Christian congregations probably sang the service in unison. As the still illegal but increasingly popular religion gained hosts of new converts, the singing became antiphonal: the older members sang and the newer ones, not yet familiar with the musical ritual, answered. When Christianity became the official state religion of Rome, the dignity of its new status required a more formal organization. The orderly performance of church music followed: a musical clergy arose, trained in the newly formalized ritual but continuing to draw on Mediterranean culture. In the beginning this schooled group alternated with the congregation in the chanting of the service. Later the entire function was assumed by the initiate, the clerical choir singing in antiphony with the officiating priest. It took many centuries for the participating audience to be transformed to the passive one. But in the transition from spontaneous singing assembly to professional choir, the bridge was not destroyed: the church music of medieval Europe was, as it is today, the direct descendant of the Greek art of the Muses.

This music, the traditional music of the Latin rite, is called plainsong. Although it is the ancestor of modern Western music it has some distinctively different qualities: it is single-voiced and exclusively vocal; it is unmeasured, its rhythms being those of prose speech; and it is based on scales approximating the Greek modes.

The names most conspicuously associated with plainsong are those of Bishop Ambrose of Milan in the fourth century and Pope Gregory I in the sixth. Ambrose was one of the first to systematize the haphazard music of the democratic early congregations. Though Pope Gregory's name is attached to plainsong, the extent of his contribution to its development is unclear. He had not much use for any kind of intellectuality, and his attitude toward music probably echoed his inclination. However, he was very much interested in the uniformity of the ritual— an element in his design to strengthen the structure of the Church— and the codification of liturgical music followed. It is now believed that Pope Gregory's work was a continuation of earlier efforts, originating in Antioch or Jerusalem, to impose order on the liturgy.

Plainsong is satellite music, enhancing the litany but subordinate to it. Almost as early as plainsong a kind of ecclesiastical music developed which would eventually free the art from its bondage to language: the metrical hymn. Roman Gaul, ahead in this as in other cultural fields, was the home of this musical innovation. Hilary of Poitiers, in the fourth century, set sacred songs to music. His hymns were lost, as Hilary himself was all but forgotten in the century after his death. But his idea had taken root, and a few years after Hilary's death the genius of Ambrose uplifted the form to a new spiritual beauty. Ambrose was an accomplished poet, and his sacred verses were cast in flawless Latin iambic dimeters harmoniously constructed so that the natural accent of the word fell on the accent of the musical verse. The result is a genuine and simple soulfulness. In the early sixth century Benedict of Nursia continued the tradition, and later in that century Fortunatus wrote, among others, the two great hymns, "Pange Lingua" and "Vexilla Regis," still sung in the Catholic service.

The words of the sacred song determined the rhythm of the music, and as the Latin language broke down, adulterated by simpler tongues with strong verbal accents, poetry and music became increasingly intertwined. It was the beginning of music's freedom from language domination and its emergence as an independent art form. The composition of hymns has changed materially since the Merovingian age. Plainsong has remained intact, and we can hear today the chants that heartened the spirits of premedieval worshippers. In the mid-nineteenth century a team of Benedictine musicologists, headed by Dom Joseph Pothier, worked to restore the authentic texts and music of the Catholic service as they had been performed in the high period, the late sixth century. The headquarters of their research was the Benedictine Abbey of Solesmes, near Le Mans, and the results can be heard there every Sunday morning and afternoon at High Mass and Vespers.

The monastery, a group of great gray granite buildings, looms over the tree-lined bank of the slow-flowing little river Sarthe. The abbey Church of Saint Peter has a stern plainness mitigated by the rays of the morning sun streaming through the tall clear-glass windows. The Mass begins, and the listener is at once in another age. The homophonic voices, in perfect unison, resonate with the syllables of the Mass in the natural rhythms of prose speech. The monodic cadences are not inexpressive; they have an intense, restrained emotion with understated crescendos and diminuendos accenting the meaning of the Latin words. No voice stands out. In singing, as in daily life, the choir demonstrates the monastic ideal of anomymous cooperation. No monk, however talented, may assert his personal entity; every skill must be exercised in concert for the glory of God alone. The absence of vibrato adds to the immanence of otherworldly motivation: the voices have an ethereal directness, as if they had a clear course to Heaven. Although to the uninstructed listener plainsong has a deeply moving simplicity—the very breath of an age which never questioned its faith—the music is clearly not primitive, but an achievement of high human artistry. As the song quietly rises and falls, the hearer is transported back even beyond the sixth-century apogee of the music, to its antecedents many centuries earlier. One is listening, through the premedieval cadences, to the music of Plato. There is an immediacy at Solesmes that conveys a compelling sense of the continuity of history.

The art of architecture in the Merovingian period was confined to churches. The villas and palaces of the long-haired kings are hardly mentioned in contemporary chronicles: the fighting Franks paid little attention to their living quarters. But for reasons of prestige and propaganda as much as of religious devotion, they attempted to outdo one another in the construction and decoration of places of worship.

In the early Merovingian years the Frankish builders, unschooled, made no attempt at originality in architectural design. A nomadic, hunting people, they had no tradition of building in stone, and even their use of wood was unskilled. Their wooden churches, small and flimsy, did not survive even until the time of Gregory of Tours, when no one knew anymore even where they had stood.

The Franks learned to build from their conquered subjects. The Gallo-Roman tradition of church building went back to the fourth century, when Constantine's Edict of Milan brought Christians out of the private houses where they had worshipped in secret. With the new freedom came the need for places to congregate. They naturally modeled their houses of worship on the Roman buildings they knew—preferably secular. The ideal neutral building for conversion to religious use was the basilica, which in imperial times was used for the law court or as the local administrative seat for the emperor or his deputy. For these practical purposes the structure had a big central space, usually rectangular, side aisles with colonnades and a focal point near one end where the presiding official sat. This was an exemplary arrangement for a priest and his congregation.

Another Roman style adopted by the Christians was the octagonal tomb; in Christian Gaul it was usually dedicated, appropriately, to a martyr saint. The tomb style soon became too small for the growing congregations, and these buildings were converted to use as baptisteries.

Basilicas and martyria in Gaul date back to the Roman occupation. They had been constructed in the style that prevailed all over the Roman Empire, since the needs of the imperial establishment did not vary greatly from one province to another, and architects and masterbuilders traveled easily from east to west. Still, the extant examples of Gallo-Frankish church building are natively Gallic; even the dome, the feature so typically associated with Byzantine churches, appeared in Gaul before it came to the Roman East.

The little stone churches of the early Merovingian period were soon outgrown. Either they were abandoned or, more usually, incorporated into larger buildings, their solid foundations and low thick walls making them ideal crypts. Sometimes the whole history of Gallic Christian architecture lies within the generous walls of one church. There is a fine example in Auxerre, the home of the fifth-century Saint Germain, a gracious Renaissance town rising on the steep bank of the Yonne, at the western edge of Burgundy. Near the river is the Gothic Church of Saint Germain, which encloses the saint's cell, the sixth- to ninth-century abbey basilica built over it, and part of the twelfth-century Romanesque successor.

The only remainder of the Romanesque period is a lovely square twelfth-century bell tower. But the little basilica that Queen Clotild built in the early sixth century over the tomb of Auxerre's austere monk-bishop, and which was rebuilt in the ninth, is still intact beneath the altar—a massive low-arched structure of several chambers. In one niche a stone slab displays a carved square cross within a circle, known as Clotild's Cross, probably part of the original altar.

Under the floor of the crypt is an even older sanctuary, the dank stone hole which was Germain's retreat at the rare intervals of rest in the busy life of a political ecclesiastic. This unfriendly cave is the repository of the saint's sarcophagus—a plain heavy stone coffin which, it is claimed, contains the veritable ashes of the saint. The authenticity of these has been ascertained by the presence of fragments of the cypress-wood coffin in which the Empress Galla Placidia had caused the bishop's remains to be transported from Ravenna, by the saint's dying wish, back home to Auxerre.

Parts of a church even older than the crypt of Saint Germain have been excavated beside the sixteenth-century Church of Saint Martin in the Abbey of Ligugé, near Poitiers (called the oldest monastery in the West). Ligugé was Martin's first monastery, founded by him in 361 while he was still a disciple of Bishop Hilary of Poitiers. The ancient buildings adjoin the main Renaissance church at right angles; the unadorned, round-arched façade contrasts with the intricate curves of the flamboyant Gothic doorway beside it. The interior is a maze of rooms going back even before Martin's time, to the Gallo-Roman villa around which he built. The only visible remnants of Martin's fourth-century church are the foundation stones of the apse; from them extends the nave of the basilica erected in the seventh century over the original church. This is a treasure house of Merovingian stonework: a seventh-century sarcophagus with tall narrow lettering; an engaging fifth-century deer in high relief, arching upward to graze upon tree leaves above its head; a seventh-century floor of stone tiles in a graceful arrangement of varied geometric figures; a fourth-century square column with a sheaf of wheat decorating its Ionic capital; part of a sixth-century pillar carved with interlaced stone embroidery; a seventh-century rude graffito of a haloed Christ, which resembles a twentieth-century abstract; a fifth-century crucifixion, extremely primitive, picturing a lordly, staring Christ between the two robbers, cookie-cutter figures one quarter his size.

In this crowded chamber one has little impression of a functioning church. But the overtones of the transitional age ring clear: one is responsive to the essays of the artists of the centuries of change. Disillusioned with the stale phrases of classicism, they are experimenting with their art, groping for genuine ways to express their living faith.

The other frequent Roman derivative in church architecture, the tomb style, has a remarkable example in the Baptistery of Saint John in Poitiers. The octagonal building, said to be the oldest intact Christian building in France, was erected in the fourth century, when Gaul was still a Roman province. The additions made in the sixth and later centuries did not fundamentally change the Roman pattern. It is a compact structure of Roman brick, plain and heavy. Inside, the east wall has a blind arcade of marble columns with foliated Merovingian capitals, and around all the walls is an impressive parade of upended stone sarcophagus covers, carved in low relief. The designs are of formal geometric flourishes and stylized flowers and birds. The carving, though simple, has a clean elegance: it shows that Frankish stonecutters were, by the seventh century, developing a sophisticated technique and an original sense of design.

In the center of the chamber is the baptismal font, a square hole in the floor (now blocked off), as deep as a man is tall. The candidate for baptism (they were almost always adults in those days), having left his clothes in the robing room, walked down the stone steps to immerse himself totally in the cold holy water, while the priest intoned the baptismal ritual above him. On emerging he was clad in a white tunic and led next door to the cathedral for his initiation into the solemn mysteries. The ceremony must have had a convincing entireness: the converted heathen would have felt he was incontestably redeemed.

The procedure, besides, would have appealed to him for its hint of pagan sorcery.

The Christians often took over existing Roman buildings which suited their needs. One such is the Hypogée des Dunes, a mausoleum in a suburb of Poitiers, outside the original Roman town (the Romans never buried their dead within the city walls). The mausoleum had been the central building of their cemetery, dating probably to the third century. In the seventh century the Christians of Poitiers adapted both tomb and cemetery to their use, keeping the architecture intact and adding their own decorative carving. The severe rectangular brick building lies amid its early Christian gravestones in a quiet garden of grass and trees. It was an oratory, as well as a burial place for one Abbot Mellebaude, and the interior designs suit its multiple use. Ten stone steps lead into the underground chapel. On the three top ones are crudely graceful carvings of evident magical purport: intertwined snakes (a Teutonic motif that goes back to a time when the Franks were not yet Christian), fishes, and tendrils of ivy. Their incantational intent is reinforced by a cabalistic rune on the bottom step. The figure carving of apostles, saints and angels within the chapel is rough and childish, but the inscription on the abbot's tomb is not only finely executed but is in correct Latin. It carries a message apposite to seventh-century Merovingian Gaul: "All things go from bad to worse and the end of time is near!"[6]

Most of these early oratories and baptisteries have the plain exterior that was a feature of Roman architecture, and which also suited the early Christians. Decoration was confined to the interior, where the mysteries were celebrated for the initiated—in contrast to the later Romanesque policy of displaying religion resplendently on the outsides of churches for propaganda purposes. During the fourth century, after the Edict of Milan, interior decoration began to blossom. The Catholic Church, ever practical, saw to it that its congregation, most of whom led lives of cheerless tedium, should be lifted out of themselves in every area of consciousness. The churches, as well as the services, pleased the senses with incense, music and painting at the same time that they instructed the mind and uplifted the soul.

Gallic churches were lavish in ornamentation, but most Gallic artists were not familiar, as were the artisans of cities such as

Ravenna, with the art of mosaic, and painted interiors earlier than the tenth or eleventh centuries have mostly vanished. We learn of the ornate beauty of the churches of Frankish Gaul only through contemporary chronicles. The walls, altars and side chapels, we read, were decorated with paintings, frescoes, richly embroidered silks and linens, and multitudes of lamps. Gregory of Tours describes, among others, the Church of Saint Stephen outside Clermont-Ferrand, built by Bishop Namatius, which had forty-two windows, seventy columns and eight doorways, and whose walls were glorious with paintings. "In it one is conscious of the fear of God and of a great brightness, and those at prayer are often aware of a most sweet and aromatic odour which is being wafted toward them." The bishop's wife directed the artisans in the painting of the wall frescoes: "She used to hold in her lap a book from which she would read stories of events which happened long ago, and tell the workmen what she wanted painted on the walls."[7]

The most moving Gallo-Frankish art which still survives is that in stone. Gallic stonecutters of the sixth and seventh centuries display an affinity for Byzantine art—eastern influence infiltrated through Gaul's Mediterranean ports and over the Pyrenees from Spain. The native artists integrated what they learned into the illumination of their own naïve, visionary faith. Concomitant with their piety was the intent to communicate and teach. As in early medieval hagiography, dramatic simplicity was purposeful, the better to appeal to the uneducated.

Examples of this style can be seen at Jouarre, a small, quiet and pretty town near Paris. The double monastery founded by the Luxeuil monk Adon, in the seventh century, still functions as a Benedictine convent. Its Gothic church retains a Romanesque remnant in the square bell tower. Across a little plaza from the convent is the Merovingian crypt, all that remains of the original seventh-century church. This underground chamber contains the bones of its founder as well as those of early patrons and abbesses. The lordly corpses, all members of a family strong in the councils of King Dagobert, are entombed in decorated stone sarcophagi.

The west wall of the crypt consists of dressed stones in reticulated patterns of squares, lozenges and octagons, joined by pink clay cement. The design, peculiar to the Merovingian period, is neither specifically Roman nor barbarian; and the perfection of its execution shows that the art of the stonecutter and the mason had not suffered through the postimperial centuries. This and similar masonwork were executed by professional Gallic artisans, trained by Byzantine masters, who had graduated from eastern models into native expression. They traveled about the country hiring themselves out to rich Frankish landowners and politicians—the new aristocracy wished to perpetuate its prestige by exhibiting in durable form its support of the Church in general and the local bishop or abbot in particular.

The Jouarre crypt has seven stone sarcophagi along the walls, containing the remains of the founders; and here we see an expressive display of the art of the era—an art neither imitative nor primitive, and glowing with faith. On the tomb of Telchild, the first abbess, an inscription extolling her virtues runs around both sides, divided by a double row of elegant scallop shells. The fine Latin lettering is reminiscent of contemporary Frankish manuscripts. Another abbess is commemorated with a frieze in a Greek key-pattern surrounding a network of fleur-de-lys. A third inhabitant is an Irish princess named Osanne who, it is said, was a nun at Jouarre and died there. Her presence is witness to the close ties between Jouarre and the Irish mother house at Luxeuil.

The conventionalized decoration of the tombs of the abbey ladies contrasts with the dramatic religious theme on the tomb of Bishop Agilbert, brother of the first abbess. Agilbert was a leading churchman, first in Britain, later in Gaul; learned, hardworking and unflinchingly attuned to the power politics of his day. Of Frankish birth, he received an excellent education in Ireland, then was appointed bishop of Dorchester. He was not successful there, as he never managed to accustom his tongue to the Wessex dialect. The king of Wessex divided the see without consulting him, and Agilbert, annoyed, departed. He next appeared testifying against the Irish, his erstwhile mentors, at the Synod of Whitby, where the Celtic Church was on trial versus the Roman. Here, too, he was impeded by his clumsiness with the local language; he gave over his seat and went back to Gaul. In 668 he was made bishop of Paris, and he ensured the security of his tenure by cultivating the patronage of the rascally Ebroin, Mayor of the Palace of Neustria. Agilbert kept this prestigious bishopric for sixteen years. In 686 advancing age persuaded him to retire to his sister's foundation at Jouarre, and here he died, very old, about four years later. It is difficult to find anything in the performance of this worldly career bishop that entitles him to the honorary title of saint. Presumably he had, besides his questionable secular connections, respectable affiliations in ecclesiastical circles. Whatever his earthly character, the souvenir bequeathed to posterity by his heirs—his Jouarre sarcophagus—is a memorial of inspired spirituality.

On one side of the tomb is a row of elemental figures: the enthroned Christ of the Day of Judgment flanked by the Twelve Apostles, their arms upraised in ecstatic adoration. The panel expresses a stark and innocent faith. The end of the tomb has a carved representation of the haloed Christ in an interlaced mandorla, an irreducible figure hieratic to an extreme degree. Outside the oval frame stylized flowers surround the four symbols of the Evangelists, facing away from Christ.

From the styles of these two panels, it seems probable that Greek and Coptic artisans, fleeing Arab invasions, found refuge north of the Pyrenees—even disorderly Gaul was preferable to the terror in the south—and there set up workshops where native sculptors trained. Some of the refugees migrated to northeastern Gaul: the Marne Valley, where Jouarre is located, became one of the most productive centers of the stone-carver's art. It was a bountiful region for religious artists. Starting with the proliferation of Columbanian houses (Jouarre was one of seven founded in the region by the Irish missionary or his successors) there was an explosion of the monastic population here—over two hundred houses were founded from the late sixth to the early eighth centuries. Consequently this strongly Teutonic corner of Gaul became the inheritor of Mediterranean culture. Though the teachers were eastern masters, the pupils evolved from their training a clearly indigenous art. Its plain beauty and lively faith belong to Frankish Gaul; its quality has nothing in common either with the sterile formality of late imperial art or with the later Romanesque flights of religious fantasy. The Jouarre monuments are not unique in France, although they are among the most beautiful. The country has enough examples of contemporaneous stone carving to attest to the genius of Frankish artists. Though the style was derivative the creative originality of the designs and the intensity of the motive behind them was a spontaneous generation.

Portable art forms also demonstrate that the Merovingian period, far from being a retrogressive Dark Age, was a changing era of imitation, experiment and invention. Motifs from Roman classical and contemporary Byzantine art mingled with styles introduced from the East by invading barbarians, and with Nordic themes. From this prodigal diversity there began to develop a beautiful, basically simple native art. Religious objects were crafted—chalices, reliquaries and book covers—in which one can trace the diverse ancestry, and which yet have a harmonious consistency.

Few objects remain: banditry, religious prejudice and changing tastes have accomplished the destruction, dismemberment or melting down of much of that rich heritage. A carved ivory piece, probably not considered worth looting, was found in Kranenburg, in today's West Germany. Made in Clovis's time, the early sixth century, it shows Roman influence with a distinctively Gallic cast. The frieze of lambs and the classical folds of the Apostles' garments are early Christian in design—the style found over most of the Roman Empire at that time. But the two saints have an ingenuous piety that was native to Gaul even this early. The stout figures are rudimentary but not primitive. Their simplicity was purposeful. The sculptor intended to express a higher holiness than the merely personal. Worship not us, the reduced figures signify, but the unknowable which we symbolize.

In stone and ivory Gallic craftsmen depended on Mediterranean antecedents, infusing the classical techniques with their own disposition; for the northern barbarians had no tradition of working in these materials. In metalwork and enamel, however, the invaders added new techniques and styles to the imperial legacy. Cloisonné— the art of inlaying enamel on metal within partitions of wire fillets— was introduced into Europe by invading northern tribes about the third century A.D., and adopted by Byzantine craftsmen, who brought the barbarian import to a high state of intricate elegance. Gallic workers had a natural affinity for this northern craft, and their work, although it has not the elaborate delicacy of the eastern, has a blithe grace. In a throwback to the craft's pagan origin, the piety of the subject matter is almost submerged by the heathen gaiety of the color patterns.

In Gourdon, a village climbing the flanks of a rocky hill in the Dordogne, was found a beautiful piece, of the time of Clovis: a chalice and paten of gold, filigree and cloisonné that combines the lacy precision of eastern work with the saturated reds and greens beloved by Frankish craftsmen, the whole merged into primally simple patterns. The work is at the same time gaudy and fine—a striking example of the felicitous sixth-century blend.

In Poitiers, in the handsome modern museum on the site of Queen

Radegund's Convent of the Holy Cross, is the queen's own wooden
lectern, one of the few wooden objects still extant from the sixth
century. The little desk, dark with age, is carved with Byzantine
motifs executed with Frankish simplicity. In the center is a sheep with
square-cut fleece; a cross flanks the animal on either side; below, two
crowlike birds guard a Greek cross with flared arms; and the symbols
of the evangelists fill the four corners. The piece has a neat
aristocratic plainness reminiscent of the chaste nun-queen.

Not all the genius of Merovingian craftsmen was dedicated to
religion. The military successes of the early generations of Frankish
kings, beginning with Clovis's father, Childeric, brought them
wealth, with its natural side effect, indulgence in personal finery. The
kings liked to dress up and to adorn their ladies; and the silks and
furs of their robes were set off by large-scale jewelry of gold and gems.
The ornate fancy of contemporary Byzantine aristocracy was not to
the Frankish taste; nor did western craftsmen, though they learned
much from eastern masters, ever achieve the meticulousness of
Byzantine work. The jewelry of the Frankish kings and queens is
heavy and primitive but not uncouth.

Childeric, Clovis's father, was the first Frankish chief whose
personal adornment we know, because the cache in his tomb at
Tournai has survived intact. The body was clothed in a purple silk
cloak embroidered with three hundred bees or grasshoppers in gold
and garnets. (These appealing Merovingian insects so pleased Napo-
leon that he adopted the bee as his emblem.) Near the chief lay the
skull of a horse, decorated, like its owner, with gold and jewels.
Around the chief's body were four Frankish weapons, their sheaths
richly ornamented with gold and cloisonné enamel: a long sword, a
scramasax (short saber), a lance and a *francisc* (throwing hatchet).
Besides the battle implements there were a number of decorative or
good-luck objects, among which were an impudently barbaric little
bull's head in gold and cloisonné with eyes and nostrils of garnet, and
a heavy gold signet ring with the inscription *Childerici regis* (whatever
his world named him, the Frankish conqueror evidently appropriated
royalty to himself) encircling the crudely executed head with its two
thick braids of hair. Other personal effects included gold, cloisonné
and gem-studded jewelry, and several hundred Roman and German
coins, indicating Childeric's cosmopolitan sphere.

Some of this magnificent hoard is clearly Roman-inspired and some portrays a Teutonic turn of mind: the variegation is a symptom of the ambivalence of Childeric and his Franks, independent in fact but desirous of maintaining ties with the nominal emperor of the West in Constantinople. In the field of artistry Frankish workers still depended upon eastern craft: Merovingian decorative art was manifestly influenced by Gothic goldsmiths from southern Russia. Some centuries earlier these craftsmen had brought their own barbaric techniques to Byzantium, where they were refined and perfected. Then, when the Ostrogoths and Visigoths established themselves in Italy and Spain, their decorative skills came with them to the West.

Along with this Gothic-Byzantine influence in Childeric's tomb, there is a clear pagan slant—in the burial of the horse with its master, the swarms of golden insects, and the fetishlike bull's head. The mixture of styles indicates that easy communication still existed over the far-stretched boundaries of the Roman Empire, and operated even in the outer regions of the barbarian invasions.

Lothair I, Clovis's youngest son, took as his second wife Arnegund, sister of his first, Ingund. When Arnegund died in 570, aged about forty, Lothair buried her splendidly in the church built by Saint Geneviève about one hundred years before, over the grave of Saint Denis. During recent excavations under the present-day cathedral the tomb was discovered, miraculously untouched. There was the lady, dressed in silk and linen and lavishly adorned with silver, gold and gemmed jewelry. During the ninety years that had elapsed since the burial of Childeric with his treasure, Merovingian secular art had matured into a native aristocratic Frankish style, its original elements thoroughly blended. Arnegund's jewelry is beautifully crafted; gone is the unskilled naïveté of the earlier hoard, and the evidence of multiple origin. The filigree of rings, brooches, earrings and buckles is equal in fineness to contemporary Byzantine work. It has, besides, some typically Nordic qualities—particularly the abstract treatment of animal motifs—which the Frankish craftsmen developed with high style. The premedieval artists of northern Europe avoided naturalism. Animals and flowers are convoluted and interlaced in surrealistic harmony. Often decoration is entirely formal—geometric displays of shadow and light produced by chip-carving metal, or vivid designs of color in enamel, gems and glass.

Toward the end of our period Merovingian art reached its zenith in the illuminated gospels. This exquisite and exuberant art, executed by unknown scribes in the austere anonymity of the cloister, exhibits more conclusively than stone carving and metalwork the creative virtuosity of Frankish craftsmen.

Monks had been copying manuscripts in scriptoria since the time of John Cassian. Cassian's motives were remedial, not creative. By the sixth century, scriptoria were becoming purposefully educational. Cassiodorus, the Italian scholar and monk, was the first to instruct his monks to copy Greek, Latin and Christian manuscripts for their study and preservation. The hours in the scriptoria were long and the emphasis on perfectionism tiring. Possibly to relieve the tedium of merely copying, the brothers began to ornament their script. The early practice was the enlargement of the initial letter at the start of each gospel. As the scribes' skill grew, inventiveness flourished and they began to twist their letters into figures, sometimes with pious intent, sometimes with a kind of innocent frivolity.

In time the capital letters assumed a fantasy life of their own. In flights of zoomorphic fancy an undulant fish delineates the curve of the letter "P"; "D" is a bright-feathered, long-necked bird; a row of birds and fishes stand on their tails to form the downstrokes in a row of initial letters; a serpent and a monster wind in sinuous battle to create the letter "Q". In literal realism, a prayer for novices opens with a letter shaped into a pair of scissors cutting the beard of a young monk; the "D" at the start of the Mass of Finding the Cross is a small man digging a hole wherein are the crosses of Golgotha; in a splendid illumination of the gospel account of the Crucifixion, the initial "T" is transformed into the Crucifixion itself. All these fantasy creations are executed in color, sometimes subtle and muted, sometimes barbarically gay—inks which have not faded through the centuries.

Alongside the painstaking elaboration of initial letters the inscribing artist sometimes permitted himself an offhand levity, sketching humorous little people and birds running between the lines and spilling into the margins. These casual, inventive graffiti are clearly modeled after the figures on Coptic textiles; much of the provenance of the Gallic illuminations lies in the art of the East. Only the imaginative freshness is Gallic, and the wit with which the lively images are fashioned into designs.

As manuscript illumination grew to be an art in itself, specially talented painters were assigned to create full-page illustrations. Some of these were purely decorative, others were literal depictions of events in the gospels. In one frontispiece, or portico page, two graceful long-tailed parrots uphold with their beaks the alpha and omega which signify Christ's rule of the universe. The Greek letters in turn depend from the arms of a cross embellished with rosettes and animals. The whole is enclosed with a double portico decorated with colorful little horses.

Another portico page exhibits a cross partitioned into triangles, each containing a small contorted beast; on the top triangle perches a jewellike eagle. Within the portico frame are animals with attenuated legs terminating in oversized claws; serpents coming out of or going into the mouths of these animals entwine themselves around the flimsy limbs. The canon tables have a page to themselves whereon the canon numbers are enclosed by pilasters and formed of religious verses. At the bottom of each column an evangelist writes and at the same time gazes upward at his attribute, which adorns the head of the column.

These examples are culled from five great Gallic books, all made before the demise of the Merovingian dynasty: the *Gelasius Gospel*, the manuscript of *Saint Augustine on the Heptateuch*, the *Flavigny Gospels*, the *Chronicle of Fredegarius* (from which we have often quoted in these pages) and the *Corbie Psalter*. It was the same period which saw the composition of the magnificent insular manuscripts, the *Book of Kells*, the *Lindisfarne Gospels* and the *Echternach Gospels*. These beautiful works of art represent the extraordinary early medieval monastic phenomenon in the West: by the end of the Merovingian era the monasteries had become the centers of creative art and literature, the repositories of all surviving scientific knowledge and the fountainhead of the agricultural revolution. We saw the tentative beginnings in John Cassian's concern to keep his monks from the sins born of idleness, and Saint Honoratus's compassionate welcome to refugee scholars at Lérins. But those early teachers could not have envisaged the exuberant plant that would grow from their chaste sowing.

Looked at from a historical perspective the flowering of the monastic genius was only one aspect of the fluid evolution from the Gaul of the Roman Empire to the Gallo-Germanic empire of Charlemagne, out of which, among other results, was born the nation of France. An unimpressive group of barbarians, inching over the northern borders of Roman Gaul, had metamorphosed themselves into Europe's most successful barbarian kingdom, and their chieftains had become the paramount leaders in the age of transition. The history of the Merovingian centuries, a saga at once bloodthirsty and creative, is the first chapter in the history of modern Europe.

NOTES

PRELUDE: THE FORGOTTEN KINGS

1. Quotations in this chapter are from Gregory of Tours, *The History of the Franks.*

CHAPTER ONE: ROMAN GAUL

1. The account of the Celtic invasion of Italy is from [Titus Livius], *Livy*, ed. and trans., E. H. Warmington.
2. Lucian of Samosata, *Heracles, an Introduction*, trans. A. M. Harmon (Cambridge, Mass.: Harvard University Press, Loeb Classics, 1962).
3. Lucan, *The Civil War*, trans. J. D. Duff (Cambridge, Mass.: Harvard University Press, Loeb Classics, 1969).
4. Material and quotations in this chapter concerning Julius Caesar in Gaul are from Caesar, *The Conquest of Gaul.*
5. Theodor Mommsen, *The History of Rome.*
6. Decius Magnus Ausonius, *Ephemeris*, as quoted in Norah Chadwick, *Poetry and Letters in Early Christian Gaul.*
7. Gregory of Tours, *The History of the Franks.*
8. Quotations from Sidonius in this chapter are from Sidonius, *Poems and Letters.*
9. Saint Jerome, *Commentary on Ezekiel, Preface to Book I*, in *The Principal Works.*
10. Material and quotations in this chapter concerning the Huns and Attila are, unless otherwise specified, from [Jordanes] *The Gothic History of Jordanes.*
11. Priscus, *Fragmenta*, as quoted by John Bangell Bury, in Bury, *A History of the Later Roman Empire.*

CHAPTER TWO: THE GERMANS

1. Quotations throughout this chapter concerning the customs of the German tribes are, unless otherwise specified, from Gaius Cornelius Tacitus, *Germany and Its Tribes*, in *Complete Works of Tacitus*, and from Caesar, *The Conquest of Gaul*.

2. Edward Gibbon, *The Decline and Fall of the Roman Empire*.

3. Material and quotations in this chapter concerning the Teutonic pantheon are from I. A. Blackwell, trans., *The Edda of Saemund* and *The Saorri Edda* (see Benjamin Thorpe, trans., *The Eddas*).

4. Material and quotations in this chapter concerning Ariovistus are from Caesar, *The Conquest of Gaul*.

5. Material and quotations concerning Civilis are from Tacitus, *The History*, in *Complete Works of Tacitus*.

6. Flavius Vopiscus, *Historiae Augustae scriptores* (Bonn: Historia-Augusta-Colloquium, Beiträge von Geza Alfoldy, et al., R. Habelt, 1966).

7. [Julian the Apostate], *Misopogon*, in *The Works of the Emperor Julian*.

8. Bernard S. Bachrach, ed. and trans., *Liber Historiae Francorum*.

9. Gregory of Tours, *The History of the Franks*.

CHAPTER THREE: CHRISTIANITY

1. Gregory of Tours, *The History of the Franks*.

2. Hilary of Poitiers, *On the Trinity*, in *Select Works*.

3. Gregory of Tours, *The History of the Franks*.

4. Sulpicius Severus, *Sacred History*, in *The Works of Sulpicius Severus*.

5. Jerome, *Ep. 58.*, in *The Principal Works*.

6. Hilary of Poitiers, *Homily on Psalm 65*, in *Select Works*.

7. Dorotheos of Thebes, as quoted in *Palladius, His Life and Travels*, in Ernest A. Wallis Budge, trans., *The Paradise or Garden of the Holy Fathers*.

8. Athanasius, *Festal Letters: Letter I, Easter*, Archibald Robertson, trans., A Select Library of Nicene and Post-Nicene Fathers of the Christian Church, eds. Philip Schaff and Henry Wace (Grand Rapids, Mich.: Wm. B. Eerdmans Publishing Co., 1978).

9. Sulpicius Severus, *Dialogue I*, in *The Works of Sulpicius Severus*.

10. Quotations of Cassian in this chapter are from John Cassian, *Institutes of the Coenobia*.

11. Salvian, *The Governance of God*, in *The Writings of Salvian the Presbyter*.

12. Material and quotations in this chapter concerning Saint Honoratus are from Hilary of Arles, *A Discourse on the Life of St. Honoratus, Bishop of Arles*, in F. R. Hoare, ed. and trans., *The Western Fathers*.

13. Bishop Eucherius of Lyon, as quoted in Charles René Forbes, Comte de Montalembert, *The Monks of the West*.

14. Material and quotations in this chapter concerning Saint Martin are from Sulpicius Severus, *The Life of St. Martin*, in *The Works of Sulpicius Severus*.

15. John Cassian, *Institutes of the Coenobia*.

16. Gregory of Tours, *The History of the Franks*.

17. Ibid.

18. Gregory of Tours, *Liber in Gloria Martyrum*, as quoted in Sumner McKnight Crosby, *The Abbey of Saint Denis.*

19. Material and quotations in this chapter concerning Saint Germain are from Constantius of Lyon, *The Life of St. Germanus*, in F. R. Hoare, ed. and trans., *The Western Fathers*, and from Bede, *A History of the English Church and People.*

20. *Life of St. Patrick* in the *Book of Armagh*, quoted in Mary Frances Cusack, *The Trias Thaumaturga* (Edinburgh: Ballantyne, Hanson, 1875).

21. Jocelyn, Monk of Furness, *The Life and Acts of St. Patrick*, J. C. O'Haloran, trans. (Philadelphia: Atkinson & Alexander, 1923).

CHAPTER FOUR: CLOVIS

1. Quotations in this chapter concerning the legendary history of the Franks are, unless otherwise specified, from Bachrach, ed. and trans., *Liber Historiae Francorum.*

2. Gregory of Tours, *The History of the Franks.*

3. Fredegar, *The Chronicles of the So-Called Fredegarian Scholars, Book III.*

4. Priscus, *Fragmenta*, as quoted in Dill, *Roman Society in Gaul in the Merovingian Age.*

5. Gregory of Tours, *The History of the Franks.*

6. Ibid.

7. Fredegar, *The Chronicles of Fredegar, Book III.*

8. Gregory of Tours, *The History of the Franks.*

9. The story of Clovis's courtship of Clotild is from Fredegar, *The Chronicles of Fredegar, Book III.*

10. Material and quotations concerning the conversion of Clovis in this chapter are, unless otherwise specified, from Gregory of Tours, *The History of the Franks.*

11. Fredegar, *The Chronicles of Fredegar, Book III.*

12. Bishop Avitus of Vienne, letter to Clovis, as quoted in Dill, *Roman Society in Gaul.*

13. Bachrach, ed. and trans., *Liber Historiae Francorum.*

14. Quotations concerning the Battle of the Ouche are from Gregory of Tours, *The History of the Franks.*

15. Jordanes, *The Gothic History of Jordanes.*

16. Sidonius, *Poems and Letters.*

17. Material and quotations concerning Clovis's conflict with Alaric and the Battle of Vouillé are from Gregory of Tours, *The History of the Franks.*

18. Bachrach, ed. and trans., *Liber Historiae Francorum.*

19. J. H. Hessels, ed., *lex Salica: Prologue*, translated by John Gross, in *lex Salica: The Ten Texts with the Glosses and the lex emendata.*

20. Gregory of Tours, *The History of the Franks.*

21. *lex salica.*

22. Material and quotations concerning Clovis's annihilation of Frankish chieftains are from Gregory of Tours, *The History of the Franks.*

CHAPTER FIVE: THE SONS OF CLOVIS

1. Gregory of Tours, *The History of the Franks.*

2. Jordanes, *The Gothic History of Jordanes.*

3. Material and quotations throughout this chapter concerning the sons of Clovis are, unless otherwise specified, from Gregory of Tours, *The History of the Franks*.

4. Quotations concerning Saint Radegund are from Fortunatus, *De Vita Sanctae Radegundis*, in *Opera Omnia*.

5. Quotations from the poetry of Fortunatus are from Fortunatus, *A Basket of Chestnuts*.

CHAPTER SIX: GREGORY'S KINGS

1. Material and quotations concerning the grandsons of Clovis throughout this chapter are, unless otherwise specified, from Gregory of Tours, *The History of the Franks*.

2. Fortunatus, *Miscellanea, Lib. VI*, Kay Fleming, trans., in *Opera Omnia*.

3. Bachrach, ed. and trans., *Liber Historiae Francorum*.

4. Ibid.

5. Ibid.

6. Fortunatus, *Carmen IX*, in *Opera Omnia*.

7. Bachrach, ed. and trans., *Liber Historiae Francorum*.

CHAPTER SEVEN: FREDEGUND AND BRUNHILD

1. Material and quotations concerning Queen Fredegund throughout this chapter are, unless otherwise specified, from Gregory of Tours, *The History of the Franks*.

2. Bachrach, ed. and trans., *Liber Historiae Francorum*.

3. Gregory of Tours, *The History of the Franks*.

4. Material and quotations concerning the pretender Gundovald are from Gregory of Tours, *The History of the Franks*.

5. Ibid.

6. Quotations concerning delinquent bishops are from Gregory of Tours, *The History of the Franks*.

7. Ibid.

8. Material and quotations concerning Saint Columbanus throughout this chapter are from Saint Columbanus, *Sancti Columbani Opera* and from Jonas, Monk of Bobbio, *Life of Columban*.

9. Fredegar, *The Fourth Book of the Chronicle of Fredegar & Continuations*.

10. Ibid.

11. Bachrach, ed. and trans., *Liber Historiae Francorum*.

12. Fredegar, *The Fourth Book of the Chronicle of Fredegar*.

CHAPTER EIGHT: THE MAYORS OF THE PALACE

1. Material and quotations throughout this chapter concerning the last Merovingian kings and the Mayors of the Palace are, unless otherwise specified, from Fredegar, *The Fourth Book of the Chronicle of Fredegar & Continuations*.

2. Bachrach, ed. and trans., *Liber Historiae Francorum*.

3. Ibid.

4. Bede, *A History of the English Church and People*.

5. Material concerning Saint Willibrord is from Bede, *A History of the English Church and People.*

6. Archbishop Hincmar of Rheims, as quoted in Perry, *The Franks.*

7. Bishop Wolfran of Sens, as quoted in Sergeant, *The Franks.*

8. Einhard, *The Life of Charlemagne.*

9. As quoted in Perry, *The Franks.*

10. *The Correspondence of Pope Gregory VII; selected letters from the Registrum,* translated with an introduction by Ephraim Emerton (New York: Columbia University Press, 1932).

11. Boniface, *The Letters of Saint Boniface.*

13. Alcuin, as quoted in Perry, *The Franks.*

14. As quoted in Alcuin.

CHAPTER NINE: THE MEROVINGIAN LEGACY

1. Severus, *Dialogue I,* in *The Works of Sulpicius Severus.*

2. Gregory of Tours, *The History of the Franks.*

3. Vita S. Karilefi, as quoted in Montalembert, *The Monks of the West.*

4. Jonas, Monk of Bobbio, *Life of Columban.*

5. Severus, *The Life of St. Martin,* in *The Works of Sulpicius Severus.*

6. Hubert, *Europe of the Invasions.*

7. Gregory of Tours, *The History of the Franks.*

BIBLIOGRAPHY

PRE-MEROVINGIAN EUROPE

Brogan, Olwen. *Roman Gaul*. Cambridge, Mass.: Harvard University Press, 1953.

Bury, John Bagnell. *A History of the Later Roman Empire: from Arcadius to Irene*, 2 vols. London: Macmillan & Co., 1889.

[Caesar, Julius.] *Caesar: The Conquest of Gaul*, trans. S. A. Handford. New York: Penguin Classics, 1982.

Chadwick, Norah K. *Poetry and Letters in Early Christian Gaul*. London: Bowes & Bowes, 1955.

Duckett, Eleanor Shipley. *The Gateway to the Middle Ages*, 3 vols. Ann Arbor, Mich.: University of Michigan Press, 1938.

Gibbon, Edward. *The Decline and Fall of the Roman Empire*, 6 vols. New York: E. P. Dutton & Co., Everyman's Library, 1950.

Herm, Gerhard. *The Celts: The People Who Came Out of the Darkness*. New York: St. Martin's Press, 1977.

Jones, Arnold Hugh Martin. *The Later Roman Empire: 284–603. A Social, Economic and Administrative Survey*, 2 vols. Oxford: Basil Blackwell, 1964.

[Julian the Apostate.] *The Works of the Emperor Julian*, 3 vols., trans. Wilmer Cave Wright. New York: Macmillan Co., Loeb Classics, 1913.

[Titus Livius.] *Livy*. The Loeb Classical Library, ed. E. H. Warmington. Cambridge, Mass.: Harvard University Press, 1967.

McNeill, William. *The Rise of the West: A History of the Human Community*. Chicago: The University of Chicago Press, 1963.

Mommsen, Theodor. *The History of Rome*, 4 vols., trans. W. P. Dickson. New York: E. P. Dutton & Co., Everyman's Library, 1920.

Norris, Herbert. *Costume and Fashion: The Evolution of European Dress Through the Earlier Ages*. London: J. M. Dent & Sons, 1924.

Owen, Francis. *The Germanic People: Their Origin, Expansion and Culture.* New York: Bookman Associates, 1960.

Peake, Harold. *The Bronze Age and the Celtic World.* London: Benn Bros., 1967.

[Salvian.] *The Writings of Salvian the Presbyter,* trans. Jeremiah F. O'Sullivan. New York: Cima Publishing Co., 1947.

[Sidonius Apollinaris.] *Sidonius: Poems and Letters,* 2 vols., trans. W. B. Anderson, Cambridge, Mass.: Harvard University Press, Loeb Classics, 1965.

[Tacitus, Gaius Cornelius]. *Complete Works of Tacitus,* ed. Moses Hadas, and trans. Alfred John Church and William Jackson Brodribb. New York: Modern Library, 1942.

Thorpe, Benjamin, trans. *The Elder Edda of Saemund Sigrusson,* and I. A. Blackwell, trans. *The Younger Edda of Snorri Sturluson.* London: Norroena Soc., Anglo-Saxon Classics, 1907.

EARLY CHRISTIANITY IN GAUL

Athanasius, Saint. *The Life of Saint Anthony,* trans. Archibald Robertson. A Select Library of Nicene and Post-Nicene Fathers of the Christian Church, ed. Philip Schaff and Henry Wace. Grand Rapids, Mich.: Wm. B. Eerdmans Publishing Co., 1978.

Budge, Ernest A. Wallis, ed. and trans. *The Paradise or Garden of the Holy Fathers, Being Histories of the Anchorites, Recluses, Monks, Cenobites and Ascetic Fathers of the Deserts of Egypt Between* A.D. CCL *and* A.D. CCCC *Circiter.* London: Chatto & Windus, 1907.

Campenhausen, Hans von. *The Fathers of the Latin Church,* trans. Manfred Hoffmann. London: Adam & Charles Black, 1964.

Cassian, John. *The Twelve Books on the Institutes of the Coenobia,* trans. Edgar C. S. Gibson. A Select Library of Nicene and Post-Nicene Fathers of the Christian Church, ed. Philip Schaff and Henry Wace. Grand Rapids, Mich: Wm. B. Eerdmans Publishing Co., 1978.

Chadwick, Henry. *The Early Church. The Pelican History of the Church,* Vol.1. Harmondsworth, England: Penguin Books, 1967.

Chadwick, Owen. *John Cassian: A Study in Primitive Monasticism.* Cambridge, England: Cambridge University Press, 1950.

Chitty, Derwas James. *The Desert a City.* Oxford: Basil Blackwell, 1966.

Crosby, Sumner McKnight. *The Abbey of St. Denis. 475–1122.* New Haven: Yale University Press, 1942.

Cross, F. L., and Livingstone, E. A. ed. *The Oxford Dictionary of the Christian Church.* Oxford: Oxford University Press, 1978.

Delaney, John J. *Dictionary of Saints.* Garden City, N.Y.: Doubleday & Co., 1980.

Farmer, David Hugh. *The Oxford Dictionary of Saints.* Oxford: Clarendon Press, 1978.

Hilary of Poitiers, Saint. *Select Works,* trans. Rev. E. W. Watson, Rev. L. Pullan et al. A Select Library of Nicene and Post-Nicene Fathers of the Christian Church, ed. Philip Schaff and Henry Wace. Grand Rapids, Mich.: Wm. B. Eerdmans Publishing Co., 1978.

Hoare, F. R., ed. and trans. *The Western Fathers. Being the Lives of SS. Martin of*

Tours, Ambrose, Augustine of Hippo, Honoratus of Arles and Germanus of Auxerre. New York: Sheed & Ward, 1954.

[Jerome, Saint.] *The Principal Works of St. Jerome,* trans. Hon. W. H. Fremantle, with Rev. G. Lewis and Rev. W. G. Martley. A Select Library of Nicene and Post-Nicene Fathers of the Christian Church, ed. Philip Schaff and Henry Wace. Grand Rapids, Mich.: Wm. B. Eerdmans Publishing Co., 1978.

Johnson, Paul. *A History of Christianity.* New York: Atheneum, 1977.

Medford, J.C.J. *Dictionary of Christian Lore and Legend.* London: Thames & Hudson, 1983.

[Severus, Sulpicius.] *The Works of Sulpicius Severus,* trans. Rev. Alexander Roberts. A Select Library of Nicene and Post-Nicene Fathers of the Christian Church, ed. Philip Schaff and Henry Wace. Grand Rapids, Mich.: Wm. B. Eerdmans Publishing Co., 1978.

Waddell, Helen, trans. *Vitae Patrum, The Desert Fathers.* London: Constable, 1936.

THE MEROVINGIAN ERA

Bachrach, Bernard S., ed. and trans. *Liber Historiae Francorum.* Lawrence, Kansas: Coronado Press, 1973.

Bede. *A History of the English Church and People,* trans. Leo Sherley-Price, rev. R. E. Latham. Harmondsworth, England: Penguin Books, 1977.

Betten, Francis Sales, S.J. *St. Boniface and St. Virgil.* Benedictine Historical Monographs, no. 2. Washington, D.C.: St. Anselm's Priory, 1927.

[Boniface, Saint.] *The Letters of Saint Boniface,* trans. Ephraim Emerton. New York: Columbia University Press, 1940.

Brehaut, Ernest. *Introduction* to his translation of Gregory of Tours, *The History of the Franks.* New York: Octagon Books, 1965.

[Columbanus, Saint.] *Sancti Columbani Opera,* ed. and trans. G.S.M. Walker. Dublin: Dublin Institute for Advanced Studies, 1957.

Dalton, O. M. *Introduction* to his translation of Gregory of Tours, *The History of the Franks,* 2 vols. Oxford: The Clarendon Press, 1927.

Dill, Sir Samuel. *Roman Society in Gaul in the Merovingian Age.* London: Macmillan & Co., 1926.

Einhard. *The Life of Charlemagne,* trans. Samuel Epes Turner. Ann Arbor, Mich.: The University of Michigan Press, Ann Arbor Paperbacks, 1960.

Finney, Theodore M. *A History of Music.* New York: Harcourt, Brace and Co., 1947.

[Fortunatus, Venantius.] *A Basket of Chestnuts: From the Miscellanea of Venantius Fortunatus,* trans. Geoffrey Cook. Cherry Valley, New York: Cherry Valley Editions, 1981.

_____. *Opera Omnia. Patrologiae Cursus Completus,* ed. J. P. Migne. Paris: SEU Petit-Montrouge, 1854.

[Fredegar.] *The Chronicles of the So-Called Fredegarian Scholars,* Book III. Ed. Bruno Krusch. Hanover: Impensis Bibliopolii Hahniani, 1888.

_____. *The Fourth Book of the Chronicle of Fredegar and Continuations,* trans. J. M. Wallace-Hadrill. London: Thomas Nelson & Sons, 1960.

Gies, Frances. *The Knight in History.* New York: Harper & Row, 1984.

Gregory of Tours, Saint. *The History of the Franks*, trans. Lewis Thorpe. Harmondsworth, England: Penguin Books, 1979.

Guérard, Albert. *France: A Modern History*. Ann Arbor Mich.: University of Michigan Press, 1969.

Hubert, Jean, Jean Porcher, and W. F. Volbach. *Europe of the Invasions*, trans. Stuart Gilbert and James Emmons. New York: George Braziller, 1969.

Jonas, Monk of Bobbio. *Life of Columban*. trans. and reprints, vol. 2, no. 7. Philadelphia: Pennsylvania University History Dept., 1895.

[Jordanes]. *The Gothic History of Jordanes in English Version*, trans. Charles Christopher Mierow. New York: Barnes & Noble, 1915.

Lasko, Peter. *The Kingdom of the Franks: North-West Europe Before Charlemagne*. London: Thames & Hudson, 1971.

Lehane, Brendan. *The Quest of Three Abbots*. London: Murray, 1968.

Lettsom, William Nanson. *The Fall of the Nibelungs*, otherwise *The Book of Kriemhild*. London: Williams & Norgate, 1850.

Lex Salica: The Ten Texts with the Glosses and the Lex Emendata, synoptically ed. J. H. Hessels. By H. Kern. London: J. Murray [etc.], 1880.

Montalembert, Charles Forbes René, Comte de. *The Monks of the West*, trans. F. A. Gasquet. London: John C. Nimmo, 1896.

Oman, Charles. *The Dark Ages: 476–918*. London: Rivingtons, 1901.

Perry, Walter C. *The Franks, from Their First Appearance in History to the Death of King Pepin*. London: Longman, Brown, Green, Longmans & Roberts, 1857.

Peters, Edward, ed. *Monks, Bishops and Pagans: Christian Culture in Gaul and Italy, 500–700*. Philadelphia: University of Pennsylvania Press, 1981.

Ranke, Leopold von. *Weltgeschichte*, Vol. II. 4 vols. Leipzig: Duncker & Humblot, 1910.

Scherman, Katharine. *The Flowering of Ireland: Saints, Scholars and Kings*. Boston: Little, Brown & Co., 1981.

Sergeant, Lewis. *The Franks: From Their Origin as a Confederacy to the Establishment of the Kingdom of France and the German Empire*. London: T. Fisher Unwin, 1898.

Thorpe, Mary. *The Study of the Nibelungenlied*. Oxford: Clarendon Press, 1940.

Wallace-Hadrill, J. M. *The Long-Haired Kings*. New York: Barnes & Noble, 1962.

Wemple, Suzanne Fonay. *Women in Frankish Society: Marriage and the Cloister, 500 to 900*. Philadelphia: University of Pennsylvania Press, 1981.

INDEX